Pirkei

DR. ARI

MOSAICA PRESS

Pirkei

DR. ARI

Connecting

Pirkei Avos

to the Parashah

DR. ARI CIMENT

ISBN-10: 1-946351-91-1
ISBN-13: 978-1-946351-91-3

Published by Mosaica Press, Inc.
www.mosaicapress.com
info@mosaicapress.com

עֲטֶרֶת זְקֵנִים בְּנֵי בָנִים וְתִפְאֶרֶת בָּנִים אֲבוֹתָם

Sponsored in loving memory of

אריה לייב בן אהרן ז"ל

בלימה בת יצחק ז"ל

Louis and Barbara Ciment, z"l

יחיאל שמואל בן צבי יצחק ז"ל

חנה פנינה בת אפרים פישל ז"ל

Samuel and Ann Weintraub, z"l

Ari, *mazel tov* for writing this book, and we love you and your family.

LARRY AND HELEN CIMENT AND FAMILY

Dedicated in the loving memory of

נפתלי בן אהרן ז"ל

פשע בת צבי הרש ז"ל

Harry and Paula Enis, z"l

הרב אברהם מאיר בן הרב חיים דוב ז"ל

פעריל בת הרב אברהם ליבר ז"ל

Rabbi Abraham and Pearl Zdanowitz, z"l

They sat at the feet of great teachers, and Ari continues to share
their legacy with Klal Yisroel. From strength to strength!

JAY AND SUE ENIS AND FAMILY

וְשִׁנַּנְתָּם לְבָנֶיךָ וְדִבַּרְתָּ בָּם בְּשִׁבְתְּךָ בְּבֵיתֶךָ
וּבְלֶכְתְּךָ בַדֶּרֶךְ וּבְשָׁכְבְּךָ וּבְקוּמֶךָ

Dedicated in loving memory of

יוסף בן סלים סקה ז"ל
ברכיה בת שמואל סקה ז"ל

Joseph and Becky Saka z"l

יהי זכרם ברוך

ת.נ.צ.ב.ה.

We are forever indebted to the leaders of our families
who set the path for us to walk on.

THE SAKA FAMILY

מָה אָהַבְתִּי תוֹרָתֶךָ כָּל הַיּוֹם הִיא שִׂיחָתִי

Dedicated in loving memory of our dear nephew and cousin

הרב ברוך צבי בן ראובן נתן זצ"ל

Rabbi Dr. Brian H. Galbut

His endless love for the Torah knew no boundaries.
May his memory continue to inspire us to learn and engage
each and every *parshah* with a full heart and to always remember
that our bond with the Torah is eternal.

ABRAHAM AND NANCY GALBUT
ELCHONON BORUCH AND SARKI GALBUT

Rabbi Ephraim Shapiro

It is truly an honor to have been asked to write an approbation for the *sefer* of my dear friend, Dr. Ari Ciment. I have had the extraordinary privilege, for many years, of being extremely close to Dr. Ciment and his entire family. He is the consummate physician, relating to every patient with incredible concern and devotion. Even more inspiring is his thirst for *Divrei Torah*. Ari has been blessed with a unique talent of being *mechadesh* beautiful and thought-provoking *Divrei Torah*, and is sought after by many shuls and organizations to present his exciting *shiurim* and brilliant lectures. May Hashem grant Dr. Ari the ability and the good health to continue being *mekadesh Shem Shomayim b'rabim*, as a healer and a teacher.

Rabbi Bixon

Dr. Ari Ciment is a beloved member of our Beth Israel Congregation. His weekly insights, now bound together in a book, are a cherished part of our weekly announcements. Dr. Ciment's beautiful words of Torah are inspiring and meaningful. The reader is always left with a take-home message that helps with our connection with Hashem. May the entire Ciment family have much happiness and satisfaction from the great contributions that Dr. Ari makes through the written word.

TABLE OF CONTENTS

Sefer Bereishis

BEREISHIS

NOACH

LECH LECHA

VAYEIRA

Sefer Shemos

SHEMOS

Sefer Bamidbar

Sefer Devarim

FOREWORD

By the author's father, Dr. Larry Ciment

Pirkei Avos begins with establishing the *mesorah*: Moshe passing the tradition on and serially to successive generations. Implicit in this mode is the *yeridas hadoros*: the loss of nuance and detail as the time passes. The challenge of every Jewish generation is to slow this attrition.

It is with great pride that my wife and I have been blessed with four wonderful children (and their progeny) who have taken this challenge seriously. They have achieved "וְהֵשִׁיב...לֵב בָּנִים עַל אֲבוֹתָם." They have turned the cycle retrograde, bringing us closer to *Matan Torah*. In this volume, Dr. Ari Ciment has linked the advice and wisdom of our scholars and demonstrated the roots of such thought to its source in the Torah. I proudly sponsor this work, and may the lessons contained herein inspire and guide us all.

ACKNOWLEDGMENTS

"דַּע מֵאַיִן בָּאתָ—*Know from where you come*" (*Avos 3:1*)

"Know from where (מֵאַיִן) you come" is apropos to introduce my acknowledgments.

The אַיִן from מֵאַיִן can mean "nothingness," and it is with a sense of "nothingness" and consequent humility that leads me to have an extra-special *hakaras hatov* to the whole professional team at Mosaica Press for agreeing to publish this work connecting the *parshiyos* to *Pirkei Avos*. A special thank you to Rabbi Reuven Butler and Rabbi Doron Kornbluth for making sure the Torah was pure and for the careful editing.

After my Uncle Perry Ciment retired from writing the weekly *divrei Torah* five years ago, after over thirty years of service, I have had the fortune of writing the weekly *divrei Torah* for Beth Israel of Miami Beach. I chose to connect the *parashah* to *Pirkei Avos* because the Torah is not supposed to be a history book but rather our guide to teach us perpetual lessons in life. *Pirkei Avos* then is derived by learning the *parshiyos* and it is only natural to seek such connections and lessons.

אַיִן may also be seen as an acronym: א-י-ן. The א stands for אבות, our fathers. The י stands for ידידים, beloved supporters, relatives, and friends. The ן stands for the נסים, the unexpected gifts and miracles along the way. We are what we are because of our fathers, mothers, friends, and family, along with G-d's benevolence.

אבות—This book is written to honor my parents, Helen and Dr. Larry Ciment. It was written for their *refuah sheleimah* and continued health.

It is impossible to have more loving and selfless parents, and I have tremendous *hakaras hatov* and dedicate this book to חיה דבורה בת חנה and אלעזר מיכאל בן בלימה. My upbringing was flavored by my Holocaust-surviving grandparents Samuel and Ann Weintraub. Samuel was an unbelievably learned man who had a photographic memory and always inspired me to "love a good *vort*." Ann personified hospitality. Louis and Barbara Ciment were bastions of the Miami Beach community. I am named after Louis (Aryeh), and Barbara's soft yet cunning nature permeates the whole extended Ciment family.

ידידים—My best supporters are my family and extended family. I first would like to thank my wife, Elissa Ciment, for her constant support. Raising three children is not easy, and I am indebted to her for that. My brother Elie Ciment and his wife Chana, my sister Alisa Barth and her husband David, and my sister Atara Mendelsohn and her husband Zivi, and their families are truly my inspiration! A special shout-out goes to my best friends Avraham Ciment and Jon Fisher, who are forever ידידים par excellence. My Uncle Harvey and his wife Sharon and family, and Uncle Perry and his wife Sharon and family, have harbored me from time to time, and I owe them thanks continuously.

My *rebbis* growing up included my shul rabbi, Rabbi Mordechai Shapiro, *zt"l*, whose deep insights made an imprint on me; Rabbi Elias Hochner, whose warm demeanor still impacts all of us; Rabbi Yochanan Zweig, whose methodology and insight are unparalleled (I try to model my approach based on his); Rabbi Mordechai Shifman, whose breadth of knowledge is shared selflessly; Rabbi Donald Bixon, who is a great friend and community *rav* with amazing guidance and the most meaningful ideas week in and week out; Rabbi Tzvi Neuhaus, who gives phenomenal *shiurim* and insights, along with constant inspiration including *daf yomi*; and Rabbi Chaim Friedman, whose infectious personality uplifts all those around him. My partner, Robert Galbut, MD, deserves a special thank you as he is the most unbelievably giving person I have ever met and I am honored to work with him for many years. His family is legendary and this book should serve as a special honor for my recently deceased friend and role model Rabbi Dr. Brian Galbut, *zt"l*, who I had the merit to share many of these *divrei Torah* with.

A special *hakaras hatov* goes to my shul neighbor, Jay Ennis, who encouraged me early on to write my ideas down for a book. His constructive criticism is the backbone of this *sefer*, and he is beloved by all at Beth Israel—and not just because he is the candyman. Thanks to Lionel Stein as well for distributing my *divrei Torah* all across South Africa for the past five years. A special thank you to all of Beth Israel congregation and my cousins Aryeh, Aharon, Elchanan, and Yechiel for reading my *divrei Torah* week in and week out, and for encouraging me to continue.

נסים—The miracles I have beholden as a physician have been many. I am thankful for the natural and the unnatural miracles that I have witnessed and have been a part of, which are too many to mention here. But the three greatest miracles wrought for me and to whom I dedicate this book to are my children: Tehilah Ahavah, Yaakov Moshe, and Shmuel Yitzchak. Through this book, I bless them with שיבה, זקנה, חכמה, כבוד, עושר, כח, נוי, ובנים. Enjoy!

SEFER

Bereishis

Bereishis

THE LESSON OF THE
SNAKE'S PUNISHMENT

בֶּן זוֹמָא אוֹמֵר: אֵיזֶהוּ עָשִׁיר, הַשָּׂמֵחַ בְּחֶלְקוֹ,
שֶׁנֶּאֱמַר (תהלים קכח) יְגִיעַ כַּפֶּיךָ כִּי תֹאכֵל
אַשְׁרֶיךָ וְטוֹב לָךְ. אַשְׁרֶיךָ, בָּעוֹלָם הַזֶּה.
וְטוֹב לָךְ, לָעוֹלָם הַבָּא.

*Ben Zoma would say: Who is rich? One who is satisfied with
his lot, as is stated: "If you eat of **toil of your hands**, fortunate
are you, and good is to you" (Tehillim 128); "fortunate are
you" in this world, **"and good is to you"** in the World to
Come. (Avos 4:1)*

QUESTIONS

1. The Mishnah seems to be making the following point: Who is
   "wealthy" in spirit and purpose? The person who gets to reap
   the fruits of his labor. Where in *Bereishis* do we see the quintessential example of this concept?

2. Also, the standard reading of the Mishnah is: "אֵיזֶהוּ עָשִׁיר הַשָּׂמֵחַ
   בְּחֶלְקוֹ—Who is rich? One who is happy **with his part**." But
   why use the word בְּחֶלְקוֹ as opposed to בְּעָשְׁרוֹ—his wealth, or

3

בִּנְכָסִים שֶׁלּוֹ—his belongings? Happy *with his part* seems to possibly connote something else, especially when coupled with the confirmatory verse, "יְגִיעַ כַּפֶּיךָ כִּי תֹאכֵל אַשְׁרֶיךָ—If you eat of **toil of your hands**, fortunate are you," which does not clearly jive with this idea.

—————————— ANSWERS ——————————

וַיֹּאמֶר ה' אֱלֹקִים אֶל הַנָּחָשׁ כִּי עָשִׂיתָ זֹּאת אָרוּר אַתָּה מִכָּל הַבְּהֵמָה
וּמִכֹּל חַיַּת הַשָּׂדֶה עַל גְּחֹנְךָ תֵלֵךְ וְעָפָר תֹּאכַל כָּל יְמֵי חַיֶּיךָ.

And the Lord G-d said unto the serpent: "Because you have
done this, cursed are you from among all cattle, and from
among all beasts of the field; upon your belly shall you go, and
dust shall you eat all the days of your life. (Bereishis 3:14)

What type of punishment did the snake receive after all? If the snake in fact lives on his belly all day, then having the easy-to-access dust to eat would seemingly be a good thing and thus be quite pleasurable!

Rabbi Mordechai Shapiro, *zt"l*, would often say: The answer is that this ease of life made the snake bored and left him feeling unfulfilled. Only when you eat of your toil can you enjoy emotional satisfaction! This is the paradigm of the verse: "יְגִיעַ כַּפֶּיךָ כִּי תֹאכֵל אַשְׁרֶיךָ—If you eat of **toil of your hands**, fortunate are you." When you get something for free, it does not have the same effect as "earning" a prize.

I would like to add that this idea may nicely jive with the first half of the Mishnah as well.

"אֵיזֶהוּ עָשִׁיר הַשָּׂמֵחַ בְּחֶלְקוֹ—Who is rich? He who is happy with his part" may not be about *being happy with your lot*, but rather *being happy by giving your part*—בְּחֶלְקוֹ! This is actually most consistent with the supporting verse now of "יְגִיעַ כַּפֶּיךָ כִּי תֹאכֵל אַשְׁרֶיךָ—If you eat of toil of your hands, fortunate are you," which highlights the *toil of your hands*. By giving up a part of yourself and not getting everything so easy, that is the best way to achieve happiness. Similarly, "כל ישראל יש להם חלק לעולם הבא" can homiletically read: "Everyone has the chance to get to the next world, if you give your חלק—do your part!" Most often it is the יגיע—effort, that is commensurate with the satisfaction/reward. Thus, the quintessential example of being happy with what you have is actually a lesson in being happy with what you are able to earn; this is the lesson taught to us by the snake. By having the dust as his food, he had life too easy and was unable to become rich, as he was unable to *work* for his food. Not having to give up any of his portion, he was destined to live an unfulfilling life!

─────── TAKEAWAY MESSAGES ───────

The twofold lesson of the snake's punishment is the following:

1. True happiness is only derived from reaping the fruit of your own hard work: "יְגִיעַ כַּפֶּיךָ כִּי תֹאכֵל, אַשְׁרֶיךָ—If you eat of **toil of your hands**, fortunate are you" (Rabbi Shapiro).

2. Happiness is achieved by doing your part! By giving up a part of yourself, and thus doing your part, you can truly achieve happiness. Because of the snake's sin, things became too easy for him, and fulfillment in life became difficult to achieve.

The lesson of the snake's punishment is: Achieving success is more in the mind than in the actual wealth.

IN WHAT WAY DO WE RULE OVER ANIMALS?

עֲקַבְיָא בֶּן מַהֲלַלְאֵל אוֹמֵר: דַּע מֵאַיִן בָּאתָ,
וּלְאָן אַתָּה הוֹלֵךְ ...

*Akavia the son of Mahalalel said: Know from where you come
and to where you are going…(Avos 3:1)*

שַׁמַּאי אוֹמֵר: יֵאמֹר מְעַט וַעֲשֵׂה הַרְבֵּה...

Shammai said: Say a little and do a lot…(Avos 1:15)

QUESTIONS

1. The simple interpretation of the first ethic is that we come from nothingness and leave with nothing. Is there another idea lurking beneath this statement?
2. Also, does Shammai really espouse that we should be relatively quiet?

ANSWERS

An approach may be derived by analyzing a verse from our *parashah*:

וַיֹּאמֶר אֱלֹקִים נַעֲשֶׂה אָדָם בְּצַלְמֵנוּ כִּדְמוּתֵנוּ וְיִרְדּוּ בִדְגַת הַיָּם וּבְעוֹף
הַשָּׁמַיִם וּבַבְּהֵמָה וּבְכָל הָאָרֶץ וּבְכָל הָרֶמֶשׂ הָרֹמֵשׂ עַל הָאָרֶץ.

6

And G-d said, "Let us make man in our image, after our
likeness, and they shall rule over the fish of the sea and over
the fowl of the heaven and over the animals and over all the
earth and over all the creeping things that creep upon the
earth." (Bereishis 1:26)

This verse highlights our superiority over animals. But what qualities do we humans have that give us our advantage over animals anyway? A well-known verse says, "וּמוֹתַר הָאָדָם מִן הַבְּהֵמָה אָיִן—the advantage of man over the animal is אָיִן," i.e., nothing!

I once heard from Rabbi Ephraim Shapiro in the name of his *rav* that this could be homilized and read: "וּמוֹתַר הָאָדָם מִן הַבְּהֵמָה, א-י-ן." The advantage of man over the animal is א=אמירה—the ability to speak; י=ידיעה—the ability to comprehend; and ן=נשמה—the ability to have a soul. Animals cannot generally speak, do not have advanced cognition, and do not have the same type of lofty soul as do humans. When G-d created humankind, these three traits were instilled within them to really separate them from animals.

His *rav* then said that this may be what is meant by the statement: "דַּע מֵאַיִן בָּאתָ, וּלְאָן אַתָּה הוֹלֵךְ." Homiletically, it means to say: Know that you came in this world with אַיִן—the ability to speak (א=אמירה), to gain knowledge (י=ידיעה), and with a soul (ן=נשמה). However, when you leave this world, i.e., "וּלְאָן אַתָּה הוֹלֵךְ," your knowledge does not accompany you as you ascend to Heaven; you only leave this world with the things you said (א=אמירה) and your *neshamah* (ן=נשמה) alone!

A possible *mussar* from this is that G-d fashioned us to reign over animals by virtue of our speech, intellect, and our souls. Our intellect is used only in this world but does not truly impact the world unless we "say" it over so that others can record it. When we leave this world, what we say or said still lives on. The knowledge is what dissipates!

Therefore, when Shammai said, "אֱמוֹר מְעַט וַעֲשֵׂה הַרְבֵּה," perhaps he was not only saying "speak a little and do a lot" but he was rather demonstrating the power of even just a little speech. By speaking even a little bit, you can do so much. אֱמוֹר מְעַט—speak a little, and by virtue of this gift, you can do so much! Converting the potential (intellect) into kinetic (statements) is what makes humankind reign supreme. We need to take advantage of this gift!

What we say in this world can be recorded for time immemorial, but the personal knowedge we gain (i.e., excluding Torah knowledge, which is kinetic in the sense that it continuously transforms a person) does not accompany us. We must focus on ways to transfer the knowledge into speech so that our messages can be transmitted forever. Our three-pronged advantage dissipates to two when we leave this world, and so steps should be taken to ensure our immortality!

─────────────── TAKEAWAY MESSAGES ───────────────

And G-d said, "Let us make man in our image, after our likeness, and they *shall rule* over the fish of the sea and over the fowl of the heaven and over the animals and over all the earth and over all the creeping things that creep upon the earth."

How do we rule over the animals? We have אָיִן: the advantage of man over the animal is the ability to speak, to comprehend, and to have a soul! We also have to remember that we leave this world with just the spoken transmitted word and our soul, as hinted in the ethic: "וּלְאָן אַתָּה הוֹלֵךְ." The *mussar*, perhaps, is that we need to cherish the gift of the spoken word, which separates us from animals. In what way do we rule over animals? By our speech, comprehension, and soul: א-י-ן.

TWO DOGS, THE SERPENT, AND BLESSINGS/CURSES

וְהַתּוֹרָה נִקְנֵית בְּאַרְבָּעִים וּשְׁמֹנָה דְבָרִים.
וְאֵלּוּ הֵן, בְּתַלְמוּד, בִּשְׁמִיעַת הָאֹזֶן, בַּעֲרִיכַת
שְׂפָתַיִם...הַמַּכִּיר אֶת מְקוֹמוֹ...

*The Torah is aquired in forty-eight ways. They are: by
learning, listening, speaking eloquently...**knowing your
place**...(Avos 6:6)*

וּרְדוּ בִדְגַת הַיָּם וּבְעוֹף הַשָּׁמַיִם וּבְכָל חַיָּה
הָרֹמֶשֶׂת עַל הָאָרֶץ.

*And **have dominion** over the fish of the sea, and over the fowl
of the air, and **over every living thing that creeps on the
earth**. (Bereishis 1:28)*

QUESTIONS

What does it mean to "know your place" stated in the ethic above?

Also, the Gemara in *Sanhedrin* (29b) states that "having dominion over every living thing" is referring specifically to the serpent. This can be paraphrased to imply that had the serpent *not* been cursed, each human would have two pet serpents dragged by leashes that would be used to retrieve objects for us humans.

The obvious question that I have (which I was surprised not to see in the *mefarshim* there) is this: Why is it so much better that the serpent was cursed by not having legs? If he wouldn't have been cursed, his destiny wouldn't have looked too much brighter being the co-servant to a human, retrieving objects and being dragged around by a leash! That's called a blessing?

ANSWERS

Some time ago, I took care of a former Iraqi war hero, an army medic CW who had a seizure while swimming in the Keys (he had a chronic seizure disorder from an injury sustained during a terrorist attack during combat; he freely shares this). He was placed on a ventilator and airlifted to Mount Sinai. After a thorough evaluation of his respiratory status, I decided to rest him overnight and take out his breathing tube in the morning. When the morning came and his numbers looked great, I gave the order to extubate. The nurse told me, "Sorry, doctor, but the patient requested to wait for his dog that is being driven up from the Keys before taking the tube out." I told her, "I take orders from other humans, but have never been ordered by a dog!" I respected his unusual wish and took the tube out later in the day when the dog arrived. One day later in the ICU, the CW was doing great until he had a breakthrough seizure and fell from the bed. If not for his gigantic amazing German Shepard service dog that literally sprung beneath him and broke his fall, the CW would have sustained a significant head injury. Now I realized why this CW never traveled far from his VA-trained service dog!

In contrast to this dog, I took care of a GP about eight years ago (the story was featured on CNN) in the ICU. She famously gave one million dollars to each of her bodyguards and three million dollars to her pet chihuahua! (I got nothing, by the way!)

Which dog do you think is happier? The CW's service dog, or the GP's chihuahua, living it up with weekly spa treatments costing thousands of dollars?

When G-d commanded humans to "have dominion over every living thing," animals were given a special opportunity to be helpful to humans. The Gemara in *Sanhedrin* is so crystal clear in saying that the serpent would have been thrilled being on a leash and helping humans find gems and the like. We interpret blessings and curses relative to our G-d-given expectations, and the initial expectation of the serpent was to serve the human. What greater blessing is there than being led around on a leash! In fulfilling G-d's desire, the CW's dog undoubtedly was happier. (Of course, the CW's dog was also royally treated—by no fault of the chihuahua, by the way.)

The bigger point is that blessings and curses are not absolute, but rather are relative to everyone's G-d-given expectations.

"הַמַּכִּיר אֶת מְקוֹמוֹ—knowing your place" is one of the forty-eight ways of acquiring Torah because it is the prerequisite of being able to maximize your blessings in life. Fulfilling your individual task in life begins by knowing what your ideal task is!

─────────── TAKEAWAY MESSAGES ───────────

We are commanded to have dominion over animals. The Gemara says that this refers to the serpent who, if not cursed, would have been happy to be a servant to humans. How is it not a curse itself to be a human's servant? The answer is that blessings and curses are relative to G-d-given expectations. A blessing to you may be a curse to someone else and vice versa. "הַמַּכִּיר אֶת מְקוֹמוֹ—knowing your place" is listed as one of the forty-eight ways of acquiring Torah because blessings depend on individual expectations. CW's service dog likely is living a more fulfilled existence than GP's chihuahua, despite its lavish necklaces. Two dogs and a serpent remind us of the relativity of blessings and curses.

WAS NOACH RIGHTEOUS?

יְֽהוֹשֻׁעַ בֶּן פְּרַחְיָה אוֹמֵר: עֲשֵׂה לְךָ רַב, וּקְנֵה לְךָ
חָבֵר, וֶהֱוֵי דָן אֶת כָּל הָאָדָם לְכַף זְכוּת.

Yehoshua ben Perachia would say: "Make for yourself a
master, acquire for yourself a friend, and judge every man to
the side of merit." (Avos 1:6)

QUESTIONS

The simple meaning of this ethic implies that one should engage in
three distinct parts of a mission: (a) go get yourself a rabbi, (b) acquire
a friend, and (c) judge people favorably.

1. Is there a connection between these ideas?
2. Also, the wording here of "עֲשֵׂה לְךָ רַב—Make for yourself a rabbi" is
   rather unusual. Shouldn't it rather say, "Go get yourself a rabbi"?

ANSWERS

The Torah says that Noach was a righteous man "in his generation."
Rashi says the following:

בְּדֹרֹתָיו: יש מרבותינו דורשים אותו לשבח, כל שכן שאלו היה בדור
צדיקים היה צדיק יותר, ויש שדורשים אותו לגנאי, לפי דורו היה
צדיק, ואלו היה בדורו של אברהם לא היה נחשב לכלום.

In his generations: Some of our Sages interpret it [the word
בְּדֹרֹתָיו *] favorably: How much more so if he had lived in a*
generation of righteous people he would have been even more
righteous! Others interpret it derogatorily: In comparison
with his generation he was righteous, but if he had been in
Avraham's generation, he would not have been considered of
any importance. (Sanhedrin 108a; Bereishis Rabbah 30:9;
Midrash Tanchuma, Noach 5)

Rabbi Ephraim Shapiro once said: Why does *Rashi* say that "some of our Sages" interpret it favorably, and then say that "others" interpret it derogatorily, leaving out the word "sages" or "rabbis"? An answer may be because it is not becoming to be derogatory of others, especially of our forefathers. Rabbis or respected folk should, and usually will, find a way to find the good in people, and thus likely analyze Noach in a positive light, while "others" (i.e., not really "rabbi-like" in the sense that a rabbi would not be proud of having to say this) will find a way to deem Noach in a negative light. Bottom line, it is generally derogatory to be derogatory, and thus not the ideal purpose of a *rav*. To be clear, it was Sages who interpreted it to be a less than good thing about Noach, and of course rabbis need to criticize when there is a purpose or lesson. Nevertheless, the term "rabbi" is still not mentioned in relation to the derogatory view because harsh criticism is just an unfortunate albeit necessary by-product of being a rabbi, and not the ideal primary purpose.

Perhaps the Mishnah in *Avos* may be saying the same thing: Do you know how to truly make yourself into a *rav*? First you must find a friend and together judge people favorably! Each and every one of us has the potential of becoming a *rav*, or a respected person in some way, by adhering to the simple tenet of being friendly and judging people favorably. And so, in fact, these three seemingly disparate elements of getting a rabbi, finding a friend, and judging others favorably, represent one unifying concept.

———————————— TAKEAWAY MESSAGES ————————————

Noach was righteous "in his generation." The fact that *Rashi* states that "some rabbis" interpret "in his generation" favorably, and that "others (i.e., not rabbis) interpret" the same words negatively may indeed reflect a point that it is not ideal or "rabbi-like" to be disparaging of others. The best way we can each become "rabbi-like" (i.e., respectable people) may not be by knowing *Shas* inside and out, but rather by simply not being overly judgmental of others.

How can I become a *rav*? By judging others favorably along with the friends you acquire along the way. So was Noach righteous? "Others" may say not, but many "rabbis" will judge favorably.

HOW COULD NOACH BE A *TZADDIK* IF THE MIDRASH SAYS HE HAD LITTLE FAITH?

יְהוֹשֻׁעַ בֶּן פְּרַחְיָה אוֹמֵר: עֲשֵׂה לְךָ רַב, וּקְנֵה לְךָ חָבֵר, וֶהֱוֵי דָן אֶת כָּל הָאָדָם לְכַף זְכוּת.

Yehoshua ben Perachia would say: "Make for yourself a master, acquire for yourself a friend, and judge every man to the side of merit." (Avos 1:6)

QUESTIONS

In our *parashah*, it states:

וַיָּבֹא נֹחַ וּבָנָיו וְאִשְׁתּוֹ וּנְשֵׁי בָנָיו אִתּוֹ אֶל הַתֵּבָה מִפְּנֵי מֵי הַמַּבּוּל.

And Noach went in and his sons and his wife and his sons' wives with him into the Ark because of the flood waters"
(Bereishis 7:7).

Rashi quotes the midrash on this verse:

מִפְּנֵי מֵי הַמַּבּוּל: אַף נֹחַ מִקְטַנֵּי אֲמָנָה הָיָה, מַאֲמִין וְאֵינוֹ מַאֲמִין שֶׁיָּבֹא הַמַּבּוּל וְלֹא נִכְנַס לַתֵּיבָה עַד שֶׁדְּחָקוּהוּ הַמַּיִם.

Because of the flood waters: Noach, too, was of those who had little faith, believing and not believing that the Flood would come, and he did not enter the ark until the waters forced him to do so. (Bereishis Rabbah 32:6)

15

Now isn't this very unexpected, that Noach is declared a *tzaddik* by the Torah, but the midrash posits that Noach had little faith? Since we are taught in the above ethic to give everyone the benefit of the doubt, shouldn't we assume Noach was not belittling G-d by delaying his boarding onto the Ark? Also, the wording here is a bit strange in *Rashi*: "אַף נח מקטני אמנה היה." Why start a sentence with the word אַף, which means "even"?

─────────────── ANSWERS ───────────────

An idea brought down in Aharon Greenberg's *Iturei Torah* is that you can read *Rashi* differently by moving over the comma: "אַף נח מקטני אמנה היה מאמין—that Noach believed even in those with small faith"—that they would appease G-d by virtue of their small faith. Not that Noach was with small faith, but rather that he even placed hope/belief in those with very little faith, and thus he didn't believe that G-d would ultimately destroy the world. He was a believer in the potential of humanity. He was forced into the Ark not because he was of small faith, but rather because he believed in those with "small faith" that they would suffice to ratchet up G-d's mercy to save the world! In other words, he was an optimist par excellence.

With the understanding of *Rashi* that Noach was the optimist, holding out until the very end, perhaps *Rashi* starts with the unusual word אַף to further illustrate this idea:"אַף נח מקטני אמנה היה—Noach's nose [אַף also means nose] did not have faith." Noach was a "מאמין ואינו מאמין." He had such firm belief in his fellow man that they would repent and that G-d would renege on His doomsday pledge that, "ולא נכנס לתיבה עד שדחקוהו המים—he didn't go into the Ark until the waters *climbed up to his nose* [and he couldn't breathe anymore!]." In other words, Noach had put so much faith in mankind/humanity (perhaps a bit too much) that he waited until being forced by his nose (because he couldn't breathe any longer!) to enter the Ark.

─────────────── TAKEAWAY MESSAGES ───────────────

Although the classical way to read the *Rashi* and midrash is seemingly disparaging in questioning Noach's belief in G-d, there is also another way to read it that rather glowingly espouses his belief in the concept of judging others favorably. אַף/Even Noach believed in those with little faith, i.e., that they could ultimately sway G-d's decree. Being a *tzaddik* therefore means trying to see the good in others, even if it means having to hold out until the waters are climbing and reaching your אַף/nose! Noach teaches us not to give up on humanity so fast. He was thus indeed a *tzaddik* who did not have little faith, but rather had faith אַף/even in those with little faith!

הִלֵּל אוֹמֵר, הֱוֵי מִתַּלְמִידָיו שֶׁל אַהֲרֹן,
אוֹהֵב שָׁלוֹם וְרוֹדֵף שָׁלוֹם, אוֹהֵב אֶת הַבְּרִיּוֹת
וּמְקָרְבָן לַתּוֹרָה.

*Hillel says: Love peace and run after peace, love people, and
bring them closer to Torah. (Avos 1:12)*

אֵלֶּה תּוֹלְדֹת נֹחַ נֹחַ אִישׁ צַדִּיק תָּמִים
הָיָה בְּדֹרֹתָיו.

*These are the generations of Noach: Noach was a just man,
and perfect in his generations…(Bereishis 6:9)*

*Rabbi Yochanan said: In his generations, but not in other
generations. Reish Lakish maintained: [Even] in his
generations—how much more so in other generations! Rabbi
Chanina said: As an illustration of Rabbi Yochanan's view,
to what may this be compared? To a barrel of wine lying in a
vault of acid: in its place, its odor is fragrant [by comparison
with the acid]; elsewhere, its odor will not be fragrant.
(Sanhedrin 108a)*

─────────── QUESTIONS ───────────

1. What does Hillel mean when he says, "love peace" and then "run after peace"? Is there any connection to the latter half of this statement, or is he making four disparate statements?

2. Also, the Torah is not a history lesson, and devaluing Noach seems sacrilegious, especially since he literally saved the human race. What then is Rabbi Yochanan's point? Also, what is added by the statement of Rabbi Chanina? Can't we easily understand Rabbi Yochanan without the analogy of the barrel of wine? Finally, *Rashi* brings down the midrash that Noach specifically built the Ark for 120 years so that people would see what he was doing and possibly do *teshuvah*. How does this extraordinary detail fit with Rabbi Yochanan's opinion that he was perfect only in comparison with his generation?

─────────── ANSWERS ───────────

In fact, Rabbi Yochanan was not giving us a history lesson. The hidden key is in Rabbi Chanina's addendum: The focus of this comparison is on the wine's pleasant odor but equally on the point of "in its place"! The odor is fragrant in comparison with the acid around, much like Noach was good in comparison to the evil people surrounding him. The words "in its place," though, are really the key: If you bring the acid to wine that is stationary, "in its place," that's when you recognize the greatness of the wine. Similarly, Noach's effect on the people was only when the acid, i.e., the evil people, would come to him.

It seems then that Rabbi Yochanan isn't knocking Noach as much as he is highlighting a salient teaching point: As a leader, it is not enough to sit back and let others be affected by your greatness when they are exposed to you. If given extraordinary gifts like Noach, you should go out and actively affect others (like Avraham, about whom the Torah tells us, "וַיֵּלֶךְ לְמַסָּעָיו" [*Bereishis* 13:3]). Perhaps Rabbi Yochanan specifically felt compelled to point out this lesson to Reish Lakish because, in many ways, Rabbi Yochanan was actually Reish Lakish's teacher! It is not enough for a teacher to sit back and let their students learn passively by role-modeling; the teacher must go out and actively affect the students!

Summarized homiletically: Noach was in a sense "*tamim b'dirosav*, in his own dwelling," as he relied on people visiting his place (a play on words, as the Torah says, "*b'dorosav*"). This concept may finally explain how Rabbi Yochanan may downplay the midrash that Noach built the ark for 120 years so that people would see him involved and do *teshuvah*. This perhaps is a veiled criticism, that instead of going out to people, he was insular and relied on people coming to him to be influenced!

When Hillel says, "אוֹהֵב שָׁלוֹם וְרוֹדֵף שָׁלוֹם," he isn't saying that you should love peace and *separately* run after peace. Rather, he is saying that if you love peace, then you must run after it to show that love. By parallel structure, the end of the statement follows as well: If you love people, then it is not enough to just be there for them to come to you, but rather, "וּמְקָרְבָן לַתּוֹרָה," you must go out and positively influence them. The overarching idea of the ethic then is not to harbor your love and expect to impact others by remaining in your place. Rather, you have to work on spreading out your talents!

─────────── TAKEAWAY MESSAGES ───────────

Rabbi Yochanan's comments on Noach's greatness were more of a teaching point than a disparagement. As the teacher of Reish Lakish, it seems plausible that his comments were directed to his student: In order to be a great teacher, you need to actively go out and influence rather than expect people to flock to you. The Torah is not a history book, and when Noach devotedly built the Ark for 120 years, Rabbi Yochanan points out that although virtuous, he could have actively pursued people, rather than be like the wine with a pleasant odor entrenched "in its place"! When Hillel teaches us, "אוֹהֵב שָׁלוֹם וְרוֹדֵף שָׁלוֹם," he is teaching us that having love or being internally good is not enough; you must run after others and positively influence others.

Noach, Rabbi Yochanan, and wine? The downsides of "in its place" are not enough for an extraordinary person to be "*tamim b'dirosav*"!

Lech Lecha

חֲמִשָּׁה קִנְיָנִים קָנָה לוֹ הַקָּדוֹשׁ בָּרוּךְ הוּא
בְּעוֹלָמוֹ, וְאֵלּוּ הֵן, תּוֹרָה קִנְיָן אֶחָד, שָׁמַיִם וָאָרֶץ
קִנְיָן אֶחָד, אַבְרָהָם קִנְיָן אֶחָד, יִשְׂרָאֵל קִנְיָן
אֶחָד, בֵּית הַמִּקְדָּשׁ קִנְיָן אֶחָד...אַבְרָהָם קִנְיָן
אֶחָד מִנַּיִן, דִּכְתִיב (בראשית יד), וַיְבָרְכֵהוּ וַיֹּאמַר
בָּרוּךְ אַבְרָם לְאֵל עֶלְיוֹן קֹנֵה שָׁמַיִם וָאָרֶץ...

*G-d acquired five acquisitions in his world. They are: one
acquisition is the Torah, one acquisition are the heavens
and the earth, one acquisition is Avraham, one acquisition
is the people of Israel, and one acquisition is the Holy
Temple...Avraham, as it is written (Bereishis 14:19), "And he
blessed him, and said: 'Blessed be Avram to G-d Most High,
acquirer of heavens and earth." (Avos 6:10)*

עֲשֵׂה לְךָ רַב, וּקְנֵה לְךָ חָבֵר ...

*Make for yourself a master, acquire for yourself a
friend...(Avos 1:6)*

—————————— QUESTIONS ——————————

1. Why are these five things (Torah, heaven/earth, Avraham, Israel, Beis Hamikdash) specified as those things that G-d "acquired" in this world?

2. What does it mean that G-d acquired five things *in this world*; doesn't G-d acquire everything?

3. Why does the Mishnah repeat each of these elements, capping them off with the words "קִנְיָן אֶחָד"? The whole sentence seems very repetitive!

4. Why is Avraham mentioned here as opposed to the other forefathers Yitzchak and Yaakov?

5. Finally, how does the *pasuk* of "בָּרוּךְ אַבְרָם לְאֵל עֶלְיוֹן קֹנֵה שָׁמַיִם וָאָרֶץ"—And he blessed him, and said: 'Blessed be Avram to G-d Most High, acquirer of heavens and earth" explain how G-d acquired Avraham in this world, and how does this tie into a related ethic of "וּקְנֵה לְךָ חָבֵר"—acquire yourself a friend"?

—————————— ANSWERS ——————————

When the Mishnah says that "five acquisitions the Holy One Blessed Be He acquired in this world," the Tanna may not be saying that G-d acquired five things in the world, but rather that there are five examples of acquisitions whereby G-d is acquired "in His world," by using our very own earthly world. In other words, there are five prime examples of worldly elements that can connect us to G-d despite their seemingly earthy nature and essence. Perhaps then, it can be read not that G-d acquired these things, but rather that we can acquire G-d in this world by virtue of these elements! The Mishnah is then read: "There are five acquisitions that demonstrate that G-d can be acquired in our very world!"

What made Avraham unique from all of our *Avos* was his ability in amalgamating the *gashmi*, "material" and the *ruchani*, "heavenly." He was one of the "worldly" beings/elements that epitomized the concept of "acquiring G-d in this world!"

And this beautifully explains why the Tanna uses the *pasuk* from our very *parashah* to demonstrate Avraham's unique unifying strength. When the *pasuk* says, "Blessed be Avram to G-d Most High, acquirer of heavens and earth," it may not only be referring to G-d as the "acquirer of heavens and earth" (which, admittedly, is the simple classic reading), but rather to Avraham, who acquired that ability to unite the heavenly with the mundane, thus becoming *shalem*, complete. When the Mishnah repeats each of these five things and follows it with the words, "one acquisition," the author may be saying that each of these five elements represents the ultimate of what a true acquisition should entail: an אֶחָד—Oneness. By combining the heavenly elements with the mundane, one can become a true אֶחָד. The Beis Hamikdash was a place that clearly combined the mundane with spirituality: Torah, Israel, heaven/earth, and of course, Avraham, also fit the same pattern.

And now we can finally understand what the Tanna meant by "עֲשֵׂה לְךָ רַב, וּקְנֵה לְךָ חָבֵר." Rather than literally meaning, "Make for yourself a *rav* and acquire yourself a friend," perhaps the Mishnah may also be understood as follows: Make **yourself** a *rav*; i.e., each and every one of us common folk, with our physical and material needs and drives, is charged with *finding the spirituality within our mundane essence*. The word חָבֵר means "friend," but it also is the root word for חבורה, which means connection; i.e., if you are successful in combining these two crucial elements (the spiritual with the material), then you have earned a true *kinyan*, acquisition (וּקְנֵה) by virtue of your combination (לְךָ חָבֵר). "Make yourself a *rav*, and the *kinyan* will be evident in you by virtue of this חבורה!"

— TAKEAWAY MESSAGES —

When Malki-Tzedek blessed Avraham, he may have been referring to Avraham (not necessarily G-d!) as "acquiring heaven and earth" in that Avraham was the quintessential forefather who epitomized the combining of the heavenly with the mundane—he was the ultimate acquirer of heaven and earth! To be "one acquisition," one must emulate Avraham Avinu in combining the holy and mundane, and thus achieve unity in purpose. By "finding the *rav* within each of ourselves"

(עֲשֵׂה לְךָ רַב), we can successfully amalgamate (לְךָ חָבֵר) the heavenly with the mundane and best achieve the "one acquisition" (וּקְנֵה) much like Avraham did years ago.

Why is Avraham "a blessing to G-d, the acquirer of heaven and earth"? Because Avraham shows us all how to be a blessing to G-d—by acquiring both heaven and earth and fusing the spiritual with the mundane!

A HINT TO PRAYER

דַּע מַה לְּמַעְלָה מִמְּךָ...וְכָל מַעֲשֶׂיךָ בַּסֵּפֶר נִכְתָּבִין...

Know what is above you...and all of your deeds will be written in a book. (Avos 2:1)

רַבִּי אֶלְעָזָר אוֹמֵר: וְדַע מַה שֶׁתָּשִׁיב לְאֶפִּיקוֹרוֹס...

Rabbi Elazar would say: Know what to answer a heretic...(Avos 2:14)

QUESTIONS
---

1. Why doesn't the first Mishnah say, "דַּע מִי לְּמַעְלָה מִמְּךָ—Know *who* is above you (namely G-d!)"? What is signified by the word מַה?

2. What does the second Mishnah mean when it says that we should know "מַה" to respond to the *apikores*, non-believer? Why not tell us what the "what" is?

3. Finally, when Avraham asks for a sign that G-d will keep His covenant with his descendants, he states: "בַּמָּה אֵדַע כִּי אִירָשֶׁנָּה — Hashem, with what shall I know that I shall inherit it?" G-d then responds:

וַיֹּאמֶר אֵלָיו קְחָה לִי עֶגְלָה מְשֻׁלֶּשֶׁת וְעֵז מְשֻׁלֶּשֶׁת
וְאַיִל מְשֻׁלָּשׁ וְתֹר וְגוֹזָל.

*And He said to him: "Take Me a heifer of three years
old, and a she-goat of three years old, and a ram of
three years old, and a turtle-dove, and a young pigeon."*

Why does Avraham need a sign from G-d that He was going to
keep His covenant? Is G-d's word not good enough?

 ANSWERS

"דַּע מַה לְמַעְלָה מִמְּךָ" can be understood homiletically: Know that "מַה" is
defined as "לְמַעְלָה מִמְּךָ," a yearning to get close to the One above you! מַה
is a form of prayer, question, or request that is an attempt to bond us to
Hashem, who of course has His eye and ear open to such requests! This
also explains, "דַּע מַה שֶׁתָּשִׁיב לְאֶפִּיקוֹרוֹס"; instead of wasting our time trying
to rationalize G-d to a denying atheist, perhaps we should respond by
focusing on the "מַה." We should focus our efforts on solidifying our own
beseeching to Hashem.

And, at last, how can we understand Avraham's request for a sign
that he was going to inherit: "בַּמָּה אֵדַע כִּי אִירָשֶׁנָּה"?

According to *Bereishis Rabbah*, the three heifers, three goats, and the
three rams were actually references to *korbanos* eventually brought by
B'nei Yisrael, either for atonement of sins or for the sake of holidays. The
Gemara in *Megillah* (31b) actually says that Avraham was comforted in
knowing that even when the *korbanos* ceased, prayer would be in their
stead and perpetuate the connection that we have to Hashem. Perhaps
that is exactly what Avraham wanted: he was not merely requesting a
sign from G-d that He was going to come through with an inheritance.
He was saying (not asking) that with מַה, he can become closer to G-d.
With the constant ability to connect to G-d anytime and in any place,
Avraham could feel solace: בַּמָּה, with the "מַה" of prayer, "אֵדַע כִּי אִירָשֶׁנָּה," I
know I am going to inherit!

——————— TAKEAWAY MESSAGES ———————

When *Avos* says you should know "what is above you" and also "what you should respond to a non-believer," it may be hinting at the quintessential "מַה"—a question, beseeching, or prayer that connects us to לְמַעְלָה מִמְּךָ. Likewise, when Avraham was saying, "With what shall I know I will inherit?" he may have, in fact, been saying rather than asking: "With the *what* of prayer, I know I will inherit!"

Is there any hint of prayer in this *parashah*? Yes: "בַּמָּה אֵדַע כִּי אִירָשֶׁנָּה."

A SOURCE FOR TZITZIS AND TEFILLIN

עַל שְׁלֹשָׁה דְבָרִים הָעוֹלָם עוֹמֵד, עַל הַדִּין
וְעַל הָאֱמֶת וְעַל הַשָּׁלוֹם.

*On three things the world stands: on justice, on truth, and on
peace. (Avos 1:18)*

---------------------- QUESTIONS ----------------------

1. What is the difference between אמת and שקר? Where in this
    parashah do we see the quintessential case study of liv-
    ing with אמת?

2. In *perek* 14, *pasuk* 23, we read:

    אִם מִחוּט וְעַד שְׂרוֹךְ נַעַל וְאִם אֶקַּח מִכָּל אֲשֶׁר לָךְ.

    *That I will not take a thread or a shoelace from
    anything that is yours!*

After helping the King of Sodom miraculously defeat the
other kings, Avraham famously declares that he doesn't want
to take even a thread from the evil king in personal payment.
The Gemara in *Chullin* (89a) says: "Raba also said: 'As a reward
for our father Avraham having said, "I will not take a thread
or a shoestrap," his descendants were worthy to receive two
commandments: the thread of *techeiles* [i.e., on the tzitzis], and
the strap of the tefillin.'" What do tzitzis and tefillin have to
do with this aforementioned statement of Avraham? Yes, of

course tzitzis is a thread, and tefillin is a form of a strap, but is there a deeper message?

ANSWERS

Imagine that your journey is to achieve the ת, the last letter of the *aleph-beis*, representing the culmination of a life's journey. You could reach there by living in אמת, orderly and complete with א in the front, the מ smack in the middle, and finally achieving the ת. You can also get close to the ת by living in שקר (the letters that come just before ת in the *aleph-beis*), but besides for never reaching the ת, this is also tarnished by simply being incomplete and disorderly (since there is no start and no middle!). Avraham Avinu wanted to live life as a complete model of אמת, from front to middle to back; he wanted to be the model of an *ehrliche Yid* with nothing that could tarnish him. Perhaps, by not taking a thread or strap from Sodom, he was showing that even though one could easily hide such a small prize, for him that would feel like a complete breakdown of his אמת nature! The tzitzis and tefillin are mitzvos meant to be worn on the outside, and although the thread and strap are small indeed, they are impossible not to see. Avraham was teaching us that we should value every thread or strap that we can hide inside as if they are visible for all to see. We must make an effort to be squeaky clean from beginning to end.

TAKEAWAY MESSAGES

The thread and the strap that Avraham would not take from Sodom may have led to the Jewish People meriting mitzvos of tzitzis and tefillin because just like Avraham treated every business transaction (even the seemingly small ones of threads and straps) with complete אמת from beginning to end (from א to ת), we should wear the thread of tzitzis and strap of tefillin on the outside for all to see and be cognizant that every little thread and strap counts!

A source for tzitzis and tefillin in this week's *parashah* is therefore that every thread and strap counts: "אִם מִחוּט וְעַד שְׂרוֹךְ נַעַל"!

WAS AVRAHAM'S HOMETOWN SO BAD?

רַבִּי נְהוֹרַאי אוֹמֵר: הֱוֵי גוֹלֶה לִמְקוֹם
תּוֹרָה...וְאֶל בִּינָתְךָ אַל תִּשָּׁעֵן.

*Rabbi Nehorai would say: Exile yourself to a place of
Torah...rely not on your own understanding. (Avos 4:13)*

QUESTIONS

1. If Avraham's hometown was so bad, how come he later sends
   Eliezer to search this very hometown for a lady to marry his son?
   It must be that there were some positives about his hometown.

2. Also, interestingly, if Avraham's hometown was so bad after all,
   wouldn't G-d have used the language: "צֵא מֵאַרְצְךָ" instead of "לֶךְ
   לְךָ מֵאַרְצְךָ"?

ANSWERS

My father, Dr. Larry Ciment, often says that notwithstanding the
positive virtues of one's self or hometown, part of someone's natural
growth is to go out and experience a different vantage point. לֶךְ has
the *gematria* of fifty, as does לְךָ, as if to say that you need 50 percent of
your past and 50 percent must be your own future! Just as important
as the past, the לֶךְ of life, is the challenge of לְךָ, when you can step out
of your comfort zone and explore for yourself. This, perhaps, is what
is meant in *Avos* by, "Banish yourself to a place of Torah...do not rely
on your knowledge." Less than a knock on your past, it is a highlight

30

of the importance of being able to explore on your own, out of your comfort zone!

──────────── TAKEAWAY MESSAGES ────────────

When Avraham is told "לֶךְ לְךָ מֵאַרְצְךָ," he was not really being told to leave as much as he was being encouraged to start exploring on his own. לֵךְ has the *gematria* of fifty, as does לְךָ. Life is about taking 50 percent of your past and forging ahead with 50 percent on your own. Avraham's hometown may not have been so bad after all, but he still needed to explore onward.

WAS TERACH GOOD OR BAD?

הִלֵּל אוֹמֵר: הֱוֵי מִתַּלְמִידָיו שֶׁל אַהֲרֹן אוֹהֵב
שָׁלוֹם וְרוֹדֵף שָׁלוֹם אוֹהֵב אֶת הַבְּרִיּוֹת
וּמְקָרְבָן לַתּוֹרָה.

*Hillel would say: Be of the disciples of Aharon—a lover of
peace, a pursuer of peace, one who loves the creatures and
draws them close to Torah. (Avos 1:12)*

QUESTIONS

The standard meaning of this ethic is that you should not be satisfied
with just loving peace but should constantly run after peace to ensure it
is solidified. Yet the term רוֹדֵף שָׁלוֹם is quite unusual. Is there perhaps an
additional latent idea?

Rabbi Bixon quoted a midrash or Gemara that says anytime the
Torah repeats the names of a person one after the other (i.e., "Avraham,
Avraham"), this is a sign of their righteousness. It therefore makes
sense that we see examples such as:

- "Avraham, Avraham" (*Bereishis* 22:11)
- "Yaakov, Yaakov" (ibid., 46:2)
- "Moshe, Moshe" (*Shemos* 3:4)
- "Shmuel, Shmuel" (*Shmuel I* 3:10)

No one will argue that these four people were indeed righteous. But
as *Parashas Noach* ends, Terach's name is repeated twice: "וְאֵלֶּה תּוֹלְדֹת
תֶּרַח תֶּרַח הוֹלִיד אֶת אַבְרָם." The Rabbinic tradition is that Terach was indeed

32

wicked (*Vayikra Rabbah* 19:1, 33), and he even brought his son before Nimrod, who threw him into a fiery furnace (*Bereishis Rabbah* 38:13). So why does G-d record him in the Torah with the "signature" of a righteous person?

─────────────── ANSWERS ───────────────

The answer alluded to by Rabbi Bixon is that after Avram escaped the furnace, the *Zohar* (*Bereishis* 1:77b) says that Terach repented, and Rabbi Abba bar Kahana says that G-d assured Avram that Terach had a portion in the World to Come (*Bereishis Rabbah* 30:4; 30:12).

Rabbi Bixon continues that perhaps a proof of Terach's *teshuvah* is in the fact that when G-d told him to go from his land to another land in our *parashah*, Avram was already in Charan (not his hometown of Ur Chasdim), having been sent there by Terach. Terach knew that in order for Avram to achieve true success, he needed to distance himself from his hometown and thus personally escorted him to safety. Terach then clearly repented, and for that strong decision he merited the Biblical "signature" of the righteous!

Sometimes, the winning decisions are the difficult ones, requiring self-sacrifice (such as a father sending a son away) and running away, and sometimes you have to run to achieve peace. רוֹדֵף שָׁלוֹם may hint to the idea that sometimes you have to be chased out of town or willingly leave in order to achieve peace. Interestingly, we see a similar idea when Avraham is the one who picks up and leaves Lot after their shepherds squabble continuously. Sometimes, chasing others out of town or willingly being chased out of town is the only avenue for peace. This may be Terach's legacy and through this he received repentance.

─────────────── TAKEAWAY MESSAGES ───────────────

Because Terach repented, the Torah repeats his name, which is usually only done for the righteous. This is hinted at by the fact that Avram was already in Charan and no longer in his hometown of Ur Chasdim when G-d commanded him in our *parashah* to "go from your land." Terach's piety is in his realization that his son needed to be escorted out of his hometown to best succeed and flourish. Sometimes, peace can only be achieved by allowing oneself to be chased out! Terach was bad and then good, which was good enough for him to earn the next world. (Still, I do not recommend sending your children into fiery furnaces, as you may not get a second chance at *teshuvah*!)

PREFER 318ers OVER 76ers
OR 49ers—WHY?

רַ־בִּי חֲנִינָא בֶן חֲכִינַאי אוֹמֵר: וְהַ־מְהַלֵּךְ בַּדֶּרֶךְ
יְחִידִי...הֲרֵי זֶה מִתְחַיֵּב בְּנַפְשׁוֹ.

*Rabbi Chanina the son of Chachina'i would say: One
who...travels alone on the road...has forfeited his life.*
(Avos 3:4)

───── QUESTIONS ─────

What is so bad about walking alone on a path that it makes one liable? The Bartenura explains that if you are by yourself, you may invite robbers and other great dangers. Is there possibly another lesson here?

Many modern-day sports teams are named after numbers: The Philadelphia 76ers get their name from 1776, the year that the Declaration of Independence was signed in their hometown; the San Francisco 49ers are so named because of the 1849 Gold Rush. But a truly successful team should be named the "318ers," and here's why...

The four kings just beat the five kings, showing us that these four kings were likely pretty strong. Then they take Lot hostage. Avraham brazenly takes only 318 men to fight this whole enormous army! Even more surprisingly, *Rashi* brings the midrash that says that the 318 was actually Eliezer alone, as 318 is the *gematria* of his name (*Bereishis Rabbah* 43:2; *Nedarim* 32a). What is the deep lesson here, if any? Did Avraham and Eliezer really destroy a huge army on their own? And if

35

they did, how come we don't really talk about it much as such a corner-stone miracle? In short, what's so special about 318?

—————————————— ANSWERS ——————————————

The Gemara in *Nedarim* (32a) actually says that Avraham's use of 318 Torah scholars to battle for Lot was not a good thing, and actually led to our eventual punishment in Mitzrayim. Nonetheless, as Avi Feiner once pointed out, quoting *Sukkah* (32a), the 318 warriors are the *exemplum primi* of how Jews just never give up despite adversity. How so? The word "יאוש—giving up hope," has the *gematria* of 317. One above that is 318. In order to get *over* יאוש, you go one over it and conquer it; hence 318 is the *exemplum primi* of a number signifying never giving up hope!

Besides hope, there are two more beautiful aspects of 318.

When we combine strengths, our attributes are not additive but synergistic. In *Parashas Bechukosai*, it says that when we are blessed, "Five of you shall chase a hundred, and a hundred of you shall chase ten thousand" (*Vayikra* 26:8). If 200 is 4 x 50, one would expect that the Torah would be consistent and say 100 will chase 400 (instead, it is one hundredfold!). Instead, the point is that when we combine our strengths, working together as a unit, our abilities become synergistically powered!

Eliezer was the ultimate servant of Avraham, and by saying that the *gematria* of 318 is Eliezer, the midrash may simply be saying that the 318 warriors acted as one, united and dedicated. (To be fair, Chazal seem to imply that it was really Eliezer alone who went out to fight, but this may be another *pshat* in the midrash.)

Beyond these two great lessons of 318—of hope and of unity—there may be one final idea to slam it home.

Eliezer was so focused and loyal to Avraham that perhaps the midrash is in fact saying that he alone, together with Avraham, was indeed able to root out the enemy. The Torah may be teaching that true loyalty and dedication can be so crucial that it could make one person as powerful as 318 men!

The three lessons of 318 recapped are:
1. Never giving up hope
2. Being committed with a clear unifying goal and direction
3. Being loyal to no end

רַבִּי חֲנִינָא בֶן חֲכִינַאי אוֹמֵר: וְהַמְהַלֵּךְ בַּדֶּרֶךְ יְחִידִי...הֲרֵי זֶה מִתְחַיֵּב בְּנַפְשׁוֹ.

Rabbi Chanina the son of Chachina'i would say: One who travels alone on the road...has forfeited his life.

What is so bad about walking alone on a path that it makes one liable? Maybe the answer is that if you think you can conquer everything yourself, without unifying and showing loyalty to others, you will miss out on the benefits of team synergy!

——————— TAKEAWAY MESSAGES ———————

The 318 warriors dispatched by Avraham were the *exemplum primi* of the perfect team: They never gave up hope (318 is one more than יאוש); they worked together, unified in purpose (as per an alternate *pshat* in the midrash that all 318 men were with singular focus equal to Eliezer, and hence 318 is the *gematria* of Eliezer); and Eliezer was extremely loyal and dedicated (one Eliezer was as strong as 318 men, given his immense loyalty)! As Rabbi Chanina implores us in *Avos*: "Don't ever walk on a path alone!"

318ers will no doubt defeat any team with their grit, togetherness, and loyalty, characteristics that must highlight any great team!

Vayeira

THE FIVE SENSES AND SIN— A CONNECTION?

רַבִּי אוֹמֵר: הִסְתַּכֵּל בִּשְׁלֹשָׁה דְבָרִים וְאִי אַתָּה בָא לִידֵי עֲבֵרָה: דַּע מַה לְמַעְלָה מִמְּךָ עַיִן רוֹאָה וְאֹזֶן שׁוֹמַעַת וְכָל מַעֲשֶׂיךָ בַּסֵּפֶר נִכְתָּבִין.

Rebbi said: Investigate three things and you will not come to sin: Know what is above you: a seeing eye, a hearing ear, and all of your deeds will be written in a book. (Avos 2:1)

QUESTIONS

The simple interpretation of this ethic is as the *Abarbanel* says: "An omnipotent, omniscient, and omnipresent power continuously keeps an eye on us...and with this in mind, we will not come to sin." G-d sees our every action, He hears us, and will write down all of our deeds—so we'd better watch out!

Does knowing that there is a G-d above us really stop us from sinning? Although this is certainly ideal, there are many people who believe and even fear G-d, yet still sin and regularly so. So is there another strategy here to explain this ethic?

———— ANSWERS ————

A possible answer derives from analyzing a scene from this week's *parashah*:

וַיִּפְקַח אֱלֹקִים אֶת עֵינֶיהָ וַתֵּרֶא בְּאֵר מָיִם וַתֵּלֶךְ וַתְּמַלֵּא אֶת הַחֵמֶת מַיִם וַתַּשְׁקְ אֶת הַנָּעַר.

And G-d opened her eyes, and she saw a well of water; and she went, and filled the bottle with water, and gave the lad to drink. (Bereishis 21:19)

Hagar was crying about the imminent death of her starving, thirsty child in a desert, and yet when she "opens" her eyes, a well of water is right there! Did G-d miraculously create a well for her, or was the well really there all along? The midrash states here that "all may be presumed blind until G-d enlightens their eyes" (*Bereishis Rabbah* 53:14). In other words, some things are right before our eyes, and yet because of our sins or spiritual blurriness, G-d doesn't privilege us with seeing them.

With this in mind, דַּע מֶה לְמַעְלָה מִמְּךָ may in fact be saying: דַּע, understand, that מ"ה, from five (senses), לְמַעְלָה מִמְּךָ, you can be even better than you are now. You can elevate yourself beyond where you are by using your very own five G-d-given senses, which are heightened when you are without sin! Know that "your five senses" can be elevated and magnified when you avoid sin, and it is in our hands to take advantage of this amazing gift!

The Baal Shem Tov likewise said that if one did not sin, his eyes would see much more (עַיִן רוֹאָה) and his ears would hear from the edges of the earth (אֹזֶן שׁוֹמַעַת). According to this, the phrases in the aforementioned ethic—עַיִן רוֹאָה/אֹזֶן שׁוֹמַעַת—actually refer to *our* eyes and ears and not to G-d's! Sins insulate our superhuman abilities! Perhaps Hagar's well was there all along, but her imperfections blurred that reality until she desperately and wholeheartedly pleaded with G-d. The emphasis may be less on G-d watching our every step and more on us all watching out for sin, knowing that it is self-destructive and can blur our senses.

——————— TAKEAWAY MESSAGES ———————

Rather than avoiding sin due to fear, perhaps we are being encouraged to recognize how much greater our potential is when we avoid sin, and we will have clear vision. By realizing that our human senses can become supernatural if they are not clouded by an imperfect spiritual reality, we will be motivated to avoid sin. Just like Hagar eventually came to see the well that was before her eyes the whole time, we likewise hope that our five senses will not be clouded by sin.

Our five senses can elevate us to supernatural heights. Sinning can dull the five senses, but *teshuvah* removes the impediment, as evidenced by Hagar's later detection of the well right in front of her eyes.

HOW IS YITZCHAK A MODEL FOR GEVURAH?

אֵיזֶ—הוּ גִבּוֹר הַכּוֹבֵשׁ אֶת יִצְרוֹ.

Who is strong? He who conquers his nature/desires.
(Avos 4:1)

QUESTIONS

Each of the *Avos* had their defining trait: Avraham's was חסד—kind-ness; Yitzchak's was גבורה—strength, and Yaakov's was אמת—truth.

Why does Yitzchak represent גבורה; after all, he is portrayed as rather feeble and passive throughout *Bereishis*, as he will later be brought as a *korban* during עקידת יצחק, and then is later fooled by both of his sons?

Furthermore, why is Yitzchak named so? The root of his name is צחק, which could mean "laugh," "joy," "scream," or even "cry," depending on the context. Firstly, the name conjures up disbelief, since both Avraham and Sarah, respectively, initially laughed in disbelief when they were informed of their impending child (*Bereishis* 17:17; 18:12). But when Sarah actually has a child, the Torah reports that Sarah said, "A joy G-d has done for me; all who hear the news will rejoice with me!" Here, the צְחֹק is one of sheer joy and not disbelief! So which use of the root is Yitzchak named after—the disbelief or the joy? Also, what is the sig-nificance of Yitzchak being named by G-d Himself first (as opposed to by Avraham and/or Sarah) one whole year before his actual birth (ibid., 17:19)? Finally, how does this all tie in to the concept that Yitzchak is the paradigm of *gevurah*?

─────────────── ANSWERS ───────────────

Gevurah is not about being born with some G-d-given talent and then utilizing that talent to succeed. True *gevurah* is about overcoming some obstacle and transforming it into a talent. Yitzchak was the ultimate paradox. He is portrayed as very passive and manipulated (at least according to the simple *pshat* reading of Yaakov "stealing" the blessings), and yet on the other hand, he is also portrayed as being strong and far-sighted. After all, despite this seeming weaker appearance, it is actually Yitzchak who reclaimed the wells that were being stolen from Avraham, and also later guaranteed a *berachah* to Yaakov despite Eisav's harsh objection. This paradox is illustrated even in Yitzchak's name, which was given by G-d Himself, perhaps to highlight that his essence was purposely injected into this heavenly chosen name. He started out as a disbelief, but his name was transformed into joy when he was ultimately born. Yitzchak's name was thus purposely ambiguous; its meaning, whether pejorative or complimentary, was entirely based on the context. The lesson of *gevurah* is likewise one of context. The Mishnah in *Avos* doesn't read, "אֵיזֶהוּ גִּבּוֹר הַכּוֹבֵשׁ אֶת הָאָרֶץ—Who is strong? He who conquers the earth," because that would not take transformation. True strength is being able to change or improve upon one's natural tendencies: "אֵיזֶהוּ גִּבּוֹר הַכּוֹבֵשׁ אֶת יִצְרוֹ—Who is strong? He who conquers his nature/desires."

─────────────── TAKEAWAY MESSAGES ───────────────

Why is Yitzchak named Yitzchak? Is it disbelief or joy? The answer is that Yitzchak is both! Yitzchak is an ambiguous name, which was defined and redefined by the circumstances (i.e., when Avraham and Sarah first heard, it was disbelief, but when he was actually born, it was joy!). G-d personally bestows Yitzchak's name as He endows him with the attribute of *gevurah*, teaching us that true strength is when we apply context to transform disbelief into joy. Being strong is being able to overcome and *transform*.

The very name of Yitzchak, therefore, teaches us the lesson of *gevurah*.

IS LYING AND BENDING THE TRUTH THE SAME THING? ASK AVRAHAM AVINU...

רַבָּן שִׁמְעוֹן בֶּן גַּמְלִיאֵל אוֹמֵר: עַל שְׁלֹשָׁה
דְבָרִים הָעוֹלָם עוֹמֵד, עַל הַדִּין וְעַל הָאֱמֶת וְעַל
הַשָּׁלוֹם שֶׁנֶּאֱמַר (זכריה ח) אֱמֶת וּמִשְׁפַּט שָׁלוֹם
שִׁפְטוּ בְּשַׁעֲרֵיכֶם.

*Rabbi Shimon the son of Gamliel would say: By three things
is the world sustained: law, truth, and peace, as is stated
(Zechariah 8:16), "Truth, and a judgment of peace, you
should administer at your [city] gates." (Avos 1:18)*

QUESTIONS

Are these three attributes interconnected, and how so? Wouldn't one expect a verse showing that all three things (law, truth, and peace) are important, rather than this verse from *Zechariah* that seems unusual in lumping law and peace together ("judgment of peace")?

מִדְּבַר שֶׁקֶר תִּרְחָק.

From lies you shall distance yourself. (Shemos 23:7)

There appear to be four lies in *Parashas Vayeira.* This doesn't seem consistent with Torah values. The four episodes are:

43

1. G-d "lied" by telling Avraham that Sarah said, "How am I supposed to have a child as I am so old?" when, in fact, she said, "How am I supposed to have a child as Avraham is so old?"

2. The second example is when Sarah said she didn't laugh when, in fact, she did.

3. The third is when Avraham told Sarah that she was his sister when meeting Avimelech (she, of course, was his wife).

4. When Avraham was on the way to the *Akeidah*, Yitzchak asked where the lamb was, to which Avraham responded, "G-d will show you the lamb" (*Bereishis* 22:8), not telling him that Yitzchak himself was going to be the lamb!

How can it be that the *parashah* is so replete with things that don't appear to be true?

ANSWERS

In truth, none of these were lies. The Torah may be teaching that truth is not absolute. These are all examples of "bending the truth," rather than lies, which are outright fallacies. Sometimes, bending the truth is allowed for specific reasons:

For instance, the Gemara explains, and the *Baalei Tosafos* clarify, that in the first example, G-d didn't "lie" but rather "bent the truth" so as not to cause marital issues. By saying that Sarah said that she was old (and not him), Avraham wouldn't be upset with her! In the second episode, when Sarah said, "I didn't laugh," she may have not lied in the sense that she in fact didn't laugh out loud! (Interestingly, G-d reprimands her in this instance in any event, perhaps because unlike the other examples here, this "bending of truth" didn't have a clear purpose (i.e., for peace or safety). In the third case, Avraham wasn't lying because, in a sense, Sarah could be described as his sister. After all, the *Imrei Shefer* reminds us that Avraham purposely married his brother Haran's daughter Sarah to carry on Haran's legacy. She was, in a sense, Haran's replacement; the female version of his brother is…a sister!

Finally, in the fourth anecdote, it is not farfetched to say that Avraham either knew with prophecy that he was in fact going to sacrifice a lamb, or that the "lamb" he was referring to was indeed euphemistically Yitzchak!

A lie, on the other hand, is an outright fallacy—calling black red or red black. Bending the truth, although misleading, is allowed halachically when the intent is to save from physical or mental injury.

In *Vayeira*, the Torah teaches us that the truth takes second fiddle to life and is thus not an absolute ethic! Lest you wonder, it seems so sacrilegious to allow "bending the truth" even though there are positive intentions to save from injury, there is a stronger message: Even when there is potential for mental or physical injury, we should try bending the truth rather than outright lying, the latter of which can have a deleterious effect on our nature!

"מִדְּבַר שֶׁקֶר תִּרְחָק"—From lies you shall distance yourself" may in fact be understood: "From lies, you will distance your self," i.e., you will move away from your own very essence. Therefore, avoid outright lies at all cost!

Regarding the verse brought in the aforementioned ethic, it may very well be emphasizing *emes* to point out that *emes* is not always an absolute black and white, but rather must be balanced and defined as a "judgment of peace." *Emes* can be altered (but not completely destroyed) in order to promote or restore peace!

The three attributes are interconnected in the sense that truth is defined by how it impacts peace.

─────────── TAKEAWAY MESSAGES ───────────

We find four apparent lies in this *parashah*. Or do we? In truth (not lying!), these are not lies but *bending of the truth*, which is allowed when the goal is to save from physical or mental injury. Whether for *shalom bayis*, or to save oneself from Avimelech, or to spare Yitzchak undue worry, bending the truth is clearly shown to be OK at times. Outright lying, though, is forbidden, even in tough times, to spare us the deleterious effect it may have on us! "מִדְּבַר שֶׁקֶר תִּרְחָק"—From lies you shall distance yourself!" could also be read as "From lies, you become someone/ something else—distant from your true self!"

Don't lie, even when you have to; better to bend the truth!

Chayei Sarah

CAMELS AND GOOD DEEDS?

עַל שְׁלשָׁה֙ דְבָרִים הָעוֹלָם עוֹמֵד֙ עַל הַתּוֹרָה
וְעַל הָעֲבוֹדָה וְעַל גְּמִילוּת חֲסָדִים.

On three things the world stands: On Torah, service, and good deeds. (Avos 1:2)

QUESTIONS

What is the significance of Rivkah's exemplification of doing "good deeds" have to do with camels? Perhaps she could have shown her good nature by walking a blind man across the street or feeding poor people? Why by feeding camels?

ANSWERS

The common understanding for the term גְּמִילוּת חֲסָדִים is that you are גּוֹמֵל, causing kindness to exist by doing exemplary acts. But the very word of גְּמִילוּת חֲסָדִים is also related to the word "camel." After all, the Hebrew root for גְּמִילוּת is spelled the same as the word for camel, גָמָל!

What does a camel have to do with גְּמִילוּת חֲסָדִים? After feeding camels (they can drink up to fifty-three gallons in one sitting), they can subsequently survive a long time, being "self-sufficient." When temperatures rise above 110 degrees Fahrenheit, camels can survive for about five days without drinking water. During the winter, camels can survive six or seven months without drinking water. The concept is that true גְּמִילוּת חֲסָדִים is predicated on helping someone else be self-sufficient. It is not about giving up of yours to help another as much as it is about helping another stand on his own two feet!

TAKEAWAY MESSAGES

Perhaps Rivkah's paradigmatic גְּמִילוּת חֲסָדִים involved camels (גמלים) because just like a camel becomes incredibly self-sufficient after being fed, so too the ultimate גְּמִילוּת חֲסָדִים is helping another become self-sufficient! Camels and good deeds—a lesson in גְּמִילוּת חֲסָדִים.

LESSON OF MALKA HORWITH
FROM THIS PARASHAH

הַכֹּל צָפוּי וְהָרְשׁוּת נְתוּנָה
וּבְטוֹב הָעוֹלָם נִדּוֹן...

Everything is expected and yet permission is granted, and in goodness the world is judged...(Avos 3:15)

QUESTIONS

What does it mean that "in *goodness* the world is judged"? Let's look at our *parashah*:

וְעַתָּה אִם יֶשְׁכֶם עֹשִׂים חֶסֶד וֶאֱמֶת, אֶת אֲדֹנִי הַגִּידוּ לִי וְאִם לֹא הַגִּידוּ לִי וְאֶפְנֶה עַל יָמִין אוֹ עַל שְׂמֹאל. וַיַּעַן לָבָן וּבְתוּאֵל וַיֹּאמְרוּ מֵה' יָצָא הַדָּבָר לֹא נוּכַל דַּבֵּר אֵלֶיךָ רַע אוֹ טוֹב.

"And now if you will deal kindly and truly with my master, tell me; and if not, tell me; that I may turn to the right hand, or to the left." Then Lavan and Besuel answered and said, "The thing comes from the Lord; we cannot speak to you [neither] bad nor good." (Bereishis 24:49–50)

After Eliezer tells Lavan and Besuel about the unmistakable sign that Rivkah was to be the chosen one for Yitzchak, Eliezer asks them if he should go to the "right or left," in a sense, neglecting to see the sign. They answer that "the straight path" (i.e., not right or left) that led to Rivkah was so clearly G-d-chosen that "we cannot speak to you [neither]

48

bad nor good." The *Likutei Anshei Shem* wonders why Lavan and Besuel did not say, "We cannot speak to you bad," alone, without adding the "or good" part, since after all, wasn't the miraculous sign that Rivkah passed the litmus test a *good* thing?

ANSWERS

I'll answer the question with the story of Malka Horwith, a 101-year-old patient of mine. It was *Parashas Chayei Sarah* when she was hospitalized and told me about her harrowing escape during the Holocaust (which she permitted me to share). She was transferred from the Vilna Ghetto to a concentration camp, and after both her parents and her younger sister were killed, she told me, "What did I care about being a Jew? Even Rosh Hashanah and Yom Kippur meant nothing to me. But one day, before I planned my escape from the camp, my father appeared to me in a dream, and I asked him '*Tatte*, should I go to the **right or to the left**?' and he replied, 'Go straight!'" She woke up, and the next morning she joined the partisans as they dashed for the forest (and not the towns to the right and left of the camp). This strategy, although arduous, proved to be lifesaving, and after two years of hiding in the forest, she ultimately survived. She told me clearly, "This dream made me believe again." But what was it about her dream that made her believe?

The *Likutei Anshei Shem* explained that Lavan and Besuel purposely responded, "We cannot speak to you [neither] bad nor good" because this episode was so Divinely ordained, as evidenced by the clear signs, that there was no true *bechirah*, choice. An action that we fulfill can only be truly "good or bad" if there is a choice that leads up to the reality. If it is fixed no matter what you do, the reality just "is what it is"! Even though Rivkah's "Divine" selection was clearly good in the sense that it was so amazingly coincidental, Lavan, Besuel, and Eliezer really felt no other choice in the matter, which made their personal judgment (good or bad) irrelevant. When Eliezer says to Lavan and Besuel, "[If you don't tell me I can take Rivkah], I will go to the right or to the left," he was saying this rhetorically, just like Malka Horwith rhetorically asked her father in the dream, "Shall I go to the right or to the left?" as if she really had a choice then. The dream that she had seventy-four years earlier, though, gave her sustainable belief. It made her realize that despite all her sadness, this was her destiny for which she could bear no guilt about. It was all, "מֶה' יָצָא הַדָּבָר—this came from Hashem," and it didn't pay for her to contemplate the goodness or badness of her upcoming decisions. Like the *bashert*-ness of Rivkah and Yitzchak, for better or worse, she realized that her destiny was out of her control; but this lack of control actually gave her solace at that time, removing any potential guilt (the proverbial "I could've/should've done this or that" did not apply here) and lent her the necessary resolve to somehow survive the forest.

The Mishnah in *Avos* reminds us that "וּבְטוֹב הָעוֹלָם נִדּוֹן—in goodness the world is judged." We are only judged in life by the things that can be called "good moves." If things happen out of our control, we are afforded the opportunity to just put our hands up in the air and declare, "מֶה' יָצָא הַדָּבָר, for those things, we cannot possibly be judged."

─────────── TAKEAWAY MESSAGES ───────────

Why did Lavan and Besuel say, "We cannot speak to you [neither] bad nor good," when clearly it seemed that the Divinely orchestrated *shidduch* between Rivkah and Yitzchak was a good thing? Sometimes in life, we are faced with challenges in which we rhetorically wonder or ask, "Should we go to the right or left?" knowing full well that we have *no* choice in the matter. Rather than losing hope at that time, we can pull a Malka Horwith and take solace in the concept of מֶה' יָצָא הַדָּבָר. For those things beyond our control, we can go with the flow, knowing that G-d only judges us for things that we can control.

The lesson of Malka Horwith is the lesson of Rivkah and Yitzchak's *shidduch*—taking solace and rekindling belief in מֶה' יָצָא הַדָּבָר.

SERVANT ELIEZER'S MASTER LESSON

וְהַתּוֹרָה נִקְנֵית בְּאַרְבָּעִים וּשְׁמֹנָה דְבָרִים.
וְאֵלוּ הֵן...נוֹשֵׂא בְעֹל עִם חֲבֵרוֹ.

*Torah is acquired in forty-eight ways. These
are...participating in the burden of one's fellow...(Avos 6:6)*

רַבִּי יַעֲקֹב אוֹמֵר: הָעוֹלָם הַזֶּה דּוֹמֶה לִפְרוֹזְדוֹר
בִּפְנֵי הָעוֹלָם הַבָּא. הַתְקֵן עַצְמְךָ בַפְּרוֹזְדוֹר
כְּדֵי שֶׁתִּכָּנֵס לַטְּרַקְלִין.

*Rabbi Yaakov would say: This world is comparable to the
antechamber before the World to Come. Prepare yourself in
the antechamber, so that you may enter the banquet hall.
(Avos 4:16)*

QUESTIONS

In what way does carrying the burden of others tie into the ethic of
"this world is but an antechamber to the next"? Additionally, where in
our *parashah* do we see a perfect example of נוֹשֵׂא בְעֹל עִם חֲבֵרוֹ?

ANSWERS

וַיֹּאמַר עֶבֶד אַבְרָהָם אָנֹכִי.
And he [Eliezer] said: "I am Avraham's servant."

Let me set the stage: Avraham asked his servant Eliezer to find Yitzchak a wife. Upon Eliezer's arrival into Rivkah's father Besuel's home, he revealed that he was merely "a servant of Avraham." Eliezer proactively and deliberately volunteered degrading personal information immediately as he entered Besuel's house. The Gemara (*Bava Kama* 92b) posits that from here we learn why people say that one should reveal their negative characteristics upon meeting someone else.

But why is that? The *Maharsha* on the Gemara answers that it is much harder to come crashing down from a pedestal than if one was never elevated in the first place. By stating he was a simple servant, Eliezer was less likely to feel embarrassed later on when he was "found" out.

But there is yet another surprising explanation given by the *Torah Temimah*: One should reveal degrading information proactively so as to avoid creating a scenario where the one who finds out the information might consequently embarrass the lowly one! A person should be so sensitive and thoughtful to the point that he worries less about his own embarrassment, and instead worries more about putting another in a position where they may transgress the sin of embarrassing others. Eliezer therefore proactively calls himself a servant to prevent Rivkah's father Besuel from being *over* the sin of embarrassing others if he discovers Eliezer's lowly status at a later point. This is a classic example of נוֹשֵׂא בְּעֹל עִם חֲבֵרוֹ—taking the responsibility of someone else on your own shoulders.

The theme is thoughtfulness at all times, with foresight to prevent any problems down the road.

My mother, Helen Ciment, would always teach us that in both heaven and hell are there identical banquets replete with an all-you-can-eat buffet table. In both places, everyone's elbows are locked in extension, the result being that no one can feed him or herself. Those in hell cannot understand how to partake of this most amazing feast and are thus frustrated with a hellish frustration. However, those in heaven enjoy the buffet unimpeded because they have been conditioned in the prior world by the lesson of נוֹשֵׂא בְּעֹל עִם חֲבֵרוֹ and thus simply feed each other! Locked elbows only affect the selfish!

When the Mishnah says, "הַתְקֵן עַצְמְךָ בַּפְּרוֹזְדוֹר כְּדֵי שֶׁתִּכָּנֵס לַטְּרַקְלִין"—Prepare yourself in the antechamber so that you may enter the banquet hall," the Tanna is likely saying that if you prepare in this world with the lesson of putting your friends' needs even before your own, you will easily be able to partake in the feast of the World to Come. It is not necessarily that we earn heaven by acting with benevolence, rather that our actions in this world prime us to best take advantage of the next world.

―――――――――― TAKEAWAY MESSAGES ――――――――――

When Eliezer proactively introduces himself as a lowly servant, he may have done so to prevent later humiliation (*Maharsha*). Alternatively, he was actually being נוֹשֵׂא בְּעֹל עִם חֲבֵרוֹ, and merely trying to prevent the possibility that Besuel would subsequently humiliate Eliezer by saying something derogatory and thus be *over* the sin of humiliating others (*Torah Temimah*). This is a Biblical illustration of what נוֹשֵׂא בְּעֹל עִם חֲבֵרוֹ means.

Finally, heaven and hell are both banquets replete with buffets par excellence. The attendees of both have locked elbows, but only those in heaven, primed with the concept of נוֹשֵׂא בְּעֹל עִם חֲבֵרוֹ, can enjoy the luscious food because they realize that they can feed each other. The servant Eliezer's *master* lesson is: next-worldly!

EPHRON, LAVAN...AND CHICAGO

שַׁמַּאי אוֹמֵר: אֱמֹר מְעַט וַעֲשֵׂה הַרְבֵּה...

Shammai said: Speak a little and do a lot. (Avos 1:15)

--- QUESTIONS ---

1. What are two examples of this ethic in the *parashah*?
2. Is אֱמֹר מְעַט וַעֲשֵׂה הַרְבֵּה emphasizing the speaking or the doing? In other words, what is the better virtue: the אֱמֹר מְעַט—speaking less, or the וַעֲשֵׂה הַרְבֵּה—doing more?

--- ANSWERS ---

וַיַּעַן עֶפְרוֹן הַחִתִּי אֶת אַבְרָהָם בְּאָזְנֵי בְנֵי חֵת לְכֹל בָּאֵי שַׁעַר עִירוֹ לֵאמֹר. לֹא אֲדֹנִי שְׁמָעֵנִי הַשָּׂדֶה נָתַתִּי לָךְ וְהַמְּעָרָה אֲשֶׁר בּוֹ לְךָ נְתַתִּיהָ לְעֵינֵי בְנֵי עַמִּי נְתַתִּיהָ לָּךְ קְבֹר מֵתֶךָ.

Ephron the Hittite answered Avraham in the hearing of the children of Ches, all that went in at the gate of his city, saying: "No, my lord, hear me: the field I give you, and the cave that is in it, I give it to you; in the presence of the sons of my people I give it to you; bury your dead." (Bereishis 23:10–11)

Seemingly, Ephron is giving the burial plot as a gift to Avraham as he "windily" exclaims in front of the whole town. But then he continues:

אֲדֹנִי שְׁמָעֵנִי אֶרֶץ אַרְבַּע מֵאֹת שֶׁקֶל כֶּסֶף בֵּינִי וּבֵינְךָ מַה הִוא וְאֶת מֵתְךָ קְבֹר.

"My lord, hear me: a piece of land worth four hundred shekels of silver, what is that between me and you? Bury your dead."

Rashi explains:

וַיִּשְׁקֹל אַבְרָהָם לְעֶפְרֹן: חסר וי"ו, לפי שאמר הרבה ואפילו מעט לא עשה.

"And Avraham weighed out to Ephron." עֶפְרֹן is spelled without a vav, because he promised much but did not do even a little [i.e., he promised the cave as a gift but took a great deal of money for it]. (Bereishis Rabbah 58:7; Bechoros 50a; Bava Metzia 87a)

So the duplicitous Ephron is criticized as one who speaks a lot and did not even do a fraction of what he spoke!

Later in the *parashah*, this theme comes up again:

וַיַּעַן לָבָן וּבְתוּאֵל וַיֹּאמְרוּ מֵה' יָצָא הַדָּבָר לֹא נוּכַל דַּבֵּר אֵלֶיךָ רַע אוֹ טוֹב.

Then Lavan and Besuel answered and said: "The thing comes from the Lord; we cannot speak to you [neither] bad nor good." (Bereishis 24:50)

Seemingly, Lavan is reassuring Eliezer that Rivkah can certainly leave with Eliezer ASAP to become Yitzchak's wife by this "windy" version of "yes." But yet, a few *pesukim* later, it says:

וַיֹּאמֶר אָחִיהָ וְאִמָּהּ תֵּשֵׁב הַנַּעֲרָ אִתָּנוּ יָמִים אוֹ עָשׂוֹר אַחַר תֵּלֵךְ.

And her brother and her mother said: "Let the girl stay with us a few days, at least ten; after that she shall go." (Ibid., v. 55)

Despite the initial, seemingly obliging gesture, the duplicitous Lavan is trying to weasel his way out of it. Notice that much like Ephron's name was spelled without a *vav* in the *pasuk*, demonstrating his duplicity, in this *pasuk*, which also details the duplicity of Lavan, the word נַעֲרָ

is missing a ה, perhaps to trigger our sensitivity that both Ephron and Lavan are saying one thing but trying to hide things from us!

Chicago is called the "Windy City" not because the wind speed is greater than other cities (for instance, Boston has greater average wind speeds) but rather because long-winded politicians and frequent political conventions were commonplace in early Chicago history. Both Ephron and Lavan demonstrated their "windy" nature. Unfortunately, like many politicians, the number of words they use to say they will do something is inversely proportional to the likelihood they will actually follow through. אֱמֹר מְעַט וַעֲשֵׂה הַרְבֵּה is not saying that the **saying** or the **doing** is the key, but rather that when you say a little, there is a higher chance that you are going to follow through on your word. The windiness of both Ephron and Lavan were giveaways that "something was up," and we are taught the lesson to be wary of the winded!

——————— TAKEAWAY MESSAGES ———————

Both Ephron and Lavan exhibit the lesson inherent in אֱמֹר מְעַט וַעֲשֵׂה הַרְבֵּה: When Ephron exclaimed to all "windily" that he was giving away his field for free; and when Lavan exclaimed "windily" that of course Rivkah could go with Eliezer, the long-winded response was a giveaway that they were not really planning to follow through on their words. Inherent in "windy" verbiage are hidden agendas (symbolized by the missing *vav* from Ephron and the missing *hei* from the word *naarah*). אֱמֹר מְעַט וַעֲשֵׂה הַרְבֵּה may not only mean, "speak a little and do a lot," but also "speak a little, which proves you mean to do a lot"! Like Chicago, both Ephron and Lavan were "windy" for sure.

WHAT WAS SO GREAT ABOUT
SARAH ANYWAY?

הוּא הָיָה אוֹמֵר: מַרְבֶּה בָשָׂר מַרְבֶּה רִמָּה.
מַרְבֶּה נְכָסִים מַרְבֶּה דְאָגָה.

And he [Hillel] says: The more flesh, the more worms. The
more possessions, the more worry. (Avos 2:7)

---------------- QUESTIONS ----------------

Is *Avos* really just teaching us here that "the more the merrier" is
false, or is there an even deeper understanding?

Rabbi Yaakov Garfinkel asked: Why is the *parashah* named *Chayei
Sarah* when it basically contains only her death? Wouldn't it have been
more appropriate for this *parashah* name to be applied to the *parashah*
in which she lived? After all, *chayei* means "the life of."

Rashi says that the *pasuk* states she lived one hundred years, twenty
years, and seven years to highlight that just as she didn't sin at twenty,
she was sinless at one hundred, and just as she was beautiful at seven,
she was beautiful at twenty. I would have expected a midrash highlighting Sarah's greatness to say that she was as actively doing good deeds
when she was one hundred as she was vibrant at twenty. Why did the
midrash couch her greatness in highlighting that she didn't sin, rather
than highlighting her active good deeds! Also why is it that our matri-
archs, including Sarah, were notable beauties?

שֶׁקֶר הַחֵן וְהֶבֶל הַיֹּפִי אִשָּׁה יִרְאַת ה' הִיא תִתְהַלָּל.

Grace is false, and beauty is vain; but a woman who fears G-d,
that is praiseworthy. (Mishlei 31:30)

After all, "Grace is false, and beauty is vain"! Why specifically does our midrash also highlight her beauty, saying that "when she was twenty, she was as beautiful...""?

———————————————— ANSWERS ————————————————

Rabbi Garfinkel paraphrased the Lubavitcher Rebbe, who answered that Sarah's real greatness wasn't necessarily about what she did but the legacy that she passed on. The "life of Sarah" thus belongs to the *parashah* of her death because her legacy was perpetuated in her death as she was such a righteous person.

Perhaps we can take that a step further. Rabbi Bixon analyzes why it was that Lot was saved from Sodom. The verse states, "וַיִּזְכֹּר אֱלֹקִים אֶת אַבְרָהָם—and G-d remembered Avraham" (*Bereishis* 29:19), and *Rashi* says that this is referring to Lot, who merited being saved because he didn't ruin Avraham's ruse when he told Avimelech that Sarah was his sister. (Lot could have tattled on Avraham and shattered the trick that saved Avraham and Sarah!) Rabbi Bixon asks why Lot wasn't worthy of being saved due to his great *middah* of hospitality, rather than this "inaction" of simply not tattling. He beautifully answers that sometimes it is more of an accomplishment to refrain from an urge than it is to positively do something. Going against nature and doing the right thing is more meritorious than doing what your innate proclivity leads you to do. Lot went against his nature and hushed himself, ultimately making him deserving of being saved. So the first point is that "not sinning" can sometimes be more of a positive attribute than doing an active good deed.

The Gemara recounts that once, a Roman emperor's daughter asked why Rabbi Yehoshua was so ugly if he was a wise Talmud scholar. After illustrating his point demonstrably with an interesting teaching point, she then asked, "So why is Rabbi Yosef a Talmud scholar and yet is so handsome?" Rabbi Yehoshua answered, "Can you imagine what a greater scholar he would be if he were ugly!" (*Taanis* 7). The point is that beauty usually comes at a cost. Usually the attention garnered from external beauty leads people down a road that takes them away from spirituality or genuine accomplishment. Now it makes sense why the midrash highlights the greatness of Sarah in terms of her not sinning—perhaps despite her beauty! (Now *Rashi's* description of her sinlessness at one hundred, and her beauty at twenty, make perfect sense.)

This also may explain Shlomo HaMelech's statement: The meaning of the word "that" in "that is praiseworthy" may very well be that grace and beauty can be destructive, but a woman who is beautiful and yet is *still G-d-fearing* is extra praiseworthy. "That" is referring to the achievement of being G-d-fearing, even though this is against the odds when one has beauty and other distractions.

When Hillel says, "מַרְבֶּה בָשָׂר מַרְבֶּה רִמָּה מַרְבֶּה נְכָסִים מַרְבֶּה דְאָגָה," he is not simply stating that having lots of amenities does not necessarily make you happy. He is saying that having lots of amenities brings even more challenges for you to overcome. Blessings in abundance can become curses if not tempered or controlled. If one tempers one's gifts like Sarah Imeinu, how much greater is her beauty indeed!

─────────────── TAKEAWAY MESSAGES ───────────────

Sarah is our matriarch and a role model, demonstrating that our life's mission is to ensure our legacy (the Rebbe and Rabbi Garfinkel). As Lot taught us, sometimes inaction can be more powerful than actions if those inactions defy our innate proclivity. Sometimes, greatness can be about what you don't do more than what you do (Rabbi Bixon).

Sarah was indeed great, not so much because she actively did good deeds, but also because she did so despite the odds against her.

Sarah was great because she was all about legacy and she succeeded against the odds. Being beautiful can be challenging!

NATURE OR NURTURE—IN RIVKAH'S BELLY

רַ־בִּי נְהוֹרַאי אוֹמֵר: הֱוֵי גוֹלֶה לִמְקוֹ⊏ תּוֹרָה
וְאַל תֹּאמַר שֶׁהִיא רָתְבֹא אַחֲרֶיךָ שֶׁחֲבֵרֶיךָ
יְקַיְּמוּהָ בְיָדֶךָ וְאֶל בִּינָתְךָ אַל תִּשָּׁעֵן.

*Rabbi Nehorai would say: Exile yourself to a place of
Torah; do not say that it will come after you, that your
colleagues will help you retain it. Rely not on your own
understanding...(Avos 4:13)*

QUESTIONS

Where do we learn this concept of "exiling yourself to a place of
Torah"? What does this ethic really mean, and why does one have to
specifically exile oneself?

The answer lies in analyzing Rivkah's pregnancy:

וַיִּתְרֹצְצוּ הַבָּנִים בְּקִרְבָּהּ וַתֹּאמֶר אִם כֵּן לָמָּה זֶּה אָנֹכִי וַתֵּלֶךְ
לִדְרֹשׁ אֶת ה'.

*And the children struggled together within her, and she said:
"If so, why is this to me?" And she went to inquire of Hashem."
(Bereishis 25:22)*

Rashi brings down the famous midrash here:

> *Our Rabbis (Bereishis Rabbah 63:6) interpreted it [the word*
> וַיִּתְרֹצְצוּ] *as an expression of running (ריצה): When she passed*
> *by the entrances of [the] Torah [academies] of Shem and Ever,*
> *Yaakov would run and struggle to come out; when she passed*
> *the entrance of [a temple of] idolatry, Eisav would run and*
> *struggle to come out...*

But there seems to be a basic problem with this midrash: How can we fault Eisav for being an idolater if he was created that way? Even before he was born, with no real volition of his own, he was drawn to *avodah zarah*. And just as we seemingly shouldn't fault Eisav, we also cannot credit Yaakov for his holiness, which also seemed innately inherent.

ANSWERS

Consider the following homily: When Rivkah says, "לָמָּה זֶּה אָנֹכִי," she may be referring to the eventual first commandment: "Why is there that very first commandment of אָנֹכִי ה' אֱלֹקֶיךָ אֲשֶׁר הוֹצֵאתִיךָ מֵאֶרֶץ מִצְרַיִם מִבֵּית עֲבָדִים'? After all, if my children are born with a predilection for G-dliness or for idolatry, then of what use is a commandment to believe in one G-d? Either you are born a believer or non-believer!" The answer to her own question is provided by her next action: "וַתֵּלֶךְ לִדְרֹשׁ אֶת ה'"—She went to seek G-d." The purpose of the first commandment is not simply to just believe in G-d, because as pointed out above, people are bestowed with *natural* tendencies to be believers or non-believers. Rather, the challenge is to constantly seek to grow in your belief. Growth can only come about by exiting your comfort zone, removing yourself from the innate tendencies so that you can truly exceed your capabilities, or in some cases, steer away from an unbelieving future. The focus is on the **seeking**, and in that sense, despite the innate proclivities of Eisav and Yaakov, Rivkah took solace in knowing that their challenges were one and the same!

And that is why the Tanna says, "הֱוֵי גוֹלֶה לִמְקוֹם תּוֹרָה—One needs to *ostracize* himself to a holy place." Sometimes one needs to strip oneself of the innate tendencies and/or immediate environment to truly reach their spiritual peak. This ostracizing reminds us that the trajectory is more important than where we begin because so much is merely injected in us either from our DNA or from our environment; "וְאֶל בִּינָתְךָ אַל תִּשָׁעֵן," we should not merely rely on what we inherently know.

───────── TAKEAWAY MESSAGES ─────────

When Rivkah asks, "Why me?" perhaps she is saying, "Why have a commandment to believe in G-d if we are born with innate tendencies to believe or disbelieve?" The answer is that the challenge is less about our bestowed belief tendencies and more about how we nurture such tendencies. The **seeking** is the key; one must exile oneself and not simply rely on one's own inherent knowledge in the quest to attain meaning. Nature or nurture? Nurture your nature! That is the *derashah* of Rivkah's *derishah*!

YAAKOV'S TRUTHFULNESS
AND THE TENNIS KICK SERVE

עַל־ שְׁלשָׁה דְבָרִים הָעוֹלָם עוֹמֵד עַל ־הַדִּין
וְעַל הָאֱמֶת וְעַל הַשָּׁלוֹם.

By three things is the world sustained: law, truth, and peace.
(Avos 1:18)

———————————— QUESTIONS ————————————

Is justice a prerequisite for truth, or are these disparate elements?

תִּתֵּן אֱמֶת לְיַעֲקֹב חֶסֶד לְאַבְרָהָם.

You shall show truth to Yaakov, kindness to Avraham.
(Michah 7:20)

Honesty is the virtue attributed to Yaakov. But if Yaakov indeed beguiled Eisav and Yitzchak, this seems misplaced. Furthermore, "מִדְּבַר שֶׁקֶר תִּרְחָק—Distance [oneself] from a false matter," would supposedly mean that the one saying the untruth (i.e., Yaakov), the subject/victim of the untruth (i.e., Eisav), and the public (i.e., Yitzchak), ideally should not view the matter as a lie. Being squeaky clean from all sides would be expected from the Jewish paradigm of truth, no?

———————————— ANSWERS ————————————

Firstly, Yaakov did not consider himself to be lying. When he asked his mother about wearing Eisav's garments, he said, "אוּלַי יְמֻשֵּׁנִי אָבִי וְהָיִיתִי

בְּעֵינָיו כִּמְתַעְתֵּעַ—Perhaps my father will feel me, and I will seem to him as a mocker." But if he considered himself to be a real mocker, the wording would be, "וְהָיִיתִי בְעֵינָיו מְתַעְתֵּעַ—I will be exposed as the mocker [as I am]"! The extra כ is denoting that he knows he is not a fraud!

Secondly, even when Eisav says, "וַיַּעְקְבֵנִי זֶה פַעֲמַיִם—He has supplanted me these two times," *Onkelos* purposely interprets וַיַּעְקְבֵנִי as "outsmarted" (not tricked!). Again, the object of the potential untruth, Eisav, did not perceive Yaakov's trickery as an untruth. Finally, Yitzchak acknowledged that Yaakov took the *berachah* "בְּמִרְמָה," which *Ibn Ezra* defines as "guile" or "not telling truth," but which *Onkelos* (and then *Rashi*) interpret as "בחכמה—with wisdom"!

So it turns out that Yaakov and the blessing is actually the paradigm of *emes* because even though it may look on the outside as quite the contrary, all three players here (Yaakov, Eisav, and Yitzchak) knew that the justly achieved birthright entitled Yaakov to the blessing, as all acknowledged that he was, in fact, not being untruthful!

Rashi takes it even further and quotes the midrash that Yitzchak initially yelped in anger, thinking he blessed the wrong man, but then realized through Eisav's confession that he was not transgressing the "שורת הדין" (*Rashi* actually uses the word דין to make the point). The fact that Yaakov justly acquired the *bechorah* sets up the ultimate truth that Yaakov deserved the blessing, even though he had to achieve it in this convoluted way. Justice is indeed a prerequisite for truth: עַל שְׁלֹשָׁה דְבָרִים הָעוֹלָם עוֹמֵד עַל הַדִּין וְעַל הָאֱמֶת וְעַל הַשָּׁלוֹם.

Only after playing tennis for ten years did I finally figure out how to do the perfect kick serve. To serve, one must hit the ball from one's side to a specific box on the opposite side of the court. Most amateurs make the mistake of aiming for that particular box as they hit the ball. But in reality, if one hits the ball *aiming away from the box*, one will more consistently hit the ball into the box! The point is that sometimes the only way to get it into the right box is to change one's mindset and hit away from that box. The lesson is that *emes* is a box, and sometimes (even more often) you can or must arrive at the *emes* in a somewhat convoluted fashion, but it does not take away from the *emes*.

—————— TAKEAWAY MESSAGES ——————

"מִדְּבַר שֶׁקֶר תִּרְחָק" implores us to avoid lying or even the suspicion of lying, so how is Yaakov's sneaky retrieval of the *berachah* from Yitzchak consistent with his being the poster child of *emes*? Justice is what defines what true *emes* is, and Yaakov (כִּמְתַעְתֵּעַ), Eisav (וַיַּעְקְבֵנִי) and even Yitzchak (בְּמִרְמָה) did not question Yaakov's truthfulness. Sometimes, like a wicked tennis kick serve, you have to aim *away from the box* to get it into the box; a convoluted path to *emes* does not mean it is not *emes*! Yaakov's truthfulness and the tennis kick-serve—don't confuse the path to *emes* with *emes* or *sheker* itself.

WHERE DOES "OY VEY" COME FROM AND WHY IS IT A JEWISH THING?

יוֹתֵר מִלְּמוּדְךָ עֲשֵׂה.

More [important] than your learning, do!" (Avos 6:5)

--- QUESTIONS ---

Where in the *parashah* do we see this theme espoused in *Avos*? Let's analyze two classic questions from this *parashah*:

1. How was Yitzchak fooled by Eisav? Was he really so naive?
2. Did Yaakov really pull a fast one by Eisav when he "stole" his birthright for a bowl of soup, or did Eisav actually know what he was giving up?

--- ANSWERS ---

The similarity in the verses of the taking of Eisav's birthright and the taking of Eisav's blessing are too obvious to miss, so much that they may answer both questions!

When Eisav squandered his birthright for soup, the verse reads:

וְיַעֲקֹב נָתַן לְעֵשָׂו לֶחֶם וּנְזִיד עֲדָשִׁים וַיֹּאכַל וַיֵּשְׁתְּ וַיָּקָם וַיֵּלַךְ וַיִּבֶז עֵשָׂו אֶת הַבְּכֹרָה.

And Yaakov gave Eisav bread and pottage of lentils; and he **ate and drank, and rose up, and went his way**. *So Eisav despised his birthright. (Bereishis 25:34)*

Later on, when Yaakov tricks Yitzchak and "steals" the *berachah*, the verse reads:

וַיֵּלֶךְ וַיִּקַּח וַיָּבֵא לְאִמּוֹ וַתַּעַשׂ אִמּוֹ מַטְעַמִּים כַּאֲשֶׁר אָהֵב אָבִיו.

And (Yaakov) went, and fetched, and brought them to his mother; and his mother made savory food, such as his father loved.

There is clear parallel structure in the action displayed by Eisav in the beginning of the *parashah* and the action displayed by Yaakov later on! Yitzchak perhaps wasn't really as naive as he is portrayed. He envisioned the Jewish People, who were going to have the materialistic blessings of מִטַּל הַשָּׁמַיִם and וּמִשְׁמַנֵּי הָאָרֶץ to be a people of action. Sure, Eisav had his clear faults, but Yitzchak likely admired that he was a man of action, as opposed to an אִישׁ תָּם יֹשֵׁב אֹהָלִים; he preferred, "יוֹתֵר מִלִּמּוּדְךָ עֲשֵׂה—More [important] than your learning, do!" Hinting at his kinetic nature, Eisav is seen as "וַיֹּאכַל וַיֵּשְׁתְּ וַיָּקָם וַיֵּלֶךְ," all words connoting action. Ironically, and through the coaching by G-d with two fortunate happenstances, Yaakov metamorphasized into a man of action, as hinted by the words "וַיֵּלֶךְ וַיִּקַּח וַיָּבֵא" at the end of the *parashah*. Once Yitzchak realized that Yaakov was indeed a man of action, Yitzchak declared, "גַּם בָּרוּךְ יִהְיֶה."

As to the question of whether Yaakov stole Eisav's birthright, when by Yaakov it says, "וַיֵּלֶךְ וַיִּקַּח וַיָּבֵא," the midrash says that the alliteration by these successive words sound like *"vey, vey, vey,"* hinting that Yaakov *begrudgingly* set out to trick his father. Although the midrash doesn't say the same thing by the stealing of the *bechorah*, the alliteration there is even more evident: וַיֹּאכַל וַיֵּשְׁתְּ וַיָּקָם וַיֵּלֶךְ—*vey, vey, vey, and vey,"* Eisav sounds like he begrudgingly, **yet knowingly**, was giving up his *bechorah*! The first *"oy veys"* in the Torah are perhaps related to the giving up of the birthright and the difficult circumstances surrounding Yaakov's acquisition of the *berachos*!

──────────── TAKEAWAY MESSAGES ────────────

The concept in *Avos* of "יוֹתֵר מִלִּמּוּדְךָ עֲשֵׂה" may be why Yitzchak preferred the hunter Eisav over Yaakov, the "אִישׁ תָּם יֹשֵׁב אֹהָלִים." Only after

Yaakov developed the capability of being a man of action did Yitzchak exclaim, "גַּם בָּרוּךְ יִהְיֶה," and accepted him wholeheartedly. The midrash says that the *vav-yud* of "וַיֵּלֶךְ וַיִּקַּח וַיָּבֵא" hinted that Yaakov *begrudgingly* tricked his father. The even more obvious alliteration by Eisav in the stealing of the *bechorah* (וַיֹּאכַל וַיֵּשְׁתְּ וַיָּקָם וַיֵּלֶךְ) may possibly hint that Eisav likewise *begrudgingly* but knowingly gave away his *bechorah*! The first *oy vey* indeed may explain why *oy vey* is distinctly Jewish—our Jewishness actually originates from a couple of *oy veys*!

EMES, CHESSED, OR GEVURAH— WHICH SUPERSEDES ALL?

וְד־הַתּוֹרָה נִקְנֵית בְּאַרְבָּעִים וּשְׁמֹנָה דְבָרִים. וְאֵלוּ הֵן...מַעֲמִיד־וֹ עַל הָאֱמֶת וּמַעֲמִידוֹ עַל הַשָּׁלוֹם...

Torah is acquired in forty-eight ways...standing by the truth and standing by the peace...(Avos 6:6)

QUESTIONS
---

1. What does it mean to "stand by the peace"?
2. We often ascribe key *middos*, attributes, to each of our Patriarchs

תִּתֵּן אֱמֶת לְיַעֲקֹב חֶסֶד לְאַבְרָהָם...

To Avraham kindness; Yaakov truth...(Michah 7:20)

Though not stated in the verse, Yitzchak is associated with *gevurah*, strength (*Shem MiShmuel, Vayishlach*). But it almost sounds like "Purim Torah" when you think about it. How can Avraham correspond to kindness when, after all, he sent out his wife Hagar and son Yishmael to a desert when Sarah complained about Yishmael's influences.

3. How can Yitzchak correspond to strength as, after all, he is portrayed as a gullible blind man "allowing" Eisav to manipulate him and Yaakov to deceive him?

69

4. Finally, how can Yaakov correspond to truth if, in fact, he mis-chievously "stole" Eisav's birthright?

———————————— ANSWERS ————————————

Let's analyze the three main attributes—*chessed, gevurah,* and *emes*—and then we'll be able to answer the above. Firstly, the words *chessed* and *gevurah* are not automatically associated with being right or even good. The word *chessed* is seen in *Parashas Kedoshim* as refering to an incestuous relationship. The word *gibor* is used by the evil Nimrod who was a גִּבּוֹר צַיִד. The point is not to suggest that Avraham had the "evil" connotation of *chessed,* heaven forbid, but rather that *chessed* is ambiguous and may not always be viewed by all as clearly good or bad. When Avraham sent away Hagar and Yishmael, he was commanded to do so by G-d, which de facto makes it kindness (shielding Yitzchak from Yishmael's bad influences) more than unkind (sending them out to harsh conditions). In other words, even when one faction will view the action as unkind (Hagar and Yishmael), the act was nevertheless an act of *chessed.* Kindness can sometimes be cruel, but it is kindness nonetheless.

וַיָּשָׁב יִצְחָק וַיַּחְפֹּר אֶת בְּאֵרֹת הַמַּיִם אֲשֶׁר חָפְרוּ בִּימֵי אַבְרָהָם אָבִיו
וַיְסַתְּמוּם פְּלִשְׁתִּים.

And Yitzchak digged again the wells of water, which they had
digged in the days of Avraham his father; for the Philistines
had stopped them after the death of Avraham. (Bereishis
26:18)

As for *gevurah,* my father, Dr. Larry Ciment, said that Yitzchak's *ge-vurah* may also refer to his unshakable *emunah* in tradition. Yitzchak's great strength is really in restoring the wells of his father that were plugged up by the Pelishtim; *his* focus, and therefore strength, *wasn't in innovation but in preservation.* Likewise, he wanted to hold steadfast on to the prevalent tradition that a *bechor,* a firstborn, should merit to inherit. His hope that Eisav was to be the rightful *bechor* was less a function of Yitzchak's gullibility and more a function of genuine faith in tradition. We learn, however, that sometimes tradition is meant to be broken. The fact that the word *gibor* is not only associated with good (Nimrod was a *gibor*) may hint that *gevurah* is not always necessarily a positive thing!

By Yaakov, however, *emes* is different. *Emes* is not simply "truth," and it is not an absolute ethic. Paraphrasing Dr. Velvy Posner, *emes* is more aptly defined as "what is right/appropriate" than "what is true." When Yaakov "stole" the *bechorah*, he was surely committing a ruse, but he was nevertheless exhibiting genuine *emes* in the sense of doing the right thing—enabling the inheritance of the good portion to reach the right hands!

Unlike *chessed* and *gevurah*, which can inherently have sinister associations, *emes* is always good because it is defined by being right and appropriate.

What does it mean, then, to "stand by the truth"? Standing by the "truth" means standing up for what is right or appropriate, which is a prerequisite for any lasting genuine peace!

───────── TAKEAWAY MESSAGES ─────────

Avraham's *middah* is *chessed*, even though he sent off Yishmael. The *chessed* of shielding Yitzchak had unfortunate consequences on Yishmael—not all *chessed* is clearly "good" to all parties (the word *chessed* itself is ambiguous, perhaps highlighting this idea). Yitzchak's *middah* of *gevurah* wasn't in physical strength but in steadfastly carrying on his father's traditions (i.e., the Philistine wells). This *middah* may have been detrimental at times, as it may have misled him into clinging to the tradition that Eisav, as the *bechor*, was the chosen one!

Yaakov's *middah* of *emes*, however, is not defined by absolute truth but rather in what is right, appropriate, or everlasting. Tricking Eisav was an act of *emes*, which by definition is always good. Which *middah* supersedes them all? *Emes* over *chessed* and *gevurah*, because that is the *middah* that is truly "right."

Vayeitzei

WHY DOES THE WORD FOR "AFFLICTION" DOUBLE AS THE WORD FOR "PRAYER"?

רַ—בִּי שִׁמְעוֹן אוֹמֵר: אַל תַּעַשׂ תְּפִלָּתְךָ קֶבַע...

Rabbi Shimon said: When you pray, do not make your prayers routine…(Avos 2:13)

--- QUESTIONS ---

1. If the Tanna wanted to say, "Don't make your prayers routine," then why not say it more clearly, i.e., "אַל תִּתְפַּלֵּל קֶבַע"? Why specifically use this language of תַּעַשׂ and תְּפִלָּתְךָ, which give it a very personal twinge?

2. "וַיִּפְגַּע בַּמָּקוֹם וַיָּלֶן שָׁם כִּי בָא הַשֶּׁמֶשׁ"—And he encountered the place, and tarried there all night…" (*Bereishis* 28:11). According to the Gemara (*Berachos* 27b), this verse is the source from which we learn that Yaakov is the architect of *Maariv*; this is because פגיעה means *tefillah* (אין פגיעה אלא תפילה). However, we know that פגע/ פוגע means "affliction" or "injury." Why would G-d choose such a *negative* word for *tefillah*?

3. Also, we see the word mentioned again later in the *parashah*: "וְיַעֲקֹב הָלַךְ לְדַרְכּוֹ וַיִּפְגְּעוּ בוֹ מַלְאֲכֵי אֱלֹקִים"—And Yaakov went on his way, and the angels of G-d met him." What is the significance of the

72

וַיִּפְגְּעוּ here in this context, and how is it related to the aforementioned וַיִּפְגְּעוּ?

<hr>
ANSWERS
<hr>

One approach may be that וַיִּפְגַּע בַּמָּקוֹם suggests that Yaakov felt afflicted/deficient/injured, so to speak, in his place. After all, only by feeling incomplete in one's current place can one more earnestly pray for something to change!

On the one hand, one must feel afflicted and deficient in his current place so as to pray with more *kavanah* for some positive change to take place, but on the other hand, one must "hit" that very place and shake things up, actively effectuating the change in oneself while one is praying for Divine help. The double meaning of וַיִּפְגַּע thus simultaneously shows introspection and action—what an amazing word for *tefillah* indeed!

G-d reminds Yaakov that by recognizing his inner affliction and praying in earnest and then "hitting" his place (i.e., changing in some positive way), G-d will repay Yaakov *middah k'neged middah*, in due measure. This is why at the end of the *parashah*, He sends *malachim* who "hit him" (וַיִּפְגְּעוּ בוֹ מַלְאֲכֵי אֱלֹקִים) back in perfect recompense, providing safe harbor to Yaakov.

And so now we can answer what the Tanna may have meant in *Avos*: אַל תַּעַשׂ תְּפִלָּתְךָ קֶבַע—not just, "Don't make your prayers rote/routine," but also, "Do not make your *tefillah* into something that enables you to just stay the very same way you are today! Do not remain קֶבַע or *steadfast* in your ways!" Instead, you should feel afflicted in your place to pray for change, but also hit or shake up your place to help effectuate change.

<hr>
TAKEAWAY MESSAGES
<hr>

פְּגִיעָה may in fact be a perfect word for prayer because it denotes affliction and hitting. The double meaning of וַיִּפְגַּע בַּמָּקוֹם shows simultaneous introspection and action; one best prays when they feel "afflicted" in their current place in life, and it should inspire them to "hit" or shake up the place for the better! If we change our place, G-d reassures us He will pay perfect recompense (וַיִּפְגְּעוּ בוֹ מַלְאֲכֵי אֱלֹקִים). Our *tefillos* are not meant to keep us steadfast (קֶבַע) in our place/ways, but should rather simultaneously inspire and move us to be better and better.

The word for "affliction" doubles as the word for "prayer" because prayer is most efficacious when one feels afflicted enough to pray, "שִׁיר הַמַּעֲלוֹת מִמַּעֲמַקִּים קְרָאתִיךָ…."

WHAT IS THE LESSON OF "ELOKEI YITZCHAK" AND "PACHAD YITZCHAK"?

רַבִּי יְהוֹשֻׁעַ אוֹמֵר: עַיִן הָרָע וְיֵצֶר הָרָע
וְשִׂנְאַת הַבְּרִיּוֹת מוֹצִיאִין אֶת הָאָדָם מִן הָעוֹלָם.

Rabbi Yehoshua says: An evil urge...bring[s] a man out of this world. (Avos 2:11)

אֵיזֶהוּ גִבּוֹר הַכּוֹבֵשׁ אֶת יִצְרוֹ...

Who is strong? One who overpowers his inclinations...(Ibid., 4:1)

QUESTIONS

Why is Yitzchak the poster child for *gevurah* despite being the least active of our forefathers? The two most prevalent answers are that he was willing to die at the *Akeidah* or that he strove to keep his father's accomplishments intact. However, both of those answers do not describe *gevurah* as defined in *Avos*, as having something to do with quelching the יצר הרע, the evil inclination!

ANSWERS

At the end of the *parashah*, Yaakov refers to G-d as "*Pachad* (Fear of) Yitzchak*," and the midrash explains that the pseudonym of *Pachad* is used instead of the more usual אלוקי because that holy name is reserved for when one is completely holy, which is only after death, when one is no longer challenged by their lusts. But if that is the case, why does G-d refer to Himself as וַאלֹקֵי יִצְחָק at the beginning of the *parashah*, as if Yitzchak was alive? *Rashi* explains that since Yitzchak was blind, he was no longer tempted by his *yetzer hara* and thus was considered dead.

If that is so, *Elokei Yitzchak* can be used indeed.

> וַאלֹקֵי יִצְחָק: *Although we do not find in Scripture that the Holy One Blessed be He associates His name with that of the righteous during their lifetimes by writing, "the G-d of so-and-so," for it is said (Iyov 15:15): "He does not believe in His holy ones," [i.e., G-d does not consider even His holy ones as righteous until after their deaths, when they are no longer subject to the evil inclination], nevertheless, here He associated His name with Yitzchak because his eyes had become dim, and he was confined in the house, **and he was like a dead person**, the evil inclination having ceased from him (Tanchuma, Toldos 7).*

So this may be the connection of Yitzchak to *gevurah* after all. Yitzchak is considered holy, even during his lifetime, because he unfortunately developed blindness, which squelched his *yetzer hara*. He was, perhaps unwittingly הַכּוֹבֵשׁ אֶת יִצְרוֹ, and therefore a true *gevurah* of the ultimate sense, having conquered his *yetzer hara*, as per the aforementioned dictum in *Avos*: אֵיזֶהוּ גִבּוֹר הַכּוֹבֵשׁ אֶת יִצְרוֹ!

It is also worthwhile to point out a nuance in the language of *Rashi*:

לפי שכהו עיניו וכלוא היה בבית והרי הוא כמת ויצר הרע פסק ממנו.

*Because his eyes had become dim, and he was confined in the house, **and he was like a dead person**, the evil inclination having ceased from him.*

Without the *yetzer hara*, Yitzchak was really considered dead. On the one hand, lustfulness can bring us out of this world and isolate us (רַבִּי יְהוֹשֻׁעַ אוֹמֵר: וְיֵצֶר הָרָע...מוֹצִיאִין אֶת הָאָדָם מִן הָעוֹלָם), but on the other hand, we need this challenge to overcome, as that is what living is about. Yitzchak may have been the extreme conqueror of lustfulness by virtue of his blindness, which made him "dead to the world," but for the rest of us, our very life depends on having lusts that we can hope and try to suppress and overcome.

———————— TAKEAWAY MESSAGES ————————

Yitzchak indeed is the poster child of *gevurah* because he is the prototypical forefather who overcame lustfulness (even though it was not intentional!). In fact, G-d refers to Himself as אלֹקֵי יִצְחָק while Yitzchak was alive because Yitzchak was so pure and not tempted anymore by his *yetzer hara* due to his blindness. For the rest of us, having lusts is what makes us alive, and a goal in life is to try to suppress and overcome these lusts, attaining *gevurah*. The lesson of *Pachad Yitzchak* and *Elokei Yitzchak* is that of אֵיזֶהוּ גִבּוֹר הַכּוֹבֵשׁ אֶת יִצְרוֹ.

DAVID DOBIN'S EXTRA FRIDAY NIGHT
BLESSING: כִּי מַלְאָכָיו יְצַוֶּה לָּךְ לִשְׁמָרְךָ בְּכָל דְּרָכֶיךָ

הִֿלֵּל אוֹמֵר: אַל תִּפְרֹשׁ מִן הַצִּבּוּר
וְאַל תַּאֲמִין בְּעַצְמְךָ עַד יוֹם מוֹתֶךָ.

*Hillel says: Don't distance from the congregation and don't
believe in yourself until the day you die. (Avos 2:4)*

QUESTIONS

What is wrong with "believing in oneself"? Doesn't it seem as if *Avos*
is discouraging self-confidence here?

Long-time Beth Israel member and אדם חשוב, Mr. David Dobin, recently passed away. In a very touching eulogy, his son Josh described
how every Friday night, he would bless his son with the following
prayer: "כִּי מַלְאָכָיו יְצַוֶּה לָּךְ לִשְׁמָרְךָ בְּכָל דְּרָכֶיךָ—For He shall command His angels for you, to guard you on all your paths" (*Tehillim* 91:11). I couldn't
help but wonder why he would bless his son with this prayer. The usual
prayer for boys is "Y'simcha Elokim k'Ephraim u'k'Menasheh—G-d shall
make you like Ephraim and Menasheh!" (or for girls, "...like Sarah,
Rivkah, Rachel, and Leah") and *Birkas Kohanim*. The aforementioned
"*Ki Malachav*" is sometimes used in *Tefillas Haderech*, but how and why
did Mr. Dobin use it on Friday nights?

——— ANSWERS ———

A common question asked by the Friday night blessing is why we bless our boys to be like Ephraim and Menasheh, who weren't, after all, such great *tzaddikim*, at least not like Avraham, Yitzchak, and Yaakov. An answer may be that we are blessing each and every child to value other people. Appreciate having other people in your lives that you can count on, and you will never be alone. Ephraim is always with Menasheh. The blessing on Friday night is that we should never feel isolated and always have someone accompanying us wherever we are or go! It is a blessing to avoid loneliness, which is the bane of any existence.

In our *parashah*, it states:

וַיֵּצֵא יַעֲקֹב מִבְּאֵר שָׁבַע וַיֵּלֶךְ חָרָנָה.

Yaakov departed from Beer Sheva, and he went toward Charan. (Bereishis 28:10)

More than twenty years ago, (I think,) I heard a *vort* from Isaac Weiss: The *pasuk* could have said, "וַיֵּצֵא יַעֲקֹב מִבְּאֵר שָׁבַע לְחָרָן—Yaakov left Beer Sheva to Charan," and so why the wordiness and extra words and letters of וַיֵּלֶךְ חָרָנָה?

Rabbi Zvi Elimelech Shapira, *zt"l* (1843–1924), the *Tzvi LaTzaddik* of Bluzhov, answered that the extra letters when comparing "*l'charan*" to "*vayeilech Charanah*" are the four extra letters: י, ו, and ךְ of וַיֵּלֶךְ and the ה of חָרָנָה. (The *lamed* of "*vayeilech*" is needed to convert "*Charanah*" to "*l'Charan*.") These four letters are the ending letters of the phrase "כִּי מַלְאָכָיו יְצַוֶּה לָךְ—He will charge his angels to you" (quoted in *Otzros Tzaddikei U'Geonei Hadoros*). The idea is that when Yaakov went on his journey, Hashem supplied him with the company of two angels to protect and guide him; he was not to be left alone!

To add to this idea, it is not a coincidence that the *parashah* starts off with Yaakov being "וַיִּפְגַּע בַּמָּקוֹם וַיָּלֶן שָׁם—He encountered G-d," and ends with the passage also in *Tefillas Haderech*: "וְיַעֲקֹב הָלַךְ לְדַרְכּוֹ וַיִּפְגְּעוּ בוֹ מַלְאֲכֵי אֱלֹקִים." Each encounter highlights that G-d never allowed Yaakov to be alone and constantly assigned angels to escort him.

This cute *vort* is more than cute; it is a powerful lesson in the dangers of loneliness. When it says that Yaakov went from Beer Sheva to Charan, it seems that he went on his own on this dangerous journey. These added letters hint toward G-d's reassurance to Yaakov that he would never be left alone, but in fact has two accompanying angels at all times: "כִּי מַלְאָכָיו יְצַוֶּה לָּךְ."

This idea of *Ki Malachav* can therefore very well be a lesson of "Never be alone," which fits perfectly with the *berachah* of "Y'simcha Elokim k'Ephraim u'k'Menasheh." The *berachah* that we impart to our children on Friday night is "You will never be alone" and "Cherish and seek company"!

When Hillel says, "אַל תִּפְרֹשׁ מִן הַצִּבּוּר, וְאַל תַּאֲמִין בְּעַצְמְךָ עַד יוֹם מוֹתְךָ"—Don't detach from the community and don't believe in yourself until the day you die," it is not that he is disparaging self-confidence, he is rather highlighting the virtues of knowing that you are not alone. It is comforting to know that G-d reassures us that we have others around and that we need not feel we have to shoulder everything alone!

─────────── TAKEAWAY MESSAGES ───────────

It may very well be the reason that we bless our children on Friday night to be like "Ephraim and Menasheh" so that they not only cherish having company but so they should be blessed to never feel alone. Yaakov's trip to Charan is described with extra letters (*vav, yud, kuf,* and *hei*), which remind us of the verse, "כִּי מַלְאָכָיו יְצַוֶּה לָּךְ," to teach the powerful idea that G-d never leaves us alone even in our loneliest of times. It may very well be that Mr. Dobin picked this *pasuk* to accompany his Friday night blessing so that his child and future children, and now all of us, will realize the most important blessing of "never being alone."

וְאַל תַּאֲמִין בְּעַצְמְךָ עַד יוֹם מוֹתְךָ may not simply be a warning to not be overly confident but rather a reassurance that you are never alone in this world, and that you have a *tzibbur* that you can and should rely on!

David Dobin's extra Friday night blessing is the lesson that G-d never leaves a descendant of Yaakov to be alone.

DID YAAKOV REALLY NEVER DIE?

יַעֲקֹב אָבִינוּ לֹא מֵת.

Our forefather Yaakov never died. (Taanis 5b)

—————— QUESTIONS ——————

Given that Yaakov had a whole funeral procession and was even embalmed, how can this be true? One cryptic answer utilizes a *pasuk* in *Yirmiyahu* from which a Tanna proves Yaakov is on some level still alive—that he remains alive in or by virtue of his progeny, the Jewish People. But can there be any alternative meaning?

Another answer or approach may be derived from our *parashah*, but first one more question:

וַיֵּרָא אֱלֹקִים אֶל יַעֲקֹב עוֹד בְּבֹאוֹ מִפַּדַּן אֲרָם וַיְבָרֶךְ אֹתוֹ. וַיֹּאמֶר לוֹ אֱלֹקִים שִׁמְךָ יַעֲקֹב לֹא יִקָּרֵא שִׁמְךָ עוֹד יַעֲקֹב כִּי אִם יִשְׂרָאֵל יִהְיֶה שְׁמֶךָ וַיִּקְרָא אֶת שְׁמוֹ יִשְׂרָאֵל.

And G-d appeared to Yaakov again when he came from Paddan-aram, and blessed him. And G-d said to him: "Your name is Yaakov; your name shall no longer be called Yaakov but Yisrael shall be your name," and He called his name Yisrael." (Bereishis 35:9–10)

What is the significance of changing the name Yaakov to Yisrael? What's the big deal? Also, is there any veiled message in the rather lengthy verbiage here of "your name shall no longer be called Yaakov, but Yisrael shall be your name"?

───────── ANSWERS ─────────

The name Yaakov conjures up the imagery of Yaakov holding onto Eisav's heel for dear life. The name highlights the survivalist *holding-on-for-dear-life* nature of the Jew. The concept of "Yaakov never died" then probably speaks to this idea—that a descendant of Yaakov has genetic resilience, as if to say, "Yaakov [i.e., the nature of us always holding on to the *heel*] never dies (i.e., we survive against all odds]." Yisrael, on the other hand, is an officer (שׂר) of G-d (אל); this represents the stand-alone, independent, and self-sufficient nature we achieve after we survive. This *pasuk* therefore represents what G-d ultimately wanted from Yaakov and his descendants—not to be satisfied with just being a survivor but metamorphasizing and growing into being a leader.

As for the lengthy verbiage, this *pasuk* mystically contains the blue-print for the process and transformation of leadership. Pay attention to the *trop*, the Biblical music notes of this *pasuk* (symbolized above each word to show how it is supposed to be *leined*):

$$\text{לֹא־יִקָּרֵא שִׁמְךָ עוֹד יַעֲקֹב כִּי אִם־יִשְׂרָאֵל יִהְיֶה שְׁמֶךָ.}$$

Above the לֹא־יִקָּרֵא is a *telisha ketana*; above the שִׁמְךָ עוֹד is a *kadma v'azla*; above the יַעֲקֹב is a *revi'i*; below the כִּי is a *mapach*; above the אִם־יִשְׂרָאֵל is a *pashta*; and below the יִהְיֶה שְׁמֶךָ is a *zakef katon*.

The *mussar* is that all leaders start with some small, unforeseen opportunity that helps jockey the future leader into position; this is *telisha ketana* (*telisha* literally means "uproot"). Then the person rises up, sometimes quite swiftly; this is the *kadma v'azla* (when you *lein* this, the tune just goes up and away!) into the position of leadership. But then comes a dramatic fall from grace, which is par for the course; this is the *revi'i*, which sounds like someone parachuting down from grace. Instead of giving up, though, a leader must reinvent himself; this is the *mapach* (which literally means "flip over") in the sense of being able to change yourself and adapt to conflict. The consequence of any leader's ups and downs gives him the experience to know how to best serve others; this is the *pashta* (which literally means to "put one's hand out") in the sense of putting your hand out to actually affect others. Finally, the culmination of any great leader is to not suffer undue hubris, which would take him down; this is represented by the *zakef katon* (literally "small standing") in the sense of not being haughty or conceited! And so, the transformation from a *surviving* Yaakov to a *succeeding leader* Yisrael entails going through a *telisha ketana*, *kadma v'azla*, a *revi'i*, and a *mapach* so that he can be a great *pashta*, who nevertheless doesn't succumb to hubris and is a *zakef katon*.

──────────── TAKEAWAY MESSAGES ────────────

The concept of "Yaakov Avinu never died" speaks to the idea that a descendant of Yaakov has genetic resilience: Yaakov (always holding on to the *heel*) never dies (we survive against all odds). The verbose *pasuk* has a veiled message contained in the *trop*: that a true leader starts by a small uprooting (*telisha ketana*) and then rises exponentially (*kadma v'azla*), only to then fall precipitously (*revi'i*), but then reinvents himself (*mapach*), and with this culminated experience is able to give to others effectively and wholeheartedly (*pashta*), realizing that to retain the leadership qualities, he must remain humble (*zakef katon*).

Yaakov never dies in the sense that his descendants never give up, and they survive against the odds. The challenge for all Jews is to metamorphasize from the surviving Yaakov to the succeeding leader Yisrael.

YAAKOV'S CHANGED NAME
AND THE WORD "OD"

לֹא יִקָּרֵא שִׁמְךָ עוֹד יַעֲקֹב.

Your name shall no longer be called Yaakov. (Bereishis 32:28)

וּבְמָקוֹם שֶׁאֵין אֲנָשִׁים הִשְׁתַּדֵּל לִהְיוֹת אִישׁ.

In a place where there are no persons, try to be a man.
(Avos 2:5)

The simple understanding of this ethic is that "if you find yourself in a place devoid of good people, don't despair and be like the rest, but rather try to stand out and make an impact." Or, "Be the [important respectable] man [that is otherwise lacking]." But there can be another way to read this ethic as well.

וַיֵּרָא אֱלֹקִים אֶל יַעֲקֹב עוֹד בְּבֹאוֹ מִפַּדַּן אֲרָם וַיְבָרֶךְ אֹתוֹ. וַיֹּאמֶר לוֹ
אֱלֹקִים שִׁמְךָ יַעֲקֹב לֹא יִקָּרֵא שִׁמְךָ עוֹד יַעֲקֹב כִּי אִם יִשְׂרָאֵל יִהְיֶה
שְׁמֶךָ וַיִּקְרָא אֶת שְׁמוֹ יִשְׂרָאֵל.

And G-d appeared to Yaakov again when he came from
Paddan-aram, and blessed him. And G-d said to him: "Your
name is Yaakov; your name shall no longer be called Yaakov
but Yisrael shall be your name," and He called his name
Yisrael." (Bereishis 35:9–10)

QUESTIONS

1. Why does G-d use the word עוֹד in the above verse?
2. If there is an injunction not to call Yaakov by that name, why does G-d indeed call him by this very name just a few *pesukim* later (v. 15)?
3. Finally, why the wordiness? G-d simply could have said, "Your name is Yisrael from here and on!" Certainly the words עוֹד and כִּי אִם seem wordy and redundant!

ANSWERS

Homiletically, the emphasis may not only be on not calling Yaakov by that name, but rather on not calling him an עוֹד anymore! עוֹד is defined in verse 9 by *Rashi* as "second time" or duplication. G-d is perhaps saying, "Yaakov, no longer are you to strive just to be a duplicate of what your fathers were...now you need to be a כִּי and an אִם." The words כִּי and אִם in the Tanach have multiple meanings *depending on the context*. The *mussar* for Yaakov is that instead of being cookie-cutter Yaakov, he would from then on need to dictate his own future and adapt to whatever comes his way. Much like the words כִּי and אִם, which are "adaptive words," i.e., adopting different meaning depending on their context (כִּי can mean "because/since/when/if/but/although," and אִם can mean "when" or "if"), Yaakov was going to learn to be a chameleon of sorts, navigating through an ever-changing world. Jews have adopted this important trait, and it is a key to our success.

Back to the Mishnah in *Avos*: "In a place where there are no persons, try to be a man" may actually also be read homiletically: Instead (וּבְמָקוֹם) of harboring your concept of "there are no persons" (שֶׁאֵין אֲנָשִׁים)—embarking on a cookie-cutter Yaakov path, merely aiming to produce duplicates of each other—a leader must "try to be a man" (הִשְׁתַּדֵּל לִהְיוֹת אִישׁ). Try to stand out while embracing your individual strengths to positively impact those around you!

Repeated again for clarity: Replace the concept of "there are no persons" with the concept of "try to be a man."

Perhaps G-d's message to Yaakov was to focus now on his individual strengths and to embrace his uniqueness. His name would no longer be just an עוֹד anymore, as he would no longer be known as a mere duplicate or clone. To be an effective leader, Yaakov had to be like a כִּי and a אִם, and be able to adapt depending on the context. Yaakov's name change was thus so that he would no longer be an עוֹד.

WHY IS YAAKOV ASSOCIATED WITH THE ATTRIBUTE OF TRUTH?

שִׁבְעָה דְבָרִים בַּגֹּלֶם וְשִׁבְעָה בֶחָכָם.
חָכָם אֵינוֹ מְדַבֵּר בִּפְנֵי מִי שֶׁהוּא גָדוֹל מִמֶּנּוּ
בְּחָכְמָה וּבְמִנְיָן...וְאוֹמֵר עַל רִאשׁוֹן רִאשׁוֹן
וְעַל אַחֲרוֹן אַחֲרוֹן...וְחִלּוּפֵיהֶן בַּגֹּלֶם.

*There are seven things that characterize a boor, and seven
that characterize a wise man. A wise man does not speak
before one who is greater than him in wisdom or age...He
responds to first things first and to latter things later...With
the boor, the reverse of all these is the case. (Avos 5:7)*

The lesson to take away from this ethic is that it is a sign of wisdom
to be organized in thought and delivery!

QUESTIONS

1. Why do we read about what a "wise man" says in *Avos*? Isn't
   ethics about piety?
2. If, in fact, a proof of wisdom is "responding to first things first
   and latter things later," why doesn't the author of the Mishnah
   first state what a boor does, since a boor was introduced first
   ?(שִׁבְעָה דְבָרִים בַּגֹּלֶם וְשִׁבְעָה בֶחָכָם)

To answer these questions, we first have two further questions:

87

1. Why is Yaakov ascribed the element of *emes*, truth, if he is, in fact, best known for tricking his brother? Where do we see his *emes* shine through?

2.

וַיָּשֶׂם אֶת הַשְּׁפָחוֹת וְאֶת יַלְדֵיהֶן רִאשֹׁנָה וְאֶת לֵאָה וִילָדֶיהָ
אַחֲרֹנִים וְאֶת רָחֵל וְאֶת יוֹסֵף אַחֲרֹנִים.

*And he placed the maidservants and their children
first and Leah and her children after, and Rachel and
her son Yosef last. (Bereishis 33:2)*

How is it that Yaakov shows favoritism by sending out his maidservants in front of Leah, and Leah in front of Rachel, when greeting the potentially malevolent, armed, and dangerous Eisav?

─────────── ANSWERS ───────────

As Yaakov was preparing to meet Eisav, he instructed his party:

וַיְצַו אֶת הָרִאשׁוֹן לֵאמֹר כִּי יִפְגָּשְׁךָ עֵשָׂו אָחִי וּשְׁאֵלְךָ לֵאמֹר לְמִי אַתָּה
וְאָנָה תֵלֵךְ וּלְמִי אֵלֶּה לְפָנֶיךָ. וְאָמַרְתָּ לְעַבְדְּךָ לְיַעֲקֹב **מִנְחָה הִוא שְׁלוּחָה**
לַאדֹנִי לְעֵשָׂו וְהִנֵּה גַם הוּא אַחֲרֵינוּ.

*And he commanded the first one, saying, "When my brother
Eisav meets you, and asks you, saying, 'To whom do you
belong, and where are you going, and for whom are these
before you?' You shall say, '[I belong] to your servant Yaakov;
it is a gift sent to my master, to Eisav, and behold, he himself
is behind us.'"*

Rashi brings down *Avos D'Rebbi Nasan*, which learns the concept of "אומר על ראשון ראשון ועל אחרון אחרון" from this very episode of Yaakov: "To whom do you belong?" is answered as "I belong to your servant Yaakov"; "and for whom are these before you?" is answered a "it is a gift sent."

Literally, we are just being taught by Yaakov how best to be a *chacham*: to be organized in thought and delivery and to answer the first question first and the second question later. But another way to learn the Mishnah above is to read the word *chacham* as it is presented in the Haggadah, meaning "righteous," in contrast to the *rasha*. A sign of righteousness is to be straightforward and honest with your priorities: "Say what is first in your heart and be forthright about what is not, or should not be, of import."

Yaakov was honest with his feelings and thus was attributed the element of *emes*. Whether we like it or not, he did send Leah before Rachel because he was true to himself and blatantly *emes-dik* without presumptions. He openly "said" what was first in his heart and what was last in his heart.

───────────── TAKEAWAY MESSAGES ─────────────

Avos teaches that we should aspire to be a *chacham*—to be organized in thought and speech (אומר על ראשון ראשון ועל אחרון אחרון), as learned from Yaakov's sending of his camp to Eisav before the showdown. We should aspire to be a *chacham*, righteous: openly and honestly displaying our priorities as Yaakov displayed his element of pure *emes* in dividing up his camp prior to meeting Eisav. Organization and prioritization are prerequisites of *chochmah* and *emes*, and are entrenched in our forefather Yaakov! Yaakov is designated the attribute of *emes* because he unabashedly acted upon the priorities he understood to be correct.

ANTI-SEMITISM AND THE GID HANASHEH

הִלֵּל אוֹמֵר: וְאַל תֹּאמַר דָּבָר שֶׁאִי אֶפְשָׁר לִשְׁמֹעַ שֶׁסוֹפוֹ לְ־הִשָּׁמַע.

Hillel says: And don't say something that is impossible to hear because in the end it can be heard. (Avos 2:4)

———————— QUESTIONS ————————

1. What does this ethic mean?
2. Where in the Torah do we see the first physical manifestation of anti-Semitism?
3. Why do we say the prayer of *Av Harachamim* on Shabbos morning?
4. What may be a lesson of the Torah forbidding the tasteless *gid hanasheh*, sciatic nerve?

———————— ANSWERS ————————

Reading through the passage detailing the fight between Yaakov and the angel of Eisav, I was convinced that this represented our symbolic fight against anti-Semitism and subsequently found at least two sources that corroborate this idea (*Rashba, Peirushei HaHaggados; Sefer Chinuch* §3; see *Chullin* 91a (Schottenstein Talmud Bavli), note 37). The *Rashba* essentially states that the struggle is an example of "מעשה אבות סימן לבנים—our fathers' actions portend our future," as we struggle with Eisav's descendants from generation to generation. The *Sefer Chinuch* also states: "Just as the angel of Eisav caused Yaakov to suffer, so too

90

the children of Eisav..." He adds that just like Yaakov was harmed but nevertheless emerged victorious, B'nei Yisrael will emerge similarly from their encounters with Eisav.

But perhaps we can delve even deeper and add to their general observation:

The *pesukim* start out:

1. "וַיִּוָּתֵר יַעֲקֹב לְבַדּוֹ"—And Yaakov was left alone." Yaakov was alone and "isolated." The first step of all anti-Semitic approaches is to isolate the Jew. Whether it be the yellow star or the Pale of Settlement, Jewish isolation almost always follows a mischaracterization of the Jews. Interestingly, the Gemara in *Chullin* points out that Yaakov (to his credit!) went back to get small flasks. This praiseworthy character trait of valuing every penny has been twisted into the evil trait of "stinginess" in an attempt to isolate Jews from time immemorial!

2. "וַיֵּאָבֵק אִישׁ עִמּוֹ"—There wrestled a man with him." Notice that the angel didn't merely try to hit and hurt but rather tried to drag Yaakov down. The Palestinians, Nazis, and other Jew-haters are interested in the final solution more than simply potshots. Also, the word אבק means "dust," which conjures up the "dust of destruction" that marked not only the two burned Holy Temples but also the communities burned during the Crusades. (The Gemara actually does equate this language of אבק to dust, saying that the fight lifted the dust to the Throne of Glory.) "עַד עֲלוֹת הַשָּׁחַר"—Until the breaking of the day." The fight until morning reminds us that the fight against anti-Semitism will have many different manifestations until the ultimate redemption (עֲלוֹת הַשָּׁחַר is a metaphor for the ultimate morning). This concept of the many manifestations of anti-Semitic outbreaks over time explains why we say *Av Harachamim* every Shabbos, remembering the destroyed communities of Mainz, Speyer, and Worms during the Crusades, even though this tragedy is a lesser tragedy than the later Holocaust. The overriding point is that all these tragedies are the *same* in the sense of being the manifestations of generational anti-Semitism.

3. "וַיַּרְא כִּי לֹא יָכֹל לוֹ"—And when he [the Angel] saw that he prevailed not against him." G-d reminds us that we always eventually prevail against these anti-Semites.

4. "וַיִּשְׁאַל יַעֲקֹב וַיֹּאמֶר הַגִּידָה נָּא שְׁמֶךָ וַיֹּאמֶר לָמָּה זֶּה תִּשְׁאַל לִשְׁמִי"—And Yaakov asked and said, 'Tell me your name,' and he said, 'Why do you ask my name?'" The angel was teaching Yaakov that the name of anti-Semitism is irrelevant, as the anti-Semitic entities will change from generation to generation, be it Crusaders, Cossacks, Nazis, Palestinians, and so on. He may also be hinting to Yaakov that anti-Semitic groups often masquerade under different names that may not seem so anti-Semitic and may even sound good, such as BDS and the Jewish Voice for Peace (a vehement anti-Israel group).

5. "וַיִּקְרָא יַעֲקֹב שֵׁם הַמָּקוֹם פְּנִיאֵל...וַיִּזְרַח לוֹ הַשֶּׁמֶשׁ כַּאֲשֶׁר עָבַר אֶת פְּנוּאֵל"—And Yaakov called the place Peni-el...and the day came and they passed Penu-el." The place was Peni-el for Yaakov, but when he left it was called Penu-el, reminding us that even though only some of us may have experienced these Holocausts firsthand (Peni-el is singular for Yaakov), we must all subsequently make an effort to personally relate to it (Penu-el is plural) when all is said and done. Once daybreak came and they left the place, it becomes known in the "plural" sense of Penu-el, because the rest of the people who may have not physically been there still must share the pain and learn the lessons of others' travails.

6. "עַל כֵּן לֹא יֹאכְלוּ בְנֵי יִשְׂרָאֵל אֶת גִּיד הַנָּשֶׁה"—Therefore the children of Yisrael do not eat the sciatic nerve." How does not eating the *gid hanasheh* culminate this episode? The *gid hanasheh* is the only non-kosher food that has no taste. The lesson is that we must accept that there is no real viable reason for our enemies to hate us. We should not tolerate the fabrication of reasons for our being hated, which apologetic Jews do too often (e.g., explaining the Gaza conflict as being due to us having taken away their land, or the Jews of Germany deserving to die because they were too greedy!). Just like the *gid hanasheh* had no *taam*,

taste, there simply is no reason (טעם) that anti-Semites hate us, so don't waste mental energy on trying to placate such haters.

הִלֵּל אוֹמֵר: וְאַל תֹּאמַר דָּבָר שֶׁאִי אֶפְשָׁר לִשְׁמֹעַ שֶׁסּוֹפוֹ לְהִשָּׁמַע.

Hillel says: And don't say something that is impossible to hear
because in the end it can be heard. (Avos 2:4)

Sometimes it's important to recognize that there are realities beyond our control that will never be understood. Reading the Mishnah homiletically, "Don't say about a thing 'שֶׁאִי אֶפְשָׁר לִשְׁמֹעַ—that is impossible to understand' that it will be 'שֶׁסּוֹפוֹ לְהִשָּׁמַע—understood.'" Anti-Semitism will always fit into the category of a דָּבָר שֶׁאִי אֶפְשָׁר לִשְׁמֹעַ!

─────── TAKEAWAY MESSAGES ───────

The fight between the angel of Eisav and Yaakov is the paradigm of all future anti-Semitism.

1. וַיִּוָּתֵר יַעֲקֹב לְבַדּוֹ —Yaakov and Jews are first isolated.
2. וַיֵּאָבֵק אִישׁ עִמּוֹ—They aren't looking to hurt us, but rather it is an existential fight to wrestle us down. Also, אבק means dust, which conjures up the "dust of destruction" as they may cause significant destruction.
3. עַד עֲלוֹת הַשָּׁחַר—The fight will go until the ultimate redemption (עֲלוֹת הַשַּׁחַר is metaphorically the ultimate morning).
4. כִּי לֹא יָכֹל לוֹ—But they will not defeat us.
5. לָמָּה זֶּה תִּשְׁאַל לִשְׁמִי—The name of anti-Semitism is irrelevant, as the anti-Semitic entities will change from generation to generation.
6. וַיִּקְרָא יַעֲקֹב שֵׁם הַמָּקוֹם פְּנִיאֵל...כַּאֲשֶׁר עָבַר אֶת פְּנוּאֵל—The singular experience of some (the singular פְּנִיאֵל) transitions to a communal experience (the plural פְּנוּאֵל), as we are all really targeted and affected.
7. לֹא יֹאכְלוּ בְנֵי יִשְׂרָאֵל אֶת גִּיד הַנָּשֶׁה—There is no taste or reason why anti-Semites hate us, and there should be no tolerance for apologetic Jews—its simply not kosher! Anti-Semitism and the *gid hanasheh*—it's not kosher to suggest there's a real reason (טעם) why we Jews should be hated!

HOW DID YOSEF KNOW THE FATES
OF THE CUPBEARER AND THE BAKER?

בֶּן עַזַּאי אוֹמֵר: הֱוֵי רָץ לְמִצְוָה קַלָּה כְּבַחֲמוּרָה
וּבוֹרֵחַ מִן הָעֲבֵרָה.

*Ben Azzai says: Run to do a small mitzvah like a hard one
and run from a sin. One mitzvah leads to another and one sin
leads to another sin. (Avos 4:2)*

─────────── QUESTIONS ───────────

1. I understand running to pursue a mitzvah, but why do I need to
   flee from sin? How about just *avoiding* sin?
2. Also, the Gemara (*Berachos* 57a) says that if you dream that you
   are standing naked in Yisrael, it is a sign that you are "naked of
   merits." Is it because you are naked, or because you are standing
   in the dream that makes it a bad dream?

─────────── ANSWERS ───────────

The answers to these questions, and a profound lesson, are found in
our *parashah* by analyzing the dreams (and their respective interpretations) of the Cupbearer and Baker:

וַיַּחַלְמוּ חֲלוֹם שְׁנֵיהֶם אִישׁ חֲלֹמוֹ...וַיְסַפֵּר שַׂר הַמַּשְׁקִים אֶת חֲלֹמוֹ
לְיוֹסֵף וַיֹּאמֶר לוֹ בַּחֲלוֹמִי וְהִנֵּה גֶפֶן לְפָנָי...וְכוֹס פַּרְעֹה בְּיָדִי וָאֶקַּח
אֶת הָעֲנָבִים וָאֶשְׂחַט אֹתָם אֶל כּוֹס פַּרְעֹה וָאֶתֵּן אֶת הַכּוֹס עַל כַּף
פַּרְעֹה...וַיֹּאמֶר לוֹ יוֹסֵף זֶה פִּתְרֹנוֹ...בְּעוֹד שְׁלֹשֶׁת יָמִים יִשָּׂא פַרְעֹה
אֶת רֹאשֶׁךָ...

And they dreamed a dream, both of them...and the Cupbearer
told his dream to Yosef and said, "Pharaoh's cup was in my
hand; and I took the grapes, and pressed them into Pharaoh's
cup, and I gave the cup into Pharaoh's hand"...And Yosef said
unto him: "This is the interpretation of it: The three branches
are three days; within three days Pharaoh will lift up your
head and restore you to your position."

וַיַּרְא שַׂר הָאֹפִים כִּי טוֹב פָּתָר וַיֹּאמֶר אֶל יוֹסֵף אַף אֲנִי בַּחֲלוֹמִי וְהִנֵּה
שְׁלֹשָׁה סַלֵּי חֹרִי עַל רֹאשִׁי...וּבַסַּל הָעֶלְיוֹן מִכֹּל מַאֲכַל פַּרְעֹה מַעֲשֵׂה
אֹפֶה וְהָעוֹף אֹכֵל אֹתָם מִן הַסַּל מֵעַל רֹאשִׁי...בְּעוֹד שְׁלֹשֶׁת יָמִים יִשָּׂא
פַרְעֹה אֶת רֹאשְׁךָ מֵעָלֶיךָ וְתָלָה אוֹתְךָ עַל עֵץ.

When the Chief Baker saw that the interpretation was
good, he said to Yosef, "I also saw in my dream, and, behold,
three baskets of white bread were on my head...the birds ate
them out of the basket upon my head"..."Within three days
Pharaoh will lift up your head from off of you, and you shall
hang on a tree; and the birds shall eat your flesh from off of
you..." (Bereishis 40:5–19)

How did Yosef know how to interpret those dreams of the Cupbearer
and the Baker? The standard answer is to say that normally birds are
fearful of approaching humans, and so since in the Baker's dream the
birds ate directly from his head, it was the clear sign that he was a
"walking dead man!" But a different approach might be the following:

The Cupbearer's dream was full of action; he was constantly on the
move: "I **took** the grapes, and **pressed** them into Pharaoh's cup, and
I **gave**..." On the other hand, the Baker was completely passive and
the birds did all the work: "The **birds ate them** out of the basket **upon**

my head." Life is defined by actions. Being passive is being dead to the world; when you are green, you are growing, and when you are ripe, you are rotting!

The reason the Tanna in *Avos* says that one should run toward a mitzvah and should **flee** sin (as opposed to merely **avoiding** sin) is likewise to demonstrate that action is needed at all times to stave off degradation. Standing still is a recipe for degradation. Active steps are needed to ensure we don't inevitably decline.

This may also be why the Gemara in *Berachos* says that if you dream of yourself *standing* naked, it is a bad sign. If you dream that you can just get by unscathed by *standing still*, despite the currents pulling you down, you will inevitably decline. The Gemara is hinting that we each need to take active steps to prevent our otherwise inevitable spiritual decline!

—————— TAKEAWAY MESSAGES ——————

When Ben Azzai says you need to flee from a sin as you need to run toward a mitzvah, he may have purposely taught us the lesson that inaction is akin to negative action. Yosef recognized that the Cupbearer was going to live and the Baker was to die because the Cupbearer's dream was full of action, whilst the Baker's was passive. The dreamer who dreams of himself standing naked is perhaps naked by virtue of the standing! Yosef knew the Cupbearer was going to live because he was on the move. When you dream, make sure you are not standing still!

TO AVOID EMBARRASSING ANOTHER— WHERE IS THE TORAH'S SOURCE?

רַבִּי אֶלְעָזָר הַמּוֹדָעִי אוֹמֵר: וְהַמַּלְבִּין פְּנֵי חֲבֵרוֹ
בָּרַבִּים...אַף עַל פִּי שֶׁיֵּשׁ בְּיָדוֹ תּוֹרָה וּמַעֲשִׂים
טוֹבִים אֵין לוֹ חֵלֶק לָעוֹלָם הַבָּא.

Rabbi Elazar of Modi'in would say: And one who humiliates his friend in public...although he may possess Torah knowledge and good deeds, he has no share in the World to Come! (Avos 3:11)

— QUESTIONS —

From *Avos*, we see that it is really egregious to humiliate a friend in public. In fact, you can lose the next world if you embarrass another! In this *parashah*, we learn this ethic par excellence by Tamar's actions. But a serious question arises after we set the stage:

Yehudah found out that his daughter-in-law was pregnant, not figuring that he himself had impregnated her, and thus called for her immediate death. Then it states:

הוּא מוּצֵאת וְהִיא שָׁלְחָה אֶל חָמִיהָ לֵאמֹר לְאִישׁ אֲשֶׁר אֵלֶּה לּוֹ אָנֹכִי
הָרָה וַתֹּאמֶר הַכֶּר נָא לְמִי הַחֹתֶמֶת וְהַפְּתִילִים וְהַמַּטֶּה הָאֵלֶּה.

She was taken out, and she sent to her father-in-law, saying, "From the man to whom these belong I am pregnant," and she

97

said, *"Please recognize whose signet ring, cloak, and staff are
these." (Bereishis 38:24–26)*

Rashi says:

> *She did not want to embarrass him and say, "From you I am
> pregnant," but, "From the man to whom these belong." She
> said, "If he confesses by himself, let him confess, and if not, let
> them burn me, but I will not embarrass him." From this they
> [our Rabbis] said, "It is better for a person to be cast into a fiery
> furnace than to embarrass his fellow in public." (Sotah 10b)*

We know that there are only three sins for which we are supposed to
die rather than transgress them: incestuous relations, murder, and idolatry. So how was Tamar willing to die rather than to embarrass Yehudah
if embarrassing another is not one of those cardinal sins?

──────────── ANSWERS ────────────

Here are three possible approaches:

1. Since embarrassing another person is like putting them to
   death, she saw her death and causing his death as equivalent
   choices! Rabbeinu Yonah in *Shaarei Teshuvah* actually obligates
   self-sacrifice rather than shaming another person, and he
   equates embarrassing others with *avak retzichah*, an equivalent,
   derivative sub-category of murder, in his commentary to *Pirkei
   Avos* (see *Kol Torah* by Rabbi Daniel Feldman). Rabbi Yaakov
   Ettlinger concludes that in his view, the majority position
   indeed forbids humiliating another, even at the expense of
   one's life.

2. A similar question arises as to how Chananiah, Mishael and
   Azariah were allowed to jump into a fiery furnace despite not
   being forced to do one of the cardinal sins by Nevuchadnetzar.
   (*Tosafos* says that all Nevuchadnetzar was forcing them to do was
   to bow to his image, which would have only brought him more
   respect.) The commentators explain that these three prophets
   were allowed to potentially sacrifice their lives because of the

unique *kiddush Hashem* they would create by refusing to bow to the evil king. Likewise, here, Tamar could possibly allow herself to be put into the fire as long as she created a *kiddush Hashem* by showing the extent one should go to not embarrass another! In other words, it is not obligatory but a *heter*, allowed only in lieu of the potential great *kiddush Hashem*.

3. When Yehudah sentenced her to death, she was already considered in the throes of death. Since embarrassing Yehudah would actually just make her suffer more, she had no obligation to attempt to remove her death status in lieu of the suffering it entailed. This is tantamount to someone actively dying who is not forced or obligated to take a pill that causes pain and suffering, even if that pill may save their life!

—————————— TAKEAWAY MESSAGES ——————————

Tamar teaches us the lesson of how important it is not to embarrass another person, perhaps even if your life is on the line! How was Tamar actually allowed to risk her life to prevent embarrassing another (as it is not a "cardinal sin" after all!)?

1. Embarrassing another is like killing, and you can't save yourself by killing another!

2. Perhaps she had a *heter* only because, like Chananiah, Mishael, and Azariah, she could create a *kiddush Hashem*.

3. Since she was considered a dead woman walking, she had no obligation to endure any more suffering (it would cause her to suffer by embarrassing Yehudah) in the dying state! Embarrassing another person may not be a cardinal sin, but it should be cardinally avoided—your *Olam Haba* depends on it!

WHY ISN'T AKEIDAS YOSEF AS CELEBRATED AS AKEIDAS YITZCHAK?

רַבִּי יְהוֹשֻׁעַ אוֹמֵר: עַיִן הָרָע וְיֵצֶר הָרָע וְשִׂנְאַת הַבְּרִיּוֹת מוֹצִיאִין אֶת הָאָדָם מִן הָעוֹלָם.

Rabbi Yehoshua says: An evil eye, an evil urge, and hatred of beings bring a man out of this world. (Avos 2:11)

רַבִּי אֶלְעָזָר הַקַּפָּר אוֹמֵר: הַקִּנְאָה וְהַתַּאֲוָה וְהַכָּבוֹד מוֹצִיאִין אֶת הָאָדָם מִן הָעוֹלָם.

Rabbi Elazar Hakapar says: Jealousy, lust, and honor bring a man out of this world. (Avos 4:21)

QUESTIONS
---

1. Given the clear parallel structure, what is a message here?
2. Also, the *Torah Temimah* asks how Yosef could have been harmed if, after all, there is a concept of "שְׁלוּחֵי מִצְוָה אֵינָן נִזּוֹקִין—One who is sent for a mitzvah is not harmed." Yosef was sent by his father Yaakov to check on his brothers—a mitzvah indeed! The answer given by the *Torah Temimah* is that this concept doesn't hold if you are placed in a location that is "שְׁכִיחָא הֶיזֵּקָא—A place that is associated with badness," and since Shechem was bad luck (i.e., Dinah was raped there), Yosef was not safe, even though he was heading over there for a mitzvah.

100

Beyond the inherent danger of the place, though, why would Yaakov send Yosef to his brothers at all, knowing how much Yosef's brothers hated him? (The verse already said, "וְאָבִיו שָׁמַר אֶת הַדָּבָר—and Yaakov knew the thing [that his brothers despised him].") Beyond Shechem, the climate with his brothers was such that it was a שְׁכִיחָא הֶיזֵקָא situation, and one must wonder why Yaakov would send Yosef there in the first place!

ANSWERS

The answer may in fact be that Yaakov recognized the dangers but felt compelled to send him anyway.

In fact, if you simply follow the verses carefully, there is a clear parallel structure of the "sacrifice of Yosef" to the "sacrifice of Yitzchak."

1. The wording by Avraham's mission to slaughter Yitzchak started "וְלֶךְ לְךָ," similar to Yosef's mission of "לְכָה וְאֶשְׁלָחֲךָ."
2. The response of Yitzchak was "הִנֵּנִי," and the response of Yosef was an identical and almost out-of-place "הִנֵּנִי."
3. Right in the middle of this plot, the Torah informs us that "וַיִּשְׁלָחֵהוּ מֵעֵמֶק חֶבְרוֹן," which is out of place, but *Rashi* informs us is a connection to Avraham Avinu, another veiled reference/connection.
4. "וַיֹּאמֶר הָאִישׁ נָסְעוּ מִזֶּה"—the man who found Yosef in the field and guided him to the brothers was an angel, reminiscent of the angel who stopped Avraham from slaughtering Yitzchak.
5. "וַיִּרְאוּ אֹתוֹ מֵרָחֹק—And they saw him from afar" has almost the identical language of "וַיַּרְא אֶת הַמָּקוֹם מֵרָחֹק," which prefaced Avraham and Yitzchak approaching the mountain where their test would take place.

The connections are undeniable. The tests, though, are clearly different. *Akeidas Yitzchak* wasn't Yitzchak's test but Avraham's. Avraham proved that he was willing to sacrifice his only son upon G-d's command. Sending off Yosef, which Yaakov knew was dangerous ("וְאָבִיו שָׁמַר אֶת הַדָּבָר"), was more of a test of the brothers than of Yosef! Knowing the score, Yaakov, in a sense, was testing his sons and tasking them with protecting this hated brother. But unlike *Akeidas Yitzchak*, which we flaunt daily to accrue merit, *Akeidas Yosef* was a tragic failure that, as Rabbi Bixon pointed out one *Shabbos Shuvah*, we are still paying for today. Rabbi Bixon reminded us that the very day Yosef was sold was, in fact, Yom Kippur, and was the very day that each of the ten *harugei malchus* (famous martyred rabbis) were killed. Interestingly, they accepted their fate in a sense, complying with the tradition that we are at fault for having let down our brother.

This concept of paying back for the misdeed is continued by the tradition of paying five *shekalim* (equal to the twenty *dinarim* accepted for Yosef's trade) to redeem our firstborn (Rabbeinu Bachya, brought down in The Stone Chumash) to this very day. It is the reason we give a half-shekel (the price of each sinning brother's contribution) every Purim (perhaps related to Yom Kippur being Yom K'Purim!). We constantly remind ourselves of our failure to redeem our brother in need.

Yaakov our father was not a feeble, gullible man to believe that his hated son would be safe in the hands of his children. He did, though, genuinely believe they would (like their grandfather Avraham) keep their temptations at bay and do the right thing. The brothers failed, and we have suffered greatly throughout the generations because of this misdeed.

Regarding the question posed above due to the parallel structure in the two quotes from *Avos*, the juxtaposition signifies that עַיִן הָרָע means קִנְאָה, that יֵצֶר הָרָע means תַּאֲוָה, and that שִׂנְאַת הַבְּרִיּוֹת occurs because of infatuation with הַכָּבוֹד. מוֹצִיאִין אֶת הָאָדָם מִן הָעוֹלָם may very well homiletically be referring to Yosef HaTzaddik, and the message is that the brothers' sin against Yosef, for which we eternally suffer, was in having jealousy, lustfulness, and honor issues that caused them to banish him from the world.

─────────── TAKEAWAY MESSAGES ───────────

The *Torah Temimah* asked how Yosef wasn't protected when he went to check on his brothers, if indeed he was commanded to go by his father and שְׁלוּחֵי מִצְוָה אֵינוֹ נִזּוֹקִין. He answered that because Shechem was a dangerous place, Yosef wasn't protected. He could have added that wherever the brothers were was also a "dangerous place" because they hated him so much—and Yaakov knew that!

Similarites abound between *Akeidas Yitzchak* and a so-called *Akeidas Yosef*:

1. "וְלֵךְ לְךָ" similar to "לְכָה וְאֶשְׁלָחֲךָ."
2. The response of Yitzchak and then Yosef of "הִנֵּנִי."
3. "וַיִּשְׁלָחֵהוּ מֵעֵמֶק חֶבְרוֹן" is a connection to Avraham Avinu in the middle of this plot.
4. "וַיֹּאמֶר הָאִישׁ נָסְעוּ מִזֶּה"—the angel imagery is similar to *Akeidas Yitzchak*.
5. "וַיִּרְאוּ אֹתוֹ מֵרָחֹק" is very similar to "וַיַּרְא אֶת הַמָּקוֹם מֵרָחֹק."

The difference is that we passed *Akeidas Yitzchak* and failed *Akeidas Yosef*. We are reminded every Yom Kippur (the very day we failed) about how we suffer because of this misdeed; the ten *harugei malchus* is the most salient example. We are also reminded when we give five shekels for every firstborn and a half-shekel every Yom K'Purim!

Our jealousy, lustfulness and honor wrongly banished him (i.e., Yosef) from the world!

Because we failed *Akeidas Yosef*, it isn't as celebrated as *Akeidas Yitzchak*, and in fact, it teaches that we should never, ever abandon our brother's need again!

Mikeitz

WHY DID YOSEF CRY WHEN HE SAW HIS BROTHERS SHOW REMORSE?

אַף הוּא רָאָה גֻּלְגֹּלֶת אַחַת שֶׁצָּפָה עַל
פְּנֵי הַמָּיִם. אָמַר לָהּ, עַל דַּ אֲטֵפְתְּ, אַטְפוּךְ.
וְסוֹף מְטִיפַיִךְ יְטוּפוּן.

*He also saw a **skull** floating upon the water. He said to it:
Because you drowned others, you were drowned; and those
who drowned you, will themselves be drowned. (Avos 2:6)*

--- QUESTIONS ---

1. Hillel is looking at a skull and saying the above. I understand the message to be, "what goes around, comes around," but that could have more simply been made by saying the following: "You were drowned, but in the end, those who drowned you will be drowned!" Why does Hillel have to add the point that the person may have drowned someone first, which started the cascade?

2. After Yosef's brothers come to Egypt without Binyamin, Yosef devises a scheme to get them to fetch Binyamin. In perfect disguise, he accuses them of being spies and commands that one of them stays behind while the others get Binyamin. The

brothers exclaimed that they were being paid back for their treatment of Yosef (אֲבָל אֲשֵׁמִים אֲנַחְנוּ עַל אָחִינוּ), and hearing this while in disguise, Yosef weeps! How did this episode trigger the brother's epiphany, and why does it cause Yosef to weep?

—————— ANSWERS ——————

The *Meshech Chochmah* relates that the halachah is that if a group of people are held up by terrorists, and the terrorists say, "Give us one and the rest can be saved," all should die rather than to hand one over willingly. But if one volunteers to save the rest, it is a different story. The brothers realized here that one person would have to stand up and have compassion on the rest in order to ensure their survival. They realized that this sense of brotherly compassion had been lacking when they had dealt with Yosef, and thus they "figured out" that this was payback from G-d!

As to why Yosef cried, *Rashi* posits it was because Yosef realized his brothers regretted their actions. But how does their regret alone cause Yosef to cry? One approach is that this regret simply stirred his compassion toward them. Another approach may be that regret from one side of any warring or opposing faction often triggers regret from the other side. It is only natural that actions or gestures of reconciliation are often reciprocated with those same feelings. When Yosef cried, then, one can easily imagine that he reciprocated their feelings of regret with feelings of regret as well. Whereas there is no direct Chazal stating that Yosef ever demonstrated regret per se for causing his brothers to hate him, it would be unlikely that Yosef would not feel at least uncomfortable about the fact that his brothers' (and father's) anguish were, at the very least, connected to his actions. He saw their regret at having lacked compassion, which may have triggered his regret and subsequent cry, in kind.

A point to take home is that sometimes only upon vindication do people recognize they bear at least some fault in any difficult situation. The goal, though, is to try to recognize fault before vindication.

This may be the lesson of "Because you drowned others, you were drowned, and in the end those who drowned you will be drowned."

Often, only once one sees that those who drowned them will be drowned does one then take ownership of having started the circle of misfortune. In this quintessential Biblical example, Yosef may have only pondered his role in the cascade when he saw that his brothers were being punished by having to show brotherly compassion for their lack of brotherly compassion when they sold Yosef! עַל דַּאֲטֵפְתְּ—So because you, Yosef, "drowned" your brothers, so to speak, by stimulating their jealousy (albeit unintentionally); אַטְפוּךְ —you were sold away as a slave; but, סוֹף מְטִיפַיִךְ—your brothers, who lacked brotherly compassion; יְטוּפוּן—are also forced to "drown" by having to sacrifice one of their own to save the others.

And so, in short, the עַל דַּאֲטֵפְתְּ אַטְפוּךְ is a call to action for us all to assume responsibility for our part in misunderstandings or disputes, even before we are vindicated!

────────────── TAKEAWAY MESSAGES ──────────────

The *Meshech Chochmah* states that Yosef's brothers realized that they were being paid back for selling Yosef because they were being forced to show compassion to save themselves—a compassion that they lacked earlier when it came to their selling of Yosef. Yosef cried after seeing the brothers demonstrating regret. Their regret either triggered Yosef's compassion, which led to his crying, or perhaps triggered his own regret in the sense that he now realized that maybe he could have had more compassion when telling over his dreams. Yosef perhaps cried, though, because only upon "vindication" did he realize his part (even if it wasn't his fault!) in the cascade of his brothers' and father's anguish. עַל דַּאֲטֵפְתְּ אַטְפוּךְ וְסוֹף מְטִיפַיִךְ יְטוּפוּן teaches us that although we can yearn for vindication when we are wronged, we must also recognize our part in contributing to whatever problem stimulated the conflict. We should be mindful not to drown others! Yosef cried when he saw his brothers show remorse, perhaps showing his own remorse at having been a part of the cascade.

YOSEF'S PARADIGMATIC CRITICISM— THE LESSON OF M'AYIN AND KASHOS

עֲקַבְיָא בֶּן מַהֲלַלְאֵל אוֹמֵר: הִסְתַּכֵּל בִּשְׁלשָׁה
דְבָרִים וְאִי אַתָּה בָא לִידֵי עֲבֵרָה. דַּע מֵאַיִן בָּאתָ,
וּלְאָן אַתָּה הוֹלֵךְ, וְלִפְנֵי מִי אַתָּה עָתִיד לִתֵּן
דִּין וְחֶשְׁבּוֹן ...

Akavia the son of Mahalalel would say: Reflect upon three
things and you will not come to the hands of transgression.
Know from where you came, *where you are going, and before*
whom you are destined to give a judgment and accounting.
(Avos 3:1)

וַיַּרְא יוֹסֵף אֶת אֶחָיו וַיַּכִּרֵם וַיִּתְנַכֵּר אֲלֵיהֶם
וַיְדַבֵּר אִתָּם קָשׁוֹת וַיֹּאמֶר אֲלֵהֶם מֵאַיִן בָּאתֶם
וַיֹּאמְרוּ מֵאֶרֶץ כְּנַעַן לִשְׁבָּר אֹכֶל.

And Yosef saw his brethren, and he knew them, but made
himself strange to them, and **spoke roughly with them;** *and*
he said to them: "From where do you come?" And they said,
"From the land of Canaan to buy food." (Bereishis 42:7)

107

─────────────── QUESTIONS ───────────────

1. What is meant by Yosef "speaking roughly with them" (וַיְדַבֵּר
   אִתָּם קָשׁוֹת)?

2. What is the connection of this *pasuk* to our Mishnah in
   Avos above?

─────────────── ANSWERS ───────────────

It is very possible that this may be the first *mussar shmuess* in the
Torah! וַיְדַבֵּר אִתָּם קָשׁוֹת may hint that Yosef was giving them good old fashion *mussar*, rebuke. Inherent in the very word is a description of *mussar*'s very intent: קָשׁוֹת means "harden," as well as "harshly." Although
criticism should be superficially harsh, it must be used to "harden" or
improve somebody. This is constructive criticism par excellence. And
what is that *mussar* lesson that Yosef chooses here? מֵאַיִן בָּאתֶם—not
only "Where are you brothers going," but rather akin to the דַּע מֵאַיִן בָּאתָ
espoused by *Avos* above: "Know that you came from nothing, and so
how can you sin!" Homiletically interpreted: Not "where (מֵאַיִן) are you
from?" but "From nothing (מֵאַיִן) you have come."

The lesson of מֵאַיִן can be further elaborated with two points showing
how criticism can be directed from pure critique to constructive advice:

1. "אֶשָּׂא עֵינַי אֶל הֶהָרִים מֵאַיִן יָבֹא עֶזְרִי"—I will lift up my eyes to the moun-
   tains; from where (*ayin*) shall my help come?" (*Tehillim* 121:1)
   - *Criticism*: We are puny compared to the mighty
     mountains!
   - *Constructive Criticism*: אַיִן means that despite the odds
     against us, from "nothing," our help will come. From rec-
     ognizing our humility and lowliness, only then can we be
     hardened and deserve help from Above! (Adapted from a
     derashah of Rabbi Mordechai Shapiro, thirty years ago.)

2. "וּמוֹתַר הָאָדָם מִן הַבְּהֵמָה אָיִן"—And the superiority of man over the
   animal is nothing (*ayin*)..." (*Koheles* 3:19)
   - *Criticism*: we are nothing more than animals!
   - *Constructive Criticism*: אָיִן stands for אמירה (we can talk),
     ידיעה (we understand), and נשמה (we have souls) (adapted

from Rabbi Ephraim Shapiro). Only by realizing that we are essentially very much like animals can we appreciate our subtle superiority to them (being able to speak, know, and have a soul), which can make us more adept at using our faculties for good.

—————— TAKEAWAY MESSAGES ——————

When Yosef said to his brothers, "מֵאַיִן בָּאתֶם," he could very well have been saying, "You come from nothing and are no more than animals." But he was actually giving them a message of hope, since once a person hears this *mussar*, he is reminded of his humility—and once a person knows his place, deliverance and superiority are inevitable. "מֵאַיִן יָבֹא עֶזְרִי," from the understanding of being from little, you can get help! More simply put, Yosef was saying to his brothers the very same *mussar* that the Tanna in *Avos* would espouse years later, "מֵאַיִן בָּאתָ," the truth of knowing your lowliness is what will set you up for success! Yosef's paradigmatic criticism was as constructive as it was harsh, but was meant to harden (קָשׁוֹת).

DREAMS 101—THE FIRST STEP
IN DREAM ANALYSIS

הוּא הָיָה אוֹמֵר: וְאַל תָּדִין אֶת חֲבֵרְךָ עַד שֶׁתַּגִּיעַ לִמְקוֹמוֹ...

He used to say: Do not judge your fellow until you have stood
in his place [until you find yourself in a similar situation].
(Avos 2:4)

QUESTIONS
---

1. Wouldn't you expect the Mishnah to say: "*Never* judge your friend, as it is not your place to judge another"! Rather, the ethical statement leaves open a possibility of when you in fact can judge another, namely, when you reach their place? Is there perhaps another message here?

2.

וַיְהִי מִקֵּץ שְׁנָתַיִם יָמִים וּפַרְעֹה חֹלֵם וְהִנֵּה עֹמֵד עַל הַיְאֹר.

It came to pass at the end of two full years that
*Pharaoh was dreaming, and behold, he was **standing***
by the Nile. (Bereishis 41:1)

How did Yosef know how to interpret Pharaoh's dream?

110

———————— ANSWERS ————————

Let's analyze by studying a key Talmudic passage regarding dream interpretation: "If one dreams that he is **standing** unclothed: If in Babylon he will remain sinless, if in the Land of Israel he will be bare of pious deeds" (*Berachos* 57a).

If the man is standing unclothed in the dream, why does it matter if he is standing in Babylon or Israel?

The answer will hinge on the emphasis in the dream on either the *standing* element or the *unclothed* element! "Standing" represents merely surviving, while "unclothed" represents not fulfilling significant achievements. The major point that will ensue will be that all dreams must be interpreted in relation to the expectations.

If I am in the less holy Babylon and I am *standing* unclothed, the fact that I am able to stand by myself and not fall is certainly consistent with overcoming the potential.

If I am situated in the Land of Israel with such great potential, though, and I dream of standing *unclothed*, the dream/hope/aspiration is not commensurate with the potential!

The point is clear: The place where you choose or happen to be sets your potential, for which all your eventual dreams/hope/aspirations will be relevant or compared to!

The backdrop of Pharaoh's dream was the Nile River. Rabbi Shimshon Raphael Hirsch reminds us that the Nile's overflow determined the agricultural fate of Egypt. It is thus no wonder that Yosef was able to connect the dots on the further aspects of the dream. The rest of the dream, again, is dependent and relevant to the very **place** one finds oneself in. Yosef knew Pharaoh's dream was tied to the agricultural fate because Pharaoh gave away the locale/backdrop of the dream, which was econo-centric!

You can tell a lot about how a person will be like based on where they make their place. "אַל תָּדִין אֶת חֲבֵרְךָ עַד שֶׁתַּגִּיעַ לִמְקוֹמוֹ" may not simply have the negative connotation of "Don't judge someone," but may be saying, "You can tell a lot about someone when you see the places they choose to be!" Once you see the places people value, שֶׁתַּגִּיעַ לִמְקוֹמוֹ, their dreams/

hopes/aspirations become self-evident, just like the dreams of Pharaoh became evident to Yosef once he saw Pharaoh's frame of reference.

———————————— TAKEAWAY MESSAGES ————————————

Yosef applied an inherent lesson of "אַל תָּדִין אֶת חֲבֵרְךָ עַד שֶׁתַּגִּיעַ לִמְקוֹמוֹ" in analyzing Pharaoh's dream. "אַל תָּדִין אֶת חֲבֵרְךָ עַד שֶׁתַּגִּיעַ לִמְקוֹמוֹ" implies that you actually *can judge someone* based on their *makom*, the place they are in or dream to be in. Pharaoh's dream started out on the Nile, and so Yosef was tipped off that this dream was going to be about the economy of Egypt. If we are standing naked in our dreams, better to be standing in Babylon, because being naked in Israel would not be a dream commensurate with the place's potential! Dreams 101—where the dream takes place shapes the future dreams (and aspirations).

MIKEITZ AND CHANUKAH— THE TRUE "KANEH"CTION

הוּא הָיָה אוֹמֵר: בַּטֵּל רְצוֹנְךָ מִפְּנֵי רְצוֹנוֹ
כְּדֵי שֶׁיְּבַטֵּל רְצוֹן אֲחֵרִים מִפְּנֵי רְצוֹנֶךָ.
הִלֵּל אוֹמֵר: אַל תִּפְרֹשׁ מִן הַצִּבּוּר.

And he [Rabban Gamliel] said: Overcome your own desire for
His desire so that He overcomes the will of others in lieu of
your will! Hillel says: Do not distance from the congregation.
(Avos 2:4)

QUESTIONS

In many editions of *Avos*, this is listed as one Mishnah. Isn't it un-usual for this to be one Mishnah, especially given that there are two statements by two different people—Rabban Gamliel and Hillel?

Why is it that *Parashas Mikeitz* almost always falls out on Shabbos Chanukah?

These are perhaps a few potential answers:

1. *Parashas Mikeitz* has Pharaoh's dreams, and in the first dream he saw seven weak cows eating seven robust cows, while in the second dream he saw seven good ears of grain getting swallowed up by seven thin ears of grain. Similarly, by Chanukah, the weaker Jewish nation was able to overcome the much stronger nation of Greece!

2. The miracle of "the improbable seven" cows and ears of grain in Pharaoh's dream mirrors the seven days of the miraculous extension of the oil of Chanukah.

3. The symbol of Chanukah is the *Menorah*, which is wisdom, and *Mikeitz* features Yosef, who harbors wisdom and foresight.

4. The Vilna Gaon comments that there are 2,025 words in *Mikeitz*, which is a *remez* to the Gemara in *Shabbos* (21b) that says we should light *ner ish u'beiso* for eight days. The *gematria* of the word *ner* is 250, and if you multiply that by eight days, 8 x 250 = 2,000. The remaining 25 is for the 25ᵗʰ of Kislev!

With all of these interesting answers, I searched for a meatier, more substantial connection and the answer is derived from the *Baal Haturim* and the *Kli Yakar* on the *parashah*.

─────────── ANSWERS ───────────

The Torah says:

וְהִנֵּה שֶׁבַע שִׁבֳּלִים עֹלוֹת בְּקָנֶה אֶחָד בְּרִיאוֹת וְטֹבוֹת.

Behold, seven ears of corn came up upon one stalk, healthy and good. (Bereishis 41:5)

When it talks about the unhealthy stalks, though, the Torah says:

הִנֵּה שֶׁבַע שִׁבֳּלִים דַּקּוֹת וּשְׁדוּפֹת קָדִים צֹמְחוֹת אַחֲרֵיהֶן.

Behold, seven ears, thin and blasted with the east wind, sprung up after them. (Ibid., v. 6)

Note that it leaves out the word בְּקָנֶה. The *Kli Yakar* explains that when people or things work together in unison (בְּקָנֶה signifies oneness), then that is בְּרִיאוֹת וְטֹבוֹת—healthy and good, but when scattered and disconnected, they become weakened and thin! He also points to the language of אַחֲרֵיהֶן, "afterward," in the *pasuk*, "עֹלוֹת אַחֲרֵיהֶן מִן הַיְאֹר רָעוֹת מַרְאֶה," which conjures up a "separatist" feel because אַחֲרֵיהֶן and אֲחֵרוֹת are very similar words, connoting that the cows were ugly *because they came separated from one another!*

Isn't that the Chanukah story par excellence? A smaller faction (the Maccabim), *albeit unified*, was able to overcome the mightier, less cohesive (mostly because of their bulky army) Seleucid army.

Perhaps to bolster this idea, it is more than a coincidence that this word בְּקָנֶה is only used two more times in the whole Chumash and both times about the *Menorah*, which is the symbol of Chanukah.

שְׁלֹשָׁה גְבִעִים מְשֻׁקָּדִים בַּקָּנֶה הָאֶחָד כַּפְתֹּר וָפֶרַח וּשְׁלֹשָׁה גְבִעִים מְשֻׁקָּדִים בַּקָּנֶה הָאֶחָד.

Three cups made like almond-blossoms in one branch, a knop and a flower; and three cups made like almond-blossoms in the other branch, a knop and a flower.

And what is the connection of the בְּקָנֶה by Yosef's dream and the בְּקָנֶה of the *Menorah*, the symbol of Chanukah? The answer is that it is well-known that the *Menorah* could not be made of disparate parts but rather as one: "מִקְשָׁה תֵעֲשֶׂה הַמְּנוֹרָה—Fashioned (i.e., not welded) you shall make the *Menorah*." Just like the seven ears of corn came together as one and were beautiful because of it, the *Menorah* was beautiful because it too was made from one big piece. Despite its seeming disparate parts, it was really essentially from one קָנֶה הָאֶחָד. So too, the victorious Jews in the Chanukah story worked together; and this unity wasn't a consequence but a cause of their success.

הוּא הָיָה אוֹמֵר: בַּטֵּל רְצוֹנְךָ מִפְּנֵי רְצוֹנוֹ כְּדֵי שֶׁיְּבַטֵּל רְצוֹן אֲחֵרִים מִפְּנֵי רְצוֹנֶךָ. הִלֵּל אוֹמֵר: אַל תִּפְרֹשׁ מִן הַצִּבּוּר.

And he [Rabban Gamliel] said: Overcome your own desire for His desire so that He overcomes the will of others in lieu of your will! Hillel says: Do not distance from the congregation.
(Avos 2:4)

Perhaps this is listed in many editions as one Mishnah to make a point: When does G-d battle for you? When you don't distance yourself from the *tzibbur*. Success comes to you when you work together. This, then, is the same message of בַּקָּנֶה!

———————— TAKEAWAY MESSAGES ————————

Parashas Mikeitz is almost always read on Chanukah. One reason may be the connection between בְּקָנֶה by the dreams that make the corn beautiful, and the בְּקָנֶה by the *Menorah*. The overriding theme of Chanukah is how great we can all be when we work together. When the corn was בְּקָנֶה, it was beautiful. The *Menorah* was essentially one בְּקָנֶה made of one material as well. The Maccabim fought as one, and the Jewish unity wasn't a consequence but a cause of their success!

The connection of *Mikeitz* to Chanukah is the "*kaneh*"ction—a unified Jewish People is cause of, and not a consequence of, success.

Vayigash

HOW CAN YOSEF FAVOR BINYAMIN AFTER SEEING THE DAMAGE DONE BY FAVORITISM?

וְהַגַּבָּאִים מַחֲזִירִים תָּדִיר בְּכָל יוֹם וְנִפְרָעִין מִן הָאָדָם מִדַּעְתּוֹ וְשֶׁלֹּא מִדַּעְתּוֹ וְיֵשׁ לָהֶם עַל מַה שֶּׁיִּסְמֹכוּ.

The collection officers make their rounds every day and exact payment from man, with his knowledge and without his knowledge. Their case is well-founded, the judgment is a judgment of truth, and ultimately, all is prepared for the feast. (Avos 3:16)

QUESTIONS

What does it mean that "collection officers" exact payment without his knowledge?

After Yosef reveals himself to his brothers in this *parashah*, it seems very odd that he seemingly favors Binyamin by giving him much more than the others; didn't he learn the lesson that favoring one person over another leads to tragedy!

117

לְכֻלָּם נָתַן לָאִישׁ חֲלִפוֹת שְׂמָלֹת וּלְבִנְיָמִן נָתַן שְׁלֹשׁ מֵאוֹת כֶּסֶף וְחָמֵשׁ חֲלִפֹת שְׂמָלֹת.

To all of them he gave to each man changes of clothing; but to Binyamin he gave three hundred shekels of silver, and five changes of clothing. (Bereishis 45:22)

Yosef gives Binyamin three hundred shekels more than each of his brothers, as well as five times the amount of clothing. In fact, the Gemara in *Megillah* (16a) asks precisely this question and answers that Yosef giving five times as much clothing as the others hints to a future time where a Binyaminite will get a fivefold of clothing, namely Mordechai, who will be rewarded with five cloaks from Achashverosh for saving him from death! But would Yosef risk upsetting his brothers and renewing the cycle of jealousy just to "foreshadow" that a heroic descendant will be rewarded in a similar fashion? That doesn't answer the question at all...or does it?

—————————— ANSWERS ——————————

The *Torah Temimah* points out, in the name of Rabbeinu Bachye, that each of the ten brothers owed thirty shekels for selling him as a slave; 30 x 10 = 300. Technically the brothers then collectively owed Yosef three hundred shekels. Since Binyamin did not sell Yosef, it is only fair to pay Binyamin the three hundred shekels that he waived for the other ten brothers. (Think about it this way: Yosef gifted the brothers three hundred shekels by absolving their debt and so he owed three hundred shekels to the one who had no debt!) OK, while that takes care of the three-hundred-shekel piece, how do we then explain the fivefold gift of clothing?

(The *Torah Temimah* does point out, artistically, that although Yosef seemingly gave more clothing to Binyamin, the wording in the *pasuk* hints that he actually gave them the same amount. The word חֲלִפוֹת by the ten brothers is מלא—full in the sense that it is spelled with a *vav*, and the word חֲלִפֹת by Binyamin is חסר—missing in the sense that it is spelled without the *vav*. Even though at first glance it seems that Yosef gave Binyamin more clothing than his brothers, in fact the Torah hints that Yosef gave them מלא clothing and an equivalent amount of cloth-ing (חסר clothing), monetarily speaking to Binyamin. In other words, five garments of חסר equals one garment of מלא. This answer is quite a stretch, though.)

In fact, using the *Torah Temimah*'s approach in separating out the ten brothers who sold Yosef versus Binyamin (back by the three-hundred-shekel discussion), who didn't, the Gemara in *Megillah* (16a) finally makes sense! Yosef gave the brothers ten cloaks that they didn't de-serve, and thus should owe Binyamin ten cloaks. But Yosef only gave five cloaks to Binyamin, which should make us wonder what happened to the other five! The Gemara thus points out that in the future, he will get his due. His descendant will be rewarded with five cloaks by Achashverosh. And so it is actually completely flipped on its head here: you initially thought that Yosef was provoking jealousy by giving Binyamin fivefold clothing, but in reality, he may have been favoring his ten brothers by giving them ten cloaks and only giving Binyamin five, but then consoling him in a sense by assuring him an extra five cloaks in the future, rewarded to his heroic descendant.

Although seemingly convoluted, the point is that we go to great lengths to try to explain how Yosef would not be foolish enough to make the same mistake that his father seemingly did by favoring one child over another. Yet another point is that "collection officers" are sent to exact payment in ways we simply do not understand (וְהַגַּבָּאִים מַחֲזִירִים תָּדִיר בְּכָל יוֹם וְנִפְרָעִין מִן הָאָדָם מִדַּעְתּוֹ וְשֶׁלֹּא מִדַּעְתּוֹ). Although it seems as if Yosef is favoring Binyamin, G-d has His own machinations, and per-haps He is merely giving to him what he is owed (three hundred shekels per the *Torah Temimah*'s explanation), or even perhaps hinting that he will receive his full reward in the future (the future five garments of Mordechai that He "owes" him to complete the ten).

────────── TAKEAWAY MESSAGES ──────────

Yosef actually did not favor Binyamin by giving him three hundred shekels and fivefold of clothing. The three hundred seemingly super-fluous shekels given to Binyamin were in fact owed to him as Yosef absolved the brothers of their three-hundred-shekel debt to him. Using that same logic, Binyamin was owed ten garments but only got five, but was destined to get the other five later on in the form of his heroic descendant Mordechai. One can actually make an argument that the ten brothers were favored by Yosef over Binyamin, but this highlights that it is imperative for us to understand that "collection officers" sent out by G-d execute the retribution machinations without our knowledge, in ways that we do not fully comprehend. Yosef did not favor Binyamin; his "half-gift" signaled that the other half was awaiting him in the future!

TRAVEL ADVICE FROM THE AVOS

רַבִּי שִׁמְעוֹן אוֹמֵר: הַמְהַלֵּךְ בַּדֶּרֶךְ וְשׁוֹנֶה
וּמַפְסִיק מִמִּשְׁנָתוֹ וְאוֹמֵר מַה נָּאֶה אִילָן זֶה
מַה נָּאֶה נִיר זֶה מַעֲלֶה עָלָיו הַכָּתוּב כְּאִלוּ
מִתְחַיֵּב בְּנַפְשׁוֹ.

*Rabbi Shimon says: One who is walking on a path and
learning and stops from his learning and says, "How beautiful
is this tree and how nice is the plowed field," then the Torah
considers him culpable with his life.*
(Avos 3:7)

One explanation of this ethic is that when you travel, you can protect
yourself from the dangers of traveling by having some spiritual focus;
involvement with some sort of spiritual endeavor/purpose can save you
from the lurking dangers of travel.

QUESTIONS

In our very *parashah*, we perhaps see a completely different approach
to traveling as Yosef warns his brothers, as they were returning home
post his revelation: "אַל תִּרְגְּזוּ בַּדָּרֶךְ—Don't quarrel on the way!" The simple meaning is that Yosef warned them not to fight with one another
on the way home, blaming each other for selling Yosef. But *Rashi* brings
down two other possibilities:

1. Do not engage in a halachic discussion, lest the way cause you to stray.
2. Do not walk with large steps (*Taanis* 10b).

Didn't *Pirkei Avos* just teach us the travel safety tip of being involved in learning? Also, presumably "Don't walk with large steps" would mean "Don't rush too fast"; is it not odd that these two interpretations brought in *Rashi* are actually complete opposites: (1) Don't go too slow, and (2) Don't go too fast. Which one is right?

—————————— ANSWERS ——————————

The Gemara in *Taanis* (10b) actually answers this question indirectly. When Yosef said, "Don't get engrossed in learning, lest you stray," he was referring to cogitation or deep learning for the first time. Perhaps by our Mishnah, however, the Tanna who espouses learning to protect from danger is referring to a less intense form of learning, such as in repetition or review. (The Gemara there doesn't bring down our Mishnah, by the way, but has yet another source that learning is protective; see Gemara inside!) The lesson is clear: On the one hand, you need to have some spiritual focus to protect you from the dangers lurking in travel. But don't get so over-engrossed in your learning that you don't take heed of the actual dangers. Don't be too spiritual, or you can overshoot your target.

Interestingly, when that very same Gemara talks about the second interpretation of not taking large steps, the prevalent opinion is that taking large steps robs a man of one five-hundredth of his eyesight. Why is this so? Perhaps the message is that if you try to rush too fast to your destination and do not cherish (to some degree) the actual trip itself, you "blind yourself" and are perhaps missing out on some of the rare amenities of the travel itself.

So, putting it all together: Our Mishnah in *Avos* teaches us that we must understand that G-d protects us while we travel. Besides saying *Tefillas Haderech*, we have to have some spiritual focus—הַמְהַלֵּךְ בַּדֶּרֶךְ וְשׁוֹנֶה. That spiritual focus must be on something light because being over-engrossed in some Torah matter can have a paradoxical dangerous effect, as we may lack focus on the inherent perils of travel—אַל תִּרְגְּזוּ

בַּדָּרֶךְ! The next message is that we shouldn't try to get to our destination too fast, lest "we become blinded" and not appreciate the actual travel itself, which has something to offer—אַל תִּרְגְּזוּ בַּדָּרֶךְ.

———————— TAKEAWAY MESSAGES ————————

הַמְהַלֵּךְ בַּדֶּרֶךְ וְשׁוֹנֶה—When you travel, have some spiritual endeavor. Don't get too over-engrossed in that spiritual endeavor, as you may miss your exit! Also, don't travel too fast, as you might be blinded and miss out on some of the great aspects of the travel itself. Yosef's travel advice: Get there fast, but not too fast—אַל תִּרְגְּזוּ בַּדָּרֶךְ.

YOSEF'S "PRIVATE" LESSON
TO HIS BROTHERS

הוּא הָיָה אוֹמֵר: וְאַל תֹּאמַר דָּבָר שֶׁאִי אֶפְשָׁר
לִשְׁמֹעַ שֶׁסּוֹפוֹ לְהִשָּׁמַע.

He [Hillel] says: And don't say something that's impossible to
hear because in the end it can be heard. (Avos 2:4)

─────────── QUESTIONS ───────────

What can this ambiguous statement mean?

Right after Yosef famously reveals himself to his brothers, saying, "I am Yosef; is my father still alive," the Torah recalls how the brothers became startled in his presence. Seemingly to placate their fears, he summons them to huddle closer with the words: "גְּשׁוּ נָא אֵלַי וַיִּגָּשׁוּ—Please, come closer to me."

Rashi quotes the midrash that

ראה אותם נסוגים לאחוריהם אמר עכשיו אחי נכלמים קרא להם
בלשון רכה ותחנונים והראה להם שהוא מהול.

He saw they were going backward, and he said, "Now my
bothers are embarrassed," and so with gentle touch, he showed
them that he was circumcised. (Bereishis 45:3)

The *Sifsei Chachamim* adds that Yosef simply wanted to remind the brothers that they were all on the same squad (ברית אחוה), so to speak, by showing them he was a Jew just like them.

124

If Yosef was sold into slavery at seventeen years of age, then clearly the brothers knew that Yosef was circumcised. So then why didn't he just say, "Remember, brothers, I am circumcised just like you!" What is the utility in *showing* them that he was circumcised?

———————— ANSWERS ————————

The answer perhaps is derived from analyzing the words invoking the huddle: "גְּשׁוּ נָא אֵלַי וַיִּגָּשׁוּ." This is reminiscent of when Yitzchak wanted to huddle with Yaakov to make sure he was Eisav by the "stealing of the blessing": "גְּשָׁה נָא וַאֲמֻשְׁךָ בְּנִי—Come here so I can touch you." In fact, the root word of וַיִּגַּשׁ is used a whopping six times in six *pesukim* over there, highlighting the dramatic test of strength—that Yaakov was still able to carry on the ruse, despite being in such close proximity. Think about it from Yaakov's perspective; he must have been tempted to say at any moment, "Mommy put me to this; I didn't mean to trick you!" In other words, despite the huddle and the temptation to go back on his plan, Yaakov persevered and passed the test set by his mother to acquire the blessing that was rightfully his. This story of determination was undoubtedly passed over to his sons.

When Yosef then summons his brothers, "גְּשׁוּ נָא אֵלַי וַיִּגָּשׁוּ," he is reminding them of his father's "גְּשָׁה נָא וַאֲמֻשְׁךָ בְּנִי," and how despite the odds/temptation, he did not back out of it and make excuses. He is telling his brothers as they are "נְסוֹגִים לְאֲחוֹרֵיהֶם—backing up," as they are about to come up with excuses and regret, that they need not resort to blaming one another, making excuses, or rewriting history, but rather to move on and accept the past.

By showing them his circumcision, as opposed to just reminding them of it, he is making the same point: Don't abandon ship, disown reality, and try to rewrite history. It was a practice of some Jews who were ashamed of their Jewishness to surgically correct the circumcision to make it look like they were uncircumcised. (In fact, Elazar Hamodai says in *Avos* that this reversion of the *bris* is a grave sin—the so-called מֵפִיר בְּרִיתוֹ שֶׁל אַבְרָהָם). Being disowned from his father's house, it would not be farfetched to assume that Yosef would correct his circumcision to fit in better with his Egyptian brethren. By *showing* his brothers that he *still* was circumcised, he is again making the point that "just like I accepted my fate even in duress and didn't disown my past, please take ownership of your misdeed and do not try to go backward and blame one another." In response to this secretive plea, it is thus no surprise that a unified collective responsibility ensued.

הוּא הָיָה אוֹמֵר: וְאַל תֹּאמַר דָּבָר שֶׁאִי אֶפְשָׁר לִשְׁמֹעַ שֶׁסּוֹפוֹ לְהִשָּׁמַע.

He [Hillel] says: And don't say something that's impossible to hear because in the end it can be heard. (Avos 2:4)

This ambiguous statement may be an encouragement to confront your inner fears. Everybody has something they once did that they are ashamed about. Don't think that whatever bad thing you did is "אִי אֶפְשָׁר לִשְׁמֹעַ—impossible to hear or understand," because in the end it can be understood, "שֶׁסּוֹפוֹ לְהִשָּׁמַע." Confronting our prior misdeeds and acknowledging them is the first step toward rehabilitation! Yosef reminded his brothers: "וְאַל תֹּאמַר דָּבָר שֶׁאִי אֶפְשָׁר לִשְׁמֹעַ."

——— TAKEAWAY MESSAGES ———

Yosef's brothers were at his *bris* and certainly knew he was circumcised, so why did he gather them in to *show* him his *bris*? The *Sifsei Chachamim* said it was to show that "we are all brothers!" The "גְּשׁוּ נָא אֵלַי" by Yosef and his brothers mirrors the "גְּשָׁה נָּא וַאֲמֻשְׁךָ בְּנִי" by Yaakov taking Yitzchak's redirected blessing to Eisav. Yosef reminded his brothers that just like Yaakov was steadfast despite the dramatic temptation to renounce his plan, they should also not start going backward and rewriting history, but rather should take ownership of their misdeeds. Yosef showed his *bris* in the sense that he still had a *bris* and didn't "undo" it amid his acculturation in Egypt. He took ownership of his past and did not try to fabricate his history.

Yosef's "circumcision" lesson to his brothers is a lesson to us: Don't try to renegotiate the past. Take ownership of your misdeeds and don't blame others! When in a state of גְּשׁוּ נָא אֵלַי, don't be נְסוֹגִים לְאַחוֹרֵיהֶם, as we should never be מֵפִיר בְּרִיתוֹ שֶׁל אברהם!

IS THIS THE BEST D'VAR TORAH EVER?

רַבִּי יְהוֹשֻׁעַ אוֹמֵר: עַיִן הָרַע וְיֵצֶר הָרַע וְשִׂנְאַת הַבְּרִיּוֹת מוֹצִיאִין אֶת הָאָדָם מִן הָעוֹלָם.

*Rabbi Yehoshua says: An **evil eye**, an evil urge, and hatred of beings bring a person out of this world. (Avos 2:11)*

─────── QUESTIONS ───────

What does it mean to have an "evil eye" after all? My fellow friend/candyman/mentor Jay Ennis explained to me that, indeed, if you want others to fail, and you "evil eye" them, that effectively makes you isolated and is to your detriment. But if that was true, the "evil eye" that the Tanna mentions would merely be repeating the subsequent, disparate idea of "hatred of others." What does "evil eye" really mean then?

בֵּן פֹּרָת יוֹסֵף בֵּן פֹּרָת עֲלֵי עָיִן בָּנוֹת צָעֲדָה עֲלֵי שׁוּר.

*Yosef is a fruitful vine, **a fruitful vine by a fountain**; its branches run over the wall. (Bereishis 49:22)*

Rashi, noticing the word עָיִן can also mean "eye," interprets the phrase, "by a fountain," as "his charm **attracts the eye** that beholds him." The Gemara in *Berachos* (20a) tells a cryptic story about the handsome Rabbi Yochanan who wasn't worried about receiving עַיִן הָרַע

127

because he was from the tribe of Yosef. Why is Yosef protected from an עַיִן הָרָע, and what's the possible message here? The Gemara itself answers that the *pasuk* can be read, "בֵּן פֹּרָת עֲלֵי עָיִן," as if to say, "he is the son that is **over** the [evil] eye." In other words, Yosef was blessed with being protected from the evil eye. The problem with that interpretation, though, is that it doesn't really explain why Yosef was granted such a supernatural gift.

ANSWERS

Michtav M'Eliyahu explains the evil eye as follows: The "evil eye" works like this…The blessings bestowed by G-d upon an individual should not serve as a source of anguish to others. If one allows his blessings (wealth, etc.) to cause pain to others less fortunate, and certainly if one flaunts these, one arouses G-d to reconsider the blessings bestowed and possibly rescind them! (Adapted from *Berachos* 20a [Schottenstein *Talmud Bavli*].)

Now, when the Gemara says, "בֵּן פֹּרָת עֲלֵי עָיִן," the עֲלֵי may not mean "over" or "on top," but perhaps "burden" (root of עֹל). The Gemara may then be consistent with this *Michtav M'Eliyahu*: "Yosef is עֲלֵי עָיִן" means that Yosef understood the **burdens** that his beauty created for him! Cognizance of and sensitivity to others are genetically imbued in Yosef and his descendants so that they are "free from *ayin hara*"—they are not going to arouse the jealousies of others heretofore. Yosef understood (perhaps from experience) that the best way to ward off the evil eye was to best underplay his sundry gifts so as not to arouse unpredictable jealousy from others! As opposed to just receiving some supernatural blessing from Yaakov (עֲלֵי עָיִן—**on top of** *ayin*), this is a more down-to-earth, practical approach (עֲלֵי עָיִן—Yosef's greatness was that he understood the **burdens** his grace led to).

And so perhaps the Mishnah in *Avos* is likewise saying that we need to work on underplaying our great assets so that we don't provoke undesired jealousy. עַיִן הָרָע doesn't mean that we should be wary not to be jealous of others (שִׂנְאַת הַבְּרִיּוֹת covered that). Rather, that we should be wary not to be overly showy so that others won't be naturally jealous!

─────────── TAKEAWAY MESSAGES ───────────

Yosef was able to be protected from an evil eye, perhaps not only because the blessing from Yaakov hinted that he will be "עוֹלֵי עָיִן," or **above** the evil eye, but also because he was "עוֹלֵי עָיִן," as in "burden." Yosef knew as the *Michtav M'Eliyahu* teaches—that an evil eye is when our positives provoke unwanted jealousies, which may provoke G-d to reconsider our blessings. Even if this is the best *d'var Torah* ever (which it probably is), let's just pretend it isn't and try to be Yosef-like!

WHAT DOES IT MEAN TO BE B'TZELEM ELOKIM?

חָבִיב אָדָם שֶׁנִּבְרָא בְצֶלֶם. חִבָּה יְתֵרָה נוֹדַעַת
לוֹ שֶׁנִּבְרָא בְצֶלֶם, שֶׁנֶּאֱמַר (בראשית ט) כִּי בְּצֶלֶם
אֱלֹקִים עָשָׂה אֶת הָאָדָם.

It is a great love that it was made known to man that he was created in the image of G-d, as it is stated, "For in the image of G-d (אֱלֹקִים) did He make man" (Bereishis 9:6). (Avos 3:14)

QUESTIONS

Really?! How many of us really go around and think about how lucky we are to be created in the image of G-d? Also, is there any specific reason that G-d's name used here is אֱלֹקִים?

ANSWERS

"יְשִׂמְךָ אֱלֹקִים כְּאֶפְרַיִם וְכִמְנַשֶּׁה—G-d will place you like Ephraim and Menasheh." Yaakov blessed Yosef's children saying that Yisrael would bless their children to be like Ephraim and Menasheh. The custom of blessing the children on Friday night is in fact based on this *pasuk*. But why are we blessing our children to be like the two sons who were ultimately not so overtly successful? In fact, eventually the tribes of Ephraim and Menasheh were both lost, as in the "the ten lost tribes." The answer is hinted in the cantillation marks of the *pasuk*: a *zakef katon* as seen here אֱלֹקִים should be registered as a pause by the reader. Since the *zakef katon* is by the word אֱלֹקִים, the *pasuk* should be understood as follows: "Place G-dliness [in your lives]," pause, "[as exemplified] by Ephraim and Menasheh." As opposed to being the "goal," Ephraim and Menasheh are actually examples of G-dliness, which is the object/goal here.

And how are Ephraim and Menasheh the paradigm of G-dliness? In the midst of brotherly fights and jealousy that mark the first *parshiyos* of *Bereishis*, Ephraim and Menasheh are two brothers who are, at the very least, nearly always mentioned in unison. Do you ever talk about the Biblical Menasheh without talking about Ephraim, or vice versa? And so we bless our children, "You should have G-dliness [in the sense of coming together and working as one unit] as Ephraim and Menasheh."

The "plurality" inherent in the singular G-d's name is not accidental. He wants us to emulate Him and went so far as calling Himself by a plural name, אֱלֹקִים, thus potentially adding critical fodder to sectarians, all to teach us that we need to yearn for plurality. He wants us to work together and not try to succeed alone. And thus, the great love that G-d shows us in creating us in the image of אֱלֹקִים, according to Rabbi Akiva, may be that we are guaranteed to never be alone if we truly emulate G-d as in His Name of אֱלֹקִים. How comforting it is to know that we all need each other and thus can rely on each other; it is also no coincidence that the author (Rabbi Akiva) of this statement is also known for his comments of "Love your neighbor as yourself."

—— TAKEAWAY MESSAGES ——

G-dliness and spirituality, along with an emulation of G-d, are best accomplished by working together. Like Ephraim and Menasheh are always in unison, we bless our children to be teammates with one another and others—working together is truly being בְּצֶלֶם אֱלֹקִים!

בְּצֶלֶם אֱלֹקִים means knowing that to be G-dlike is to be able to work with others in unison, like Ephraim and Menasheh!

IS THERE A CONNECTION BETWEEN DENTISTRY AND BEING KING?

שַׁמַּאי אוֹמֵר: עֲשֵׂה תוֹרָתְךָ קֶבַע אֱמוֹר מְעַט
וַעֲשֵׂה הַרְבֵּה וֶהֱוֵי מְקַבֵּל אֶת כָּל הָאָדָם
בְּסֵבֶר פָּנִים יָפוֹת.

*Shammai says: Do a lot, and greet everyone with a
pleasant face. (Avos 1:15)*

QUESTIONS

1. Is there any Biblical source for Shammai's ethic?
2. Is וֶהֱוֵי מְקַבֵּל אֶת כָּל הָאָדָם בְּסֵבֶר פָּנִים יָפוֹת a separate idea from עֲשֵׂה הַרְבֵּה?

ANSWERS

"חַכְלִילִי עֵינַיִם מִיַּיִן וּלְבֶן שִׁנַּיִם מֵחָלָב"—He is red-eyed from wine and white-toothed from milk (*Bereishis* 49:12)."

The *berachah* that Yaakov gives Yehudah seems pretty straight-forward; Yehudah's descendants shall have plenty of wine and milk. As the white milk flows by one's teeth, it will leave the white residue behind (as in the "Got Milk" commercials), and the teeth will shine bright.

Rabbi Motti Shifman points out that although many commentaries interpret this passage literally as a description of Yehudah's suitability for royalty (that he was a man of regal appearance), the Talmud offers the following homiletic interpretation: "The person who makes his teeth white, i.e., by smiling affectionately at his fellow man, has done more good than the person who offers his fellow man milk to drink." Rather than interpreting the verse, "וּ לְבֶן שִׁנַּיִם מֵחָלָב—teeth white from milk," one should read, "וּלְבֶן שִׁנַּיִם מֵחָלָב—showing the whiteness of your teeth is more beneficial than milk" (*Kesuvos* 111b). Rabbi Shifman pondered the connection between the homiletic and literal interpretations: Why should this message be relayed in the blessing of Yehudah? Furthermore, the Gemara elsewhere (*Kiddushin* 82b) teaches that were it not that Hashem provided for the animals, each animal would be suited for a particular profession: The fox would be most competent as a storekeeper, the lion as a porter, etc. Why would the mighty lion be a porter (a person hired to carry burdens or baggage)? You'd expect a *mightier* job given to the king of the jungle!

An answer is that genuine Jewish might is defined in terms of being willing and able to help others. A mighty lion's job would be a porter because true strength is seeing beyond oneself. Like the lion he is named for, Yehudah was willing to be a slave to free Binyamin, again demonstrating the Jewish regal trait of trying to help others. Yehudah is similarly blessed with "וּלְבֶן שִׁנַּיִם מֵחָלָב," greeting everyone with a smile; setting aside your own worries/thoughts to try and make others feel worthy is a trait worthy of a king!

Similarly, when Shammai says, "Do a lot and receive everyone with a pleasant face," he may in fact be saying, "Do a lot, which is defined by how you treat others!" Doing a lot in a Jewish ethical perspective is not about what you personally accomplish but by how you affect and receive other people! And so the "עֲשֵׂה הַרְבֵּה" is *defined* by "הֱוֵי מְקַבֵּל אֶת כֹּל הָאָדָם בְּסֵבֶר פָּנִים יָפוֹת."

––––––––––– TAKEAWAY MESSAGES –––––––––––

When Yehudah is blessed with having an abundance of milk that would whiten his teeth, we are also taught about an important kingly nature that we should strive toward: "Show your white teeth and smile when you greet others!" Making other people feel comfortable is the ultimate Jewish might. A lion would be a porter if he had a job.

Doing a lot in Jewish terms (עֲשֵׂה הַרְבֵּה) is defined by how you affect others (הֱוֵי מְקַבֵּל אֶת כֹּל הָאָדָם בְּסֵבֶר פָּנִים יָפוֹת). A kingly trait is to smile with white teeth when greeting others—to be a good king, you need a good dentist!

IS THERE A KINDNESS THAT IS FALSE?

הוּא הָיָה אוֹמֵר: אַל תִּהְיוּ כַּעֲבָדִים הַמְשַׁמְּשִׁין אֶת הָרַב עַל מְנָת לְקַבֵּל פְּרָס אֶלָּא הֱווּ כַּעֲבָדִים הַמְשַׁמְּשִׁין אֶת הָרַב שֶׁלֹּא עַל מְנָת לְקַבֵּל פְּרָס וִיהִי מוֹרָא שָׁמַיִם עֲלֵיכֶם.

He said: Be as slaves who serve their master not for the sake of reward, and the fear of heaven should be upon you. (Avos 1:3)

QUESTIONS

1. Is the idea of "having fear of heaven upon you" a consequence of, or a prerequisite for, the "serving not in order to reap reward"?
2. Why use this unusual reference to שָׁמַיִם in this ethic?
3.

> וַיִּקְרְבוּ יְמֵי יִשְׂרָאֵל לָמוּת וַיִּקְרָא לִבְנוֹ לְיוֹסֵף וַיֹּאמֶר לוֹ אִם נָא מָצָאתִי חֵן בְּעֵינֶיךָ שִׂים נָא יָדְךָ תַּחַת יְרֵכִי **וְעָשִׂיתָ עִמָּדִי חֶסֶד וֶאֱמֶת** אַל נָא תִקְבְּרֵנִי בְּמִצְרָיִם.
>
> *And the time drew near that Yisrael must die; and he called his son Yosef, and said to him: "If now I have found favor in your eyes, please put your hand under my thigh, and **deal kindly and truly with me**; please don't bury me in Egypt."*

What does this message of חֶסֶד וֶאֱמֶת entail?

———————————— ANSWERS ————————————

One answer discussed by Rabbi Shlomo Wolbe is the following: There is discussion regarding those living outside of Israel who die and then want to be buried in Israel. (I found a *Midrash Tanchuma* in *Vayechi* that actually pits Rebbi against Rabbi Elazar: Rebbi opposed the practice while Rabbi Elazar supports it.)

A natural reaction one might have is: "Israel wasn't good enough for you to live in, but it's good enough to be buried there?" Yaakov was telling Yosef that burying me in Israel would be אֱמֶת, truthful—i.e., consistent with my true Israel loyalty—because I only came to Egypt from Israel to ensure our survival.

Nowadays there is a seemingly healthy trend of people "resting their bones" in Israel while living their lives outside of Israel. Much like Yaakov's directive to Yosef of וְעָשִׂיתָ עִמָּדִי חֶסֶד וֶאֱמֶת, an understanding that makes this custom rational is that such people may live physically outside of Israel but have a real stake in Israel by virtue of their spiritual (and some physical) dedication to the Land.

But there is another understanding. *Rashi* quotes the *Midrash Rabbah* that "kindness done to the dead is the truest kindness, because one does not expect reward." Yaakov considered the deed of Yosef burying him as the ultimate of *chessed*, as he could never repay him for that mitzvah.

Nowadays, we have our local *chevra kadisha* that ensures that the bodies of deceased Jews are prepared for burial according to Jewish tradition and are protected from desecration, willful or not, until burial (a huge issue lately has been the growth of cremation). At the heart of the *chevra kadisha's* function is the ritual of *taharah*, purification. The body is first thoroughly cleansed of dirt, bodily fluids and solids, and anything else that may be on the skin, and then is ritually purified by immersion in, or a continuous flow of, water from the head over the entire body. Once the body is purified, the body is dressed in *tachrichim*, shrouds, of white pure linen or muslin garments (made up of ten pieces for a male and twelve for a female), which are identical for each Jew and symbolically recalls the garments worn by the *Kohen Gadol*, High Priest. Once the body is shrouded, the casket is closed. The society may also provide *shomrim*, or watchers, to guard the body from theft, vermin, or desecration until burial. Special individuals that you may know have performed such beautiful acts of this truest form of kindness, the kindness that cannot be repaid, and such individuals continuously fulfill Yaakov's plea to Yosef: וְעָשִׂיתָ עִמָּדִי חֶסֶד וֶאֱמֶת.

The reference to שָׁמַיִם in the ethic brought above may very well specifically be used here to remind us that true ultimate reward is in שָׁמַיִם, the next world. We are adjured not to work for a reward in this world but rather for reward in the next world. The fear of heaven here is a reference that working for G-d should be done with a goal of accruing heavenly reward alone.

———— TAKEAWAY MESSAGES ————

וְעָשִׂיתָ עִמָּדִי חֶסֶד וֶאֱמֶת is Yaakov's plea to Yosef. It may have been said to remind Yosef that his desire to be buried in Israel was אֱמֶת, truthful, in the sense that his loyalty to Israel never desisted even when he left for Egypt. וְעָשִׂיתָ עִמָּדִי חֶסֶד וֶאֱמֶת may also mean that Yaakov was asking Yosef to do the ultimate charity, which is that done without reward: taking care of the needs of the dead. *Chevrei kadisha* across the world fulfill Yaakov's plea daily through each of their Yosef HaTzaddiks. This is the חֶסֶד שֶׁל אֱמֶת of Yaakov and Yosef. Our work in this world should be done knowing that the real reward is in the next world. Yaakov's request of truthful kindness; but is there a kindness that could be false? (1) One can be buried in Israel as one's soul/dedication is there, even if one's body isn't, and (2) the truest *chessed* is one that doesn't have any earthly recompense!

SEFER
Shemos

Shemos

MOSHE GIVES US THE KEY TO HAPPINESS

רַבִּי אוֹמֵר: אֵיזוֹהִי דֶרֶךְ יְשָׁרָה שֶׁיָּבֹר לוֹ הָאָדָם
כֹּל שֶׁהִיא תִפְאֶרֶת לְעוֹשֶׂיהָ וְתִפְאֶרֶת לוֹ
מִן הָאָדָם.

Rebbi would say: What is the right way for man to choose?
Whatever is pleasant to those who do them and pleasant for
man. (Avos 2:1)

─── QUESTIONS ───

The Bartenura explains that not only should you enjoy your occupation, but it should be a job that brings joy to others. In his words, "תִפְאֶרֶת לוֹ מִן הָאָדָם" means that "יהיו נוחין בני אדם ממנו—people/mankind will derive pleasure from him." Perhaps, however, we can explain a different *pshat*. After all, "תִפְאֶרֶת לוֹ מִן הָאָדָם" technically means that "it brings **him** joy from the man [singular]," and not "brings **them** joy from him"?

─── ANSWERS ───

The verse says, "וַיִּגְדַּל מֹשֶׁה וַיֵּצֵא אֶל אֶחָיו וַיַּרְא בְּסִבְלֹתָם—He went out to his brothers, and looked on their suffering" (*Shemos* 2:11).

The *Midrash Rabbah* explains:

141

He saw great burdens put upon small people, and light burdens upon big people; a man's burden upon a woman, and a woman's burden upon a man; the burden which an old man could carry on a youth, and of a youth on an old man. So he left his suite and rearranged their burdens, pretending all the time to be helping Pharaoh.

I understand the suffering of great burdens upon small people, and possibly a man's (backbreaking hard labor) being placed on a woman, but is it really considered *suffering* to put light burdens upon big people or the typically easier woman's burden upon a man?

The answer is an important truism for happiness. Famous marketing consultant and TED Talk extraordinaire Simon Sinek says that over 90 percent of people do not find fulfillment in their jobs and it's not because of the job, work, or pay, but rather because "we don't help anybody anymore." Fulfillment, he insightfully espouses, is directly proportional to generosity.

The suffering that a big strong person feels when he is given a light burden is likewise the lack of fulfillment in knowing that he is not maximizing his generous potential and contributing to society all that he can. Moshe Rabbeinu recognized that true happiness is derived by each individual, when potential is matched with action, thereby improving mankind.

When the Mishnah in *Avos* says that the way to live your life is "וְתִפְאֶרֶת לוֹ מִן הָאָדָם," the focus is perhaps not as the Bartenura says, "יהיו נוחין בני אדם ממנו—that people (mankind) will derive pleasure from him," which may create an overly externally dependent scenario that would be more likely to fail than to succeed. Rather, the goal is a more internal personal goal of deriving your own pleasure (תִפְאֶרֶת לוֹ) by recognizing you are מִן הָאָדָם—part of mankind. More clearly, happiness will not be derived from "people taking from you" as much as it is from "you giving to the people." Simon Sinek echoes Moshe Rabbeinu's point that the job done is less important in terms of happiness than the feeling of giving your utmost to the כלל.

When Moshe Rabbeinu recounts the suffering of the Jews, the *Midrash Rabbah* remarks that "he saw great burdens put upon small people, and light burdens upon big people; a man's burden upon a woman, and a woman's burden upon a man..." What was the suffering of putting "light burdens upon big people"? We all feel most fulfilled when we know we are matching our potential to contribute. An individual's fulfillment will be less about what "people take from him" and more about what "each individual gives to mankind." "תִּפְאֶרֶת לוֹ מִן הָאָדָם" doesn't mean that he will derive pleasure when he sees **others taking from him per se** (מִן הָאָדָם meaning "from others," i.e., he derives pleasure from seeing mankind benefit from him), but it means he will derive pleasure when he simply focuses on the **giving itself** that makes him more aware that he is one of mankind (מִן הָאָדָם meaning "he is part of mankind"; he derives pleasure from contributing and thus being part of mankind).

Moshe gives us the key to happiness: giving all you can to be מִן הָאָדָם.

WHAT'S IN A NAME?

רַ—בִּי שִׁמְעוֹן אוֹמֵר: שְׁלֹשָׁה כְתָרִים הֵם
כֶּתֶר תּוֹרָה וְכֶתֶר כְּהֻנָּה וְכֶתֶר מַלְכוּת
וְכֶתֶר שֵׁ=ם טוֹב עוֹלֶה עַל גַּבֵּי–הֶן.

*Rabbi Shimon would say: There are three crowns—the
crown of Torah, the crown of priesthood and the crown of
sovereignty—but the crown of a good name surmounts them
all. (Avos 4:13)*

——— QUESTIONS ———

1. Does a good name really supersede being satiated with Torah or perhaps born into monarchy or priesthood?
2. Furthermore, what does "עוֹלֶה עַל גַּבֵּיהֶן—rises above them all," really mean?

וְאֵלֶּה שְׁמוֹת בְּנֵי יִשְׂרָאֵל הַבָּאִים מִצְרָיְמָה אֵת יַעֲקֹב אִישׁ וּבֵיתוֹ בָּאוּ.

*Now these are the **names** of the sons of Israel, who are
coming into [came into] Egypt with Yaakov. (Shemos 1:1)*

The *Chiddushei HaRim* (1799–1866) asks two questions: (1) Why does the *pasuk* say הַבָּאִים, which literally means "coming," as opposed to אֲשֶׁר בָּאוּ, which means "came"? (2) Why does it say that the שְׁמוֹת, names, came into Egypt as opposed to אנשים, people?

144

He responds homiletically that whenever we come upon a מְצָרִים, so to speak, or a difficult scenario (from the root word מָצוֹר—hardship), we have the *names of our ancestors* that can be utilized to invoke merits, which subsequently protect us.

But what is really in those actual *names* that protect us, if anything? Can *names* really protect us or is this voodoo Judaism?

ANSWERS

One approach, perhaps, is simply that we remind G-d how the B'nei Yisrael meritoriously kept their Jewish names despite the external pressures of assimilation: "They didn't call Reuven, 'Rufus' and they didn't call Shimon, 'Luliani'; nor Yosef, 'Listim'; nor Binyamin, 'Alexander'..." (*Shir Hashirim Rabbah* 4). But it must be more than just the fact that they kept their Jewish-sounding names!

In fact, the *Yalkut Midrash*, as brought down by Rav Peninim, takes it a step further: The names of each son have some relation to גאולה. For instance, Shimon hints to "וַיִּשְׁמַע אֱלֹקִים אֶת נַאֲקָתָם—and G-d hears their cries." In other words, Leah may have named her sons with one thing in mind in the present tense, but the names carried a spiritual significance that became applicable only later on. Rav Peninim emphatically states that the names had a רושם—impact, on their redemption because of the names' inherent Jewish messages of redemption.

Dr. Steven Oppenheimer quotes Rabbi Shimshon Raphael Hirsch as saying that the word שֵׁם—name comes from the word שָׁם—place. A person's name indicates his place in the world. When someone is given a name, that name has a profound effect on that person's essence. In fact, the Baal Shem Tov points out that the middle letters of the word נשמה, soul, spell the word שֵׁם, name.

Let us apply this concept to the aforementioned ethic from *Avos*: "כֶּתֶר תּוֹרָה וְכֶתֶר כְּהֻנָּה וְכֶתֶר מַלְכוּת וְכֶתֶר שֵׁם טוֹב עוֹלֶה עַל גַּבֵּיהֶן." Many are troubled by the concept that a good name is better than these other erstwhile great attributes. Perhaps homiletically this can be understood as follows: Whether you are born to be a future Torah scholar or holy priest or even a king, do not underestimate the power of a good (Jewish) *name*, which can עוֹלֶה עַל גַּבֵּיהֶן, further take you above and beyond where you may have been without such a great bestowed *name*. My father, Dr. Larry Ciment, added an additional homily utilizing the names of the five books of the Torah: בְּרֵאשִׁית—In the beginning, שְׁמוֹת וַיִּקְרָא—you are called by your names, בְּמִדְבַּר דְּבָרִים—and by virtue of that name, *even in a desert you can be something*!

The point is to not underestimate the power of a name in taking you to an even higher plane than your destiny may have intended initially—שֵׁם טוֹב עוֹלָה עַל גַּבֵּיהֶן.

─────────── TAKEAWAY MESSAGES ───────────

Jewish names have inherent spiritual significance and should be a source of pride for us as we embark on the challenges presented on our way. Names are "presently" impacting our destiny in ways we may not fully fathom. They have the power to be עוֹלָה עַל גַּבֵּיהֶן and take us a step beyond our destiny. What's in a name? No, the name affects the what!

IT AIN'T OVER TILL THE FAT LADY SINGS?
THE LESSON FROM TZIPPORAH'S HEROISM

רַ־בִּי אֱלִיעֶזֶר אוֹמֵר: יְהִי כְבוֹד חֲבֵרְךָ חָבִיב
עָלֶיךָ כְּשֶׁלָּךְ, וְאַ־ל תְּהִי נוֹחַ לִכְעוֹס. וְשׁוּב יוֹם
אֶחָד לִפְנֵי מִיתָתְךָ.

*Rabbi Eliezer would say: The honor of your fellow should be
as precious to you as your own, and do not be easy to anger.*
Repent one day before your death...*(Avos 2:10)*

QUESTIONS

How can one repent the day before their death if the time and date
of death is not known?

ANSWERS

There are at least three answers to the question. One original answer
is admittedly tongue-in-cheek: Although we always say or pretend we
are actively doing *teshuvah* all of the time, how many of us really actively do earnest *teshuvah*? The Tanna may be saying this with a touch
of sarcasm, as if exasperated: "Do *teshuvah* at least for one day before
you die!" Often, we just need a spark, and once we dedicate a small bit of
time toward a goal, Hashem helps us with the rest. In that sense, if we
repent even for one day, it could lead to much more—הבא ליטהר מסייעין לו.

A more straightforward (and most accepted answer) is from the
Talmud (*Shabbos* 153a):

*Rabbi Eliezer would say: Repent one day before your death.
Asked his disciples: "Does a man know on which day he will die?"
Said he to them: "So being the case, he should repent today, for
perhaps tomorrow he will die; hence, all his days are passed
in a state of repentance." Indeed, so said Shlomo HaMelech in
his wisdom (Koheles 9:8): "At all times, your clothes should be
white, and oil should not lack from your head."*

A third answer, however, can perhaps be derived from our *parashah*.
But before we see that answer, there is an additional question: Why is
it that the *vidui* prayer, a confessional that is supposed to specifically be
recited on one's deathbed, has within the prayer a request for a *refuah
sheleimah*? If the person is on their deathbed saying this *tefillah*, seemingly all hope is lost, so why add those words that almost seem like a
ברכה לבטלה? The answer can be found here:

וַיְהִי בַדֶּרֶךְ בַּמָּלוֹן וַיִּפְגְּשֵׁהוּ ה' וַיְבַקֵּשׁ הֲמִיתוֹ. וַתִּקַּח צִפֹּרָה צֹר וַתִּכְרֹת
אֶת עָרְלַת בְּנָהּ וַתַּגַּע לְרַגְלָיו וַתֹּאמֶר כִּי חֲתַן דָּמִים אַתָּה לִי.

*And it came to pass on the way at the lodging-place, that
Hashem met him, and sought to kill him. Then Tzipporah took
a flint, and cut off the foreskin of her son, and cast it at his
feet; and she said: "Surely a bridegroom of blood you are to
me." (Shemos 4:24–25)*

The Gemara brings down that an angel, disguised as a snake, partially
ate up Moshe. Tzipporah figured out this was because he failed to do a
bris on his son. She promptly performed the circumcision and Moshe's
life was spared.

The *mussar* is really that our sins prompt our dying process. Everyone
has a certain allowance that we are not privy to, but as soon as that
allowance is gone, our fate is set at any time. Yet, G-d's mercy is such
that He allows us to "bring back the clock," so by remedying whatever
wrong we may have committed, we can clean the slate and avoid the
"dying" inevitability!

How much more dead could Moshe have been than to have been
swallowed up from his head down, and yet Tzipporah knew that if she

performed the *bris* on her son, she could save him. How much more dead can a dying man be on his deathbed and yet he recites a prayer for his own *refuah sheleimah*! This is thus the third meaning of "שׁוּב יוֹם אֶחָד לִפְנֵי מִיתָתְךָ"—"Turn back the clock," so to speak, by going back/returning (שׁוּב) to the *day before your death* by correcting your wrongs that put you in this deathly situation. It's not over, even after the fat lady sings!

─────────── TAKEAWAY MESSAGES ───────────

שׁוּב יוֹם אֶחָד לִפְנֵי מִיתָתְךָ may mean that you should try to do *teshuvah* at least for one day before you die. Or it may mean that since we do not know the day of our death, we should do *teshuvah* every day. Finally, the episode of Tzipporah saving Moshe after he was nearly swallowed whole teaches us a third possibility that explains why a dying person asks for *refuah sheleimah* even on his deathbed: G-d gives us the miraculous ability to turn back the clock by remedying our sins even when all hope is seemingly lost—*return back to the way you were just one day before you died*! It ain't over even after the fat lady sings (unless you're at the opera).

הִלֵּל ⟵אֹומֵר: הֱוֵי מִתַּלְמִידָיו שֶׁל אַהֲרֹן ⟵אֹוהֵב שָׁלֹום⟶ וְרֹודֵף שָׁלֹום⟶ אֹוהֵב אֶת הַבְּרִיֹות⟶ וּמְקָרְ⟵בָן לַתֹּורָה.

Hillel would say: Be of the disciples of Aharon—a lover of peace, a pursuer of peace, one who loves the creatures and draws them close to Torah. (Avos 1:12)

רַבִּי יְ⟵הֹושֻׁעַ אֹומֵר: עַיִן הָרָע וְיֵצֶר הָרָע וְשִׂנְ⟵אַת הַבְּרִיֹות מֹוצִיאִ⟵ין אֶת הָאָדָם מִן הָעֹולָם.

Rabbi Yehoshua says: An evil eye, an evil urge, and hatred of beings bring a person out of this world. (Avos 2:11)

רַ⟵בִּי אֶלְעָזָר הַקַּפָּר אֹומֵר: הַקִּנְאָ⟶ה וְהַתַּאֲוָה וְהַכָּבֹוד מֹוצִיאִין אֶ⟵ת הָאָדָם מִן הָעֹולָם.

Rabbi Elazar says: Jealousy, lust, and honor bring man out of this world. (Avos 2:21)

There is clear symmetry between these two latter Mishnayos. The עַיִן הָרָע, evil eye, may correspond to קִנְאָה, jealousy, the יֵצֶר הָרָע to תַּאֲוָה, and

שְׂנְאַת הַבְּרִיּוֹת to כָּבוֹד. Also, both Mishnayos end cryptically: מוֹצִיאִין אֶת הָאָדָם
מִן הָעוֹלָם!

─────── QUESTIONS ───────

1. What does מוֹצִיאִין אֶת הָאָדָם מִן הָעוֹלָם mean? Most commentators
   interpret it to mean that these evil traits will "remove (מוֹצִיאִין)
   man from the world (מִן הָעוֹלָם)," but that is quite an unusual way
   of saying this. Is there another way to understand this classic
   statement?

2. In our *parashah*, we see the loving nature (described above in
   Avos) of Moshe's brother Aharon. G-d wanted to reassure Moshe
   that Aharon would not be jealous of him and so the *pasuk* reads:
   "וְרָאֲךָ וְשָׂמַח בְּלִבּוֹ—And he saw and was happy in his heart." The
   Gemara in *Shabbos* (139a) states that Aharon's lack of jealousy
   merited him the *Choshen*, the priestly breastplate, to be placed
   on his heart. OK, the heart-heart connection (i.e., Aharon was
   happy "in his heart" and the *Choshen* was thus placed "on his
   heart") makes sense, but why was it specifically the *Choshen*?
   Also, why is Aharon *rewarded* for not being jealous; wouldn't
   that be expected behavior?

─────── ANSWERS ───────

It is not that we are all born angels and then we succumb to a nascent
עַיִן הָרָע וְיֵצֶר הָרָע וְשִׂנְאַת הַבְּרִיּוֹת. Rather, we unfortunately are born with these
evil tendencies. Aside from its literal meaning, that they "take us out of
this world," מוֹצִיאִין אֶת הָאָדָם מִן הָעוֹלָם may also be homiletically understood
as meaning that these traits are מוֹצִיאִין (they are "found" in each and
every human), from the very beginning of our essence (מִן הָעוֹלָם). In that
sense, it is actually a worthy endeavor indeed that Aharon *overcame* his
yetzer and was not jealous of Moshe!

This homiletic interpretation of the Mishnah likewise explains why
the *Choshen* specifically was placed on his heart. The *Choshen*, of course,
housed the *Urim V'Tumim*, the jewels that were used to determine G-d's
will in a particular situation, which represents the heavenly decree.
This representation of an immutable nature rests upon the heart of

Aharon to show that despite our inherent innate characteristics, we can potentially influence them positively with our heart. Aharon is thus the paradigmatic individual who gives us hope in overcoming our innate evil characteristics.

──────────── TAKEAWAY MESSAGES ────────────

The traits of being jealous and despising other people not only "מֹוצִיאִין אֶת הָאָדָם מִן הָעֹולָם—take us out of this world," but are unfortunately expected innate characteristics that are "מֹוצִיאִין—found, אֶת הָאָדָם מִן הָעֹולָם—in us all from our birth."

"וְרָאֲךָ וְשָׂמַח בְּלִבֹּו"—The fact that the great Aharon saw Moshe and was happy in his heart makes him the paradigmatic individual who gives us hope in overcoming our innate evil characteristics. The *Choshen* resting on the heart symbolizes that G-d allows a symbol of His "immutable" nature to rest/rely/mutate on a human heart. Aharon merited the *Choshen* to rest on his heart to teach us that lesson. Aharon was an example how we can improve those characteristics that unfortunately are מֹוצִיאִין אֶת הָאָדָם מִן הָעֹולָם—found in all of us from birth.

KNOWING WHAT KNOWING MEANS
IS IMPORTANT TO KNOW

רַבִּי אֶלְעָזָר אוֹמֵר: הֱוֵי שָׁקוּד לִלְמֹד תּוֹרָה
וְדַע מַה שֶּׁתָּשִׁיב לְאֶפִּיקוֹרוֹס. וְדַע לִפְנֵי
מִי אַתָּה עָמֵל...

*Rabbi Elazar says: You should learn Torah; know what
to answer a heretic and know in front of whom you are
toiling...(Avos 2:14)*

--------- QUESTIONS ---------

The Mishnah says, "Know what to answer the heretic," but doesn't
give us any instruction as to what?

וַיָּקָם מֶלֶךְ חָדָשׁ עַל מִצְרָיִם אֲשֶׁר לֹא יָדַע אֶת יוֹסֵף.

Now there arose a new king over Egypt, who knew not Yosef.

How could it be that the new Egyptian king didn't know Yosef? Didn't
Yosef just save the whole nation from certain starvation and possible
extinction? One answer comes right from *Rashi*, who says, "He acted as
if he did not know about him." Another answer attributed to the *Sefas
Emes* is that Yosef represented the ability to bust through hardships
(such as escaping from Potifar's wife and jail) and be better off because
of them. When it says that the king didn't "know Yosef," it meant that
he didn't understand that hard times can be utilized for creating better

times like Yosef did. He instead folded under pressure and started persecuting others. Yet another answer can perhaps be derived from analyzing the very next time it says *yada*, "know," in the Torah:

> Now it came to pass in those many days that the king of Egypt died, and the Children of Israel sighed from the labor, and they cried out, and their cry ascended to G-d from the labor. G-d heard their cry, and G-d remembered His covenant with Avraham, with Yitzchak, and with Yaakov. And G-d saw the Children of Israel, and G-d **knew**. (Shemos 2:23–25)

───────────── ANSWERS ─────────────

Rabbi David Holzer quotes Rav Joseph B. Soloveitchik as asking a very straightforward question: If G-d indeed heard B'nei Yisrael's crying (it even says that G-d remembered His covenant with the forefathers!), then what does "and G-d **knew**" add? The answer he gives is basically that B'nei Yisrael sighed "from the labor," and they didn't appreciate the spiritual havoc their slavery was having on them. When it says that "G-d knew," it is saying that G-d knew beyond even what B'nei Yisrael knew, in the sense of knowing them better and what they really needed. He adds a point culled from the words in *Shemoneh Esreh*: "Hear our voice, have pity and mercy on us and accept our prayers with compassion and with **desire** (תקבל ברחמים וברצון)." What is meant by "וברצון"? The Rav explained: We ask that G- should only fulfill the prayers that He desires to fulfill, for only He knows what is truly best for us. In the Rav's own words: "We beseech of G-d: 'You choose which prayer to realize and fulfill, and which prayers to reject, because we don't rely on ourselves.'" We might pray for something that would actually be bad for us, and so it makes more sense to pray for what G-d thinks is best for us! G-d heard the cries of B'nei Yisrael when they worked, but He "knew" they needed a spiritual healing as much as a physical redemption.

So "knowing" means more than hearing and knowing some facts; it is a deeper understanding beyond even that recognized by the personal subject of the knowing. When it says that the new king didn't know

Yosef, it could very well mean that he knew Yosef's historical connection to Egypt, but didn't understand or know the extensive details surrounding his very essence.

When Rabbi Elazar says in *Avos*, "Know what to answer the *apikorus*," but doesn't give us any instruction, homiletically it could mean that וַדַע—the fact that G-d knows us (as in "and G-d knew"), is what we need to respond to an *apikorus*. G-d knows our very essence and what we need more than we know ourselves. This special connection is what we should relate to an *apikorus*!

———————— TAKEAWAY MESSAGES ————————

How can Pharaoh not know the savior Yosef? He did know but chose or pretended not to know (*Rashi*). Or he didn't know "Yosef," i.e., he didn't understand that trials and tribulations can lead to bigger successes as we learn from Yosef (*Sefas Emes*). A novel understanding is derived from the great *vort* of the Rav on "and G-d knew"—G-d knew more than what we actually knew when we were crying from physical labor. He "knew" our unappreciated spiritual suffering. "Knowing" sometimes means understanding a person deeper than they actually know themselves! When we say *Shema Koleinu* every day, the Rav reminds us that we should ask that G-d answers us "בְרָצוֹן," that G-d should grant us whatever *we should be praying for* and maybe not what we are praying for! Pharaoh didn't "know" Yosef in the way that G-d "knew" B'nei Yisrael; he didn't see the stories behind the story and thus underappreciated the great nation that he had under his reign. Knowing what knowing means is important to know, because now your *Shema Koleinu* prayer will never be the same!

Va'eira

WHAT'S THE CONNECTION BETWEEN THE FROGS AND ANGER?

רַ־בִּי אֱלִיעֶזֶר אוֹמֵר: וְאַל תְּהִי נוֹחַ לִכְעֹס
וְשׁוּב יוֹם אֶחָד־ לִפְנֵי מִיתָתְךָ ...

*Rabbi Eliezer says: And don't be quick to get angry, and
repent one day before your death. (Avos 2:10)*

--- QUESTIONS ---

Most commentators interpret these two phrases in the above ethic
as completely unrelated separate statements. But is there a possible
connection? What does anger have to do with being able to repent
before you die?

--- ANSWERS ---

וַתַּעַל הַצְּפַרְדֵּעַ וַתְּכַס אֶת אֶרֶץ מִצְרָיִם.
*And the frog went up and covered the land of Egypt.
(Shemos 8:2)*

There is a *Midrash Tanchuma*, also brought in *Rashi*, that quotes Rabbi
Akiva as saying that there was initially only one frog, but miraculously,

156

as the Egyptians would smite the frog, many frogs came forth from that one frog!

Rabbi Yaakov Kanievsky, the Steipler Gaon, asked the obvious question: If the abundance of frogs were a nuisance, why didn't the Egyptians simply stop smiting them once they realized that hitting them actually caused their multiplication?

The answer he gives in his *sefer*, *Birkas Peretz* (which I saw in Rabbi Yaakov Edelstein's *B'Rinah Yiktzoru*) is essentially that anger always muddles reason. Though the Egyptians should have rationally stopped hitting the frogs, their anger made them out of control. Reason and really good intent can be squashed in one minute by one fit of rage. I will add that it is likely no coincidence that this message of anger is taught to us by the צְפַרְדֵּעַ—frog. The word צְפַרְדֵּעַ can be broken up to mean צְפַר, "morning" and דַע, "to know." One strategy I have learned that helps prevent anger in any situation is to "sleep on it" and "know the morning." The lesson of anger is indeed to דַע—know, the צְפַר—morning.

When the Tanna in *Avos* says, "Don't be quick to get angry, and repent one day before your death," he is likely saying that anger leads us to lose control and eventually relinquish well-meaning and good intent. In order to assure we will die having done sincere *teshuvah*, repentance, we thus have to avoid anger, which is the root of losing rationality! Anger and repentance are thus very much connected.

—————— TAKEAWAY MESSAGES ——————

Rabbi Yaakov Kanievsky asked why the Egyptians didn't simply stop smiting the frogs once they realized that hitting them actually caused their multiplication. The Egyptians got angry, and reason and rationality is squashed when anger takes control!

So what's the connection between the frog and anger? To דַע—know the צְפַר—morning. Sleep on it, as anger just leads to irrationality!

WAS MOSHE'S SPEECH IMPEDIMENT
A BLESSING OR A CURSE?

שַׁמַּאי אוֹמֵר: אֱמֹר מְעַט וַעֲשֵׂה הַרְבֵּה.

Shammai says: Say a little and do a lot. (Avos 1:15)

The standard approach to this well-known ethic is: You should do more than you say you are going to do. Don't be so flashy and ostentatious, but rather let your actions speak louder than your words.

—————————— QUESTIONS ——————————

1. But what would be so bad if you were אֱמֹר הַרְבֵּה as long as you were עֲשֵׂה הַרְבֵּה?
2. In the *parashah*, Moshe says that the Jews and Pharaoh will not listen to him because he does not speak well. G-d replies, "Command them!" How does the second *pasuk* answer Moshe's concern?

—————————— ANSWERS ——————————

An answer may lie in the mystical {פ} that ends the first *pasuk* and the {ס} that ends the second. Look at these *pesukim*:

וַיְדַבֵּר מֹשֶׁה לִפְנֵי ה' לֵאמֹר הֵן בְּנֵי יִשְׂרָאֵל לֹא שָׁמְעוּ אֵלַי וְאֵיךְ יִשְׁמָעֵנִי פַרְעֹה וַאֲנִי עֲרַל שְׂפָתָיִם. {פ} וַיְדַבֵּר ה' אֶל מֹשֶׁה וְאֶל אַהֲרֹן וַיְצַוֵּם אֶל בְּנֵי יִשְׂרָאֵל וְאֶל פַּרְעֹה מֶלֶךְ מִצְרָיִם לְהוֹצִיא אֶת בְּנֵי יִשְׂרָאֵל מֵאֶרֶץ מִצְרָיִם. {ס}

And Moshe spoke before Hashem, saying: "Behold, the
Children of Israel have not listened to me, how then shall
Pharaoh hear me, when I am of uncircumcised lips?" {P} And
Hashem spoke to Moshe and to Aharon, and gave them a
charge to the Children of Israel, and to Pharaoh king of Egypt,
to bring the Children of Israel out of the land of Egypt. {S}

The פ stands for the word פתוחה—open, meaning that the *"parashah"* ends with a space after it (hence the word "open"), and that a new *parashah* begins on a new line below it. The ס stands for סתומה—closed, and indicates a smaller space with a new *parashah* beginning on the same line.

It could very well be that Hashem was teaching Moshe that his impediment was actually his strength. Moshe starts out wanting and yearning for the ability to be a master of words, able to deliver lengthy discourses. He wanted to be a פתוחה, someone who can speak openly and freely. But Hashem reminds Moshe that it is not about Moshe but rather about Hashem! Hashem wants him to "command" and not give lengthy discourses. He wanted Moshe to be a סתומה, or someone stingy with words, wisely choosing what to say. And so, instead of being a פתוחה, or an open-ended speaker, which would leave Moshe vulnerable to misinterpretation, he can be more of a סתומה, more assertive and "to the point" in directing Pharaoh, as well as B'nei Yisrael!

Similarly, when Shammai says, אֱמוֹר מְעַט וַעֲשֵׂה הַרְבֵּה, it may not be a direction: "Speak a little and do a lot." (If so, what would be so bad if you spoke a lot, as long as you accomplished a lot as well!) Rather, it is a description of the benefits of speaking concisely: "Speak a little *so that you can accomplish a lot!*"

─────────── TAKEAWAY MESSAGES ───────────

When Moshe complained to Hashem that B'nei Yisrael and Pharaoh wouldn't listen to him because he had a speech impediment, Hashem aptly answers him obliquely by reminding him that it is actually ideal to be סתום, or "close-worded." וַיְצַוֵּם אֶל בְּנֵי יִשְׂרָאֵל וְאֶל פַּרְעֹה מֶלֶךְ מִצְרָיִם—G-d teaches Moshe the lesson that speaking concisely and resolutely can accomplish a lot. Moshe's speech impediment forced him to speak less but be more concise, which is a lesson for us all! אֱמוֹר מְעַט וַעֲשֵׂה הַרְבֵּה are not two disparate ideas but one: Speak a little and thus accomplish a lot. Moshe's speech impediment was a blessing indeed!

THE LESSON OF HAIL

אִם אֵין חָכְמָה אֵין יִרְאָה.

If there is no wisdom, then there is no fear [of G-d].
(Avos 3:17)

―――――― QUESTIONS ――――――

1. What does wisdom have to do with fearing G-d? How and why is knowledge a prerequisite for fearing G-d?
2. When G-d warned the Egyptians in this week's *parashah* about the upcoming hail, the determining factor of whether the people stayed indoors was their belief:

> הַיָּרֵא אֶת דְּבַר ה' מֵעַבְדֵי פַּרְעֹה הֵנִיס אֶת עֲבָדָיו וְאֶת מִקְנֵהוּ
> אֶל הַבָּתִּים. וַאֲשֶׁר לֹא שָׂם לִבּוֹ אֶל דְּבַר ה' וַיַּעֲזֹב אֶת עֲבָדָיו
> וְאֶת מִקְנֵהוּ בַּשָּׂדֶה.

> *Those who feared G-d sheltered their servants and*
> *cattle into their homes. **But he who did not pay***
> ***attention to the word of G-d** left his servants and*
> *his livestock in the field.*
> *(Shemos 9:20–21)*

The opposite of "those who feared G-d" shouldn't be "he who did not pay attention to the word of G-d," but rather "those who don't fear G-d!" Also, what does the plague of hail have to do with the lesson of fearing G-d anyway?

161

—————————————— ANSWERS ——————————————

In the Passover Haggadah, when discussing the Four Sons, we learn that the opposite of the *rasha*, evil son, is not a *tzaddik* but rather a *chacham*. This teaches us an important lesson: Sometimes doing the right thing is merely a matter of being smart. A *rasha* is someone who is smart but not wise; he is given the tools and knowledge to easily choose the right path, but he negligently places a smokescreen that enables himself to get it wrong. The *rasha* has knowledge, and yet he is not a *chacham*.

Often, we fool ourselves and purposely cloud our judgment in order to enable ourselves to sin. At the basic level, true *yiras Hashem* is not something mysterious, in the clouds, or difficult to reach. It's not something that you can only grasp if you can read *Rashi* and *Tosafos*, or if you teach or learn Gemara every day. It can most often be achieved by not being purposely blind or stupid! By simply being careful, placing your attention on the task at hand, and not letting yourself be clouded with improper machinations or justifications in order to sin, anyone can achieve this goal. Rabbi Yerucham similarly says that "those who did not pay attention" is indeed the opposite of "those who feared the word of G-d" because not paying attention to your heart and creating smokescreens to enable sin creates ultimate disbelief.

And now, perhaps, we can understand our Mishnah in *Avos*. Indeed, the plague of hail teaches us this important lesson: אִם אֵין חָכְמָה, אֵין יִרְאָה—If there is no wisdom, i.e., if you let yourself be blinded to knowledge and create smokescreens to see certain things that are clearly wrong as acceptable behavior, thus enabling yourself to sin, then there is no fear of G-d. The absence of knowledge creates an unfaithful environment. We always say that fire is akin to Torah ("אֵשׁ דָּת לָמוֹ," *Devarim* 33:2), and we know that the hail had fire enveloped by ice. The fire, representing Torah knowledge, is often only realized when you peel off the cool icy covering representing our evil tendencies to cover such clear fire.

—————————— TAKEAWAY MESSAGES ——————————

"Those who did not pay attention" is indeed the opposite of "those who feared the word of G-d" because not paying attention to the knowledge of what is right and creating smokescreens to enable sin creates ultimate disbelief. The hail perfectly symbolizes the challenge of recognizing our tendency to hide or obscure the hidden fire with a ground-glass "smokescreen" ice cover. The opposite of the *rasha* is thus clearly the *chacham*, and this led to our Tanna of *Avos* teaching: אֵין חָכְמָה אֵין יִרְאָה. Hail taught us how best to fear G-d—by paying attention!

IS IT ANTI-ZIONIST TO NOT HAVE
A FIFTH CUP ON PESACH?

גָּלוּת בָּאָה לָעוֹלָם עַל עוֹבְדֵי עֲבוֹדָה זָרָה
וְעַל גִּלּוּי עֲרָיוֹת וְעַל שְׁפִיכוּת דָּמִים
וְעַל הַשְׁמָטַת הָאָרֶץ.

Banishment comes to the world because of idol worship,
promiscuity, murder, and not resting the Land. (Avos 5:9)

QUESTIONS

What is the message of listing the cardinal sins such as idol worship, promiscuity, and murder, specifically with the punishment of exile?

לָכֵן אֱמֹר לִבְנֵי יִשְׂרָאֵל אֲנִי ה' **וְהוֹצֵאתִי** אֶתְכֶם מִתַּחַת סִבְלֹת מִצְרַיִם
וְהִצַּלְתִּי אֶתְכֶם מֵעֲבֹדָתָם **וְגָאַלְתִּי** אֶתְכֶם בִּזְרוֹעַ נְטוּיָה וּבִשְׁפָטִים
גְּדֹלִים. **וְלָקַחְתִּי** אֶתְכֶם לִי לְעָם וְהָיִיתִי לָכֶם לֵאלֹקִים וִידַעְתֶּם כִּי אֲנִי
ה' אֱלֹקֵיכֶם הַמּוֹצִיא אֶתְכֶם, מִתַּחַת סִבְלוֹת מִצְרָיִם. **וְהֵבֵאתִי** אֶתְכֶם
אֶל הָאָרֶץ אֲשֶׁר נָשָׂאתִי אֶת יָדִי לָתֵת אֹתָהּ לְאַבְרָהָם לְיִצְחָק וּלְיַעֲקֹב
וְנָתַתִּי אֹתָהּ לָכֶם מוֹרָשָׁה אֲנִי ה'.

Therefore say to the Children of Israel: I am Hashem, and I
*will **bring you out** from under the burdens of the Egyptians,*
*and I will **deliver you** from their bondage, and I will **redeem***
you with an outstretched arm, and with great judgments; and
I will take you to Me for a people, and I will be to you a G-d;
and you shall know that I am the Lord your G-d, who brought

you out from under the burdens of the Egyptians. And I will
bring you *into the Land, concerning which I lifted up My hand*
to give it to Avraham, to Yitzchak, and to Yaakov; and I will
give it to you for a heritage: I am Hashem. (Shemos 6:2–8)

The *Talmud Yerushalmi* (*Pesachim* 10:1) relates: "[The four cups] correspond to the four [languages] of redemption: וְהוֹצֵאתִי וְהִצַּלְתִּי וְגָאַלְתִּי וְלָקַחְתִּי."

Why do we have four cups if there are really five expressions of G-d's redemption? Why is וְהֵבֵאתִי left out?

ANSWERS

The *Torah Temimah* beautifully explains that "הארץ מסורה בידי זרים—the Land has been handed over to 'strangers,'" and so how can we raise a glass to that! He also adds that it may be called the Cup of Eliyahu because in the future time of Eliyahu and Mashiach, we will have the Land back and we can then have the fifth cup! It is worth noting that the *Torah Temimah* (Rabbi Baruch Epstein) died in 1941 before the State of Israel. How would he explain the lack of the fifth cup today? Also, notice that Rabbi Yochanan's opinion was recorded in the very *Talmud Yerushalmi* and at a time when Jews inhabited Israel obviously, so why then wasn't וְהֵבֵאתִי celebrated with its own cup? (It is worth noting that there was a minority opinion brought down in the *Talmud Bavli* [*Pesachim* 118] of Rabbi Tarfon, who did hold of a fifth cup. Apparently, the *Rambam* holds that a fifth cup is optional, but the fifth cup may be called the Cup of Eliyahu as we know that Eliyahu will eventually answer our halachic questions [תיקו]. We thus call it the Cup of Eliyahu as he will determine if we should or should not have this fifth cup!) But what about the *Yerushalmi*, and why they didn't have a fifth cup, even as they inhabited Israel and would naturally have wanted to celebrate the fulfillment of that promise to come to the Land?

One answer I derive from both the *Ohr Hachaim* and the *Seforno* is that this promise of וְהֵבֵאתִי is (unlike the prior four) completely dependent on the words immediately preceding it: "וִידַעְתֶּם כִּי אֲנִי ה' אֱלֹקֵיכֶם הַמּוֹצִיא אֶתְכֶם מִתַּחַת סִבְלוֹת מִצְרָיִם." In other words, whereas the וְהוֹצֵאתִי וְהִצַּלְתִּי וְגָאַלְתִּי

וְלָקַחְתִּי וְלָקַחְתִּי are essentially gifted by G-d without further conditions, the וְהֵבֵאתִי is contingent on us recognizing and obeying G-d, Who graciously gave Israel to us and can take it back from us if we don't behave obediently. The lack of the fifth cup today, then, is not because we aren't celebrating being in Israel, but rather out of recognition that our challenge in keeping Israel in our possession is never over. We must continuously know that each and every one of us is responsible for our State of Israel. We sit at the table with the fifth cup continuously staring us in the face to remind us that the fifth cup is ours to continuously earn. Because we do not know if we, in fact, pass G-d's obedience test, perhaps that is why we call it the Cup of Eliyahu, as he knows the score! Perhaps the reason that even the Yerushalmites didn't celebrate the fifth cup is because they realized that the cup was continuously up for grabs, presently dependent on our fulfillment of "וִידַעְתֶּם כִּי אֲנִי ה' אֱלֹקֵיכֶם הַמּוֹצִיא אֶתְכֶם מִתַּחַת סִבְלוֹת מִצְרָיִם."

So, what is the message of listing the cardinal sins such as idol worship, promiscuity, and murder specifically with the punishment of exile? We have such a unique connection to the Land of Israel that it is almost like one of us. Just like a person has to forfeit one's life rather than do these sins, the Land cannot tolerate such sins as well. This is a testimony of our interconnectivity to the Land of Israel!

───────────── TAKEAWAY MESSAGES ─────────────

Why don't we have a fifth cup corresponding to וְהֵבֵאתִי like we have a cup for the four other expressions of redemption? One answer, according to Rabbi Tarfon, is that we should! Another answer is that Israel isn't ours, but that was stated by a rabbi who lived before the State of Israel (Rabbi Baruch Epstein)! Another answer may be that despite having Israel in our possession, this blessing is dependent on us continuously performing obediently and fulfilling the imperative directly preceding this blessing in the Torah of "וִידַעְתֶּם כִּי אֲנִי ה' אֱלֹקֵיכֶם הַמּוֹצִיא אֶתְכֶם מִתַּחַת סִבְלוֹת מִצְרָיִם." Since this blessing is so dependent on our actions, we can't drink a glass to it, but must face the Cup of Eliyahu, the fifth cup, all night and realize that our destiny is 100 percent intertwined with our obedience. This is not a warning as it is a comfort knowing that we directly impact our very own State of Israel by how we act!

Not having a fifth cup on Pesach shows one's true Zionism!

Bo

PHARAOH'S HARDENED HEART
AND THE NEW MOON

הַכֹּל צָפוּי וְהָרְשׁוּת נְתוּנָה.

Everything is expected and yet permission is granted.
(Avos 3:15)

— QUESTIONS —

How is this concept evident in our *parashah*?
Shemos 11:10 states:

וַיְחַזֵּק ה' אֶת לֵב פַּרְעֹה וְלֹא שִׁלַּח אֶת בְּנֵי יִשְׂרָאֵל מֵאַרְצוֹ.

*Hashem hardened Pharaoh's heart and he did not let the
Children of Israel go out of his land.*

The very next chapter begins:

הַחֹדֶשׁ הַזֶּה לָכֶם רֹאשׁ חֳדָשִׁים רִאשׁוֹן הוּא לָכֶם לְחָדְשֵׁי הַשָּׁנָה.

*This month shall be unto you the beginning of months; it shall
be the first month of the year to you. (Ibid. 12:2)*

Is there any connection between Pharaoh's stubborn reluctance to let
the Jews go and the first mitzvah given to the Jewish nation, namely
kiddush hachodesh, sanctifying the new moon?

ANSWERS

My father, Dr. Larry Ciment, stated that the common denominator here is in "free will."

Many argue that Pharaoh lacked free will because G-d hardened his heart, and so how could he be held accountable? An interesting approach, at least partially attributed to the *Seforno* (7:3), is that G-d restored his free will by hardening his heart! The *makkos* delivered to the Egyptians were removing his inherent desire to enslave them, and thus He hardened the heart of Pharaoh to once again restore his "free choice."

Similarly, by the sanctifying of the new month, we learn about destiny versus will. The members of the Sanhedrin were experts in astronomy and knew exactly when the new moon would have appeared and where it would have been visible. Nevertheless, the sanctification depended on the testimony of two witnesses who saw the crescent of the new moon (*Rosh Hashanah* 22). G-d left the declaration of our months up to the "free will" of the *beis din* in this way!

In both cases, then, G-d is showing us that He doesn't want us to view Him as a rigid controller; a completely fatalistic approach is, in fact, not Jewish. And this is what Rabbi Akiva means in *Avos* when he says, "הַכֹּל צָפוּי וְהָרְשׁוּת נְתוּנָה—Everything is expected, and yet permission is given!"

TAKEAWAY MESSAGES

Although the all-knowing G-d may know our destiny, free will is given to each one of us to shape and flavor that destiny. Hence, the connection between Pharaoh's stubborn reluctance to let the Jews go and the first mitzvah given to the Jewish nation, namely *kiddush hachodesh* (sanctifying the new moon): They are both examples of G-d giving heed to "human choice." Pharaoh's hardened heart and the new moon are thus examples of free will.

THE CONSTELLATION RA'AH
IS A LESSON IN...

הַכֹּל צָפוּי וְהָרְשׁוּת נְתוּנָה.

Everything is expected and yet permission is granted.
(Avos 3:15)

QUESTIONS

How is this concept evident in our *parashah*?

ANSWERS

וַיֹּאמֶר אֲלֵהֶם יְהִי כֵן ה' עִמָּכֶם כַּאֲשֶׁר אֲשַׁלַּח אֶתְכֶם וְאֶת טַפְּכֶם רְאוּ כִּי רָעָה נֶגֶד פְּנֵיכֶם.

He (Pharaoh) said to them, "Let it be so that Hashem will be with you when I send you and your children. Look! For Ra'ah is against your faces!"

Rashi brings down the midrash that the constellation רָעָה—*Ra'ah* symbolized blood, and it was this star that was out during the Jews' planned three-day hiatus. *Rashi* continues that, in fact, this explains why Moshe later exclaims that the Egyptians will declare that the Jews were annihilated because *"b'Ra'ah hotzi'am*—they were taken out during the constellation of *Ra'ah*," which was in fact a "bloody" and unfortunate time. To satisfy the nature that G-d sets, and the success of the Jewish People, He altered the "bloody" outcome of *Ra'ah* to mean the blood of the circumcision of Yehoshua, which would take place later in history.

170

"הַכֹּל צָפוּי וְהָרְשׁוּת נְתוּנָה"—Everything is expected and yet permission is granted." *Ra'ah* predicted a bloody outcome, but given what the Jews merited (through Moshe's support), the blood required was changed to the *dam milah* of Yehoshua (before the celebration of Pesach, Yehoshua had the Jewish males circumcised at Gilgal specifically before they entered Canaan).

—————— TAKEAWAY MESSAGES ——————

The Jews left under the constellation *Ra'ah*, which necessitated some bloody outcome. "הַכֹּל צָפוּי וְהָרְשׁוּת נְתוּנָה—Everything is expected and yet permission is granted"; *Ra'ah* predicted a bloody outcome, but given that the Jews had merit (through Moshe's support), the blood that was required of them was not their death but rather their life! It was changed to *dam milah* of Yehoshua. The constellation *Ra'ah* is a lesson in...inevitable choice!

IS REWARD RESERVED FOR ONLY
THE COMPLETION OF A MITZVAH?

אַרְבַּע מִדּוֹת בְּהוֹלְכֵי לְבֵית הַמִּדְרָשׁ. הוֹלֵךְ
וְאֵינוֹ עוֹשֶׂה שְׂכַר הֲלִיכָה בְּיָדוֹ. עוֹשֶׂה וְאֵינוֹ
הוֹלֵךְ שְׂכַר מַעֲשֶׂה בְּיָדוֹ. הוֹלֵךְ וְעוֹשֶׂה חָסִיד
לֹא הוֹלֵךְ וְלֹא עוֹשֶׂה רָשָׁע.

There are four types among those who attend the study hall.
One who goes but does nothing—has gained the rewards
of going. *One who does [study] but does not go to the study*
hall—has gained the rewards of doing. One who goes and
does, is a chassid. One who neither goes nor does is wicked.
(*Avos 5:14*)

─────────── QUESTIONS ───────────

According to this ethic, if you go to do a good deed like learning or
visiting the sick, and you either don't learn anything that day or the sick
person you went to visit was not there, you still get reward for going. But
where is the source for such reward? And why should you get reward?

─────────── ANSWERS ───────────

Moshe teaches the whole Pesach service to be observed for all time.
At the end of the fifth *aliyah*, the Torah says:

וַיֵּלְכוּ וַיַּעֲשׂוּ בְּנֵי יִשְׂרָאֵל כַּאֲשֶׁר צִוָּה ה' אֶת מֹשֶׁה וְאַהֲרֹן כֵּן עָשׂוּ.

172

*And the Children of Israel **went and did so**; as Hashem had
commanded Moshe and Aharon, so they did. (Shemos 12:28)*

But if the elders are being instructed on the first of Nissan to do
something on the fourteenth of Nissan, why does it say that B'nei
Yisrael "went and did so"? There could not have been any "did so"
because "did so" didn't occur until the fourteenth! Quoting a midrash,
Rashi beautifully answers the enigma:

וַיֵּלְכוּ וַיַּעֲשׂוּ בְּנֵי יִשְׂרָאֵל: וכי כבר עשו והלא מראש חודש נאמר להם
אלא מכיון שקבלו עליהם מעלה עליהם כאלו עשו. וַיֵּלְכוּ וַיַּעֲשׂוּ: אף
ההליכה מנה הכתוב ליתן שכר להליכה ושכר לעשיה.

*So the Children of Israel **went and did**: Now did they already
do [it]? Wasn't this said to them on Rosh Chodesh? But since
they accepted upon themselves [to do it], Scripture credits
them for it as if they had [already] done [it]...**[They] went
and did**: Scripture counts also the going, to give reward for
the going and reward for the deed. (Mechilta)*

The Tanna in *Avos* likewise says that "הוֹלֵךְ וְאֵינוֹ עוֹשֶׂה שְׂכַר הֲלִיכָה בְּיָדוֹ," there
is an aspect of going that, irrespective of the deed accomplished, is rewardable in and of itself!

But the next step is understanding why. Why should going count as
a mitzvah, and which mitzvah would it count as? The answer can be
derived from the other quintessential example of the power of **going** to
do a mitzvah, irrespective of whether you can perform an actual deed:

הַקְהֵל אֶת הָעָם הָאֲנָשִׁים וְהַנָּשִׁים וְהַטַּף וְגֵרְךָ אֲשֶׁר בִּשְׁעָרֶיךָ
לְמַעַן יִשְׁמְעוּ...

*Assemble the people, the men and the women and the **little
ones**, and the stranger that is within your gates, that they
may hear, and that they may learn, and fear Hashem your
G-d, and observe to do all the words of this law.
(Devarim 31:12)*

Why should little ones go and hear the reading of the Torah by the king? Surely it is no mitzvah for them, as they can't comprehend what they are listening to? *Rashi* says the children come "לתת שכר למביאיהם—so that reward would be given to those who bring them along" (*Chagigah* 3a). But if you read the alternate reading in the Hebrew, brought down by the *Maseches Sofrim*: "לקבל שכר מביאתם"—just the fact that the children were there gave them (the children themselves!) a reward beyond any requirement of comprehension but just for being there! And so the two reasons that going itself (even without performing a deed) is a mitzvah itself is because:

1. There is the training aspect and the preparation itself, which is a mitzvah (this fits with the version that the טַף are brought to give reward to *those bringing them*—מצות חינוך).

2. Going is an actual mitzvah itself! The טַף themselves, although not bar mitzvah, can actually fulfill the mitzvah of *Hakhel* by being in the right place at the right time.

———— TAKEAWAY MESSAGES ————

We learn the profound concept that merely intending or going to do a mitzvah is itself a rewardable act disparate from completing the actual deed from the *pasuk* in our *parashah*: "וַיֵּלְכוּ וַיַּעֲשׂוּ בְּנֵי יִשְׂרָאֵל." Even before saying נַעֲשֶׂה וְנִשְׁמָע, the Jewish People demonstrated this incredible ability to commit to mitzvos, projects, and good deeds when they were commanded on Rosh Chodesh Nissan. They are rewarded for their commitment even before "fulfilling the pledge," which reminds us all of how powerful our commitments are even before they are actually fulfilled! Why are we rewarded for merely committing ourselves? This is learned from *Hakhel*: (1) it is an aspect of training ourselves to be better, or (2) it is an actual mitzvah itself—a mystical element of going to do the right thing. Is reward reserved for only completing a mitzvah? No, the going itself is reward-worthy!

DEALING WITH YOUR EVIL CHILD—
THE LESSON FROM THE *PARASHAH*

אַרְבַּע מִדּוֹת בָּאָדָם: הָאוֹמֵר שֶׁלִּי שֶׁלִּי וְשֶׁלְּךָ
שֶׁלָּךְ זוֹ מִדָּה בֵּינוֹנִית... שֶׁלִּי שֶׁלִּי וְשֶׁלְּךָ שֶׁלִּי
רָשָׁע.

There are four characteristics in a person: One who says,
"What is mine is mine and what is yours is yours," is a
boor...and one who says, "What is mine is mine, and what is
yours is mine" is wicked. (Avos 5:10)

QUESTIONS

1. Why does the Mishnah say: "There are four characteristics in a person"? Shouldn't it rather say, "there are four types of people"? It almost seems like the four characteristics are in each and every person, rather than four different entities!

2. Our *parashah* states the source of telling over the Haggadah:

וְהִגַּדְתָּ לְבִנְךָ בַּיּוֹם הַהוּא לֵאמֹר: בַּעֲבוּר זֶה עָשָׂה ה' לִי
בְּצֵאתִי מִמִּצְרָיִם.

*And you will tell **your son** on that day, saying: "It is*
because of that which Hashem did for me when I left
Egypt." (Shemos 13:8)

175

Why does it say "tell your **son**" rather than "tell your **sons**"? After all, we know the Haggadah is directed to four different categories of children (the wise, simple, one who doesn't know how to question, and wicked).

3. Is it not quite odd that the very source of Haggadah (namely this *pasuk* of "הִגַּדְתָּ לְבִנְךָ") is directed not to the wise son, who we would imagine to be the paradigmatic son, but rather to the *rasha* in the actual Haggadah:

> The rasha asks: "מָה הָעֲבֹדָה הַזֹּאת לָכֶם—*What does this ritual mean to you?*" (Shemos 12:26). By using the expression "to you," he excludes himself from his people and denies G-d. Hit him in the teeth and say to him: "בַּעֲבוּר זֶה עָשָׂה ה' לִי בְּצֵאתִי מִמִּצְרָיִם—*It is because of what Hashem did for me when I left Egypt*" (ibid., 13:8). "For me" and not for him—for had he been in Egypt, he would not have been freed.

4. Finally, it doesn't seem to be an appropriate Jewish response to hit your son in the face, even if he's a *rasha*!

─────────────── ANSWERS ───────────────

The Gemara (*Sanhedrin* 37a) says that each and every one of us has to view himself as if the "world was created for me." The *rasha* is, in fact, the target of the Haggadah because he's the most at-risk, yet salvageable son. His problem is evident by the exclusion he professes. He may not be denying G-d by excluding himself from the fold, but rather denying that he is special! כפר בעיקר may perhaps not mean "denying G-d," but rather "denying that he's the *ikar*—that he's special! See, every child (even your most difficult child) must feel that he is the עיקר, special in his own way. This is why the verse states לְבִנְךָ in singular tense; *each son has to be afforded his due attention.*

This is also why the Mishnah in *Avos* is set in the singular tense — בָּאָדָם—to show that each individual has the tools to become righteous (as opposed to separate individuals with inherent evil, etc.).

And how can we make him feel special? Only by recognizing that we are each part of a bigger unit and thus have "backup" and purpose in life. Knowing that we are part of a team is the ultimate solace and guarantee that we won't become isolated and isolate others. "בַּעֲבוּר זֶה עָשָׂה ה' לִי"—we tell the *rasha* that it is "because of זֶה—this," referring to the *gematria* of זֶה (12), which represents the twelve tribes. G-d makes me feel special because of זֶה—because we can safely say we are part of a squad. Widely considered the best basketball player of all time, Michael Jordan has often remarked that he did not shine because he was compared to his subpar teammates, but rather was enabled for greatness because he was given the comfort of his team's acceptance!

Lastly, Alisa Barth says that we don't hit the רשע, but rather try to bring him into the fold. We הקהה את שניו—we don't hit him in the teeth, as popularly understood, but rather remove the *shin* from his name and make him a *re'ah*, a friend (רשע minus the *shin*). By bringing the רשע into the fold and by showing him that he can be part of זֶה (the team of the twelve tribes), he can ultimately shed the evil nature as he feels that he is special, an עיקר.

TAKEAWAY MESSAGES

Judaism espouses directing great attention to each individual. הִגַּדְתָּ לְבִנְךָ—we need to give each son his due, singular attention. אַרְבַּע מִדּוֹת בָּאָדָם reminds us that each son can turn out a variety of ways depending on that attention (rather than simply being born into their category!). The *rasha* feels that he is not special (כפר בעיקר), but when we remind him that he is really part of the זֶה (the Jewish communal fold), we can hit the *shin* off of his name רשע and make him a רֵעַ—friend, who sees that *bishvili nivra ha'olam*! How to deal with your evil child? Don't hit him in the teeth, but rather remove the "tooth" out of his name!

בֶּן עַזַּאי אוֹמֵר: הֱוֵי רָץ לְמִצְוָה קַלָּה כְּבַחֲמוּרָה וּבוֹרֵחַ מִן הָעֲבֵרָה. שֶׁמִּצְוָה גּוֹרֶרֶת מִצְוָה וַעֲבֵרָה גּוֹרֶרֶת עֲבֵרָה. שֶׁשְּׂכַר מִצְוָה מִצְוָה וּשְׂכַר עֲבֵרָה עֲבֵרָה.

Ben Azzai says: Run to do a small mitzvah like a hard one and run from a sin. One mitzvah leads to another and one sin leads to another sin. The reward for one mitzvah is a mitzvah and the reward for a sin is a sin. (Avos 4:2)

——— QUESTIONS ———

What is meant by "the reward for a sin is a sin"?

וַה' נָתַן אֶת חֵן הָעָם בְּעֵינֵי מִצְרַיִם וַיַּשְׁאִלוּם וַיְנַצְּלוּ אֶת מִצְרָיִם.

And G-d gave the grace of the nation in the eyes of the Egyptians and they borrowed and plundered the Egyptians. (Shemos 12:36)

Doesn't it seem strange that the Jews would find the Egyptian nation gracious to them when, after all, we just terrorized them with ten harsh plagues? Also, to fulfill G-d's promise of exiting "with great wealth," why did B'nei Yisrael borrow the items rather than outright taking them, since we deserved the spoils anyway?

—————— ANSWERS ——————

One answer is simply that this was yet another miracle. Of course, the Jews shouldn't have found favor in their eyes, and yet G-d miraculously made that happen.

Yet another answer may be derived from analyzing a midrash on the *parashah* that highlights that the Jews could have plundered the Egyptians during the three days of intense darkness but didn't (the midrash sought to explain that the Egyptians "lent" them their gold and silver accoutrements, since they were essentially impressed with their honesty). The Jewish "honest" approach of plundering Egypt was respectable and the Egyptians acknowledged it by graciously acquiescing to their planned plunder. Important for the development of our Jewish character, we couldn't look like thieves stealing these items in the middle of the night, but rather more gracefully and acceptingly "borrowing" items albeit with a plan of never returning them! Some may call this "semantics" and others may describe this as an example of the Torah talking in *lashon sagi nahor* (speaking in opposites as a type of euphemism, i.e., they really stole but doesn't want to talk in "negative language"), but it can equally just be B'nei Yisrael merely trying to fulfill G-d's pledge of "You will exit in great wealth" in the cleanest way possible without "getting their hands too dirty!"

We must not view ourselves as thieves even when plundering an oppressive nation that deserved to be plundered!

Rabbi Bixon asks why it was that by the plague of hail we see an apologetic Pharaoh, for the first time admitting that "G-d is righteous, and my nation and I are evil"? He beautifully answers that B'nei Yisrael function as an *ohr l'goyim*, a light unto the nations, which is supposed to carry the moral compass directed by G-d. Practically, this was accomplished by warning our Egyptian enemies about the hail so that those who obeyed the warning could have protected their animals. So much so, he points out, that the *Mechilta* says that the very horses that eventually pursued the fleeing Jews by the sea were only alive because of this Jewish warning! Almost to a fault, the Jewish People continuously make every effort to be a moral compass despite what fake news media may report, i.e., the Israeli army graciously and morally warns even the darkest terrorists about their planned attacks so that lives and infrastructure can be spared.

The lesson of hail is the lesson of the Egyptian spoils "borrowed" and not stolen during the plague of darkness. We go out of our way not to connive and steal surreptitiously as we bear the mantle of carrying the moral compass, despite being unfairly castigated by the media, etc.

Regarding the ethic brought above, the Bartenura on *Avos* explains, "The reward for a sin is a sin." The "benefit" or "high" that one feels from doing a sinful act is considered a sin in itself. The reason the Jews went out of their way not to do a sinful act (even though they were entitled to the spoils) is because the act itself would have brought an illicit "benefit" or "high," which is sinful in some way. The point is that there are clear-cut sins, but there are also some not-so-clear sins accompanied with sinful acts. We should avoid both!

―――――――――― TAKEAWAY MESSAGES ――――――――――

How did the Jews find grace within the Egyptians' eyes? Why did they borrow and not steal or plunder the spoils outright? The answer is the same reason why only by the hail did Pharaoh acknowledge his moral inferiority. B'nei Yisrael exhibited great morality and compassion when warning the Egyptians to save their lives and livestock by hail, even though this ultimately even put them at a disadvantage! The Jews could have easily "stolen" the gold and silver from the Egyptians during the darkness but opted for the more morally acceptable "borrowing" during the day. Despite being the object of continuous criticisms and despite the reality that they are placed in compromising situations because of their graciousness, we must recognize that our IDF is just emulating its forefathers in Egypt!

Egyptian plunder, hail, and the IDF—examples of unbelievable Jewish morality to be proud of!

Beshalach

IS G-D OUR FATHER OR OUR MOTHER— AND DOES IT MATTER?

רַבִּי אוֹמֵר: הִסְתַּכֵּל בִּשְׁלֹשָׁה דְבָרִים וְאִי אַתָּה בָא לִידֵי עֲבֵרָה דַע מַה לְמַעְלָה מִמְּךָ עַיִן רוֹאָה אֹזֶן שׁוֹמַעַת וְכָל מַעֲשֶׂיךָ בַּסֵּפֶר נִכְתָּבִין.

*Rebbi said: Investigate three things and you will not come to sin: See **what** is above you: (1) a seeing eye; (2) a hearing ear; and (3) all of your deeds will be written in a book. (Avos 2:1)*

QUESTIONS

What is meant by saying, "דַע מַה לְמַעְלָה מִמְּךָ"? "What is above you" is a strange way to reference G-d? Also, why are עַיִן רוֹאָה and אֹזֶן שׁוֹמַעַת written in feminine? Are we supposed to think of G-d as our father or mother? As a He or a She?

To answer this question, we will ask another question on our *parashah*: As the Jews incredulously complain after they are saved from Egypt, an exasperated Moshe and Aharon say, "וְנַחְנוּ מָה כִּי תַלּוֹנוּ (קרי תַלִּינוּ) עָלֵינוּ"—And what are we that they complain to us?" What were Moshe and Aharon really saying by using the word מָה? Also, is there any significance to the difference between the *kri* and the *ksiv* here (the *kri* is how it sounds without reading the words and just listening to the words being read)?

181

--------- ANSWERS ---------

In the Song of the Sea that we say every day in *Pesukei D'Zimrah*, which comes from this *parashah*, there's a verse that states: "אִישׁ ה' מִלְחָמָה—G-d is a Man of War," i.e., battling our battles for us, so to speak, and so His "masculinity" is undeniable. But there is also a not-so-subtle backdrop of "femininity" as well when you analyze the whole "birth process" of B'nei Yisrael, as G-d *delivers* us out of Egypt. I have to confess that despite my desperate searching, Tannaic and midrashic literature is noticeably absent regarding a seemingly obvious connection between the splitting of the sea and the breaking of the water prior to a woman's delivery. (There is one midrash about the Jews eating fruit directly from the Yam Suf, which draws up syllogism to the protective amniotic fluid that serves as a cushion for the growing fetus, but also serves to facilitate the exchange of nutrients, water, and biochemical products between mother and fetus.) The *Arizal* apparently says that the crossing of the Yam Suf corresponds to the baby coming through the birth canal. Be it as it may, the "delivery" of B'nei Yisrael by the Yam Suf conjures up G-d as our Mother.

The point is that when B'nei Yisrael found themselves literally בין המצרים, in their utmost time of need, they needed G-d to support them like a man (as an אִישׁ מִלְחָמָה), but also as a loving, empathetic mother. The Mishnah in *Avos* may be alluding to this by reading homiletically: Know that מָה is above you—know that your "Ma," or mother, is above you. The words עַיִן רוֹאָה and אֹזֶן שׁוֹמַעַת are written in feminine because they are supporting this idea: not that "מָה—what is above you," but rather that your "מָה—Ma[ma] is above you." The Jews needed to be reassured that their pain was understood (עַיִן רוֹאָה) and that their cries were being heard (אֹזֶן שׁוֹמַעַת), just as much as they needed the manly power to actually take them out of the furnace called Egypt!

This idea beautifully explains the apparently exasperated Moshe and Aharon saying, "וְנַחְנוּ מָה, כִּי תַלִּינוּ (קְרִי תַלִּינוּ) עָלֵינוּ." If you simply read the words of the *pasuk*, it makes sense to interpret the verse as מָה meaning "**What** are we," hinting at their exasperation of the people's incessant complaining (תַלִּונוּ means "complaining"). But remember that the *kri* is how the *pasuk* sounds, and if Moshe and Aharon say, "We are Ma," it sounds like they are saying, "We are the mothers (of B'nei Yisrael)." And then notice that the second part of that *pasuk* also changes as it is supposed to be verbalized: "כִּי תַלֹּונוּ (קְרִי תַלִּינוּ) עָלֵינוּ"—that is why they **rely** (קְרִי תַלִּינוּ) on us." In the *kri* form, Moshe and Aharon do not sound exasperated but rather are explaining why the Jews so heavily rely on them; because they are viewed as empathetic mother figures!

A *mussar* from this is that when any of us have difficult times, we all need to have manly support to do some heavy lifting (the אִישׁ מִלְחָמָה), but also need some feminine empathy (the mother nurturing us through the *k'rias Yam Suf*). Seeing and hearing our pain is often just as important as taking us out of Egypt with a mighty forearm!

—————— TAKEAWAY MESSAGES ——————

G-d is defined as a "Man of War" battling our battles, but is also our mother, guiding us through the amniotic Yam Suf and *delivering* us out of Egypt. This reminds us that in times of need, as a nation and as individuals, we need not only manly, strong-arm support, but the equally important (if not more important) feminine empathy. "Know that מֶה is above" is as in "Ma[ma]" who has an עַיִן רֹואָה and אֹזֶן שֹׁומַעַת (written in feminine). Moshe and Aharon understood the lesson of empathy—that one must be a מֶה, mother-like, in order to be תַלִּינוּ, relied on!

For us, G-d is both a father who fights our battles and a mother who empathizes. To emulate G-d is to realize what we need when we are facing our personal בֵין המצרים—that "Ma" is above you!

WHO IS THE FIRST DOCTOR MENTIONED IN THE TORAH?

רַבִּי אֱלִיעֶזֶר בֶּן יַעֲקֹב אוֹמֵר: הָעוֹשֶׂה מִצְוָה
אַחַת קוֹנֶה לוֹ פְּרַקְלִיט אֶחָד וְהָעוֹבֵר עֲבֵרָה,
אַחַת קוֹנֶה לוֹ קַטֵּגוֹר אֶחָד. תְּשׁוּבָה וּמַעֲשִׂים
טוֹבִים כִּתְרִיס בִּפְנֵי הַפֻּרְעָנוּת.

Rabbi Eliezer ben Yaakov says: He who does one mitzvah
acquires an advocate, and if one transgresses, he acquires an
adversary. Repentance and good deeds act as shields from the
punishment.(Avos 4:11)

QUESTIONS

1. Presumably, *teshuvah* is referring to the person who does bad things and then truly repents, and *maasim tovim* are referring to the person who does good deeds from the start. Then why does *teshuvah* precede *maasim tovim*?

2.

וַיֹּאמֶר אִם שָׁמוֹעַ תִּשְׁמַע לְקוֹל ה' אֱלֹקֶיךָ וְהַיָּשָׁר בְּעֵינָיו
תַּעֲשֶׂה וְהַאֲזַנְתָּ לְמִצְוֹתָיו וְשָׁמַרְתָּ כָּל חֻקָּיו כָּל הַמַּחֲלָה אֲשֶׁר
שַׂמְתִּי בְמִצְרַיִם לֹא אָשִׂים עָלֶיךָ כִּי אֲנִי ה' רֹפְאֶךָ.

And He said, "If you hearken to the voice of Hashem,
your G-d, and you do what is proper in His eyes, and
you listen closely to His commandments and observe

184

> all His statutes, all the sicknesses that I have visited
> upon Egypt I will not visit upon you, for **I, Hashem,**
> **heal you.**"

Who needs G-d to heal us if we are doing good deeds? Isn't healing only necessary if we develop the sicknesses that He Himself told us that we are protected from if we simply adhere to the mitzvos? The *pasuk* then sounds odd: If you listen to G-d, He won't give you sickness, and He is the doctor who heals you!

3. Why do we wish someone "a *refuah sheleimah*" even when he has a terminal disease—and even to someone on his deathbed? Clearly, when he's about to die, he will not have a *refuah sheleimah*, so why do the deathbed prayers contain such a weird statement?

─────── ANSWERS ───────

There are essentially two approaches to understanding the above ethic, and according to each approach, you can best understand the *pasuk* in our *parashah*.

Approach #1: When the Tanna says, "תְּשׁוּבָה וּמַעֲשִׂים טוֹבִים כְּתְרִים בִּפְנֵי הַפֻּרְעָנוּת," he is specifically referring to someone who does bad and then repents. The *Rambam* explains that since "בְּמָקוֹם שֶׁבַּעֲלֵי תְּשׁוּבָה עוֹמְדִין אֵין צַדִּיקִים גְּמוּרִים יְכוֹלִין לַעֲמֹד—The place where *baalei teshuvah* stand, even *tzaddikim gemurim* can't stand," i.e., doing *teshuvah* is actually an even stronger greatness than doing good from the start (in some way), so this is why *teshuvah* precedes *maasim tovim*!

Applying this to our *pasuk*: When the Torah says, "If you listen, I won't give you diseases," the implication is that if you don't listen, you *will* get diseases. To this second possibility, G-d speaks out that He is the ultimate Healer; even if you *don't listen* initially, the power of *teshuvah* is there to protect you from the diseases that I place upon you! Even the seemingly insurmountable Egyptian diseases are cured by the ultimate Healer if you do *teshuvah*.

Approach #2: The *Rashbam* actually says that the Mishnah has a different text; it should really read, "תּוֹרָה וּמַעֲשִׂים טוֹבִים כְּתְרִים בִּפְנֵי הַפֻּרְעָנוּת"

According to that text, the Mishnah has nothing to do with *teshuvah* at all. Observing the Torah and doing good deeds prophylactically shields you from punishments/ailments!

Likewise, our *pasuk* here may not have anything to do with *teshuvah*, but is rather denoting the optimal prophylaxis. When G-d says that "He is the Healer," he may be the Healer in the sense of prophylactically protecting us from the ailments by making sure we follow the commandments. In this sense, the word *rofeh* doesn't necessarily mean "healer," but rather one who softens, ameliorates, and protects from the burdens of sickness.

This is why we say *"refuah sheleimah"* to even someone on his deathbed and why we say that even a *goses*—one in the throes of death—should have a *refuah sheleimah*, because the word *rofeh* doesn't only mean "to heal" but also to "soften/protect/ameliorate" (*rofeh* has *rafah*, "soften," as its root)!

─────────────── TAKEAWAY MESSAGES ───────────────

If a *rofeh* is defined only as someone who heals, then the *pasuk* אֲנִי ה' רֹפְאֶךָ is referring to a situation where one initially doesn't adhere to the mitzvos and then repents. G-d will heal him or her post-repentance—תְּשׁוּבָה וּמַעֲשִׂים טוֹבִים כְּתָרִיס בִּפְנֵי הַפֻּרְעָנוּת.

If a *rofeh* is also defined as someone who not only heals but also ameliorates, softens, protects and mollifies, then אֲנִי ה' רֹפְאֶךָ refers to G-d putting in place a proper *derech* to avoid illness, a regimen of prophylaxis: תּוֹרָה וּמַעֲשִׂים טוֹבִים כְּתָרִיס בִּפְנֵי הַפֻּרְעָנוּת.

Saying *refuah sheleimah* to someone on his deathbed is not a *berachah l'vatalah*. As the doctor, it is not only about healing but also about ameliorating, protecting, or softening! The first doctor in the Torah? Hashem.

THE MANNA—PUNISHMENT OR REWARD?

עֲשָׂרָה נִסְיוֹנוֹת נִסּוּ אֲבוֹתֵינוּ אֶת הַמָּקוֹם בָּרוּךְ הוּא בַּמִּדְבָּר ...

Ten trials our forefathers tested G-d in the desert...(Avos 5:4)

One of the trials in the desert in which we "provoked" G-d was when the Jewish People complained to Moshe:

מִי יִתֵּן מוּתֵנוּ בְיַד ה' בְּאֶרֶץ מִצְרַיִם בְּשִׁבְתֵּנוּ עַל סִיר הַבָּשָׂר בְּאָכְלֵנוּ לֶחֶם לָשֹׂבַע.

Who could have brought us death by the hand of Hashem in the land of Egypt, when we sat by pots of meat, when we ate bread to our satiety. (Shemos 16:3)

──────── QUESTIONS ────────

1. Were the Jews seriously not satiated with meat and bread as slaves in Egypt?
2. Why does G-d bring the manna as a response to this apparent hallucination?

──────── ANSWERS ────────

The answer is a profound analysis into the art of propaganda, which begins with the very *pasuk* that preceded their complaint: "וַיִּלֹּנוּ (קרי וַיִּלּוֹנוּ) כָּל עֲדַת בְּנֵי יִשְׂרָאֵל—And they complained." וַיִּלֹּנוּ is how it is written, but וַיִּלּוֹנוּ is how it is said (this is one of the relatively few *kri-ksiv* examples in the

187

Chumash). Things that are written are clear as day, but you can distort them when you read them aloud. So too, B'nei Yisrael distorted their reality, as hinted by the *kri-ksiv*! In reality, they relied (the meaning of וַיִּלֹנוּ) on Moshe and Aharon, but they distorted this reality and complained (קְרִי וַיִּלּוֹנוּ) instead.

And this beautifully fits with why the manna remedies this seeming maniacal fantasy. You can only take a manna portion to provide for that very day alone: "וְלָקְטוּ דְּבַר יוֹם בְּיוֹמוֹ." Perhaps this is because saving up for the future requires one to "imagine" what he needs, and G-d saw that the Jewish People's imagination was clearly too primitive at that point! Before employing your imagination, you must first have a genuine, honest assessment of your present, which is a deep lesson of the manna. Collecting the manna was thus practicing daily self-evaluation.

Homiletically, this fits best with the end of this paragraph, as Moshe and Aharon state:

"וְנַחְנוּ מָה כִּי תלונו (תַלִּינוּ) עָלֵינוּ"—And what are we that they complain to us." This could be understood as, "We are **what** [we are] (i.e., we understand our reality) and so their complaints are not sensible."

─────────── TAKEAWAY MESSAGES ───────────

Complaining is often the sign of disconnection from our very own reality and imagination. Instead of focusing on the "מִי יִתֵּן," we must first understand, "וְנַחְנוּ מָה," our own potential and present reality. The manna was the heavenly gift that shows us the power of self-reflection, which can stave off becoming a complainer! The manna was a reward in teaching us the value of self-awareness and reflection.

GOVERNMENT SHUTDOWN, THE WALL, AND PARASHAS BESHALACH?

וְ־הַתּוֹרָה נִקְנֵית בְּאַרְבָּעִים וּשְׁמוֹנָה דְ־בָרִים.
וְאֵלּוּ הֵן ...בְּלֶ־ב טוֹב...

*The Torah is aquired in forty-eight ways...a good
heart...(Avos 6:6)*

QUESTIONS

The twenty-fourth *middah* of the forty-eight ways to acquire Torah is "having a good heart." Is there any significance to its placement in the middle?

וַיָּבֹאוּ בְנֵי יִשְׂרָאֵל בְּתוֹךְ הַיָּם בַּיַּבָּשָׁה וְהַמַּיִם לָהֶם חוֹמָה
מִימִינָם וּמִשְּׂמֹאלָם...וּבְנֵי יִשְׂרָאֵל הָלְכוּ בַיַּבָּשָׁה בְּתוֹךְ הַיָּם וְהַמַּיִם לָהֶם
חֹמָה מִימִינָם וּמִשְּׂמֹאלָם.

*The Children of Israel went on **in the midst of the sea, on
dry land**; the water was a wall for them, on their right and
on their left (Shemos 14:22)...The Children of Israel went
on dry land in the midst of the sea; the water was a wall for
them, on their right and on their left (ibid., v. 29).*

The first *pasuk* has B'nei Yisrael jumping into the water first, and the water was a חוֹמָה (including an extra *vav*), but the second *pasuk* has them going into the dry land,(and חֹמָה is written without a *vav*!). Why is this?

189

Furthermore, what is the significance of saying that the water was a wall "to the right and to the left"?

ANSWERS

An answer famously attributed to the Vilna Gaon is that many of the Jews were idolaters much like the Egyptians, and the angels questioned why the Jews should in fact be saved. Nachshon jumped into the waters with full *emunah*, and it only then became dry land; they merited a "full wall" of חוֹמָה. Others with less *emunah*, who only went in once it was dry land, only had a partial and angry wall (חֹמָה without the *vav* also spells חמה—anger!).

Perhaps we can add to this famous Vilna Gaon (which wasn't famous till you heard about it!): What is the significance of being a wall to the right and to the left? The *Rambam* (*Dei'os* 4:1) says:

דרך הישרה היא מדה בינונית שבכל דעה ודעה מכל הדעות שיש לו
לאדם. והיא הדעה שהיא רחוקה משתי הקצוות ריחוק שוה ואינה
קרובה לא לזו ולא לזו.

He essentially espouses the concept of avoiding extremisms of both sides and on focusing on a "middle of the road" path. There are people who are extreme in their ideas because they have sacrificed so much for whatever cause they are "extreme" about: The Torah (euphemism of וְהַמַּיִם) still cautions those extremists to put up a wall and avoid veering all the way to the right or to the left. The full חוֹמָה is written out perhaps because such an invested person will have to make more of an effort to avoid such expected extremist behavior. The less-invested people, who simply walks over dry land and never sacrifices much for whatever cause they are promoting, draw more ire from the Torah (/וְהַמַּיִם לָהֶם חֹמָה חמה) and they are more strongly advised not to be fake extremists! In short, וְהַמַּיִם לָהֶם חוֹמָה, מִימִינָם וּמִשְּׂמֹאלָם may be a lesson from G-d that we should avoid being fully extreme, whether it be to the right or to the left. This is consistent with the *Rambam*'s exhortation!

The twenty-fourth *middah* of the forty-eight ways to acquire Torah is "having a good heart." In order to have a good heart, one must strive to be "in the middle," not too much to the right and not too much to the left. וְהַמַּיִם לָהֶם חוֹמָה—For the water (i.e., Torah), one ideally has to place a wall to the right and to the left and stay in the straight path.

―――――――――― TAKEAWAY MESSAGES ――――――――――

Why does it say the Jews jumped in the sea and in the land in the first *pasuk*, but then says they went on the land and into the sea in the next *pasuk*? Why is חוֹמָה/wall written first and חֹמָה (without the *vav*) written second? The Vilna Gaon points out that Nachshon really saved the Jews by jumping in with full *emunah* and thus merited a full wall, while the people with less *emunah* had less of a wall (as if the wall was mad at them, spelled like חמה—anger!). In either scenario, it is worth noting that there was a wall from the right and from the left, perhaps reminding us of the *Rambam*'s exhortation to put up a wall and avoid extensive extremism to one pole or the other, whether right or left. Instead, stay in the straight path!

The wall of water reminds us Jews to strive for the straight path—to be neither all the way to the right nor the left.

Yisro

WHAT IS THE LESSON OF THE MIZBEI'ACH STONES?

אֵיזֶ—הוּ מְכֻבָּד הַמְכַבֵּד אֶת הַבְּרִיּוֹת שֶׁנֶ—אֱמַר
(שמואל א ב) כִּי מְכַבְּדַי אֲכַבֵּד וּבֹזַי יֵקָלּוּ.

Who is honorable? Those who honor beings, as it says,
"Because those who honor Me, I honor; and those that
disrespect Me, I will disrespect." (Avos 4:1)

הוּא הָיָה אוֹמֵר: אַל תְּהִי בָז לְכָל אָדָם, וְאַל
תְּהִי מַפְלִיג לְכָל דָּבָר, שֶׁאֵין לְךָ אָדָם שֶׁאֵין לוֹ
שָׁעָה וְאֵין לְךָ דָ—בָר שֶׁאֵין לוֹ מָקוֹם.

Do not scorn any man, and do not discount anything. For
there is no man who has not his hour, and no thing that has
not its place. (Avos 2:3)

--- QUESTIONS ---

1. Why is the Scriptural source for honoring other human beings
    about G-d (כִּי מְכַבְּדַי אֲכַבֵּד)? After all, the apparent respect here
    that we are talking about is the one directed toward G-d's

192

beings and not G-d Himself. There seems to be an obvious yet purposeful disconnect! I would have expected a *pasuk* like this: "Those who honor men will be honored," and not a *pasuk* about honoring G-d!

2. Is "אַל תְּהִי בָז לְכָל אָדָם, וְאַל תְּהִי מַפְלִיג לְכָל דָּבָר" one unified idea, sequential ideas, or consequential ideas? Also, I would have expected a more positive spin to this Mishnah, such as: "Be respectful to every person, and even inanimate objects!" So why deliver the same lesson in the negative (i.e., "Don't be disrespectful")?

─── ANSWERS ───

"וְלֹא תַעֲלֶה בְמַעֲלֹת עַל מִזְבְּחִי" (*Shemos* 20:22). Why is the Kohen instructed to walk up a ramp by the *Mizbei'ach* as opposed to steps? One beautiful, elaborate approach espoused by Zivi Mendelsohn is that by spirituality, it's "all or nothing"—you are either going up or going down. Steps are *ambiguous* in the sense that you can stay level and then go up or down; however, with a ramp, you're either going up or going down. But the *Midrash Rabbah* has another approach: the Kohanim do not walk up steps so as not to expose the covered parts of their body to the stones below. A *kal v'chomer* ensues: Just like the Kohanim should not in any way disrespect the stones of the Altar, all the more so, we should not disrespect one another.

Amazingly, this is in fact a Biblical source of not disrespecting others.

This then explains why the Mishnah in *Avos* uses the *pasuk* about G-d (כִּי מְכַבְּדַי אֲכַבֵּד וּבֹזַי יֵקָלּוּ), because, in fact, the *Mizbei'ach* that was used to honor/respect G-d is where we learn this very ethic of not disrespecting others. It is the *kal v'chomer* by G-d's Altar that teaches us to be respectful of others. Furthermore, this also nicely explains why the Mishnah has a negative connotation, even though it's teaching us a sublimely positive idea: simply because the ethic of respect is couched within the negative commandment of "וְלֹא תַעֲלֶה בְמַעֲלֹת עַל מִזְבְּחִי"—Not ascending on steps." This negative commandment teaches us about respect, and it is only fitting then to frame the lesson of respect in *negative* language ("do not desecrate"), which is an allusion to its origin! Finally, "אַל תְּהִי בָז לְכָל אָדָם" is not a separate issue from "וְאַל תְּהִי מַפְלִיג לְכָל דָּבָר," but rather is the reason why you shouldn't disrespect: Don't be despicable to mankind *because* we learned [by the *Mizbei'ach*] that we shouldn't desecrate even its stones. If you respect objects, you will respect people!

──────────── TAKEAWAY MESSAGES ────────────

The fact that the Kohanim could not ascend the *Mizbei'ach* by steps but rather a ramp was to teach:

1. In spiritual matters, it's either an up or down phenomenon (Zivi Mendelsohn, *shlita!*).
2. They should not desecrate the stones by exposing covered parts of their body; we learn that just like the Kohanim shouldn't disrespect even the stones, we must respect all beings.

The negative language (לֹא תַעֲלֶה בְמַעֲלֹת) may explain why the Mishnah is worded negatively (אַל תְּהִי בָז לְכָל אָדָם), perhaps reminding us again that our moral ethical code is derived from the Torah. Since the lesson of respect derives from the *Mizbei'ach* of G-d, it makes perfect sense to quote the *pasuk* "כִּי מְכַבְּדַי אֲכַבֵּד" as proof.

What is the lesson of the *Mizbei'ach* stones? Don't disrespect anyone!

HOW TO APPRECIATE SHABBOS

עֲשָׂרָה דְבָרִים נִבְרְאוּ בְּעֶרֶב שַׁבָּת בֵּין
הַשְּׁמָשׁוֹת וְאֵלוּ הֵן: פִּי הָאָרֶץ וּפִי הַבְּאֵר וּפִי
הָאָתוֹן וְהַקֶּשֶׁת וְהַמָּן וְהַמַּטֶּה וְהַשָּׁמִיר וְהַכְּתָב
וְהַמִּכְתָּב וְהַלּוּחוֹת. וְיֵשׁ אוֹמְרִים, אַף הַמַּזִּיקִין
וּקְבוּרָתוֹ שֶׁל מֹשֶׁה וְאֵילוֹ שֶׁל אַבְרָהָם אָבִינוּ.
וְיֵשׁ אוֹמְרִים אַף צְבָת בִּצְבָת עֲשׂוּיָה.

Ten things were created at twilight of Shabbos eve. These are: the mouth of the earth [that swallowed Korach]; the mouth of [Miriam's] well; the mouth of [Bilaam's] donkey; the rainbow; the manna; [Moshe's] staff; the shamir; the writing, the inscription, and the tablets [of the Ten Commandments]. Some say also the burial place of Moshe and the ram of Avraham Avinu. And some say also the spirits of destruction as well as the original tongs, for tongs are made with tongs.
(Avos 5:6)

QUESTIONS

The Mishnah in *Pirkei Avos* says that ten miracles were created on Erev Shabbos at night as Shabbos was about to start. Why did G-d wait until the very last second of the week to create these special

195

miracles to be used in the future? He could have created them any time during the week!

─────────── ANSWERS ───────────

זָכוֹר אֶת יוֹם הַשַּׁבָּת לְקַדְּשׁוֹ שֵׁשֶׁת יָמִים תַּעֲבֹד וְעָשִׂיתָ כָּל מְלַאכְתֶּךָ.

*Remember the Sabbath day, to keep it holy; six days you shall labor and **do all your work**. (Shemos 20:8)*

A possible trick to appreciate Shabbos is to recognize that Shabbos is made during the week. How so? The answer is in the words: "וְעָשִׂיתָ כָּל מְלַאכְתֶּךָ—You shall do all your work [by the arrival of Shabbos!]." An integral part of keeping Shabbos is trying to complete projects before Shabbos arrives, so that you feel accomplished (based on the *Mechilta* brought by *Rashi* here). The "rush" to complete tasks is the ultimate **motivator**, but the subsequent "mission accomplished" just as Shabbos arrives **adds to our self-esteem** weekly. To review, Shabbos is the ultimate motivator, and if you keep the Shabbos by looking at it not as a disparate entity but as the culmination of a week's hard work, with the Shabbos deadline in mind, then it will add to your self-esteem. And now I can finally understand the following cryptic Mishnah we all say every week right as Shabbos begins after במה מדליקין:

חייב אדם למשמש בגדיו בערב שבת עם חשכה שמא ישכח ויצא.
אמר רב יוסף הלכתא רבתא לשבתא.

A person is required to examine his clothing just before Shabbos for he may forget (שמא ישכח) and go out (ויצא) [inadvertently carry on Shabbos!] Rav Yosef says: This is a fundamental law of Shabbos!

At first glance the Mishnah seems to just be talking about not carrying on Shabbos. But then what is so fundamental about this law? The answer is in the homiletic interpretation: "A person is required to examine himself"—i.e., what did I accomplish this week? Did I think about completing some element of my work by Shabbos? Did I have Shabbos in mind during the week? This must be done as Shabbos arrives, because if you forget this examination (שמא ישכח) then you may lose out (ויצא) on the optimal fulfillment of Shabbos! "Rav Yosef says: That is the great and deep lesson (הלכתא רבתא) of Shabbos"—that it is fulfilled by your attention to it during the very preceding week!

─────────── TAKEAWAY MESSAGES ───────────

If you view Shabbos as a culmination of one week's hard work, with fulfillment contingent on attention to Shabbos *during the week*, then it will be a **motivator** and simultaneously **add to your self-esteem**. One must examine if they specifically worked during the week with Shabbos in mind—חייב אדם למשמש בגדיו בערב שבת—because otherwise, if they forget, their Shabbos may have been lost—שמא ישכח ויצא.

How to appreciate Shabbos? Its fulfillment is contingent on the attention given to it during the week!

PARASHAS YISRO AND SHEL SILVERSTEIN—A CONNECTION?

רַבִּי חֲנִינָא בֶּן חֲכִינַאי אוֹמֵר: הַנֵּעוֹר בַּלַּיְלָה,
וְהַמְהַלֵּךְ בַּדֶּרֶךְ יְחִידִי וְהַמְפַנֶּה לִבּוֹ לְבַטָּלָה
הֲרֵי זֶה מִתְחַיֵּב בְּנַפְשׁוֹ.

*Rabbi Chanina the son of Chachina'i would say: One who
stays awake at night, or **travels alone on the road**, and turns
his heart to idleness, has forfeited his life. (Avos 3:4)*

QUESTIONS

What does it mean that someone traveling alone on the road has forfeited his life? The simple explanation is that it's referring to someone who literally wanders alone—that embarking on dangerous, solitary paths makes one responsible should danger befall him. Another approach may be derived from analyzing one of the Ten Commandments from this week's *parashah*:

ANSWERS

כַּבֵּד אֶת אָבִיךָ וְאֶת אִמֶּךָ לְמַעַן יַאֲרִכוּן יָמֶיךָ עַל הָאֲדָמָה אֲשֶׁר ה'
אֱלֹקֶיךָ נֹתֵן לָךְ.

Honor your father and your mother *so that your days will be
long upon the Land that Hashem your G-d gave you.
(Shemos 20:12)*

198

The Stone Chumash (ArtScroll) reminds us that the term "honor" refers to deeds that raise the status of parents or provide them with comfort, such as "giving them food and drink, dressing them, and escorting them" (*Rashi* in *Vayikra* 19:3). This of course is the classic way to interpret "honor," but there may be another lesson inherent in this interesting language.

There are fourteen prior instances of the word כבד before it is used in this commandment to honor one's parents. The first one is:

וַיְהִי רָעָב בָּאָרֶץ וַיֵּרֶד אַבְרָם מִצְרַיְמָה לָגוּר שָׁם כִּי כָבֵד הָרָעָב בָּאָרֶץ.

*Behold, famine was on the land, and Avram descended to Egypt to dwell there, for the famine was **heavy/burdensome** in the land. (Bereishis 12:10)*

The point is that most of the time, כָּבֵד means "heavy" or "burdensome." If so, how would this change the understanding by "כַּבֵּד אֶת אָבִיךָ וְאֶת אִמֶּךָ"?

As children mature, many will distance themselves from their parents, either because they want to demonstrate their independence or simply because they find love elsewhere. For example,

עַל כֵּן יַעֲזָב אִישׁ אֶת אָבִיו וְאֶת אִמּוֹ וְדָבַק בְּאִשְׁתּוֹ וְהָיוּ לְבָשָׂר אֶחָד.

Therefore shall a man leave his father and his mother, and shall cleave unto his wife, and they shall be one flesh. (Bereishis 2:24)

The Torah itself points out the reality that man eventually "abandons" his parents and cleaves to his wife!

By using the term כַּבֵּד, the Torah may be reminding us that "burdening" our parents may actually be a good thing, because it perpetuates a connection that will forever be mutually beneficial. "כַּבֵּד אֶת אָבִיךָ וְאֶת אִמֶּךָ" may not only mean "**honor** your father and mother," but may also mean "**burden** your father and mother." Our fathers and mothers would rather feel burdened and retain a connection to their children than have no connection at all.

Consider the classic children's book, *The Giving Tree* by Shel Silverstein: In his childhood, the boy enjoys playing with the tree, climbing her trunk, swinging from her branches, and eating her apples. However, as time passes, he starts to make requests of the tree. After entering adolescence, the boy wants money, and the tree suggests that he pick and sell her apples, which he does. After reaching adulthood, the boy wants a house, and the tree suggests he cut her branches to build a house. After reaching middle age, the boy wants a boat, and the tree allows him to cut her trunk to make a boat, leaving only a stump. Each such stage of giving by the tree ends with the sentence: "And the tree was happy." The tree was *burdened* with providing, albeit being *honored* to have the connection. Meanwhile, the boy was only able to persevere because of the tree's help along the way.

When the Tanna in *Avos* says: "וְהַמְהַלֵּךְ בַּדֶּרֶךְ יְחִידִי—One who travels alone on the road has forfeited his life," he may be saying that we need to feel comfortable with being able to ask others for help and guidance. We need to cherish our parents and/or grandparents and realize that burdening them actually fortifies our connection, which enables us to live more fulfilled lives. Ultimately "the tree is happy," and the boy succeeds only because of the tree's help. Maturity is less about breaking away from your parents and "burdening" them less, and more about being comfortable in burdening them more, albeit for the purpose of maintaining a connection that is mutually beneficial!

TAKEAWAY MESSAGES

The problem of "וְהַמְהַלֵּךְ בַּדֶּרֶךְ יְחִידִי—one who travels alone on the road" is because one will miss out on the advantage of enabling others to help guide him/her.

"Well, an old stump is good for sitting and resting. Come, boy, sit down. Sit down and rest." And the boy did. And the tree was happy.

"כַּבֵּד אֶת אָבִיךָ וְאֶת אִמֶּךָ." *Parashas Yisro* reminds us of a lesson from Shel: You may be honoring by burdening.

MOSHE'S LESSON IN THE BEST RESPONSE WHEN CHALLENGED

אַרְבַּע מִדוֹת בְּהוֹלְכֵי לְבֵית הַמִּדְרָשׁ: הוֹלֵךְ
וְאֵינוֹ עוֹשֶׂה שְׂכַר הֲלִיכָה בְּיָדוֹ. עוֹשֶׂה וְאֵינוֹ
הוֹלֵךְ שְׂכַר מַעֲשֶׂה בְּיָדוֹ. הוֹלֵךְ וְעוֹשֶׂה חָסִיד.
לֹא הוֹלֵךְ וְלֹא עוֹשֶׂה רָשָׁע.

Four types of people who go to the house of learning: Those
who go but don't do get reward for going. Those who do
but don't go get reward for doing. Those who go and do are
righteous. Those who don't go or do are evil. (Avos 5:14)

QUESTIONS

Why does the Mishnah focus on the word "הוֹלֵךְ—go," as opposed to
using another word that connotes that the person was situated in the
learning hall (a word like נמצא—found)? Is it the actual traveling process
en route to the learning hall or does the fact that you are situated in the
learning hall give you the credit of being there, irrespective of whether
you learn a thing? In other words, is the word "go" here just synonymous with "being present," or does it in fact highlight "traveling to"?

ANSWERS

וַיַּעֲמֹד הָעָם מֵרָחֹק וּמֹשֶׁה נִגַּשׁ אֶל הָעֲרָפֶל אֲשֶׁר שָׁם הָאֱלֹקִים.

201

> *And the people stood afar off, but Moshe drew near unto the*
> *thick darkness where G-d was. (Shemos 20:21)*

Right after hearing the Ten Commandments, the Jewish People essentially had sensory overload and were shell-shocked into place. The midrash actually comments that מֵרָחֹק implies the following:

> *They were drawn backward twelve mil, as far as the length of*
> *their camp. The ministering angels came and assisted them [in*
> *order] to bring them back, as it is said: "Kings of hosts wander;*
> *yea they wander."(Shabbos 88b, quoting Tehillim 68:13)*

Where else in the Torah do we see מֵרָחֹק used?

1. "...[Avraham] בַּיּוֹם הַשְּׁלִישִׁי וַיִּשָּׂא אַבְרָהָם אֶת עֵינָיו וַיַּרְא אֶת הַמָּקוֹם מֵרָחֹק—" saw the place *from afar*," en route to the *Akeidah. (Bereishis 22:4)*

2. "The brothers וַיִּרְאוּ אֹתוֹ מֵרָחֹק וּבְטֶרֶם יִקְרַב אֲלֵיהֶם וַיִּתְנַכְּלוּ אֹתוֹ לַהֲמִיתוֹ— saw Yosef *from afar* when he was on his way to them as they conspired to hurt him." (Ibid. 37:18)

3. "Miriam stood *from afar* to know וַתֵּתַצַּב אֲחֹתוֹ מֵרָחֹק לְדֵעָה מַה יֵּעָשֶׂה לוֹ— what would happen to [baby Moshe]." *(Shemos 2:4)*

Isn't it unusual that in these other episodes of מֵרָחֹק there is no similar explanation of the midrash detailing the distance of how far they were (i.e., twelve *mil*)? Why specifically by the Ten Commandments do we see this unusual midrash, stating that the Jews were flung back twelve *mil* and were escorted back by angels?

My daughter, Tehilah, nonchalantly answered that all these episodes are marked by *fear*: Avraham was *frightened* by the sacrifice of his son (although not spelled out in the *parashah*, if Avraham hadn't feared slaughtering his son, it arguably wouldn't have been much of a test!); the brothers *feared* Yosef (and his dreams); Miriam *feared* for Moshe's sake; and the Jews *feared* G-d by the commandments. מֵרָחֹק perhaps then does not signify a physical distance per se as much as a metaphysical state of mind! The difference between מֵרָחֹק by the commandments and the other three is that ours is highlighted by the inaction that precedes it: "וַיַּעֲמֹד הָעָם מֵרָחֹק." The fact is that the Jewish People were shell-shocked and paralyzed by fear. Whereas Moshe was (to his credit) able to overcome the fear and move forward (וּמֹשֶׁה נִגַּשׁ אֶל הָעֲרָפֶל—see *Ibn Ezra*, who contrasts Moshe approaching the challenge while the rest of the Jews stood shocked!), the Jews were stuck in the mud. It is likely the stagnancy in face of adversity (the וַיַּעֲמֹד הָעָם, and not the מֵרָחֹק) that led the midrash to state that the Jews were dragged backward. The Jewish philosophy is that if you are not moving forward, you are moving backward! If you are ripe, you are rotting (Ray Kroc).

Back to our Mishnah in *Avos*, the reward may not simply be that you find yourself *situated* in a *beis midrash*, but rather that you are *moving* toward the *beis midrash*! Movement in the right direction is itself venerable and is what makes שָׂכָר הֲלִיכָה בְּיָדוֹ.

──────── TAKEAWAY MESSAGES ────────

Why does the midrash assume that the Jews moved backward if it states that they stood in place, וַיַּעֲמֹד הָעָם מֵרָחֹק? Is it from analyzing the מֵרָחֹק or the וַיַּעֲמֹד? We see that מֵרָחֹק was used in at least three other instances, and perhaps actually connoted fear rather than place (with no prior midrash pointing out the distance of מֵרָחֹק). The midrash may have been contrasting the way the Jewish People unfortunately stood still in the wake of sensory overload, while Moshe rightly and confidently walked into the עֲרָפֶל (*Ibn Ezra*). Standing in the wake of adversity or challenge is actually walking backward! Our challenge is to be more Moshe-like and move forward, even when the horizon looks nebulous. שָׂכָר הֲלִיכָה בְּיָדוֹ—Reward awaits those who simply take on challenges and don't keep their feet in the mud.

What's the best response when challenged? Move forward, but don't stand still, or you'll be moving backward.

THE REAL ELEVATED REASON WE STAND
FOR THE TEN COMMANDMENTS

אַבְטַלְיוֹן אוֹמֵר: חֲכָמִים הִזָּהֲרוּ בְדִבְרֵיכֶם
שֶׁמָּא תָחוּבוּ חוֹבַת גָּלוּת וְתִגְלוּ לִמְקוֹם מַיִם
הָרָעִים וְיִשְׁתּוּ הַתַּלְמִידִים הַבָּאִים אַחֲרֵיכֶם
וְיָמוּתוּ וְנִמְצָא שֵׁם שָׁמַיִם מִתְחַלֵּל.

Avtalyon would say: Scholars, be careful with your words,
lest you incur exile to a place of evil waters, and the disciples
who come after you will then drink [of these evil waters] and
be destroyed, and the name of heaven will be desecrated.
(Avos 1:11)

--- QUESTIONS ---

1. What is meant by a "place with evil waters"?
2. Also, the *Rambam* states (*Tamid* 5:1) that the Ten Commandments are the essence of our faith. The *Maharsha* quotes Rav Saadya Gaon (*Berachos* 11b3, Schottenstein *Talmud Bavli*, note 33) that this may be because all 613 of the mitzvos are contained within the Ten Commandments! Interestingly, the Gemara in *Makkos* (24a) says that the *gematria* of תּוֹרָה contained in the *pasuk* תּוֹרָה צִוָּה לָנוּ מֹשֶׁה has the *gematria* of 611, containing all the mitzvos of the Torah within the eight latter commandments, while the first two commandments were heard directly from G-d!

If that is in fact the case, why don't we include the Ten Commandments in our daily liturgy, like we include the *Shema*? To make the question stronger, the *Talmud Yerushalmi* (*Sukkah* 84:3) actually says that the reason we say *Shema* everyday is because there are hidden allusions to the Ten Commandments within the very *Shema*. For instance, "שְׁמַע יִשְׂרָאֵל ה' אֱלֹקֵינוּ" corresponds to "אָנֹכִי ה' אֱלֹקֶיךָ," and "וְאָסַפְתָּ דְגָנֶךָ" (collect your grain and not someone else's!) corresponds to "לֹא תִּגְנוֹב." Now, why would we say *Shema* every day to recall the Ten Commandments, but not say the actual Ten Commandments?

3. And if you were thinking that maybe it's because we don't want to show "favoritisim" to this part of the Torah over other parts, then why would we stand up while reciting the Ten Commandments when it's read on Shabbos? Isn't that showing favorites? What makes this whole question even more troubling is that Aharon Ziegler points out that the *Rambam* actually says that we *shouldn't* stand during the *leining* of the Ten Commandments! So why do we?

━━━━━━━━━━ ANSWERS ━━━━━━━━━━

Truth be told, the Mishnah in *Tamid* recalls that in the Holy Temple, the Kohanim (who were in charge of prayer) did in fact recite the Ten Commandments before *Shema* daily! It was discontinued (see *Berachos* 12a) because we were worried that sectarians would prove from the recitation that this was the only Torah of ours and nothing else! So that explains why we don't say the Ten Commandments in our prayer daily, but why do we then stand for the Ten Commandments this Shabbos, which seemingly should provoke the same concern?

An answer may be derived from a piece I saw in the name of the Rav (by Aharon Ziegler): There are two ways of reading the *Aseret Hadibros*: One by the טַעַם הַתַּחְתּוֹן (literally, "the lower tunes," i.e., reading the cantillation notation from the bottom notes) and one by the טַעַם הָעֶלְיוֹן (literally, "the higher tunes," i.e., reading the cantillation notation from the top notes). The Rav says that really we cannot stand while *leining* this Ten Commandment section with the regular טַעַם הַתַּחְתּוֹן, but when we switch to the טַעַם הָעֶלְיוֹן, which is more of a *remembrance of the event of Har Sinai*, then we can stand. In my understanding of the words, the standing is not out of reverence per se to the Ten Commandments, but rather to the whole episode of *Maamad Har Sinai*!

But at the very basic level, this should provoke a serious insight: We are willing to give up saying the Ten Commandments daily, which according to the *Rambam*, is the essence of our religion, for the fear that some sectarians will use this to cause others to disbelieve? Perhaps this unfortunate reality is homiletically precisely why we call the *trop* under the Ten Commandments section the טַעַם הַתַּחְתּוֹן (טַעַם can also mean "reason/meaning," and הַתַּחְתּוֹן can mean "the lower") or the טַעַם הָעֶלְיוֹן (הָעֶלְיוֹן can mean "exalted"). If we apply the lower basic reality/reason/meaning, we, in fact, shouldn't stand on Shabbos of *Parashas Yisro* by the ten commandments because some may be swayed to think that this is our only important section (consistent with why we don't say the Ten Commandments during daily *tefillah*!). But when we read it with the exalted meaning (i.e., the ideal situation, where we don't have to contend with evil sectarians who can sway the masses!), then we indeed can stand proudly when reading these Ten Commandments!

The Bartenura on *Avos* explains that a "place with evil waters" is referring to the *minim*, sectarians, those people who distort our Torah. Avtalyon is exhorting his rabbis to be very careful because, unfortunately, the reality is that there are people who are "evil water," ready to distort the Torah and poison the masses.

─────────── TAKEAWAY MESSAGES ───────────

Do we stand for the Ten Commandments during *leining*? The answer is that, unlike the fear that we have during our daily *tefillah*, which has discontinued recital of the Ten Commandments (for fear that sectarians would prove from here that it is our only important section), we in fact should stand. The Rav says we can stand, and perhaps by reading it with the special *trop* of טַעַם הָעֶלְיוֹן, it can be catapulted into a different category of a remembrance of the whole historic miraculous occurrence, rather than an emphasis on the Ten Commandments. Maybe we can add to that idea that, homiletically, the טַעַם הַתַּחְתּוֹן can be thought of as the down-and-dirty reason why we would not stand for the Ten Commandments, namely because we fear the sectarian influence. But ideally, or with an elevated utopian outlook (the טַעַם הָעֶלְיוֹן), we in fact can proudly stand for what the *Rambam* calls the essence of our religion—the Ten Commandments! The real *elevated* reason we stand for the Ten Commandments is in fact hidden in the real *elevated* reason (טַעַם הָעֶלְיוֹן)—the utopia in which others won't mistake our reason as saying it is the only Torah we have!

Mishpatim

WHY DOES THE WORD "ABANDON" ALSO MEAN "HELP"?

תֵּן לוֹ מִשֶּׁלוֹ שֶׁאַתָּה וְשֶׁלְּךָ שֶׁלוֹ.

Give from yours because you and yours is His. (Avos 3:7)

─────────── QUESTIONS ───────────

What is the essence of charity? Is it the giving or the receiving?

─────────── ANSWERS ───────────

The answer can be found in this week's *parashah*:

כִּי תִרְאֶה חֲמוֹר שֹׂנַאֲךָ רֹבֵץ תַּחַת מַשָּׂאוֹ וְחָדַלְתָּ מֵעֲזֹב לוֹ עָזֹב תַּעֲזֹב עִמּוֹ.

If you see the donkey of your enemy being overly burdened, would you not help him? Surely you should help [with] him.
(Shemos 23:5)

Rashi says that the word עֲזֹב in this context means "help." Usually, though, a word takes on the meaning it has already been used for previously in the Torah, and clearly עֲזֹב has been defined as "to leave/move away from" (back in *Bereishis*: "עַל כֵּן יַעֲזָב אִישׁ אֶת אָבִיו וְאֶת אִמּוֹ"—a man "leaves" his parents to marry) and so this seems quite odd.

The answer is very deep, and it is the key to a great team and/or relationship. The word "help" essentially focuses on the tangible benefit one receives from another. If I "help" another but he receives no benefit, I haven't really helped him. But if I sacrifice something of mine (my time/energy/money) for someone else, even if I didn't give that person anything tangible in the end, I have benefited us both. Even an "enemy" can recognize when someone donates their time or energy for him, and this can add emotional or spiritual support beyond the tangible. And so perhaps *Rashi* translating "abandon" with "help" here means that true "help" is when you leave your comfort zone for someone else. If so, then the *pasuk* can also be read: "עָזֹב תַּעֲזֹב—You shall 'leave yourself,'" (i.e., sacrifice of yourself) for another person, so that "עִמּוֹ," you can then forge a unifying connection independent of the tangible end product.

And this may explain Rabbi's Akiva's cryptic remark that, "וְאָהַבְתָּ לְרֵעֲךָ כָּמוֹךָ זֶה כְּלָל גָּדוֹל בַּתּוֹרָה—'Love your neighbor as yourself' is a great principle of the Torah." I would have thought "לֹא תרצח—Don't murder" is at least an equally giant precept, and so why did Rebbi Akiva stress this specific precept? Again, homiletically one can perhaps say: "וְאָהַבְתָּ לְרֵעֲךָ כָּמוֹךָ"—when you give (הַב) to your friend [of yourself], "זֶה כְּלָל"—this unifies us/connects us (כלל can mean "precept," but also "generality/unifying," as in כּוֹלֵל), and then "גָּדוֹל בַּתּוֹרה"—you can only then become a true great in Torah! The goal of *giving of yourself* to another (וְאָהַבְתָּ לְרֵעֲךָ or עָזֹב תַּעֲזֹב) enables us to be a *stronger team* (כלל or עִמּוֹ).

The Tanna in *Avos* may have specifically focused on the key aspect of charity, which is the giving of oneself, "תֵּן לוֹ מִשֶּׁלּוֹ שֶׁאַתָּה וְשֶׁלְךָ שֶׁלּוֹ."

Of course, charity is about helping another in need and supplying him with something he is missing. But helping someone else begins by giving of oneself. Becoming a more charitable person really derives from practicing giving from oneself. Thus, this is the essence of charity, because it is by this training that one can ultimately become charitable. Abandoning our selfish tendencies (עָזֹב תַּעֲזֹב) is a prerequisite of tzedakah.

——————— TAKEAWAY MESSAGES ———————

The Torah prescription for ideal "helping" is when one *sacrifices of oneself* for another with less emphasis placed on the final product. The mere sacrifice creates team unity and benefits both parties. "Abandonment" is then understandably clearly as "help."

Why does the word עֲזֹב, "abandon," also mean עָזֹר, "help"? By leaving "yourself," you help another.

SHOULD JEWISH TOMBSTONES READ RIP? A LESSON LEARNED FROM THE ROCKS PLACED ON TOMBSTONES

עֲקַבְיָא בֶן מַהֲלַלְאֵל אוֹמֵר: הִסְתַּכֵּל בִּשְׁלשָׁה
דְּבָרִים וְאִי אַתָּה בָא לִידֵי עֲבֵרָה: דַּע מֵאַיִן
בָּאתָ וּלְאָן אַתָּה הוֹלֵךְ וְלִפְנֵי מִי אַתָּה עָתִיד
לִתֵּן דִּין וְחֶשְׁבּוֹן.

*Akavia ben Mahalalel says: Look at three things and you
won't come to sin: From where you came, where you are going,
and in front of Whom you are going to come for דִּין (judgment)
and חֶשְׁבּוֹן (an accounting)! (Avos 3:1)*

What is the difference between דִּין—judgment and חֶשְׁבּוֹן—an
accounting? My father, Dr. Larry Ciment, quotes Rabbi Mordechai
Shapiro as saying that when you go up to heaven, although you get
judged by your own merits, represented by the personal, direct דִּין, you
can also claim extra continual merits by the impact you have on others,
including family members and community, which are included in the
more flexible and continually accumulating variable חֶשְׁבּוֹן!

——————————— QUESTIONS ———————————

Where in our *parashah* do we see such an idea of דִּין and חֶשְׁבּוֹן?

---------------- ANSWERS ----------------

וַיִּכְתֹּב מֹשֶׁה אֵת כָּל דִּבְרֵי ה' וַיַּשְׁכֵּם בַּבֹּקֶר וַיִּבֶן מִזְבֵּחַ תַּחַת
הָהָר וּשְׁתֵּים עֶשְׂרֵה מַצֵּבָה לִשְׁנֵים עָשָׂר שִׁבְטֵי יִשְׂרָאֵל.

And Moshe wrote all the words of Hashem, and arose early in
*the morning, and built an **altar** under the mount, and twelve*
***pillars**, according to the twelve tribes of Israel. (Shemos 24:4)*

We see Moshe building a מִזְבֵּחַ and a מַצֵּבָה. What is the difference between a מִזְבֵּחַ and מַצֵּבָה?

In *Devarim* (16:22), we see the injunction of utilizing a מִזְבֵּחַ to worship G-d but not building a מַצֵּבָה for that purpose: "וְלֹא תָקִים לְךָ **מַצֵּבָה** אֲשֶׁר
שָׂנֵא ה' אֱלֹקֶיךָ—And you shall not set up for yourself a **monument**, which
Hashem, your G-d hates." *Rashi* states over there that a מַצֵּבָה is made up
of one stone, while a מִזְבֵּחַ is made up of many stones. The classic *mussar*
here is that G-d prefers the plural over the singular. If you can worship
Him with a מִזְבֵּחַ made of *several* stones representing a congregation,
that is more pleasant than worshipping him as one as in a *single* מַצֵּבָה.

In a similar vein, my father wondered why we bring stones to the
tombstone (also called a מַצֵּבָה) of a dead person in the cemetery. He answered that the מַצֵּבָה of a person represents a single person's lifework.
Once dead, the person has but one מַצֵּבָה, a single stone reflecting his
accomplishments. We bring other stones to add on top of the מַצֵּבָה
to represent that the person should not be merely assessed for their
accomplishments but also for the influence that he had on so many others. The singular מַצֵּבָה thus becomes a מִזְבֵּחַ (many stones), reflecting a
congregation of people who were positively influenced by the deceased
and who then cause continual merit for the deceased.

When it says in *Avos*—"לִפְנֵי מִי אַתָּה עָתִיד לִתֵּן דִּין וְחֶשְׁבּוֹן"—the מַצֵּבָה is the
דִּין; we are assessed stand-alone for our personal accomplishments. But
the מִזְבֵּחַ is the חֶשְׁבּוֹן, where we are granted continual merits for influencing others beyond our demise. We must realize that we not only have
an opportunity for personal growth (דִּין), but also have a concomitant
ability to accrue continual merit by influencing others (וְחֶשְׁבּוֹן).

———— TAKEAWAY MESSAGES ————

Moshe builds a מִזְבֵּחַ as well as twelve מַצֵבוֹת in our *parashah*. G-d prefers worship though a מִזְבֵּחַ over a מַצֵבָה. This may be because, inherently, a מִזְבֵּחַ is made of *several* stones representing a congregation, while a מַצֵבָה is intrinsically made up of only one stone. Likewise, by a tombstone: By adding stones to one tombstone (מַצֵבָה), we are showing how the deceased is more than a singular מַצֵבָה. The person who passed away is a מִזְבֵּחַ of many stones that accrues merit based on how he continuously impacts us all currently living (my father, Dr. Larry Ciment). The דִין may be done, but the חֶשְׁבּוֹן keeps on going. RIP may not mean "rest in peace," but rather "re-live in plurality." Rocks on tombstones remind us all that the מַצֵבָה is really a מִזְבֵּחַ!

WHY DOES IT SAY "KEEP DISTANCE FROM A FALSE MATTER"?

יְהוֹשֻׁעַ בֶּן פְּרַחְיָה אוֹמֵר: וֶהֱוֵי דָן אֶת כָּל הָאָדָם לְכַף זְכוּת. נִתַּאי הָאַרְבֵּלִי אוֹמֵר: הַרְחֵק מִשָּׁכֵן רָע וְאַל תִּתְחַבֵּר לָרָשָׁע וְאַל תִּתְיָאֵשׁ מִן הַפֻּרְעָנוּת.

Yehoshua ben Perachiah says: And **judge every man to the side of merit.** *Nitai the Arbeli says:* **Distance yourself from an evil neighbor** *and beware an evil friend. (Avos 1:6–7)*

QUESTIONS

Why do we say you should "distance yourself from an evil neighbor and beware an evil friend"? Wouldn't one expect the ethical textbook to teach us not to become the evil neighbor or friend ourselves? In other words, why is the Mishnah assuming that we are the good ones who have to avoid an "evil neighbor"? Why not focus more introspectively on not becoming the "evil neighbor" ourselves in the first place?

What is the significance of this ethic directly following the ethic of "Judge all people favorably [i.e., assume they are good]"?

The answer to the above questions can be derived from our *parashah.* It says: "מִדְּבַר שֶׁקֶר תִּרְחָק—Keep distance from a false matter." The obvious question is, why doesn't it say, "תִּרְחַק מִדְּבַר שֶׁקֶר—Distance yourself from lying"? Why does it sound like the objective is to avoid the falsehood

214

that seems to be already out there from someone else, as opposed to focusing introspectively on avoiding initiating/creating the falsehood in the first place?

ANSWERS

The implicit answer is that the Torah obligates us to view ourselves in a positive light. If you think you are a reject, you will act like a reject. The Torah assumes each and every individual is inherently good and thus has to avoid exogenous evil influences (thus the דְּבַר שֶׁקֶר doesn't originate by us individually). In direct contradistinction to the concept in Christianity that "in Adam's fall we sin all," in which we all start out with a guilty slate, Jewish People are not supposed to view ourselves pejoratively! For all our deficiencies, we have to each be our own very best fan.

For example, in a league basketball game, in which I literally had more turnovers than points (plus rebounds and assists combined), when discussing the game with friends, I was careful not to point out my terrible playing (leave that to others!)

But it gets even deeper. A lack of true self-worth and self-confidence will lead to not only devaluing yourself, but also consequently devaluing others! This is precisely why דָן אֶת כָּל הָאָדָם לְכַף זְכוּת is right next to this concept of הַרְחֵק מִשָּׁכֵן רָע. In order to judge others favorably, you need to start out first judging yourself in a good light. Those who spend their time always criticizing others are usually not secure themselves.

We need to avoid the falsehoods of others because we really do have to view ourselves as pure (even when we clearly are not). מִדְּבַר שֶׁקֶר תִּרְחָק is thus entirely consistent with the Mishnah in *Avos* that stresses we must avoid "evil people." This is not about putting down others, but more about the lesson of the importance of self-worth!

TAKEAWAY MESSAGES

תִּרְחָק מִדְּבַר שֶׁקֶר and not מִדְּבַר שֶׁקֶר תִּרְחָק teaches us that the falsehoods out there don't originate by us individually. It's not that we view others poorly, but rather that we must be our very own best fans. In order to be able to judge others favorably, we must first have self-worth. "Distance yourself from an evil neighbor" because we are the good neighbors, and don't let anybody tell you otherwise. Self-esteem leads to judging others favorably—the lesson of "keep distance from a false matter."

"YOU SHALL THOROUGHLY HEAL HIM" AND THE MEASLES OUTBREAK

In this week's *parashah*, it states: "רַק שִׁבְתּוֹ יִתֵּן וְרַפֹּא יְרַפֵּא"—And you shall thoroughly heal him." The Gemara in both *Bava Kama* (85b) and *Berachos* (60a) teaches regarding the words וְרַפֹּא יְרַפֵּא: "מכאן שניתנה רשות לרופא לרפאות—From here [we learn that the Torah] gives *permission* to a doctor to heal."

QUESTIONS

1. Why would one think that doctoring is not allowed?
2. Why do we need permission to heal or seek healing?
3. How does our *parashah* speak to the controversy over immunization?

ANSWERS

It is worth noting that the term רשות, "permissibility," is likely to have flavored the famous idea of the *Ibn Ezra* that doctors are really only allowed to heal those illnesses on the external body (such as external injuries from trauma, etc.) that are self-evident, but "internal" illnesses (such as gallbladder attacks, etc.) are relegated to Heavenly healing alone! *Tosafos* clearly disagrees and actually says that the double language of וְרַפֹּא יְרַפֵּא teaches that even those illnesses "brought on by G-d" (i.e., the internal ones!) are given over to us to try to heal. *Rashi* understands like *Tosafos* and brings down that one may think that seeking a doctor is ill-advised (forgive the pun), because, perhaps, "The One who creates illness should be the One who heals," but we learn from וְרַפֹּא יְרַפֵּא *permissibility* to seek healing from humans!

217

Ramban on the Torah seems to side with *Ibn Ezra* that Heavenly healing is preferable (here he seems to be specifically dealing with a utopian society of *tzaddikim*, etc.), but upon further inspection in his work, *Toras Ha'adam*, he clearly says that doctoring and seeking doctors is, in fact, a mitzvah.

As to the wording of "permissibility," Rabbi Avraham Yitzchak Kook says that since by nature medicine in general is really not an exact science, we are only *permitted* to use medicine. On the other hand, if you know for sure that some remedy would surely help, we have another statement in the Torah that would already obligate one to help out, namely "לֹא תַעֲמֹד עַל דַּם רֵעֶךָ"— one may not stand idly by the blood of their friend.

I would like to add that the wording in the Gemara is very odd: "מכאן שניתנה רשות לרופא לרפאות." Although רשות does in fact more often mean permissibility, there are times when the word means "domain," (e.g., רשות הרבים or רשות היחיד—private or public domains). So another possible understanding, which flows very well with the *Ramban*, is that וְרַפֹּא יְרַפֵּא put the discussion of healing in a "human domain" for the first time. Once in a "human domain," it is our mitzvah to do whatever we can to further our medical prowess. In the *Ramban*'s own words: "אבל האי רשות רשות דמצוה הוא לרפאות" or "אבל האי רשות רשות דמצוה הוא לרפאות."

Early in 2019, measles unfortunately reached epidemic proportions in certain communities worldwide. Measles is one of the most contagious diseases known; 90 percent of non-immunized people will contract the disease just from being exposed to someone with measles. It can spread by simple breathing and can remain in the air even two hours after someone with measles has left the area. To further complicate things, it can be spread by someone before they even develop any symptoms themselves. Even if one received both recommended doses of the MMR (measles-mumps-rubella) vaccine, three out of every hundred vaccinated people are still susceptible to these diseases.

The major concern about the combination MMR vaccine, which is unfounded, is that MMR causes autism. This concern can be traced to a 1998 study on twelve children, which alleged that MMR damaged the intestinal lining, allowing encephalopathic proteins to enter the bloodstream and brain, thereby leading to the development of autism. The paper was retracted from the public record in 2010 and exposed as fraudulent in 2011.

Lest you think that sound factual arguments from the CDC or information of the dangers of the diseases prevented by the vaccine will sway parents who wish not to vaccinate their children, a well-designed study by Nyhan et al. has shown that essentially no informational intervention helped those with the "least favorable" attitudes toward vaccination. When the Torah says וְרַפֹּא יְרַפֵּא, this is not a simple permissibility to practice medicine when and if we want to. Once G-d put medicinal issues in our domain, it is now in our רשות—domain to conquer these challenges; we can't afford to be negligent, especially when it can affect us and others around us deleteriously.

הוּא הָיָה אוֹמֵר: אַל תְּהִי דָן יְחִידִי שֶׁאֵין דָן יְחִידִי אֶלָּא אֶחָד.
וְאַל תֹּאמַר קַבְּלוּ דַעְתִּי שֶׁהֵן רַשָּׁאִין וְלֹא אָתָּה.

He [Rabbi Yishmael] would say: Don't be a single judge because there is only One single judge! Don't say, "Accept my understanding," because they are allowed to and not you [as a singular judge]! (Avos 4:8)

Everybody is a judge of their own life. It is important to rely on the majority opinions in general when it comes to health, and not be swayed by anecdotal opinions, especially when they can harm others. As the Yiddish saying goes: "*Az tzvei zuggen shiker, leigst zich der driter shloffen*—If two people say you're drunk, the third one goes to sleep." Evidence-based medicine should help guide us all to make the appropriate decisions!

—————— TAKEAWAY MESSAGES ——————

Where in our *parashah* do we learn that practicing medicine is allowed? וְרַפֹּא יְרַפֵּא!

The Gemara says that the Torah gives us רְשׁוּת to practice medicine. The *Ibn Ezra* understands that medicine can only be performed on outside illnesses, while *Tosafos*, *Rashi*, and *Ramban* all support practicing medicine on external and internal illnesses.

Rabbi Kook strongly says that the term "permissibility" is used only given the ambiguous nature of most medicines, but if we know something will certainly work, we don't need permission, for לֹא תַעֲמֹד עַל דַּם רֵעֶךָ. Finally, when the Torah gives us רְשׁוּת, we can understand that G-d has placed medicine in our domain, and once in our domain, we have an obligation (not a mere permissibility!) to conquer it. The measles controversy is based on fear and misunderstanding, but information alone is not enough to convince the misbelievers. Perhaps increased awareness of our responsibility to heal would be more effective. מִכָּאן שֶׁנִּתְּנָה רְשׁוּת לָרוֹפֵא לְרַפְּאוֹת.

וְרַפֹּא יְרַפֵּא and the measles outbreak—it's our רְשׁוּת—domain, and we have to do our part.

Terumah

THE SIGNIFICANCE OF DIRECTION
IN THE HOLY TEMPLE

כַּךְ הִיא דַּרְכָּהּ שֶׁל תּוֹרָה: פַּת בְּמֶלַח תֹּאכֵל...

*Such is the way of Torah: **Bread with salt you shall
eat**...(Avos 6:4)*

גְּדוֹלָה תוֹרָה שֶׁהִיא נוֹתֶנֶת חַיִּים לְעֹשֶׂיהָ
בָּעוֹלָם הַזֶּה וּבָעוֹלָם הַבָּא...וְאוֹמֵר: אֹרֶךְ יָמִים
בִּימִינָהּ בִּשְׂמֹאולָהּ עֹשֶׁר וְכָבוֹד.

*Great is Torah, for it gives life to its observers in this world
and in the World to Come. And it says (Mishlei 3:16): "**Long
days in its right hand; in its left, wealth and honor.**"*
(Avos 6:7)

--- QUESTIONS ---

1. How are we to understand this ethic that the Torah way is to
   eat simple, salted bread (as opposed to yearning for delicacies)?
2. In the second ethic quoted, how does the *pasuk* from *Mishlei*
   tell us anything about the Torah's greatness? This seems completely disconnected!

The answer is found in our *parashah* by analyzing the Divine placement of the holy items in our *Mishkan*:

וְעָשִׂיתָ אֶת הַקְּרָשִׁים לַמִּשְׁכָּן עֶשְׂרִים קֶרֶשׁ לִפְאַת נֶגְבָּה תֵימָנָה.

*And you shall make the boards for the Tabernacle, twenty boards for the **south side southward**. (Shemos 26:17)*

Why is the south direction of the Tabernacle called נֶגְבָּה (literally, "dry") and תֵימָנָה (literally, "right")? The *Stone Chumash* explains beautifully that the נֶגֶב is the *southern* desert of Israel, and so נֶגְבָּה appropriately signifies south. Since the primary direction is east since it is natural for people to look toward the sun, if you bear *right* while facing in this primary direction *east*, you will be facing south! And so right (תֵימָנָה) in the Tabernacle is south (נֶגְבָּה/dry desert, south of Israel) as long as you are facing east toward the light of the sun.

But still, what lesson can be learned from the fact that "dry" and "right" defines the south side of the Tabernacle?

The answer may be that G-d's very design of the *Mishkan* was meant to teach us how to approach life. The right hand (generally the strong hand) represents the "ideal," while the left represents "less than ideal." As you head east (toward the sun), the *Menorah*, which represents the light of knowledge/Torah is on your right, and the *Shulchan*, which represents materialism (after all, bread is brought on the *Shulchan*) is on your left. The *Menorah*, as opposed to the foodstuff brought on the *Shulchan*, is rather נֶגֶב/dry indeed, but it is also the most enviable holy trait.

The *mussar* may be that although having wealth is, of course, desirable, Torah/knowledge is the ultimate true ideal. When the *pasuk* says, "אֹרֶךְ יָמִים בִּימִינָה," Shlomo HaMelech may have been saying that the *Menorah*, which is on the right side, is the ideal (on the right), while "שְׂמֹאולָה עֹשֶׁר וְכָבוֹד," the *Shulchan*, which is on the left side representing the quest for wealth and honor, is less ideal (on the left).

And so how are we to understand this ethic that the Torah way is to **eat simple, salted bread** (as opposed to yearning for delicacies)?

Ideally, we should *turn right while heading east*; we should yearn for the "dry" (the Negev) *Menorah*, representing the quest for holiness/spirituality/Torah knowledge. That is the true Torah way.

─────────── TAKEAWAY MESSAGES ───────────

The significance of the directions in the Tabernacle setup is telling, indeed. The right-hand direction (when facing east toward the sun) points south toward the *Menorah*, which represents the quest for light and for holy endeavors, while the left-hand direction facing north points toward the *Shulchan*, which represents the quest for wealth/honor. The ideal path is heading in the *right* direction, i.e., south toward the *Menorah*!

"Long days in its right hand; in its left, wealth and honor," is, in fact, very much connected to defining a Torah way of life: The right hand or direction is the spiritual, and the left hand is the materialistic. Being dry is being right *a la* פַּת בְּמֶלַח תֹּאכַל! The significance of the directions in the Temple: head right for long, meaningful life, and left for materialism.

GOOD FROM THE INSIDE-OUT
OR THE OUTSIDE-IN?

אַל תִּסְתַּכֵּל בַּקַּנְקַן אֶלָּא בְּמַה שֶּׁיֶּשׁ בּוֹ.

*Do not look at the outer appearance of a **pitcher** but rather
what is inside it. (Avos 4:20)*

——— QUESTIONS ———

1. Where do we see this idea from our *parashah*? Why does this
   Mishnah specifically talk about a קַנְקַן—pitcher, rather than a
   כּוֹס—cup?

2. There is a halachic concept that כלי חרש אינו מטמא מגבו—earthenware vessels don't contract *tumah* from their exterior. Unlike
   metal utensils (כלי מתכת), which become *tamei* from outside contact with sources of *tumah*, earthenware vessels (כלי חרש) only
   become *tamei* from the inside. What lesson is there and how is
   it related to the above concept?

3. When the Torah states, regarding the *Aron*, the Holy Ark: "וְצִפִּיתָ
   אֹתוֹ זָהָב טָהוֹר מִבַּיִת וּמִחוּץ תְּצַפֶּנּוּ—And you shall overlay it with pure
   gold; from inside and from outside you shall overlay it" (*Shemos*
   25:11), *Rashi* reminds us that Betzalel made three Arks: two
   of gold and one of wood. He placed the wooden one inside the
   golden one and the other golden one inside the wooden one.
   But if you cannot see the inner gold piece, why put it there?

4. We learn about the extensive tapestry of the coverings of the *Mishkan*. Why have ten separate coverings on top of the *Mishkan* if you can only see the outside (or innermost layer)?

─────── ANSWERS ───────

The Gemara in *Yoma* (72b) makes an analogy between the *Aron*'s three layers and a scholar: "כל תלמיד חכם שאין תוכו כברו אין תלמיד חכם—Any *talmid chacham* (Torah scholar) whose inside isn't like his outside is not a Torah scholar." Just as the *Aron* was covered with pure gold from within and from without, so too a Torah scholar must be consistent. His inner character must match his public demeanor; his actions must conform to his professed beliefs and outward appearance.

From the fact that the Gemara specifically mentions a *talmid chacham*, does it mean that its statement doesn't apply to one who isn't a *talmid chacham*? An answer may be that by nature, a *talmid chacham* is a role model, and people look to that person to teach others how to behave. It behooves someone in such a lofty position to strive extra hard to be "gold" on both the inside and out, as he is a role model; just like an *Aron HaKodesh* bestowed with great potential to shine light to others, so too a Torah scholar must be inside out.

Likewise, when the Mishnah in *Avos* says, "אַל תִּסְתַּכֵּל בַּקַּנְקַן," it may specifically relate to a flask (not an ordinary cup), which pours out and influences others because, unlike a single cup, the קנקן is held to a different stringent standard of being inside out.

When it comes to the rest of us, the ones in the *Mishkan*, the lesson may actually be more outside-in. The reason why the covers of the *Mishkan* were placed in such great detail may have been to show this lesson—that we have to work on our outside protective layers, even when we don't clearly see the immediate beauty of such finely woven tapestry. Homiletically, we are each individually a כלי חרש. As such, we aren't going to be *tamei* from the outside (כלי חרש אינו מטמא מגבו). In other words, if we strengthen our outside protective layers so much, we can preserve whatever spirituality we retain inside! Regular individuals need to work outside-in to preserve the holy lessons.

To summarize, the lesson in the *Aron HaKodesh* was inside-out, perhaps reflecting the great responsibility that rabbis and *talmidei chachamim* have in living up to a higher standard. The lesson of the *Mishkan* is that the rest of us living outside the *Kodesh HaKodashim* have to work to elaborate the outer coverings and protective layers that thereby insulate us from sin, even when those outer layers seem redundant!

———————— TAKEAWAY MESSAGES ————————

Our *parashah* teaches the lesson of תוכו כברו. A *talmid chacham* should strive to be consistent; his outside demeanor should reflect his inside nature, as taught by the *Aron HaKodesh*. But an outside-in approach may be more applicable to us common folk, signified by the multilayered covers of the *Mishkan* outside the *Kodesh HaKodashim*! "כלי חרש אינו מטמא מגבו"—A pottery shard (e.g., common folk like me) doesn't get impure only by buttressing oneself with enough insulation.

Inside-out if you are a *talmid chacham*, but outside-in if you're a regular Joe like me.

THE LESSON OF THE CEDAR TREES

יְהוּדָה בֶן תֵּימָא אוֹמֵר: הֱוֵי עַז כַּנָּמֵר ...
לַעֲשׂוֹת רְצוֹן אָבִיךְ שֶׁבַּשָּׁמָיִם. הוּא הָיָה אוֹמֵר
עַז פָּנִים לְגֵיהִנָּם.

*Yehudah ben Teima says: You should be bold as a leopard…to
do the will of your father in heaven. He said: Bold-faced
[people] go to hell. (Avos 5:20)*

QUESTIONS

So is it good to be bold or not good?

עֲצֵי שִׁטִּים: מֵאַיִן הָיוּ לָהֶם בַּמִּדְבָּר פֵּירֵשׁ רַבִּי תַנְחוּמָא יַעֲקֹב אָבִינוּ
צָפָה בְרוּחַ הַקֹּדֶשׁ שֶׁעֲתִידִין יִשְׂרָאֵל לִבְנוֹת מִשְׁכָּן בַּמִּדְבָּר וְהֵבִיא
אֲרָזִים לְמִצְרַיִם וּנְטָעָם וְצִוָּה לְבָנָיו לִיטְּלָם עִמָּהֶם כְּשֶׁיֵּצְאוּ מִמִּצְרַיִם.

*Acacia wood: Where did they get these [trees] in the desert?
Rabbi Tanchuma explained that our father Yaakov foresaw
with the holy spirit that the Israelites were destined to build
a Mishkan in the desert, so he brought cedars to Egypt and
planted them. He commanded his sons to take them with
them when they left Egypt. (Midrash Tanchuma 9)*

Rabbi Yissocher Frand asks a great question, which I will paraphrase:
If much of the material used in the desert to build or adorn the *Mishkan*
was in fact miraculously placed in the desert (e.g., the *Avnei Shoham*

227

and *Avnei Miluim*, the precious stones adorning the Kohen Gadol's vestments), then why was it that Yaakov specifically ensured that the cedar trees were imported from Egypt?

─────────────── ANSWERS ───────────────

I will try to relate this beautiful idea from the *sefer Menachem Tzion* and Rabbi Yissocher Frand:

A midrash on our *parashah* states that the "world would not ever have had a need for cedar trees had it not been for the *Mishkan*." The question on the midrash is: What is so bad about cedar trees that they wouldn't have needed to exist?

The *Menachem Tzion* answers that a Gemara in *Taanis* says: "A person should take on the personality of a reed and not of a cedar!" A reed is flexible and malleable, but a cedar tree is rigid by nature and inflexible. Therefore, when the midrash says that cedar trees are not desirable, the idea is that, in general, it is not a good trait to be rigid and inflexible. However, by the *Mishkan*, i.e., when it comes to spirituality, one needs to be rigid like a cedar and steadfast, committed without allowance. If one is a reed when it comes to their Judaism, the outcome is almost always irreligiosity.

Rabbi Frand beautifully continues with his idea (completely paraphrased): This may explain why Yaakov had to specifically import cedar trees from Egypt. Egypt was the very place that demonstrated the Jewish steadfastness in the environment of strangers (in that they didn't change their language and clothing, etc.).

Yaakov Avinu perhaps purposely insisted that the cedars come from Egypt to remind the Jews of this lesson: Just like the cedar is strong and unwavering, and just like the Jews were unwavering in their traditions even in hostile Egypt, we must continue to be unwavering in our Yiddishkeit, as symbolized by the *Mishkan*.

Regarding the question asked about the contradiction in the above quote from *Avos*, it seems that there is a necessity to be bold when it comes to religious matters. In all other matters, though, we should be more "reed-like" and leave out the boldness!

─────────── TAKEAWAY MESSAGES ───────────

Why did Yaakov import cedar wood from Egypt if other materials for the *Mishkan* miraculously appeared in the desert? Why does the midrash on our *parashah* state that the "world would not ever have had a need for cedar trees had it not been for the *Mishkan*"? The answer is that in general, "a person should take on the personality of a reed and not of a cedar." However, when it comes to the *Mishkan* (symbolizing spiritual matters), one needs to be steadfast like a cedar tree! Lessons of a cedar tree—be a reed most of the time, except when it comes to religion/tradition.

EXCESSIVE OR MISPLACED LASHON TOV—THE LESSON OF THE BELLS AND POMEGRANATES

כֹּל הַמַּרְבֶּה דְבָרִים מֵבִיא חֵטְא.

If you are too wordy, it will bring sin. (Avos 1:17)

──────── QUESTIONS ────────

The implication is that even if the speech sounds "positive," you are in danger of sinning. In fact, a classic example of so-called "*avak lashon hara*," the Rabbinical derivative of the Biblically prohibited *lashon hara*, is when one excessively compliments another. Where do we see this in our *parashah*?

──────── ANSWERS ────────

"פַּעֲמֹן זָהָב וְרִמּוֹן פַּעֲמֹן זָהָב וְרִמּוֹן עַל שׁוּלֵי הַמְּעִיל סָבִיב"—The Kohen's robe had golden bells and pomegranates. The *Baal Haturim* says that there were seventy-two of these bells and pomegranates, corresponding to the seventy-two shades of leprosy that the Kohen had to familiarize him-self with, and the robe along with those unusual designs was itself an atonement for *lashon hara* (he also homiletically explains "שַׁפָּה יִהְיֶה לְפִיו"; see there). So that explains the number seventy-two, but still, why were there golden bells and pomegranates?

230

One reason may be the following: A זָהָב is a way to term someone who is as pure as gold, and we know that a רִמּוֹן is usually describing one full of mitzvos (as in "כְּפֶלַח הָרִמּוֹן רַקָּתֵךְ"). And so homiletically: "פַּעֲמֹן"—when you clamor for someone (when you compliment excessively) that he is a זָהָב or a רִמּוֹן (i.e., that he is pure like gold or a holy person), even that could be potentially gossip that requires atonement. But what is so bad about calling someone a רִמּוֹן (or זָהָב)?

The answer may be in *Rashi's* interpretation of רִמּוֹן here. Although appearing like רמונים, they were actually "hollowed out" pomegranates that were like eggshells. So if you say someone is a רִמּוֹן, others will find a way to show you how this person in fact is an empty רִמּוֹן! In other words, when you excessively compliment someone, unfortunately others look to then disparage the complimented: "No, he's not as holy as you think," etc.

If the Kohen's *me'il* hints to *avak lashon hara*, just an offshoot of *lashon hara*, how much more so should we avoid obvious *lashon hara*.

────── TAKEAWAY MESSAGES ──────

The seventy-two bells and pomegranates of the Kohen's coat are reminiscent of the dangers of *lashon hara* (*Baal Haturim*). Why specifically golden bells and pomegranates? Even when we clamor for others, we must beware of clamoring too loud and insincerely, which only provokes others to find the "hollowed out" parts of the mitzvah-rich pomegranates. As the phrase goes: "Great people talk about ideas. Average people talk about things. Small people talk about other people!"

The lesson of the bells and pomegranates: *Lashon hara* can simply be *lashon tov* that is excessive or misplaced.

WHEN TO GO **BOLD**?
THE LESSON OF THE *TZITZ*

יְהוּדָה בֶן תֵּימָא אוֹמֵר: הֱוֵי עַז כַּנָּמֵר ...
לַעֲשׂוֹת רְצוֹן אָבִיךָ שֶׁבַּשָּׁמַיִם...הוּא הָיָה
אוֹמֵר: עַז פָּנִים לְגֵיהִנֹם וּבֹשֶׁת פָּנִים לְגַן עֵדֶן.

*Yehudah ben Teima says: You should be bold as a **leopard**...to do the will of your father in heaven. He said: **Bold-faced** [people] go to hell; **the bashful**—to paradise. (Avos 5:20)*

QUESTIONS

1. The Tanna in *Avos* says you should be "bold as a leopard," but then says that a person who is "bold-faced" is destined for hell?
2. Furthermore, why "as a leopard" and not as a "lion," which is the boldest of the animal kingdom?
3. Also, every morning, one of our first prayers is not to be עַז פָּנִים, but shouldn't we pray to be עַז פָּנִים as per Rabbi Yehudah's advice?

ANSWERS

1. The Gemara in *Zevachim* (88) says that the *Tzitz* on the forehead of the Kohen Gadol is to atone for עַזּוּת פָּנִים. Rabbi Aharon Greenberg, in the name of Rabbi Baruch Epstein, beautifully points out that this may be to remind us that in general, we must not be brash. But, he continues, by holy and spiritual matters (when it is קֹדֶשׁ לַה'), we are mandated to "wear it on our

232

forehead," as prescribed by the Tanna in *Avos* (הֱוֵי עַז כַּנָּמֵר); it is OK to brazenly "show off" our spirituality on our forehead! And so maybe one answer to the question is simple: We can't be showy or flashy or ostentatious in general but by holy matters, we can "go bold," as exemplified by the Kohen wearing the *Tzitz* on his forehead saying it is *"Kodesh"* as long as it is *"לַה*—for G-d."

2. Although the usual understanding of עַז is "brazen," "chutzpadik," "harsh," "brash," or "ostentatious," Yaakov Avinu actually defines עַז as quick and non-deliberate (אָרוּר אַפָּם כִּי עָז). Being bold is being very quick without much delay and deliberation. Most of the time, it is a good trait to be deliberate. (Dr. David Pelcowitz says in the name of the Baal Shem Tov: "וַאֲבַדְתֶּם מְהֵרָה"—we should lose "the quickness" and not be so fast all the time!) Your פָּנִים—face (signifying the majority of time) should not be עַז but rather one of בֹּשֶׁת פָּנִים. The *Tosafos Yom Tov* adds to this: "כל אדם שיש לו בשת פנים לא במהרה הוא חוטא." This can be read: "Anyone with abashedness will not easily sin." I prefer to read it homiletically: "Anyone with בֹּשֶׁת פָּנִים possesses the quality that he will not sin by being a בִּמְהֵרָה." Being בֹּשֶׁת פָּנִים is being the opposite of עַז in the sense that most of the time we need to be deliberate and thoughtful, mindful of the consequences of our actions.

3. But the caveat is that when it comes to Jewish matters, we have to place our deliberations aside! If we start pondering and deliberating about why we daven three times a day, give an inordinate amount of money to Jewish institutions, etc., we just simply wouldn't do it. That's why the Tanna says, "הֱוֵי עַז כַּנָּמֵר"—a leopard is known for being very fast (it can run at speeds of up to 36 mph), and although our פָּנִים must be one of בֹּשֶׁת פָּנִים—deliberation, we must be עַז when it comes to spiritual matters.

——————— TAKEAWAY MESSAGES ———————

The *Tzitz* was bold, but teaches us the lesson that brazenness is actually welcome as long as it is directed for the right spiritual purpose. The Tanna in *Avos* reminds us that being עַז as your daily פָּנִים, face, (in general) is not ideal, but being עַר, non-deliberate, is most desirable when it comes to holy matters, because, frankly, if we think too much about our personal dedications to spirituality, we would avoid religiosity because it is onerous indeed! And so it is the *Tzitz* that teaches us the exception of עַר.

The *Tzitz* tells us that we need to go bold with things that are קֹדֶשׁ לַה'.

SILENT = WISE? THE LESSON
OF THE JASPER STONE

רַבִּי עֲקִיבָא אוֹמֵר: סְיָג לַחָכְמָה שְׁתִיקָה.

Rabbi Akiva says: A fence for wisdom is silence. (Avos 3:13)

בֶּן זוֹמָא אוֹמֵר: אֵיזֶהוּ חָכָם הַלּוֹמֵד מִכָּל
אָדָם ...

Who is wise? One who learns from all people. (Avos 4:1)

----- QUESTIONS -----

1. Is wisdom really achieved by being a quiet person? If so, the
   chacham and the *she'eino yodei'a lishol* from the Pesach Haggadah
   should be equally wise!
2. Is סְיָג לַחָכְמָה שְׁתִיקָה supposed to imply that quietness is a *limitation*
   to wisdom or that it actually *contributes* to wisdom?
3. Lastly, is there any connection between the two ways of achieving wisdom as derived from *Avos*, namely being quiet and
   learning from others?

----- ANSWERS -----

וְהַטּוּר הָרְבִיעִי תַּרְשִׁישׁ וְשֹׁהַם וְיָשְׁפֵה מְשֻׁבָּצִים זָהָב יִהְיוּ בְּמִלּוּאֹתָם.
*And the fourth row a beryl, an onyx, and a **jasper**; they shall*
be enclosed in gold in their settings. (Shemos 28:20)

235

The *Midrash Aggadah* tries to explain why the jasper stone (called the יָשְׁפֵה) was the stone allotted for Binyamin to be placed in the fourth row of the *Choshen*, the breastplate of the Kohen Gadol. Since Binyamin knew that his brothers sold Yosef but did not reveal this information to Yaakov so as not to hurt him, he was awarded the jasper stone, which sounds like "יֵשׁ פֶּה—has mouth." This stone was chosen to represent Binyamin because its name reflects this praiseworthy trait of his. Rabbi Zweig asked that if Binyamin was indeed being lauded for his silence, why was the gem called יָשְׁפֵה—יֵשׁ פֶּה? Should the more appropriate name not be "אֵין פֶּה—has no mouth"? What trait did Binyamin exhibit through his silence?

An answer that I heard from both Rabbi Zweig and Rabbi Neuhaus is that the great attribute of Binyamin was that he *did not speak, even though he could speak*. It's one thing to not speak because you have nothing to say (שאינו יודע לשאול), but it's a real attribute to be able to refrain from speaking when you have much to say and yet choose silence when it is appropriate. Perhaps, then, a יֵשׁ פֶּה that is silent is more praiseworthy than a silent אֵין פֶּה!

I would like to add to this idea: The word for "conversation" in Hebrew is דו-שִׂיחַ. When you converse with someone, it is important that you approach it as דו, which in *gematria* is 4=ד and 6=ו. An effective conversation is when one approaches it first with "4" and then with "6"—when one says over their 40 percent, while leaving 60 percent of time (i.e., the majority), for listening to the other person. Wisdom is achieved by being לוֹמֵד מִכָּל אָדָם because you already know what you know and in order to glean the very most you can, you must be silent to some extent and listen to the perspectives or insights of others.

And so perhaps wisdom is not really achieved by being silent per se as much as it is about knowing when to be silent! In that sense, being wise is learning from others by giving pause and opening your ears, instead of your mouth.

———— TAKEAWAY MESSAGES ————

Binyamin was allotted the יָשְׁפֵה—jasper stone of the *Choshen* because he refrained from revealing to Yaakov that his brothers sold Yosef, thus protecting him from pain. The יָשְׁפֵה sounds like יֵשׁ פֶּה (has mouth), and the greatness is that despite "having a mouth" (i.e., the ability to talk), Binyamin was still silent and refrained from possibly damaging discourse. True wisdom is attained by learning from others (לוֹמֵד מִכָּל אָדָם) and not only yourself, which is essentially opening your ears to others more than your mouths. Effective communication should never be a שִׂיחַ—lecture, but rather a דּוּ-שִׂיחַ—conversation, where we talk 40 percent (ד) and ingest other vantage points 60 percent (ו) of the time.

Silence makes one smart if it is well-positioned and allows one to maximize intake of others' ideas.

WHY I NEED TO START SAYING PESUKEI D'ZIMRAH EVERYDAY

וְיָדְ־עוּ כִּי אֲנִי ה' אֱלֹקֵיהֶם אֲשֶׁר הוֹצֵאתִי אֹתָם
מֵאֶרֶץ מִצְרַיִם לְשָׁכְנִי בְתוֹכָם אֲנִי ה' אֱלֹקֵיהֶם.

And they shall know that I am Hashem their G-d, who
brought them out of Egypt, *so that I may* **dwell among**
them. *I am Hashem their G-d. (Shemos 29:46)*

—— QUESTIONS ——

In *sefer Shemos* of his great series on the Rav's Torah words, Rabbi David Holzer essentially asks what the connection between G-d taking us out of Egypt and the Beis Hamikdash is ("אֲשֶׁר הוֹצֵאתִי אֹתָם מֵאֶרֶץ מִצְרַיִם" is mentioned in the verse with "לְשָׁכְנִי בְתוֹכָם—to dwell among them," i.e., the Beis Hamikdash). In what sense does the miraculous exit from Egypt have to do with the Beis Hamikdash?

—— ANSWERS ——

Rabbi Holzer shares (and Rabbi Bixon has mentioned this many times) that the Rav reviewed how the Gemara in *Shabbos* (118b) tries to reconcile the saying of "I should share in the reward that those people who recite *Hallel* every day will receive in *Olam Haba*" with the notion that "הקורא הלל בכל יום הרי זה מחרף ומגדף—Whoever says *Hallel* every day is like one who engages in blasphemy." Simply put, is it a great thing to say *Hallel* every day or is it a terrible thing?

(I am essentially paraphrasing Rabbi Holzer and the Rav's idea from here and on:) The Gemara's answer is that we are talking about two different *Hallels*: The one contained within the *Pesukei D'Zimrah* that we indeed say every morning, including Shabbos, and the so-called *Hallel HaMitzri*, which the Jews said when they were about to depart from Egypt, said on only twenty-one special occasions throughout the year. The one we say every day (the *Hallelukah* chapters of *Tehillim* said after *Ashrei*) deal with the cosmic order that "Hashem has implanted in every blade of grass, beam of light, and drop of water." It makes sense that we say these every single day. It also makes perfect sense that recognizing G-d through nature is meritorious, as it is so often difficult to appreciate common ordinary daily events as blessings from G-d (my stretch). The *Hallel HaMitzri*, which is the *Hallel* of the holidays, contains the suspension of cosmic order, i.e., הַיָּם רָאָה וַיָּנֹס. This *Hallel* highlights how the sea split. Saying this *Hallel* every day is blasphemous then, in the sense that G-d did not intend every day to be a suspension in the cosmic order!

The Rav essentially highlighted that there are two ways we have a relationship with G-d:

1. Through nature, as represented by the *Pesukei D'Zimrah*'s daily *Hallel*.
2. Through *gilui haShechinah*, i.e., supernatural revelation, as represented by the *Hallel HaMitzri* only said by holidays.

The Beis Hamikdash is very much connected to *Yetzias Mitzrayim* because it was the place that "perpetuated the connection to the miraculous nature of Hashem." This answers our question as to what the connection is and also may explain why we (most Jews) traveled to visit the Beis Hamikdash only on certain occasions and not every day: A connection to the *gilui Shechinah* or supernatural revelation was not meant to be a daily occurrence!

I would like to add that according to the Gemara (*Megillah* 29a), G-d will dwell in the holy spaces we create, for they are the Temple in miniature; they are each a so-called מקדש מעט.

It may be our imperative to realize that the shul experience is supposed to remove us from our mundane, rote-yet-miraculous daily lives and be a little supernatural!

רַבִּי שִׁמְעוֹן אוֹמֵר: הַמְהַלֵּךְ בַּדֶּרֶךְ וְשׁוֹנֶה וּמַפְסִיק מִמִּשְׁנָתוֹ וְאוֹמֵר מַה
נָּאֶה אִילָן זֶה וּמַה נָּאֶה נִיר זֶה מַעֲלֶה עָלָיו הַכָּתוּב כְּאִלּוּ מִתְחַיֵּב בְּנַפְשׁוֹ.

*Rabbi Shimon says: One who is walking on a path and
learning and stops from his learning and says, "How beautiful
is this tree and how nice is the plowed field," then the Torah
considers him culpable with his life. (Avos 3:7)*

It may very well be that the mistake the man is making here is not
in complimenting the tree and the plowed field equally, but rather in
considering both compliments a "break" in his learning. He fails to
see the G-dliness in nature and will thus miss out on saying the daily
Hallel, which would have given him great reward. We must view nature
around us—both the pretty and the less pretty—as G-d-given miracles.
Praising the natural wonders is not a "וּמַפְסִיק מִמִּשְׁנָתוֹ"—break in our learning," but a continuation!

──────── TAKEAWAY MESSAGES ────────

Rabbi Holzer asked: What is the connection between G-d taking us
out of Egypt and the Beis Hamikdash, i.e., in what sense does the miraculous exit from Egypt have anything to do with the Beis Hamikdash?
The Rav answered that the Beis Hamikdash represented our "supernatural" connection with G-d. This wasn't meant to be our day-to-day
connection with G-d, which is supposed to be more "nature-based,"
i.e., seeing G-d through daily mini-miracles. Saying *Hallel* every day is
meritorious when you are saying the *Hallel* of *Pesukei D'Zimrah* because
then you have inculcated the lesson recited by Rabbi Yaakov Garfinkel:
Every day is a gift, and that is why it is called "the present"!

The Beis Hamikdash was purposely not meant to be visited by the
Jews every day because it was like our exit from the supernatural as we
experienced when leaving Egypt. But every day, we should say the *Hallel*
of *Pesukei D'Zimrah*, which reminds us that every bit of nature is really
a blessing.

Ki Sisa

WHAT DOESN'T KILL YOU MAKES YOU STRONGER

בֶּן הֵא הֵא אוֹמֵר: לְפוּם צַעֲרָא אַגְרָא.

Ben Hei-Hei said: According to the pain will be the reward.
(Avos 5:26)

QUESTIONS

Where is the source in the Torah that pain and hardship are actually advantageous? The *Abarbanel* on *Avos* beautifully quotes a conceptual precursor to Ben Hei-Hei's idea (*Sanhedrin* 26b): "The Torah is also termed תושיה because it is מתשת כוחו—it saps your strength." How in the world does "sapping your strength" translate into reward? The answer is derived from asking yet another simple question on our *parashah*:

וַיְחַל מֹשֶׁה...וַיֹּאמֶר לָמָה ה' יֶחֱרֶה אַפְּךָ בְּעַמֶּךָ אֲשֶׁר הוֹצֵאתָ מֵאֶרֶץ מִצְרַיִם בְּכֹחַ גָּדוֹל וּבְיָד חֲזָקָה.

And Moshe started...and said: "Why is G-d upset with His nation that He took out of Egypt with brute strength and strong hand?"

If you were Moshe trying to defend B'nei Yisrael to G-d, would you "remind Him"—in the very same *pasuk* that you are begging for their

241

forgiveness—about their complete lack of *hakaras hatov*, gratitude? Paraphrased, the *pasuk* sounds like this: "Why are you mad at B'nei Yisrael who completely disregarded the fact that You took them out of Egypt with such a mighty hand?" You would have expected Moshe to say, "Why be mad at them? They are just slaves after all!" Why remind Hashem about their complete lack of gratitude during this entreaty. It just doesn't make sense!

─────────── ANSWERS ───────────

Parents often make the mistake of shielding their children too much from common viruses, and partly because of that, the kids subsequently do not develop as robust an immune system. In other words, our very bodies need some adversity to build up a proper immune surveillance system. Similarly, our spirituality is also enhanced when we have some adversity. To keep the virus analogy going, Rabbeinu Nissim of Garundi (the *Ran*) famously tried to at least give some solace to his congregation who witnessed the bubonic plague pandemic that claimed tens of millions of lives in the fourteenth century: "What emerges is that G-d is actually being kind to His creations when He inflicts punishment upon them, for this *saps the strength* from man's evil inclination, allowing him to be subservient to his Creator." Although extreme, the point is clear. When the *Abarbanel* says that the Torah is called תושיה because it is מתשת כוחו—it saps your strength, this is indeed a reward because the lack of strength itself is a reward in the sense that you are more likely to work on yourself to become better!

When Moshe said, "You took B'nei Yisrael out with a mighty hand," he may have been explaining why B'nei Yisrael was so incapable of making the right choices. They hadn't been challenged. They were babied, and when adversity hit, they were carried out by the mighty hand of G-d instead of weathering the storm by themselves. Miracles do not build up our "spiritual" immune system, and Moshe was actually blaming G-d, so to speak, for their problems. "לָמָה ה' יֶחֱרֶה אַפְּךָ בְּעַמֶּךָ אֲשֶׁר הוֹצֵאתָ מֵאֶרֶץ מִצְרַיִם בְּכֹחַ גָּדוֹל וּבְיָד חֲזָקָה"—maybe if You hadn't take them out so miraculously, their spiritual immune system would have been stronger!

—— TAKEAWAY MESSAGES ——

Where in the Torah is the source of this concept: לְפוּם צַעֲרָא אַגְרָא?
Perhaps it is the entreaty of Moshe to G-d trying to defend B'nei Yisrael
after the Golden Calf. Instead of highlighting their lack of *hakaras hatov*
to G-d who took them out with a mighty hand, the words "בְּכֹחַ גָּדוֹל וּבְיָד
חֲזָקָה" may have actually been reminding G-d why B'nei Yisrael were so
spiritually defunct. They were never challenged!

"What doesn't kill you makes you stronger." Moshe's entreaty to G-d
that saved B'nei Yisrael may be the source of לְפוּם צַעֲרָא אַגְרָא.

"A LAND FLOWING WITH MILK AND HONEY"—GOOD OR BAD THING?

רַבִּי מֵאִיר אוֹמֵר: הֱוֵי מְמַעֵט בְּעֵסֶק וַעֲסֹק בַּתּוֹרָה...וְאִם בָּטַלְתָּ מִן הַתּוֹרָה יֶשׁ לְךָ בְּטֵלִים הַרְבֵּה כְּנֶגְדָּךְ. וְאִם עָמַלְתָּ בַּתּוֹרָה יֶשׁ לוֹ שָׂכָר הַרְבֵּה לִתֶּן לְךָ.

Rabbi Meir says: If you neglect the Torah, there will be many more causes for neglect before you; if you toil much in Torah, there is much reward to give to you. (Avos 4:10)

QUESTIONS
---

1. If we neglect the Torah, we end up punished with "having many more causes for neglect before you." What does this mean?

2. In our *parashah*, in the immediate aftermath of the sin of the Golden Calf, G-d is very upset and scolds B'nei Yisrael that He won't personally accompany them, but that they will go to a "אֶרֶץ זָבַת חָלָב וּדְבָשׁ—A land flowing with milk and honey." This positive-sounding description of Israel seems very out of place here when Hashem is obviously very mad at B'nei Yisrael! To strengthen this question, B'nei Yisrael actually confirms that going to אֶרֶץ זָבַת חָלָב וּדְבָשׁ is seemingly bad in the very next *pasuk*: "וַיִּשְׁמַע הָעָם אֶת הַדָּבָר הָרָע הַזֶּה—And when the people heard these evil tidings..." There is no Chazal that depicts the "land flowing with

milk and honey" as a bad thing, and yet it does seem misplaced that such a blessing would be couched in Hashem's rebuke of the Jewish nation!

ANSWERS

The Gemara in *Kesuvos* (112a) explains that the milk in the verse here is from goats, and the honey is from dates (not bees). So in order to be in a situation of "flowing with milk and honey," B'nei Yisrael would have to arduously cultivate and keep the land so that they could support goats and grow date trees. When B'nei Yisrael fear G-d, and work for the blessings of the land within the holy religious context, it is not just work but a spiritual endeavor as well. When work is dissociated with G-dliness, and people don't see any spirituality behind their endeavors, then such irreverent people may view having to work for the blessings as simply work. They may then erroneously view working for amazing *berachos* such as "a land flowing with milk and honey" as a bad thing. This may be the lesson: "וְאִם בָּטַלְתָּ מִן הַתּוֹרָה יֶשׁ לְךָ בְטֵלִים הַרְבֵּה כְנֶגְדָּךְ"—If you neglect the Torah, there will be many more causes for neglect before you." If you don't see the G-dliness and spirituality in your work because you neglect the Torah (וְאִם בָּטַלְתָּ מִן הַתּוֹרָה), then work just becomes work, devoid of spiritual meaning and potential *berachah*. "הֱוֵי מְמַעֵט בְּעֵסֶק, וַעֲסֹק בַּתּוֹרָה" could be understood as "lessen the [emphasis on] work [for work's sake alone] (הֱוֵי מְמַעֵט בְּעֵסֶק) [and realize your work is part of the Torah (וַעֲסֹק בַּתּוֹרָה)]."

TAKEAWAY MESSAGES

G-d giving us a "land flowing with milk and honey" is certainly a *berachah*, but if we fail to see the G-dliness in the work when we toil for the land, we may view such work negatively: וַיִּשְׁמַע הָעָם אֶת הַדָּבָר הָרָע הַזֶּה. By minimizing our work, in a sense, and realizing that there is a holy spiritual aspect attached to the labor, we can be spared this faulty viewpoint.

Is a "land flowing with milk and honey" a blessing or a curse? In order to recognize the work needed to make the land flow with milk and honey as the blessing it is, we need to stress that work and Torah are inseparable—"הֱוֵי מְמַעֵט בְּעֵסֶק, וַעֲסֹק בַּתּוֹרָה."

WHAT'S WORSE THAN JEALOUSY?
THE LESSON OF THE GOLDEN CALF

רַ־בִּי אֶלְעָזָר הַקַּפָּר אוֹמֵר: הַקִּנְאָה וְ־הַתַּאֲוָה
וְהַכָּבוֹד מוֹצִיאִין יּ֫אֶת הָאָדָם מִן הָעוֹלָם.

*Rabbi Elazar HaKapar says: Jealousy, lust, and honor remove
man from the world. (Avos 4:28)*

--------- QUESTIONS ---------

1. Are these three different elements or perhaps not?
2.

וַיִּקַּח אֶת הָעֵגֶל אֲשֶׁר עָשׂוּ וַיִּשְׂרֹף בָּאֵשׁ וַיִּטְחַן עַד אֲשֶׁר דָּק
וַיִּזֶר עַל פְּנֵי הַמַּיִם וַיַּשְׁקְ אֶת בְּנֵי יִשְׂרָאֵל.

*Then he took the calf they had made, burned it in
fire, ground it to fine powder, scattered [it] upon the
surface of the water, and gave [it to] the Children of
Israel to drink. (Shemos 32:20)*

What is the purpose of Moshe making B'nei Yisrael drink the
fine golden powder remnants of the Golden Calf? The image
immediately conjured up is the *sotah* woman. In fact, *Rashi*
says: "He intended to test them like women suspected of
adultery." To perhaps mysteriously further this connection,
just a few *pesukim* later, it says: "וַיַּרְא מֹשֶׁה אֶת הָעָם כִּי פָרֻעַ הוּא כִּי פְרָעֹה
אַהֲרֹן לְשִׁמְצָה בְּקָמֵיהֶם—And Moshe saw the people that they were

246

exposed, for Aharon had exposed them to be disgraced before their adversaries." *Rashi* again seems troubled by this unusual word and explains that פָּרֻעַ means "uncovered." Their shame and disgrace was revealed, as in "and he shall uncover (וּפָרַע) the woman's head" (*Bamidbar* 5:18). Again, this reference is to a *sotah* woman. The question is then what the purpose of connecting the waywardness of B'nei Yisrael by the Golden Calf with the episode of the *sotah*, suspected adulteress?

──────────── ANSWERS ────────────

A *sotah* is a woman suspected of adultery who undergoes the ordeal of bitter water. The wife would have to drink a specific potion administered by the Kohen. If she was guilty, then the potion would "make [her] belly to swell, and [her] thigh to fall away" (ibid., 5:22). If the woman was unharmed by the bitter water, the rules regard her as innocent of the accusation. But the Torah adds an interesting detail: "And if the woman is not defiled, but clean, then she shall be cleared, and shall conceive seed." The Gemara (*Sotah* 26a) derives from this *pasuk* that even if she was previously unable to conceive, she will now conceive and give birth to a male. But an obvious question arises: Why would the suspected adulteress wife ever want to have children with the husband who almost killed her? After all, he made her drink the bitter water as he suspected her of wrongdoing!

Perhaps an answer is that jealousy trumps apathy. When it says in *Avos*, "הַקִּנְאָה וְהַתַּאֲוָה וְהַכָּבוֹד מוֹצִיאִין אֶת הָאָדָם מִן הָעוֹלָם," one explanation may be: "What is jealousy? It is about lust (הַתַּאֲוָה) and about respect (וְהַכָּבוֹד)." There are essentially two ways jealousy manifests itself:

1. When a person lusts something that they cannot have
2. When a person feels disrespected

Either way, one is only jealous about something or someone that he cares about! In this manner, it is better to have feelings of jealousy toward a spouse than not to feel anything at all. If a man's wife was having an affair, and the man did not care, it truly shows that he has no feelings whatsoever for her. It may be that the outcome of the *sotah* event is actually paradoxically good for the accused lady, because she feels a renewed connection with her husband. The "jealous" husband cared enough to be jealous.

The connection of the *sotah* woman to the Golden Calf is certainly attributed to the fact that, like a suspected adulteress, B'nei Yisrael cheated with an idol. But we know that not all of B'nei Yisrael actually actively sinned, and so why would the remainder of B'nei Yisrael want to follow a G-d who nearly annihilated them "out of a jealous rage"? It may very well be that this act of jealousy by G-d actually furthered our connection to G-d. After all, G-d loved and cared about B'nei Yisrael enough to be jealous!

─────────── TAKEAWAY MESSAGES ───────────

There are at least two connections to the aftermath of the sin of the Golden Calf and the *sotah*, suspected adulterous wife. First, they drank a concoction like the lady drinks the potion. Second, the terminology of פָּרַע—uncovered is only used again by the *sotah*!

Jealousy manifests itself by lusting after something you cannot have (הַתַּאֲוָה) and/or about feeling disrespected (וְהַכָּבוֹד) (so הַקִּנְאָה וְהַתַּאֲוָה וְהַכָּבוֹד might therefore not be three disparate ideas). Either way, one is not jealous about something that he or she does not care about!

Just like a man is jealous of a suspected adulterous wife, G-d was "jealous" of His straying nation. Why would an exonerated lady who drank the bitter water want to resume a relationship with her husband? Why would the exonerated B'nei Yisrael want to follow a G-d who almost annihilated them? Because jealousy is better than apathy! Jealousy means you care enough to be jealous. G-d loved us, even after a chunk of the nation built a Golden Calf! What is worse than jealousy? Not caring enough to be jealous.

THE COPPER LESSON OF THE ALTAR
AND THE LAVER

הוּא הָיָה אוֹמֵר: אַל תְּהִי בָז לְכָל אָדָם,
וְאַל תְּהִי מַפְלִיג לְכָל דָּבָר, שֶׁאֵין לְךָ אָדָם
שֶׁאֵין לוֹ שָׁעָה וְאֵין לְךָ דָבָר שֶׁאֵין לוֹ מָקוֹם.

*Do not scorn any man, and **do not discount anything**, for
there is no man who has not his hour, and **no thing that has
not its place**. (Avos 4:3)*

מַפְלִיג is an unusual word to use in this sentence, but it really connotes
separation (i.e., דור הפלגה). The meaning is thus: Do not separate out or
"box" things in a corner, as even things deemed obsolete or inappropriate can become valuable elsewhere.

QUESTIONS

Where in our *parashah* do we learn this lesson?

ANSWERS

Perhaps a key *pasuk* that teaches this enormous lesson is:

אֶת מִזְבַּח הַנְּחֹשֶׁת וְאֶת מִכְבַּר הַנְּחֹשֶׁת אֲשֶׁר לוֹ אֶת בַּדָּיו וְאֶת כָּל כֵּלָיו
אֶת הַכִּיֹּר וְאֶת כַּנּוֹ.

The copper Altar, and its grating of copper, its staves, and all its vessels, the laver and its base. (Shemos 35:16)

We learn in this week's *parashah* that the Laver was built of copper from "בְּמַרְאֹת הַצֹּבְאֹת אֲשֶׁר צָבְאוּ"—from the mirrors of the women. Meanwhile, the Copper Altar was partially adorned by fire-pans of the evil Korach sympathizers, which they used to bring an incense-offering.

Let's analyze. *Rashi* explains that Moshe was hesitant to use the mirrors at first because they inherently represented the *yetzer hara*, lust and desire. But G-d explained that it was that very lust that ensured Jewish procreation and survival and so the mirrors "had their place" within the makeup of the Laver. Conversely, the Korach rebels' pans were inherently holy, but the intention was impure. G-d requested that those holy pans, although associated with evil-doers, remain holy and be an essential part of the Altar. To summarize, sometimes something inherently of dubious spirituality (e.g., the mirrors) can metamorphasize into something holy and great, while something inherently holy (e.g., the fire pans), if degraded by wrong intent or use, can nevertheless retain (or revert to) their holy potential.

It may not be a coincidence that both the Copper Altar and Laver are both made from copper (as opposed to gold and silver), because copper is essential to all living organisms as a trace dietary mineral; we need it to survive! An *element* inculcated in each of us is this lesson that everything and anything can be rehabilitated. This is an essential lesson of our survival.

—————————— TAKEAWAY MESSAGES ——————————

Don't be a מַפְלִיג and think that things are intractably useless, because even a narcissistically used mirror or an evil-doer's fire-pan can make it into the holiest of places! This copper lesson applies to inanimate objects but is an element that must be inculcated or "digested" as an essential lesson in all of us humans. The lesson of the Copper Altar and the Laver is that we must view everything as essential and mutable—don't box things in a corner: וְאַל תְּהִי מַפְלִיג לְכָל דָּבָר!

THE SIGNIFICANCE OF BETZALEL'S FULL TITLE

רַבָּן גַּמְלִיאֵל בְּנוֹ שֶׁל רַבִּי יְהוּדָה הַנָּשִׂיא אוֹמֵר:
וְכָל הָעֲמֵלִים עִם הַצִּבּוּר, יִהְיוּ עֲמֵלִים עִמָּהֶם
לְשֵׁם שָׁמַיִם שֶׁזְּכוּת **אֲבוֹתָם מְסַיַּעְתָּן וְצִדְקָתָם**
עוֹמֶדֶת לָעַד ...

Rabban Gamliel the son of Rabbi Yehudah HaNassi says:
Those who work for the community should do so for the sake
*of heaven; **for the merit of their ancestors shall aid them,***
and their righteousness shall endure forever. (Avos 2:2)

QUESTIONS

A common understanding is that if you exhibit volunteerism, you invoke *"zechus avos"*; the merit of your forefathers comes and gives you added communal benefit. For example, when Alby Galbut selflessly builds the sukkah for the shul every year, the *zechus avos* is activated and the shul and community further benefits from the link to holy ancestral good deeds. But what is meant by "וְצִדְקָתָם עוֹמֶדֶת לָעַד—And *their* righteousness shall endure forever"? Whose righteousness are we referring to?

251

─────────────── ANSWERS ───────────────

A possible answer could come from our *parashah*. When Hashem needs a skillful craftsman to help build the *Mishkan*, the *pasuk* states:

וַיֹּאמֶר מֹשֶׁה אֶל בְּנֵי יִשְׂרָאֵל רְאוּ קָרָא ה' בְּשֵׁם **בְּצַלְאֵל בֶּן אוּרִי בֶן חוּר** לְמַטֵּה יְהוּדָה.

*And Moshe said to the Children of Israel: "See, Hashem has called by name **Betzalel the son of Uri, the son of Chur**, of the tribe of Yehudah." (Shemos 35:30)*

Why do we see such a lengthy lineage description by Betzalel? The standard answer is that it is simply highlighting Betzalel's great lineage: Chur was the son of Miriam, and by recounting back to Chur, we know a little more of Betzalel's holy ancestry. Perhaps, though, there is another answer...

In *Berachos* (7a), it says, "צדיק בן צדיק? צדיק וטוב לו—Who is a righteous person (who has good things happen to him)? A righteous child of one who is righteous." The simple understanding of this Gemara is that if you see a righteous person having good fortune, it is because he is not only righteous, but because his ancestors were righteous as well. But when read homiletically, another nice idea is borne out: "What is good for a righteous person? The fact that he is known as a *tzaddik* 'the son of a *tzaddik*.'" In other words, there is no greater merit than feeling that you have successfully inculcated the messages and teachings instilled in you by your mentors and parents. The וטוב לו, i.e., reward, is being known as "צדיק בן צדיק—a son of the righteous"!

Betzalel was the quintessential example of volunteerism; he committed his time and effort, dedicating his lifework לשם שמים to B'nei Yisrael and G-d. A reward of his was being known as a righteous man, the son of the righteous Uri and Chur.

The concept is actually just the opposite of how we normally think. It's not only that by doing good things, we get *zechus avos* that helps us further. But rather, by doing good deeds, we invoke positive memories and flashbacks of those who came before us, and thus "help them" be recalled for good so that their righteousness is enduring. We are doing our ancestors a favor, so to speak, by doing good.

Alternatively, when the Mishnah in *Avos* says: "שֶׁזְּכוּת אֲבוֹתָם מְסַיַּעְתָּן," it can mean that by doing great things, you can help merit your fathers by reminding people of *their* contributions so that their צִדְקָתָם עוֹמֶדֶת לָעַד. When Betzalel dedicated his time and effort to the *Mishkan*, the people seeing him were reminded of his father Uri and his grandfather Chur. He thus helps (מְסַיַּעְתָּן) connect the community back to his great forefathers so that their righteousness is never forgotten (צִדְקָתָם עוֹמֶדֶת לָעַד). When Alby Galbut builds the sukkah, he reminds us of his father Hyman and mom Bessie and all that they did for the Miami Beach community; in this way, the parents' righteousness continues to endure endlessly—שֶׁזְּכוּת אֲבוֹתָם מְסַיַּעְתָּן וְצִדְקָתָם עוֹמֶדֶת לָעַד.

─────── TAKEAWAY MESSAGES ───────

When you contribute in any way to your community, your reward is like that of Betzalel ben Uri ben Chur in that you are known as the son of your father and grandfather and can invoke their greatness yet again. A reward for your volunteerism is not only that you invoke *zechus avos*, but also that you help your ancestors, so to speak, by recalling their holiness (שֶׁזְּכוּת אֲבוֹתָם מְסַיַּעְתָּן). There is no greater reward than being known as the son of so-and-so (צדיק וטוב לו? צדיק בן צדיק) because in that way, your ancestors' righteousness endures: וְצִדְקָתָם עוֹמֶדֶת לָעַד

The significance of Betzalel's full title? By giving to one's community, one reminds the world of one's great ancestors.

IS EACH INDIVIDUAL REALLY JUDGED FOR INDIVIDUAL MERIT?

יְ—הוֹשֻׁעַ בֶּן פְּרַחְיָה אוֹמֵר: וֶהֱוֵי דָן אֶת כָּל הָאָדָם לְכַף זְכוּת.

Yehoshua ben Perachiah says: Judge every man to the side of merit. (Avos 1:6)

--- QUESTIONS ---

Why does it say "אֶת כָּל הָאָדָם" as opposed to just saying "אֶת הָאָדָם"? Or perhaps it would flow better to use the more commonly used word for man, which is אִיש, and say "את כל איש ואיש." Why specifically does it use the word הָאָדָם?

An answer to that question can be derived from analyzing a question from our *parashah*:

וְהַנְּשִׂאָם הֵבִיאוּ אֵת אַבְנֵי הַשֹּׁהַם וְאֵת אַבְנֵי הַמִּלֻּאִים לָאֵפוֹד וְלַחֹשֶׁן.

*And the **princes** brought the shoham stones and filling stones for the Ephod and for the Choshen. (Shemos 35:27)*

Rashi brings down from a Tanna, Rabbi Nasan, who explains why נְשִׂאָם here is spelled without the usual *yud* (it should be נְשִׂיאָם): "[Since the] princes said, 'Let the community donate what they will donate, and what they are missing [i.e., whatever is left to be donated] we will complete.' Since at first they were lazy [i.e., they did not immediately donate], a letter is missing from their name!"

If the princes in fact were greedy and did not donate, secretly hoping that all the funds would be obtained from the congregation, then I could understand why they would be "punished" by being termed וְּשִׂאָם without the *yud*. But here the princes are seemingly being gracious, and generously offered their funds to fill in the gap at the end. What is wrong with that?

—————— ANSWERS ——————

The well-known *pasuk* in *Bereishis* says: "וַיִּבְרָא אֱלֹקִים אֶת הָאָדָם בְּצַלְמוֹ בְּצֶלֶם אֱלֹקִים בָּרָא אֹתוֹ—G-d created man in His image, in the image of G-d He created [man]." What does it mean that man was created in G-d's image? Do we look like Him?

An answer is in analyzing the inherently plural term אֱלֹקִים, which literally mean "gods." Although of course G-d is one, He allows Himself to be portrayed in the plural sense to teach us the lesson that G-dliness is best attained when people work together. The verse thus means: "In the image of G-d's plurality, so to speak, [His desire for us to be and work with others] did He create the הָאָדָם." The term הָאָדָם, then, is reminiscent of the concept that one person relies on others to be truly complete/whole.

When the Tanna in *Avos* says that you should judge "אֶת כָּל הָאָדָם," the כָּל similarly may be to once again remind us of the Biblically professed goal of הָאָדָם, namely, to be united and work together. Simply put, although each and every individual may not necessarily do the right thing, there is a greater likelihood that when you put all these individuals together and they work together (כָּל הָאָדָם), they will succeed and you can actually count on them (דָּן לְכַף זְכוּת).

And so, in this novel reading, וֶהֱוֵי דָן אֶת כָּל הָאָדָם לְכַף זְכוּת may actually not be referring to an isolated individual person, but rather the person who collectively works with others! When a person is a כָּל הָאָדָם, then you must be דָּן לְכַף זְכוּת!

The נְשִׂיאָם made the mistake of not fully believing in the congregation's potential. They were not דָּן אֶת כָּל הָאָדָם לְכַף זְכוּת in the sense that they did not appreciate the potential of collectivity/plurality. Their generosity notwithstanding, their error was in not believing in the collective potential of humankind! It is no surprise that it was a *yud* specifically that was left off their name because it is a *yud* that makes up G-d's name. Measure for measure, their name was deficient of a part of G-d's name because they didn't appreciate the inherent G-dliness when individuals work together.

────────── TAKEAWAY MESSAGES ──────────

וֶהֱוֵי דָן אֶת כָּל הָאָדָם לְכַף זְכוּת may not simply mean that we should judge every individual favorably. Rather, it may hint that each person should strive to be part of a unit; when singular man (הָאָדָם) realizes he's one of a team (כָּל), this collectivity and plurality of individuals affords them the ability to achieve great heights and G-dliness. בְּצֶלֶם אֱלֹקִים בָּרָא אֹתוֹ. The נְשִׂיאִם lost the *yud* of G-d's name because they were not דָן אֶת כָּל הָאָדָם לְכַף זְכוּת—they did not appreciate the potential greatness of meager individuals working together as כָּל הָאָדָם.

Do we really judge each individual for merit? Yes, if they are כָּל הָאָדָם.

ARE THE ARK OF THE MISHKAN
AND THE ARK OF NOACH CONNECTED?

יְ—הוֹשֻׁעַ בֶּן פְּרַחְיָה אוֹמֵר: עֲשֵׂה לְךָ רַ—ב וּקְנֵה לְךָ חָבֵר—.

*Yehoshua ben Perachiah says: Make for yourself a master and
acquire for yourself a friend…(Avos 1:6)*

——— QUESTIONS ———

1. Does this mean, "Get yourself a rabbi"? If so, then why not just
   say, "Get yourself a rabbi," as opposed to "Make yourself a *rav*"?
2. And what is the connection to aquiring a friend?
3.

וַיְצַפֵּהוּ זָהָב טָהוֹר מִבַּיִת וּמִחוּץ.

*And he overlaid it [the Ark of the Tabernacle] with
pure gold **within and without**." (Shemos 37:2)*

Since the Ark of the *Mishkan* and Noach's Ark are both called
"arks," I desperately searched for a connection. I looked into
Rashi, Ramban, Seforno, Kli Yakar, the *Ohr Hachaim,* and then
the *Daas Zekenim* on the Torah before perusing the midrashim
on the *parashah.* Nobody made such a connection. I almost
gave up, figuring that the similarity existed only in English,
since they are both called an "ark," while in Hebrew, one is the
אֲרוֹן הַקּוֹדֶשׁ and one is called the תֵּיבָה. Just as I'd thrown in the

proverbial towel, however, I observed the *pasuk* above and it clinched an obvious connection: The Ark [of the *Mishkan*] was covered **within and without** by gold, while the Ark [of Noach] was also covered **within and without** but with pitch: "וְכָפַרְתָּ אֹתָהּ מִבַּיִת וּמִחוּץ בַּכֹּפֶר—And you shall pitch it **within and without** with pitch" (*Bereishis* 6:14). The obvious question, then, is what is the connection between the two —the Ark of Noach and the Ark of the *Mishkan*?

─────── ANSWERS ───────

Rashi explains that Noach had to caulk the ark with pitch both inside and outside because of the force of the water: "מפני חוזק המים זפתה מבית ומחוץ."

When one is alone in tumultuous waters riding for survival, the Torah informs us of the need to bolster or fortify our defenses from the inside-out! We must surround ourselves with trusty friends and a support system that can help us survive the rough waters out there. A תיבה parenthetically also means "word" (*Sefas Emes*), and singular words depend on other words to make a sentence. The idea is that this Ark of Noach is unstable and "needy," and survival depends on a captain who surrounds himself with a trusty crew. You can survive a flood if you caulk the pitch, "מִבַּיִת וּמִחוּץ," i.e., first from within by having good family and friends, and only then without, i.e., the outside world!

However, one may think that once one is finally comfortable, settled in a *Mishkan* and surrounded by a fortified *chatzer* and away from tumultuous waters, perhaps we no longer need those strong internal support systems. Then the Torah reminds us: "וַיְצַפֵּהוּ זָהָב טָהוֹר מִבַּיִת וּמִחוּץ—And he overlaid it [the Ark of the Tabernacle] with pure gold **within and without**." Unlike a תיבה, which is a flimsy "word," an ארון is a heavy-duty, independent chest that doesn't depend on others—at first glance. But even when things are "golden" and times are secure, although you may think that you don't need those internal support systems as much, the Torah reminds us not to forget the lesson of the Ark of Noach—that we must still fortify from inside to outside *a la* מִבַּיִת וּמִחוּץ. We are as dependent on our internal support system of מִבַּיִת וּמִחוּץ by the successful, secure situation represented by the stable Ark of the Tabernacle, as we were by the Ark of Noach as it rode the tumultuous waters.

"עֲשֵׂה לְךָ רַב"—How can you make yourself successful? "קְנֵה לְךָ חָבֵר"—Acquire yourself a friend. In order to successfully ride a storm, you really need that strong support system within. But even in good times, don't foolishly think you can do it alone.

─────────── TAKEAWAY MESSAGES ───────────

What is the connection between the Ark of Noach and the Ark of the *Mishkan*? מִבַּיִת וּמִחוּץ! In order to survive a storm (מֵי נֹחַ), you need to surround yourself with trusty folks who can help you weather it through. But even in times of a secure *Mishkan* (the ארון הקודש), showing the gold exterior that represents regal serenity, you also need to fortify your security by surrounding yourself within and without. How can you make yourself successful in hard times and in good times? "קְנֵה לְךָ חָבֵר—Aquire yourself a friend"!

The Ark of the *Mishkan* and the Ark of Noach are connected מִבַּיִת וּמִחוּץ.

Pekudei

THE MASTERS AT THE BASE WITH LITTLE FANFARE—THE LESSON OF THE *ADANIM*

הוּא הָיָה אוֹמֵר: אַל תְּהִי בָז לְכָל אָדָם וְאַל
תְּהִי מַפְלִיג לְכָל דָּבָר שֶׁאֵין לְךָ אָדָם שֶׁאֵין לוֹ
שָׁעָה וְאֵין לְךָ דָבָר שֶׁאֵין לוֹ מָקוֹם.

*He would also say: Do not scorn any man, and do not
disrespect anything. For there is no man who has not his
hour, and no thing that has not its **place**. (Avos 4:3)*

QUESTIONS

1. At first glance, the Tanna here is teaching us the lesson that we should not only respect people, but must also even be careful not to neglect objects. Why is this?
2. Also, מַפְלִיג is a very unusual word, which actually means "separate" more than "disparage"?
3. Finally, why does the Mishnah state that things have their "places," as opposed to "roles" or "importance"?

ANSWERS

A pivotal idea from our *parashah* will help answer this.
The *pasuk* says:

וַיְהִי **מְאַת** כִּכַּר הַכֶּסֶף לָצֶקֶת אֵת אַדְנֵי הַקֹּדֶשׁ וְאֵת אַדְנֵי הַפָּרֹכֶת **מְאַת** אֲדָנִים **לִמְאַת** הַכִּכָּר כִּכָּר לָאָדֶן.

*And the **hundred** talents of silver were for casting the sockets
of the sanctuary, and the sockets of the veil: a **hundred**
sockets for the **hundred** talents, a talent for a socket.*
(Shemos 38:27)

Rabbi Aharon Greenberg relates a *Chiddushei HaRim* that the hundred sockets at the base of the *Mishkan* are similar to the hundred *berachos* a person is obligated to say every day. Just as the sockets are the base of the *Mishkan*, the *berachos* are the base of our holiness. The socket is called an אֶדֶן like the *lashon* of אָדוֹן—master, and as the sockets fortify the *Mishkan*, the *berachos* attest to the אַדְנוּת—mastery of Hashem.

But still, is there an even deeper message inherent in this *Chiddushei HaRim*? What is the essence of one hundred *berachos*? How do they attest to the mastery of G-d in the same way as the אֲדָנִים do?

The answer is that when you are making a hundred *berachos* a day, you are most likely making a *berachah* when you are using the bathroom, eating fruit, smelling spices, wearing a new garment, etc. If you are making so many *berachos*, you are instilling within yourself an appreciation of every little gift G-d has given you—from your bowels to the new garment you put on to cover your bowels! Respecting every fine detail as a gift from G-d is precisely why the *measly* sockets of the *Mishkan* are called אֲדָנִים—masters! Sometimes the most basic elements are indispensable to our survival and are thus our masters, so to speak.

Back to the Mishnah in *Avos*: מַפְלִיג is similar to the word in דּוֹר הַפְלָגָה, and actually means "to separate." When the Tanna uses the word מַפְלִיג, he is possibly saying: "Don't think you are **separate** from כָּל דָּבָר—every little thing." Rather, you are dependent on every little thing. Why? "אֵין לְךָ דָּבָר שֶׁאֵין לוֹ מָקוֹם" can mean not only "that every little thing has its place," but also that there is no thing that doesn't have מָקוֹם, which is a known euphemism of G-d. Every little object has a G-dly purpose and design. We should not think that we can independently survive without the small nuances around us because even the finest details have מָקוֹם—G-dliness!

———————— TAKEAWAY MESSAGES ————————

The *Chiddushei HaRim* says that the hundred אֲדָנִים—sockets at the base of the *Mishkan* remind us of the hundred *berachos* a person is obligated to say every day. Just as the sockets are the base of the *Mishkan*, the *berachos* are the base, i.e., foundation of our holiness. The lowest-level sockets are perhaps called אֲדָנִים—masters because they teach us that we cannot live without even the smallest and seemingly insignificant sockets. We can't become מַפְלִיג—separated from every little thing because every little thing has מָקוֹם—(a euphemism for) G-d within it! Masterful leson from the indispensable "masters" at the base—the אֲדָנִים.

WHAT'S THE CONNECTION BETWEEN CHARITY, A *BEKA*, AND A SKULL?

אַף הוּא רָאָה גֻלְגֹּלֶת אַחַת שֶׁצָּפָה עַל
פְּנֵי הַמַּיִם. אָמַר לָהּ, עַל דַּאֲטֵפְתְּ, אַטְפוּךְ.
וְסוֹף מְטִיפַיִךְ יְטוּפוּן.

*He also saw a **skull** floating upon the water. He said to it:
Because you drowned others, you were drowned; and those
who drowned you, will themselves be drowned. (Avos 2:6)*

QUESTIONS

The message of this cryptic ethic is that what goes around, comes around. There is a circle of life, a connectivity of events, cause and effect, which inevitability have rhyme and reason, despite not being clearly understood or foreshadowed. There could have been a million ways to show this message; why did Hillel choose a גֻלְגֹּלֶת—skull to portray this? The answer may be from our *parashah*:

בֶּקַע לַגֻּלְגֹּלֶת מַחֲצִית הַשֶּׁקֶל.

A beka a head, that is, half a shekel. (Shemos 38:26)

Rashi says that a בֶּקַע is the name given for a half a shekel, and the *pasuk* tells us that 603,550 adults from twenty years and older brought these coins that funded the *Mishkan*.

263

We know the word גֻּלְגֹּלֶת means skull. Isn't it unusual to use such a word to relay the head count? Why is that same word used to teach us the lesson of "cause and effect" in the ethic above by Hillel? Why specifically did G-d choose the בֶּקַע as the name of the coin; is there perhaps a hidden message? Why not say חֲצִי הַשֶּׁקֶל, as opposed to the more unusual wording of מַחֲצִית הַשֶּׁקֶל; it sounds as if the shekel is actively doing something?

─────────── ANSWERS ───────────

There is a famous story (*Shabbos* 156b) about Rabbi Akiva who knew from astrologists that his daughter would be killed by a snake on her wedding day. He was distressed but nevertheless attended the wedding. After the wedding ceremony, the daughter placed a needle from her dress through the opening of her wall and unknowingly pierced a snake in the eye. When she discovered the dead snake the next morning, Rabbi Akiva inquired about what she may have done to grant her this great fortune. She then recalled that a poor man had come to the banquet hall during the preparations, and since everyone was preoccupied, she herself gave the man one of her wedding gifts. To that Rabbi Akiva exclaimed: "צדקה תציל ממות—Charity saves from death!"

A point of this story is that there is a cycle of events that is really supposed to happen naturally, but charity enables us to alter the chain of events. The cycle can be broken.

The Chiddushei HaRim beautifully points out that the gematria of שקל (330) is the same as נפש (330), which again highlights the inherent connection between charity and life. This may be why the word מַחֲצִית is used instead of חֲצִי—to highlight a more proactive, action type of word. It almost sounds as if the shekel is being actively halved, as opposed to just stating a half a shekel. The life of a person is directly acted upon by the action of a giver! Ozer Alport similarly points out that the word מַחֲצִית has a צ in the middle that represents tzedakah; it is close to the inner letters ח and י, which spells חי (life!), and is distanced from the outer letters of מ and ת, which spell מת (death)! If you give tzedakah, you bring life closer and you can stave away death!

What about the word בֶּקַע, which is a half-shekel coin? In Hebrew, the word also means "split" (i.e., וַיְבַקַּע עֲצֵי עֹלָה). A גֻּלְגֹּלֶת, which means "skull," has within it the word גַּלְגַּל, which is a "wheel" or "cycle." Homiletically, בֶּקַע לַגֻּלְגֹּלֶת—the way to break or split the cycle (of natural events), is by bringing the מַחֲצִית הַשֶּׁקֶל; by bringing tzedakah, we can change the natural course of events. When Hillel saw the גוּלְגֹּלֶת floating in the river, he undoubtedly was contemplating how G-d weaves a neatly fitting cycle/wheel of life, but he was simultaneously conjuring up this *pasuk* of בֶּקַע לַגֻּלְגֹּלֶת to remind us of the one thing that can defy nature and break this cycle/wheel for the good: tzedakah!

─────── TAKEAWAY MESSAGES ───────

בֶּקַע לַגֻּלְגֹּלֶת מַחֲצִית הַשֶּׁקֶל teaches us how powerful tzedakah is: It can break a natural cycle (בֶּקַע לַגֻּלְגֹּלֶת); it is an active, impactful action that is not passive (מַחֲצִית and not חֲצִי); it impacts our life and saves from death (*Chiddushei HaRim* on מַחֲצִית הַשֶּׁקֶל). Hillel hinted that the cycle of life can be broken by tzedakah (גֻּלְגֹּלֶת-גַּלְגַּל connection) and Rabbi Akiva showed us the example of how צדקה תציל ממות. The צ (representing tzedakah) of מַחֲצִית is closest to the letters ח and י of חי (life) and distances us from the outer letters (מַחֲצִית) of מ and ת, which spell מת (death)!

Charity, *beka*, and a skull? Charity "splits the circle" of life and is a game changer.

SEFER

Vayikra

Vayikra

PARASHAS VAYIKRA AND SECRETS—CAN YOU OR SHOULD YOU DIVULGE SECRETS?

הַהִלֵּל אוֹמֵר: וְאַל תֹּאמַר דָּבָר שֶׁאִי אֶפְשָׁר
לִשְׁמֹעַ שֶׁסּוֹפוֹ לְהִשָּׁמַע.

*Hillel says: And don't say something that's impossible to hear
because in the end it can be heard. (Avos 2:4)*

The classic interpretation is: "Do not say something that should not be heard," i.e., should not be made public, rationalizing that it will not get around and will stay a secret, "for it will inevitably be revealed and made public."

─── QUESTIONS ───

Is there another way to understand this cryptic statement of Hillel? Why is it so unusually worded (דָּבָר שֶׁאִי אֶפְשָׁר לִשְׁמֹעַ)?

─── ANSWERS ───

We learn two fundamental laws of *lashon hara* in this week's *parashah*: confidentiality and duty to warn/attest.

1. Confidentiality: "וַיִּקְרָא אֶל מֹשֶׁה וַיְדַבֵּר ה' אֵלָיו מֵאֹהֶל מוֹעֵד לֵאמֹר"—And Hashem called to Moshe and spoke to him **out of the Tent of Meeting, saying**..." The Gemara in *Yoma* (4b) essentially says

269

that since G-d spoke to Moshe in a private setting (the Tent of Meeting!), מֹשֶׁה was only allowed to tell B'nei Yisrael about what Hashem said because G-d told him to do so. From here, the *S'mag* counts this as a לֹא תַעֲשֶׂה: You can't spill the beans if someone tells you something in private! In other words, confidentiality is a bona fide לֹא תַעֲשֶׂה.

2. Duty to warn/attest: Later in our *parashah*: "וְנֶפֶשׁ כִּי תֶחֱטָא וְשָׁמְעָה קוֹל אָלָה וְהוּא עֵד אוֹ רָאָה אוֹ יָדָע אִם לוֹא יַגִּיד וְנָשָׂא עֲוֹנוֹ—And if any one sin, in that he hears the voice of adjuration, he being a witness, whether he has seen or known, **if he does not utter it, then he shall bear his iniquity**" (*Vayikra* 5:1). Simply put, if you know of some testimony and keep it to yourself, that is a sin. Halachists use this *pasuk* to teach an *exception to lashon hara*: If you know of something negative about someone or something and hold it back, despite possible damaging repercussions, this is a sin!

There you have it. In the beginning of the *parashah* (מֵאֹהֶל מוֹעֵד לֵאמֹר), we learn about confidentiality, but the Torah is relatively quick in pointing out the exception (אִם לוֹא יַגִּיד וְנָשָׂא עֲוֹנוֹ) when there might be something hurtful (or when you can proactively help).

The Tanna in *Avos*, by saying, "אַל תֹּאמַר דָּבָר שֶׁאִי אֶפְשָׁר לִשְׁמֹעַ שֶׁסוֹפוֹ לְהִשָּׁמַע," he may be talking all about *lashon hara*. It is cryptic, because it is meant to have a dual message—both when something is *lashon hara* (confidentiality), and when there is an exception.

1. Confidentiality: Don't say "something that is impossible to be heard" (i.e., something told to you in privacy) based on a justification that it will be made known in any case (שֶׁסוֹפוֹ לְהִשָּׁמַע)! That is the essence of confidentiality.

2. Duty to warn: In a situation in which it is clear that we can warn the person and help, we must not think that no one will heed our warning. דָּבָר שֶׁאִי אֶפְשָׁר לִשְׁמֹעַ is thus thinking that "they will not listen to me and my warning!" As it is stated in *Sefer Hamitzvos* (*lo taaseh* 297), you **do** have an obligation to warn and your warning may in fact be heeded (שֶׁסוֹפוֹ לְהִשָּׁמַע) and, indeed, lead to the saving of a life!

———————— TAKEAWAY MESSAGES ————————

Our *parashah* contains a strong theme of *lashon hara*, containing the source of confidentiality (מֵאֹהֶל מוֹעֵד לֵאמֹר), as well as its exception, i.e., the duty to warn (אִם לוֹא יַגִּיד וְנָשָׂא עֲוֹנוֹ).

"דָּבָר שֶׁאִי אֶפְשָׁר לִשְׁמֹעַ can refer "אַל תֹּאמַר דָּבָר שֶׁאִי אֶפְשָׁר לִשְׁמֹעַ שֶׁסּוֹפוֹ לְהִשָּׁמַע to secrets—"Don't say things that 'should not be heard,'" but it can also refer to the feared attitude of people hearing a necessary divulged secret; don't think it is a "דָּבָר שֶׁאִי אֶפְשָׁר לִשְׁמֹעַ," that it will be something that will in any case not be heard.

Parashas Vayikra teaches us not to divulge secrets (confidentiality) unless there may be harm to others (duty to warn), both learned from אַל תֹּאמַר דָּבָר שֶׁאִי אֶפְשָׁר לִשְׁמֹעַ.

REWARDED FOR GOING TO SHUL—
WITHOUT PRAYING A SINGLE WORD

הוֹלֵךְ וְאֵינוֹ עוֹשֶׂה, שְׂכַר הֲלִיכָה בְּיָדוֹ.

*He who goes and does not practice, the reward of his going is
in his hand. (Avos 5:14)*

QUESTIONS

How is it that a person gets reward even without doing anything at
shul or place of study?

ANSWERS

נֶפֶשׁ כִּי תֶחֱטָא וּמָעֲלָה מַעַל בַּה' וְכִחֵשׁ בַּעֲמִיתוֹ בְּפִקָּדוֹן אוֹ בִתְשׂוּמֶת יָד אוֹ בְגָזֵל אוֹ עָשַׁק אֶת עֲמִיתוֹ.

*If one will sin, and commit a **trespass against Hashem, and
deal falsely with his neighbor** in a matter of deposit, or of
pledge, or of robbery, or will have oppressed his neighbor."
(Vayikra 5:21)*

Why does G-d interject "and trespass against Hashem," and not just
simply state "if a man sins by dealing falsely with his friend"? What is
added by the addition of "trespass against Hashem"?

The answer is derived from understanding why Betzalel, the grandson of Chur, specifically was chosen to lead the assembling of the
Mishkan. It was Chur who understood the power of positive attitude/

272

philosophy/encouragement as he (along with Aharon) lifted up Moshe's hand during the war against the Amalekites. As long as the Jews saw Moshe's hands up, they were "uplifted" and were able to make key advances. Before assembling the *Mishkan*, G-d wanted someone who would perpetuate constant positive encouragement.

During the actual completion of the *Mishkan*, the *pasuk* states:

וַיָּקֶם מֹשֶׁה אֶת הַמִּשְׁכָּן וַיִּתֵּן אֶת אֲדָנָיו וַיָּשֶׂם אֶת קְרָשָׁיו וַיִּתֵּן אֶת בְּרִיחָיו וַיָּקֶם אֶת עַמּוּדָיו.

The Gemara states that even though the *Mishkan* was brought up and down, it records only that Moshe "put it up," again highlighting the concept of "positivity" during the very first interaction with the *Mishkan*! The concept of מעלין בקודש ואין מורידין (which literally refers to going up in holiness and not down, e.g., not writing a mezuzah out of a *Sefer Torah* parchment, etc.) actually derives from here! Homiletically, I would add: "מעלין בקודש"—if you accord high respect for the things that are *kodesh*, then "ואין מורידין"—you can't possibly fall!

And so perhaps one way to understand (similar to an approach by the *Ohr Hachaim*) the verse from *Vayikra* is that if one deals negatively with places of G-d, this can ultimately trickle down to how he deals with his neighbors. If one has a negative attitude toward G-d's places, he will inevitably have negative interactions with his fellow man. This is precisely why "וּמָעֲלָה מַעַל בַּה'" precedes "וְכִחֵשׁ בַּעֲמִיתוֹ"; they are connected indeed! A Chur-like positivity-engendering approach, personified by Moshe's first act with the *Mishkan* (וַיָּקֶם...וַיָּקֶם), directed to our holy shuls and schools, thus saves us from sinning with man!

In a similar vein, even without saying a single word of prayer in shul, I will be rewarded for going because I am demonstrating the prerequisite positive attitude directed to a house of G-d—שְׂכַר הֲלִיכָה בְּיָדוֹ!

──────── TAKEAWAY MESSAGES ────────

If we deal positively with our very shuls and schools (e.g., treat them with reverence, say nice things about them, engender good feelings, avoid speaking negatively regarding its leaders, etc.), we are actually saved from sinning with our fellow man. "וּמָעֲלָה מַעַל בַּה'" precedes

"וְכִחֵשׁ בַּעֲמִיתוֹ," perhaps to remind us that speaking negatively about our institutions leads to interpersonal issues as well. Homiletically, "מעלין בקודש," if you accord high respect for the things that are *kodesh*, then "אין מורידין," you can't possibly fall!

Reward is accorded for going to shul, even without praying a single word, because it is about engendering a positive outlook on your institutions—מעלין בקודש ואין מורידין.

DAVENING AND LEARNING ALL DAY VS. DOING GOOD DEEDS—WHAT'S BETTER?

הוּא הָיָה אוֹמֵר: עַל שְׁלשָׁה דְבָרִים הָעוֹלָם עוֹמֵד עַל הַתּוֹרָה וְעַל הָעֲבוֹדָה וְעַל גְּמִילוּת חֲסָדִים.

He [Shimon the Righteous] would say: On three things the world stands: on Torah, service, and good deeds. (Avos 1:2)

——— QUESTIONS ———

1. Bartenura explains, like others, that the world's existence depends on the fulfillment of these three facets. Others suggest that this has a more personal flavor: your existence is defined by how you observe the Torah, how you serve (עֲבוֹדָה used to connote sacrifices, but now it refers to prayer), and how/if you perform good deeds. The question is: Are Torah, *avodah*, and good deeds equivalent, or is one better than the other?

2. Why is the phrase "גְּמִילוּת חֲסָדִים" chosen for "good deeds"? Since the word גְּמִילוּת is recompense, it seems to imply that you are *causing* good deeds rather than actually *doing* them!

——— ANSWERS ———

אָדָם כִּי יַקְרִיב מִכֶּם קָרְבָּן לה' מִן הַבְּהֵמָה מִן הַבָּקָר וּמִן הַצֹּאן תַּקְרִיבוּ אֶת קָרְבַּנְכֶם.

> *Speak to B'nei Yisrael and say unto them: When any man*
> *brings a korban to Hashem, you should bring your offering of*
> *the cattle, herd, or flock. (Vayikra 1:2)*

Rabbi Aharon Greenberg brings down the *Shelah* on this *pasuk*, who asks why the *pasuk* seems to be talking about two *korbanos* rather than one *korban*, as it first says the singular (קָרְבָּן לה'), but then the plural קָרְבַּנְכֶם; after all, it is literally only talking about one idea.

The answer he posits is that the *pasuk* is meant to be split into two ideas:

1. "אָדָם כִּי יַקְרִיב מִכֶּם קָרְבָּן לה'"—When one gives of oneself (אָדָם כִּי יַקְרִיב מִכֶּם), that is a true way to get close to G-d (קָרְבָּן לה' literally means to be קרוב—close to G-d).

2. "מִן הַבְּהֵמָה מִן הַבָּקָר וּמִן הַצֹּאן תַּקְרִיבוּ אֶת קָרְבַּנְכֶם"—When you give sacrifices/prayers (מִן הַבְּהֵמָה מִן הַבָּקָר וּמִן הַצֹּאן), which is just a תמורה—substitute for yourself, that is also a sacrifice, but it is actually more for yourself (קָרְבַּנְכֶם), as opposed to a way of getting closer to G-d! In other words, when you donate yourself, whether it be with your money, time, or effort, that is more powerful than donating your sacrifices or prayer.

I would like to add to this idea of the *Shelah*: The word מִכֶּם in the verse can be a mnemonic for the following: מ=ממון (money), כ=כח (energy), and מ=מקום (space). When one gives up one's own personal money, energy (time and effort), plus personal space, that is what defines being beneficent/doing good deeds. We thus see that there are times in which doing good deeds actually supercedes תּוֹרָה and עֲבוֹדָה, which are in some way less of a self-sacrifice, lacking some aspects of מִכֶּם, which is the backbone of גְּמִילוּת חֲסָדִים. And so yes, perhaps גְּמִילוּת חֲסָדִים has a leg-up on the other two virtues.

Furthermore, the very word for good deeds is גְּמִילוּת חֲסָדִים, as opposed to מעשים טובים, to remind us that sacrificing your money, energy, and space has a ripple effect and stimulates others (גומל others) to do good as well. As opposed to Torah and *avodah*, which are generally static variables (although of course one person's learning can inspire others to learn as well, and watching one person take prayer (more) seriously can serve as a real-life example for the people around him), גְּמִילוּת חֲסָדִים in-herently contains a more powerful dynamic element. Such good deeds motivate others to be involved; this is a perfect example of the effectual גְּמִילוּת חֲסָדִים in גְּמִילוּת.

—————— TAKEAWAY MESSAGES ——————

When the Tanna in *Avos* says that the world stands עַל הַתּוֹרָה וְעַל הָעֲבוֹדָה וְעַל גְּמִילוּת חֲסָדִים, he may have been suggesting that the ultimate aspect is the גְּמִילוּת חֲסָדִים (saved the best for last!). When one donates himself (אָדָם כִּי יַקְרִיב מִכֶּם), rather than merely looking for some replacement (מִן הַבְּהֵמָה מִן הַבָּקָר וּמִן הַצֹּאן), that is the best approach—the קָרְבָּן לָה' and not merely קָרְבַּנְכֶם. In sacrificing of our מ=ממון (money), כ=כח (energy), and מ=מקום (space), we are fulfilling the מִכֶּם and are not only doing good things but are גומל others to do as well.

Davening and learning are good, but goods deeds are the real way of being קָרְבָּן לָה'.

Tzav

עֲשֵׂה לְךָ רַב...וֶהֱוֵי דָן אֶת כָּל־הָאָדָם
לְכַף זְכוּת.

*Make for yourself **a master**...and judge every man to the side
of merit. (Avos 1:6)*

QUESTIONS

1. Is there any connection between the first and last parts of this
    Mishnah, quoted above?
2. Is the purpose of assuming the best of another person to
    avoid shaming them, or is it actually to better ourselves in
    some way? For example, if I see someone desecrating Shabbos,
    should I assume that he is doing so only because he has some
    permissibility?

ANSWERS

The answer may be found in this week's *parashah*:

בִּמְקוֹם אֲשֶׁר תִּשָּׁחֵט הָעֹלָה תִּשָּׁחֵט הַחַטָּאת לִפְנֵי ה' קֹדֶשׁ
קָדָשִׁים הוּא.

The place where the burnt-offering is killed, the sin-offering shall be killed before Hashem; it is most holy. (Vayikra 6:25)

The Gemara in *Sotah* (32b) says that by having the *chatas*, sin-offering, brought in the same place as the less sin-related *olah*, elevation-offering, those bringing the sin-offerings are saved embarrassment! That is to say, when you see someone bringing an offering in the Courtyard north of the Altar, you should judge him favorably and assume it is for an *olah* and not for a sin *to avoid embarrassing the sinner!*

The *Yerushalmi* in *Yevamos* (8:3) says on this very same *pasuk*: "כדי שלא לפרסם את החוטאים—In order not to publicize the sinners," which seems to be reiterating the point from *Sotah* that we wish to not shame the sinners! But if the *Yerushalmi* is simply repeating the Gemara in *Sotah*, shouldn't it have said: "כדי שלא לבייש את החוטאים—In order not to embarrass the sinners"?

The *Yerushalmi* in *Yevamos* may purposely be teaching us a disparate point: We need to avoid pointing out the sinners because that would lead to an overall detraction of holiness. That is to say, when you see someone bringing an offering in the Courtyard north of the Altar, you should judge favorably and assume it is for an *olah* and not for a *chatas* to avoid highlighting the sin thus adulterating our minds! (Seeing people we otherwise respect having sinned may subconsciously denigrate them and also the sanctity of the thing they desecrate.)

The Maharal Diskin (end of volume 1) says: "חז"ל יעצונו לדון לכף זכות, למען לא ימצא לנו פתח בלבבינו לפרוץ גדר הבושה—The Sages advise us to judge meritoriously, so that we don't find in our hearts an opening to similarly desecrate!" (I thank Rabbi Neuhaus for teaching me this). In other words, if one thinks someone else is transgressing, then it becomes more acceptable to transgress too. But if one judges him positively and thinks that he is not acting inappropriately, then it remains unacceptable to transgress. Thus, the Torah tells us to judge others positively to preserve our own spirituality.

This may beautifully explain our Mishnah in *Avos*: "עֲשֵׂה לְךָ רַב...וֶהֱוֵי דָן אֶת כָּל הָאָדָם לְכַף זְכוּת." The conventional way to learn this is "Get yourself a Rav..." but perhaps, in a sense, you can make *yourself* a *rav* by understanding the twofold lesson of "וֶהֱוֵי דָן אֶת כָּל הָאָדָם לְכַף זְכוּת." First, you should avoid shaming others, and second, try to remain on a spiritual high (לא ימצא לנו פתח בלבבינו לפרוץ גדר הבושה).

──────── TAKEAWAY MESSAGES ────────

By allowing us to offer the *chatas* in the same place as the less sin-related *olah*, G-d teaches us that we should judge others favorably to avoid shaming them and not to publicize sinning, which would cheapen/adulterate our belief system in some way. This lesson is thus, in fact, "קֹדֶשׁ קָדָשִׁים" (as the *pasuk* ends), because it keeps our belief system unscathed! If you see someone desecrating Shabbos, first assume that there are extenuating circumstances that allow the person to do what they are doing.

Why judge others positively? So that we retain spirit ourselves.

POLITICAL LESSONS FROM TZAV?

נִתַּאי הָאַרְבֵּלִי אוֹמֵר: הַרְחֵק מִשָּׁכֵן רָ—ע וְאַל תִּתְחַבֵּר לָרָשָׁע וְאַל תִּתְיָאֵשׁ מִן הַפֻּרְעָנוּת.

Nitai the Arbeli says: Distance yourself from an evil neighbor, don't attach to an evildoer, and **do not despair from punishment**. *(Avos 1:7)*

─────────── QUESTIONS ───────────

What does "אַל תִּתְיָאֵשׁ מִן הַפֻּרְעָנוּת—Do not despair from punishment" mean after all? Perhaps the most accepted interpretation is that you should not befriend an evildoer, because the evildoer will eventually be punished, and being in his proximity, you may sustain collateral damage. One reason that this explanation is difficult is that the first two statements are active imperatives (הַרְחֵק מִשָּׁכֵן רַע וְאַל תִּתְחַבֵּר לָרָשָׁע), while this third idea sounds out of place as it is quite passive (not despairing does not seem as kinetic as actively distancing and avoiding evil).

─────────── ANSWERS ───────────

A different approach may be found in this week's *parashah*:

בִּמְקוֹם אֲשֶׁר תִּשָּׁחֵט הָעֹלָה תִּשָּׁחֵט הַחַטָּאת לִפְנֵי ה' קֹדֶשׁ קָדָשִׁים הִוא.

The place where the burnt-offering is killed shall the sin-
offering be killed before Hashem; it is most holy.
(Vayikra 6:25)

In the above piece, we asked a question regarding the different words used in the Yerushalmi and the Bavli regarding the reason why the *chatas* and *olah* are brought in the same place. Another possible answer is one that teaches a powerful lesson in discipline. Sometimes, too much disciplining can have untoward effects/consequences. We know from disciplining children and studying politics that even negative attention is sometimes desirable attention. A public shaming or punishing could spark the subjected person to paradoxically pursue more perverse behavior. Punishments can lead to a further emboldening and a consequent yearning for more mischief; the attention, albeit negative, is enjoyed and reinforces behavior. If Hashem boxed off all the sinners in one area of the Courtyard, He knew that this could potentially humiliate and thus embolden at least some of them to pursue the "dark side." By having the sinners and non-sinners together in the Courtyard, we wouldn't know who is there for what, and there is no worry about being מפרסם את החוטאים.

This is perhaps precisely what the Tanna in *Avos* meant by "וְאַל תִּתְיָאֵשׁ מִן הַפֻּרְעָנוּת." Like the first two imperatives/strategies aimed at helping one avoid "the dark side," this third imperative means: "Don't give up hope because you are punished!" Don't take punishments the wrong way, and do not use the punishments as an excuse to go more wayward!

─────────── TAKEAWAY MESSAGES ───────────

When Hashem commanded that both the *olah* and the *chatas* should be brought in the same spot in the Courtyard north of the Altar, Hashem was trying not to embarrass the sinners. This also teaches us a lesson in discipline: "כדי שלא לפרסם את החוטאים"—Don't make the sinners *infamous* and thus paradoxically encourage them to pursue the "dark side." When the Tanna in *Avos* says "אַל תִּתְיָאֵשׁ מִן הַפֻּרְעָנוּת," he is likewise saying, "Don't miss the point of punishments and hardships and interpret them as an excuse to be מתיאש, or give up hope!" The political lesson from *Parashas Tzav*: Negative attention is attention, and can lead toward waywardness.

HOW ON EARTH CAN KAREIS
BE A GOOD THING?

וְאַל יַבְטִיחֲךָ יִצְרְךָ שֶׁהַשְּׁאוֹל בֵּירת מָנוֹס לָךְ.

And don't think that your grave will be a way for you to escape! (Avos 4:22)

QUESTIONS

It is only natural to expect mention of an ultimate reward for being ethical and straight in *Pirkei Avos*, i.e., such as the afterlife. When you search for mention of "the next world" in *Avos*, you find this statement, which essentially implies, "Don't expect a next world just because you die!" But what is our Jewish attitude toward the next world, given the relative paucity of references in Tanach? Are we supposed to believe that by doing good we earn or create a reality in which we can have a next world, or should our attitude be that we de facto have an afterlife but if we mess it up here in this world, we can *lose* the next world?

And since G-d creates the world as a paradigm for our behavior, which is the better motivation: to earn something by performing well (incentive-motivation), or to lose something that you already have by underperforming (fear-of-loss motivation)? An answer may possibly be derived from our *parashah*.

———————— ● ANSWERS ● ————————

וְהַנֶּפֶשׁ אֲשֶׁר תֹּאכַל בָּשָׂר מִזֶּבַח הַשְּׁלָמִים אֲשֶׁר לַה' וְטֻמְאָתוֹ עָלָיו
וְנִכְרְתָה הַנֶּפֶשׁ הַהִוא מֵעַמֶּיהָ.

*But the soul that eats of the flesh of the sacrifice of peace-
offerings that pertain to Hashem, having his uncleanness
upon him, that soul shall be cut off from his people.
(Vayikra 7:20)*

What is *kareis*, "cutting off"? The *Ramban* in *Parashas Acharei Mos*
(*Vayikra* 18:29) delves deeply into different scenarios but makes the
following point:

ותדע ותשכיל כי הכריתות הנזכרות בנפש בטחון גדול בקיום
הנפשות אחרי המיתה ובמתן השכר בעולם הנשמות כי באמרו
יתברך ונכרתה הנפש ההיא מקרב עמה (במדבר טו ל) ונכרתה הנפש
ההיא מלפני (להלן כב ג) יורה כי הנפש החוטאת היא תכרת בעונה
ושאר הנפשות אשר לא חטאו תהיינה קיימות לפניו בזיו העליון.

*You should know that the fact that there is kareis is actually
a great assurance that the souls are maintained after death
and that there is reward in the world of souls from the fact
that Hashem says, "ונכרתה הנפש ההיא מקרב עמה," and "ונכרתה
הנפש ההיא מלפני," implies that [only] the sinner is "cut off"
because of their sin, but for those that did not sin, they go to
the uppermost echelon. (Bamidbar 15:30)*

It is fascinating that there is such a paucity of statements regarding
the afterlife in the Torah, and yet it is a central tenet of our faith. One
answer, as we can see from the *Ramban*'s approach, is that it is actually
simply part of the natural sequence of events. One lives, dies, and then
goes to the next world. Only if we mess up in this world are we "cut off"
from the natural sequence!

Nobel Prize–winning Israeli economist and psychologist Daniel
Kahneman says that we typically fear loss twice as much as we relish
success, and that is why it's so hard to take a risk. From a spiritual point

of view, being less of a risk-taker is a more consistent, reliable, and solid way to live your life. The *Rambam* says (*Hilchos Dei'os* 4:1): "צָרִיךְ לְהַרְחִיק אָדָם עַצְמוֹ מִדְּבָרִים הַמְאַבְּדִין אֶת הַגּוּף"—Risk-taking behavior may lead to altered sleep-wake cycles, different eating routines, and other life-schedule changes, which can be deleterious to one's health.

"כָּל יִשְׂרָאֵל יֵשׁ לָהֶם חֵלֶק לָעוֹלָם הַבָּא"—We are born with a portion in the next world. But we can lose it by underperforming. We are instructed in *Avos* to live life as if we can lose the gift that is ours (וְאַל יַבְטִיחֲךָ יִצְרְךָ שֶׁהַשְּׁאוֹל בֵּית מָנוֹס לָךְ), as opposed to creating a gift de novo by being good.

────────── TAKEAWAY MESSAGES ──────────

Pirkei Avos seemingly portrays a relatively negative approach when defining how we can achieve the afterlife. The Torah itself assures us of the next life by introducing the negative concept of *kareis* (וְנִכְרְתָה הַנֶּפֶשׁ). Why all the negative and what about a positive approach, and why a paucity of sources? Perhaps, as the *Ramban* points out, it is actually a "בִּטָּחוֹן גָּדוֹל—great solace," when we realize that the next world is actually a natural gift that we are born with. At the same time, it is our responsibility to ensure that we live life trying not to lose this great gift. Fear-of-loss motivation trumps incentive motivation and wires us to be less risk-taking and more on the straight and narrow. *Kareis* is actually as great an assurance as it is a great punishment, for it proves that we can be cut off from something beyond our lives. Fear of loss trumps incentive motivation and keeps us on the straight and narrow.

Shemini

אַרְבַּע מִדּוֹת בָּאָדָם: הָאוֹמֵר שֶׁלִּי שֶׁלִּי וְשֶׁלְּךָ
שֶׁלָּךְ זוֹ מִדָּה בֵּינוֹנִית. וְיֵשׁ אוֹמְרִים, זוֹ מִדַּת
סְדוֹם. שֶׁלִּי שֶׁלְּךָ וְשֶׁלְּךָ שֶׁלִּי, עַם הָאָרֶץ.
שֶׁלִּי שֶׁלְּךָ וְשֶׁלְּךָ שֶׁלָּךְ, חָסִיד שֶׁלִּי שֶׁלִּי
וְשֶׁלְּךָ שֶׁלִּי, רָשָׁע.

*There are four types of people: One who says, "What is mine
is mine, and what is yours is yours" is of median character;
others say that this is the character of a Sodomite. **One who
says, "What is mine is yours, and what is yours is mine"
is a boor.** One who says, "What is mine is yours, and what is
yours is yours" is a chassid (pious person). And one who says,
"What is mine is mine, and what is yours is mine" is wicked.*
(Avos 5:10)

QUESTIONS

1. What is so boorish about saying, "What is mine is yours and
   what is yours is mine"? Isn't that the epitome of חסד—kindness?

286

2. The *Ramban* teaches that since the creatures we are prohibited to eat exhibit negative character traits, consumption of them would infuse a person with these traits. Among the non-kosher birds listed in this week's *parashah* is the חֲסִידָה—stork, and the Gemara explains that a *chassidah* is so named because the stork performs acts of *chessed* for its friends. Rabbi Motti Shifman points out that in light of this, it is difficult to reconcile the *Ramban*'s teaching with the Talmud's explanation of the name *chassidah*, which is seemingly a positive attribute!

—————————— ANSWERS ——————————

Rabbi Shifman brings a beautiful lesson from Rabbi Yochanan Zweig, who explains that viewing all that we do for friends as acts of *chessed* is indeed a negative trait! The Talmud is teaching us that kind acts that a person performs for their friends should be done out of commitment and obligation to the relationship. Therefore, the *chassidah* is being defined by a negative trait, not a positive one!

Another answer may be derived by further analyzing the word *chessed*. It is worth noting that in *Parashas Kedoshim*, it says: "A man who takes his sister, the daughter of his father, or the daughter of his mother, and sees her nakedness, it is a *chessed* and they shall be cut off in the sight of the members of their people; he will have uncovered the nakedness of his sister, he shall bear his iniquity." Clearly, *chessed* here has a pejorative connotation, as it relates to a forbidden relationship. I saw an article on Aish.com that quotes the *Malbim* as saying that *chessed* is more appropriately understood as a character trait characterized by overflowing and lack of boundaries, which can manifest itself in a positive or a negative way.

I would like to add that perhaps the word *chessed* itself hints to this "boundary" idea: the ח is bounded on three sides, while the ס is fully "boundaried," i.e., round and completely insulated, while the ד is essentially open without boundaries at all. Although it clearly isn't good to be fully enclosed like ס and not open to others, the challenge of *chessed*, perhaps, is balancing having many boundaries (like the ח) and having too few (like the ד). In other words, openness and a "lack of boundaries" can certainly be warm, inviting, and even genuinely be kindness, but an extreme unfettered openness can manifest as incest! I believe the *chassidah* is not kosher to remind us that being too open is dangerous, and we must work on boundaries.

What is so boorish about saying, "What is mine is yours and what is yours is mine"? Isn't that the epitome of חסד—kindness? It is the epitome of *chessed*, but it may not be kindness in the sense that sometimes boundaries are needed to ensure things do not get out of control.

——————— TAKEAWAY MESSAGES ———————

Rabbi Shifman and Rabbi Zweig point out that the *chessed* demonstrated by the *chassidah* toward its friends may in fact be a negative quality belying its non-kosher status. Kind acts that a person performs for his friends should be done out of commitment and obligation to the relationship and not as acts of righteousness! Another possibility is that *chessed* means overflowing and a lack of boundaries, which could be positive (i.e., charity) or negative (i.e., incest). We need to balance having several boundaries (like the ח) with having too few (like the ר). The *chassidah* is not kosher to remind us that not all *chessed* is good; there need to be boundaries and limits to openness. The lesson of the stork: *Chessed* can be good or bad.

Tazria

RABBI YEHOSHUA AND LEPROSY

רַבִּי יְהוֹשֻׁעַ אוֹמֵר: עַיִן הָרָע, וְיֵצֶר הָרָע, וְשִׂנְאַת הַבְּרִיּוֹת, מוֹצִיאִין אֶת הָאָדָם מִן הָעוֹלָם.

Rabbi Yehoshua says: An evil eye, an evil urge, and hatred of beings drive a person out of this world. (Avos 2:11)

--- QUESTIONS ---

What does Rabbi Yehoshua mean by "drive a person from the world"? Are these evil traits punished by being "driven out of the world," or is the "driven out of the world" a natural consequence of these traits? Also, what is meant by עַיִן הָרָע וְיֵצֶר הָרָע וְשִׂנְאַת הַבְּרִיּוֹת?

An answer may be hidden in the cryptic story found in *Chullin* (60a): A Tanna is challenged by the daughter of Caesar to make G-d deliver her a spool. He prays that she become smitten with leprosy, and she was thus given a spool (as was customary for lepers in Rome). How does this answer the questions?

--- ANSWERS ---

According to Reish Lakish in the Gemara (*Arachin* 15b), "This shall be the law concerning the *metzora* (leper)" (*Vayikra* 14:2) means: "This shall be the law concerning *motzi shem ra* (one who defames)." Most of

289

us are familiar with the concept that a cause of Biblical leprosy is *lashon hara*. But the Gemara states that there were actually seven reasons that brought about *tzaraas*:

א"ר יוחנן על שבעה דברים נגעים באין: על לשון הרע ועל שפיכות דמים ועל שבועת שוא ועל גילוי עריות ועל גסות הרוח ועל הגזל ועל צרות העין.

Rabbi Yochanan said: Seven traits precipitate the rashes:
gossip, murder, false oaths, adultery, haughtiness, robbery,
and evil eye. (Ibid.)

These seven evil traits actually all nicely fall into three main categories of עַיִן הָרָע וְיֵצֶר הָרָע וְשִׂנְאַת הַבְּרִיּוֹת:

• Gossip, murder, robbery and false oaths can be manifestations of *sinas ha'brios* (i.e., if I dislike someone, I may help falsely accuse him, etc.).

• Adultery and haughtiness can be seen as manifestations of *yetzer hara* (i.e., thinking I am the best is going to lead me to trying to satisfy my lusts and desires selfishly).

• Finally, evil eye is *ayin hara*.

Being a leper would lead to being forced "out of this world" and thus out of society. Hence, Rabbi Yehoshua in *Avos* may be saying: "עַיִן הָרָע וְיֵצֶר הָרָע וְשִׂנְאַת הַבְּרִיּוֹת" are three categories of sin that may lead to "מוֹצִיאִין אֶת הָאָדָם מִן הָעוֹלָם"—people being ostracized as lepers. It is no coincidence that the Tanna who prayed for Caesar's daughter to get leprosy was none other than the same Rabbi Yehoshua (a leprosy expert he must have been!) who authored the Mishnah in *Avos* that teaches us about the very traits that bring on leprosy. It is worth noting that Rabbi Yehoshua's statement looks similar to Rabbi Elazar Hakapar's statement years later: "הַקִּנְאָה וְהַתַּאֲוָה וְהַכָּבוֹד, מוֹצִיאִין אֶת הָאָדָם מִן הָעוֹלָם"—Jealousy, lust, and honor bring a man out of this world" (*Avos* 4:21). Each of the characteristics echoes one another: עַיִן הָרָע is like יֵצֶר הָרָע, הַתַּאֲוָה as הַקִּנְאָה, and שִׂנְאַת הַבְּרִיּוֹת as a quest for הַכָּבוֹד.

But it may very well be that unlike Rabbi Yehoshua, Rabbi Elazar holds that only gossip, which is the ultimate example of jealousy, lust, and yearning for personal honor, really leads to leprosy.

Whatever the case may be, we can still ask why these sins were chosen. Is the subsequent leprosy actually a form of יִסּוּרִין שֶׁל אַהֲבָה? The answer is that by having an evil eye on others, being of a salacious appetite, and harboring jealousy, we all tend to *ostracize ourselves*, which is in fact punishing ourselves. G-d used to deliver leprosy for such sinning to provoke self-introspection so that people would realize that their behavior was self-destructing. The *makkah*, or punishment, was thus part of the *refuah*, the healing process. By not having the horrible, debilitating affliction of leprosy nowadays, people are more likely to ostracize themselves if their tendencies to עַיִן הָרָע וְיֵצֶר הָרָע וְשִׂנְאַת הַבְּרִיּוֹת are left unchecked!

─────────── TAKEAWAY MESSAGES ───────────

Evil traits such as *lashon hara* (and possibly six others, with עַיִן הָרָע וְיֵצֶר הָרָע וְשִׂנְאַת הַבְּרִיּוֹת as the broad categories) may lead us to *naturally ostracize ourselves*. Leprosy was a Biblical punishment, perhaps out of love, which provided us self-awareness before we totally went off the map. Rabbi Yehoshua shows us the three aspects that remove a person from this world. עַיִן הָרָע וְיֵצֶר הָרָע וְשִׂנְאַת הַבְּרִיּוֹת cause us to ostracize ourselves, and leprosy reminds us of this isolation.

THE BIBLE'S ANSWER ON HOW
TO DEAL WITH AN ANGRY PERSON

רַבִּי שִׁמְעוֹן בֶּן אֶלְעָזָר אוֹמֵר: אַל תְּרַצֶּה אֶת
חֲבֵרְךָ בִּשְׁעַת כַּעֲסוֹ וְאַל תְּנַחֲמֶנּוּ בְּשָׁעָה,
שֶׁמֵּתוֹ מֻטָּל לְפָנָיו וְאַל תִּשְׁאַל לוֹ בִּשְׁעַת נִדְרוֹ
וְאַל תִּשְׁתַּדֵּל לִרְאוֹתוֹ בִּשְׁעַת קַלְקָלָתוֹ.

*Rabbi Shimon the son of Elazar would say: Do not appease
your friend at the height of his anger; do not comfort him
while his dead still lies before him;* **do not ask about a vow
the moment one makes it**; *and do not endeavor to see him at
the time of his degradation. (Avos 4:18)*

--- QUESTIONS ---

Where in our *parashah* do we see a reference to this ethic of "Don't ask about a vow the moment one makes it"?

The answer may be found by analyzing the following from our *parashah*:

וְאִם נְקֵבָה תֵלֵד וְטָמְאָה שְׁבֻעַיִם כְּנִדָּתָהּ וְשִׁשִּׁים יוֹם וְשֵׁשֶׁת יָמִים תֵּשֵׁב
עַל דְּמֵי טָהֳרָה.

*But if she bears a female, then she shall be unclean two weeks,
as in her impurity. (Vayikra 12:5)*

Why is it that if a woman bears a child, male or female, she has to eventually bring a sin-offering? Also, why is a postpartum woman unclean for one week if she gives birth to a boy and two weeks if she gives birth to a girl?

—————————— ANSWERS ——————————

The Gemara in *Niddah* (31b) says:

> *Rabbi Shimon ben Yochai's students asked him: "Why does the Torah command a woman to bring a sin-offering after childbirth?" He answered them: "When she crouches to give birth [in great pain], she determinedly swears (קופצת ונשבעת) [aloud or silently] that she will never again have relations with her husband. [This is obviously a false oath], so therefore the Torah ordained that she should bring a sin-offering [to atone for it]"...[On the birth of a] male, everybody rejoices and she regrets her oath after one week, [but on the birth of a female], everybody is upset and it takes her two weeks to regret her oath. (Niddah 31b)*

Maybe one can say that since there is a *bris* for a boy, the lady's pain subsides quicker as she sees everyone rejoicing around her, while "everybody is upset" merely means that there is no *bris* celebration, and so her pain lingers for the normal two-week postpartum period! She isn't distracted with a *bris* when she has a female, and the normal postpartum pain lingers for the full two weeks. So to review, the lady in childbirth excitedly (קופצת) swears that she won't have another child, and so when she calms down later, she has to bring a sin-offering. It takes her a week to regret her oath by a male and two weeks by a female, as explained above.

You may wonder, though, why the Gemara doesn't posit that when the husband sees his wife excitedly and emotionally vowing never to have another child that he should intervene and prevent such a false oath! The answer is that the Gemara purposely doesn't suggest that because the husband's intervention could potentially exacerbate the situation! G-d doesn't give the man a chance to question her oath made in pain because He teaches us the lesson that we should not try to question someone making a *neder* out of pain (likely because it will just lead to the furthering of false oaths). And that is the quintessential example of "וְאַל תְּשָׁאַל לוֹ בִּשְׁעַת נִדְרוֹ" in *Pirkei Avos*. When someone is upset or in pain, it is best to avoid trying to cool them down during their time of heightened acute emotional or physical duress, which can have the opposite effect!

─────────── TAKEAWAY MESSAGES ───────────

"אַל תְּשָׁאַל לוֹ בִּשְׁעַת נִדְרוֹ" may mean that we shouldn't try to intervene when people swear out of anger because even well-intended intervention can backfire, causing the swearer to make even more false oaths. The Biblical source for "אַל תְּשָׁאַל לוֹ בִּשְׁעַת נִדְרוֹ" may be the fact that a man is not instructed to negate, refute, or intervene to stop his wife from making a *neder* never to have relations again after giving birth. G-d teaches us the lesson that we shouldn't bother intervening when someone is in so much pain; better off settling to bring one sin-offering later rather than risk many more offerings later if many more false oaths are provoked! When someone is mad, often it's best to let him cool down on his own.

Metzora

WAS LEPROSY PUNISHMENT OR THERAPY?

רַבִּי אֶלְעָזָר אִישׁ בַּרְתּוֹתָא אוֹמֵר: תֶּן לוֹ מִשֶׁלּוֹ
שֶׁאַתָּה וְשֶׁלְּךָ שֶׁלּוֹ. וְכֵן בְּדָוִד הוּא אוֹמֵר
כִּי מִמְּךָ הַכֹּל וּמִיָּדְךָ נָתַנּוּ לָךְ.

Rabbi Elazar of Bartosa would say: Give Him what is His,
for you, and whatever is yours, are His. As David says: "For
everything comes from You, and from Your own hand we give
to You" (Divrei Hayamim I 29:14). (Avos 3:7)

הוּא הָיָה אוֹמֵר: אִם אֵין אֲנִי לִי מִי לִי. וּכְשֶׁאֲנִי
לְעַצְמִי מָה אֲנִי. וְאִם לֹא עַכְשָׁיו, אֵימָתַי.

If I am not for myself, who will be for me? If I am for myself,
what am I? If not now, when? (Avos 1:14)

--- QUESTIONS ---

1. How are these ethics related to leprosy?
2.

כִּי תָבֹאוּ אֶל אֶרֶץ כְּנַעַן אֲשֶׁר אֲנִי נֹתֵן לָכֶם לַאֲחֻזָּה וְנָתַתִּי נֶגַע
צָרַעַת בְּבֵית אֶרֶץ אֲחֻזַּתְכֶם: וּבָא אֲשֶׁר לוֹ הַבַּיִת וְהִגִּיד לַכֹּהֵן
לֵאמֹר כְּנֶגַע נִרְאָה לִי בַּבָּיִת:

295

*When you come to the land of Canaan, which
I am giving you as a possession, and I place a
lesion of tzaraas upon a house in the land of your
possession...**and the one to whom the house belongs**
comes and tells the Kohen, saying, "Something **like a
lesion** has appeared to me in the house."*
(Vayikra 14:35)

What is meant by "and the one to whom the house belongs," as
opposed to just saying "if you see a house!"

3. Also, what is meant by "*like* a lesion," as opposed to "there is a
lesion in the house," which is much less ambiguous?

———————————— ANSWERS ————————————

This verse is a source for why *tzaraas* was a Divine punishment targeting the traits of selfish behavior (*Rambam*'s approach).

1. As for the terminology of "to whom the house belongs," the
Gemara in *Yoma* (11b) says:

אלא "לו" למה לי? מי שמייחד ביתו "לו" שאינו רוצה
להשאיל כליו ואומר שאין לו .הקב"ה מפרסמו.

*Rather, "lo, [belongs] to him," why is it there? He who
designates his house "lo" (only to himself) and doesn't
wish to let others borrow his utensils and says that he
doesn't have—G-d will expose him!*

Since the man looks at his possessions selfishly, as only his, he
is "treated" by having his whole house cleared out and having to
rely on the hospitality of others for sustenance and well-being
for that week.

2. As for "like a lesion": By saying "it only appears there is a lesion,"
the man shows his unwillingness to admit that he has a fault.
Sometimes we are so private, we are scared to reveal faults as
per our natural egotistical nature. The Torah may be telling us
that if we do so, we may end up even further ostracized in being
"treated" by having our deficiencies (i.e., the leprosy) overtly

on display for everyone to see. If we hide too many faults, they might soon be as evident as leprosy.

Two lessons of *tzaraas* are as *Avos* says:

1. תֶּן לוֹ מִשֶּׁלּוֹ—Give to G-d what is His, i.e., we can't be selfish as we don't really own anything ourselves.

2. וּכְשֶׁאֲנִי לְעַצְמִי, מָה אֲנִי—If I am selfish and keep my faults to myself, I will become nothing. In this way, this Mishnah can be read: "כְשֶׁאֲנִי לְעַצְמִי"—if I keep to myself my problems/deficiencies, "מָה אֲנִי"—then I will always wonder "what (מָה) could have been of me (אֲנִי)! How could I have been if I was just honest with my shortcomings?"

—————— TAKEAWAY MESSAGES ——————

The *Rambam* teaches that *tzaraas* was afflicted not only for *lashon hara* but also for selfishness. The Gemara in *Yoma* teaches that this may be derived from the use of the word "to him" in the verse that says, "to whom the house belongs." The lesson of selfishness and ego is also learned from "*like* a lesion," because by saying "it only appears there is a lesion," man may be showing his unwillingness to admit that he has a fault. The isolationist nature of *tzaraas* is a therapy in a sense as it gives the selfish egoist time to recognize that he in fact needs others to survive, and that if you don't honestly approach your deficiencies/ faults, eventually they will be plain to see (as in evident skin welts). Leprosy was both a punishment and a therapy!

LEPROSY AND SELF-BELIEF

הוּא הָיָה אוֹמֵר: אִם אֵין אֲנִי לִ־י מִי לִי. וּכְשֶׁאֲנִי לְעַצְמִי מָה אֲנִי. וְאָם לֹא עַכְשָׁיו אֵימָתָי.

If I am not for myself, who will be for me? If I am for myself,
what am I? If not now, when? (Avos 1:14)

QUESTIONS

How is the idea of the above ethic evident in this *parashah*?

ANSWERS

וּבָא אֲשֶׁר לוֹ הַבַּיִת וְהִגִּיד לַכֹּהֵן לֵאמֹר כְּנֶגַע נִרְאָה לִי בַּבָּיִת.

And the one to whom the house belongs comes and tells the
*Kohen, saying, "Something **like a lesion** has appeared to me*
in the house." (Vayikra 14:35)

We "observed" in the previous piece that the language of the verse,
"*like a* lesion," is strange. Why isn't the man more clear in his observation, e.g., "There is a lesion in the house"? The *Toras Nefesh* says that
the man says כְּנֶגַע so as not to lead the Kohen to calling it a lesion. If
he would say נֶגַע, he would be "leading" the Kohen to actually call it a
leprous lesion. With the more ambiguous term of כְּנֶגַע, he is allowing for
more impartiality.

Another way to analyze this may be the following: On the one hand,
"אִם אֵין אֲנִי לִי, מִי לִי"—you need to be your own advocate and to not want

298

others to perceive you as bad. By saying, "I think *there may be* a lesion," as opposed to stating decisively, "There is a lesion in my house," we are telling the Kohen of a possible detrimental fault in ourselves only in a roundabout fashion, *preserving our individual dignity* and allowing him to make an impartial decision.

On the other hand, "כְּשֶׁאֲנִי לְעַצְמִי, מָה אֲנִי" we are proactively volunteering this lesion to the Kohen, rather than ignoring it, because we must realize that if we ignore an evident flaw in ourselves, it will just grow and grow leading to an unmanageable situation! We must *preserve our chance to improve ourselves,* even if it makes us looks bad to others!

──────── TAKEAWAY MESSAGES ────────

"It *seems to me* as if there is a plague in the house" is said instead of "there *is* a lesion in my house" because on one hand, אִם אֵין אֲנִי לִי, מִי לִי—we have to be our best advocate and try to portray ourselves as good, upright, and innocent. At the same time, כְּשֶׁאֲנִי לְעַצְמִי, מָה אֲנִי—we must be proactive in showing the Kohen our deficiency so we can improve ourselves.

Leprosy and self-belief—although we must try to improve ourselves, we must simultaneously be our own best advocates.

TAHOR/TAMEI = GOOD/EVIL? INSIGHTS FROM THE WHOLLY LEPROUS

רְַהְמְהַלֵּךְ בַּדֶּרֶךְ וְשׁוֹנֶה וּמַפְסִיק מִמִּשְׁנָתוֹ
וְאוֹמֵר, מַה נָּאֶה אִילָן זֶה וּמַה נָּאֶה נִיר זֶה,
מַעֲלֶה עָלָיו הַכָּתוּב כְּאִלּוּ מִתְחַיֵּב בְּנַפְשׁוֹ.

*Rabbi Shimon says: One who is walking on a path and
learning and stops from his learning and says, "How beautiful
is this tree and how nice is the plowed field," then the Torah
considers him culpable with his life. (Avos 3:7)*

QUESTIONS

What did the man do that was so bad? He said there is a beautiful
tree. He even acknowledged the beauty of a plowed field! There are
many answers to this question, but the foremost is that he failed to see
G-d in the beauty of the field while he was learning. Is there another
deep message, though? This question will be answered by asking the
following question from our *parashah*:

וְרָאָה הַכֹּהֵן וְהִנֵּה כִסְּתָה הַצָּרַעַת אֶת כָּל בְּשָׂרוֹ וְטִהַר אֶת הַנֶּגַע כֻּלּוֹ
הָפַךְ לָבָן טָהוֹר הוּא.

*Then the priest shall look; and, behold, if the leprosy has
covered all his flesh, he shall pronounce him clean; it is all
turned white: he is clean. (Vayikra 13:13)*

300

Isn't purity a good thing? Does it make sense that something entirely leprous should be pure? Another equally compelling question is that the Torah says that the Kohen reviews the lesion, and if it turns clean of leprosy, it is impure; however, earlier in the *parashah* we see that if after a fourteen-day period, a leprous lesion does not spread at all, then he can be *tahor*, presumably even if a very large surface area of his skin is clearly spread over with white lesions! In essence, you can have one scenario that is fully leprous and is *tahor*, and another scenario that is nearly fully leprous and is *tahor* or *tamei*, depending on the trajectory of the lesion!

───────────── ANSWERS ─────────────

One famous approach is that the wholly leprous person represents one who is resistant to changing. A true *achzar*, stubborn person, is one who sees that he has developed lesions in response to *lashon hara* but fails to repent. There is no sense in calling him *tamei*, impure, because he will not seek to improve upon his *tamei* state in any case. But this approach seems to "reward" the intransigent one…

Another approach may be that *tumah* and *taharah* is not clearly an issue of wrong and right, bad and good. It is about wholeness and incompleteness. One who is *tahor* has nowhere else to go; he is in a completely pure state, whether it be good or bad. One who is impure, though, has wiggle room and potential to improve his situation.

A lesson of the leper may be that in order to considered "completely evil," you have to be 100 percent covered in leprosy. But conversely, if you are a 99.9 percent leper, and then fourteen days later you are a lesser, 99 percent leper (i.e., your lesions have improved albeit a small amount), the Torah considers you to be 100 percent pure and not a leper! The *mussar* is that one's purity and impurity is defined by the trajectory, and is not necessarily a static variable, unless you are 100 percent covered up!

When Rabbi Shimon thus said that one who interrupts his learning to appreciate the beauty of the tree or field forfeits his life, he may also perhaps be referencing the mistake of interrupting the trajectory. If you are walking "on the way," don't be static because then your impure state will remain. You must constantly focus on being on the *derech*, which is the key to being wholly good.

TAKEAWAY MESSAGES

Tahor and *tamei* are about the pure and the yet-to-be pure. One can be wholly bad and more easily wholly good, but it is wholly dependent on a holy trajectory.

Acharei Mos

AMERICAN JEWS OR JEWISH AMERICANS? THE LESSON OF "CHAI BAHEM"

בֶּן בַּג בַּג אוֹמֵר: הֲפֹךְ בָּה וַהֲפֹךְ בָּה דְּכֹלָּא בָּה. וּבָה תֶּחֱזֵי וְסִיב וּבְלֵה בָּה, מִנַּהּ לֹא תָזוּעַ שֶׁאֵין לְךָ מִדָּה טוֹבָה הֵימֶנָּה.

Ben Bag Bag says: Delve and delve into it; and in it you shall see, and be mindful of it, and never leave it, for there is no greater thing than it [Torah life]. (Avos 5:22)

--- QUESTIONS ---

What is meant by "וּבָה תֶּחֱזֵי—In it, you shall see"? Why is this added, since the rather wordy Mishnah already says "הֲפֹךְ בָּה וַהֲפֹךְ בָּה—Turn it over and over," which presumably already means that you should review Jewish/Torah concepts continuously. What then is added by וּבָה תֶּחֱזֵי?

The answer is derived from asking two more questions: one from this *parashah*, and the next from the Passover Seder.

In this *parashah*, it says, "וְחַי בָּהֶם—And you shall live in them" (*Vayikra* 18:5), the source in which we learn that, in general, we *must* transgress a Torah law if our survival depends on it (save the three cardinal sins and in cases of *chillul Hashem*). But this language of וְחַי בָּהֶם is rather unusual!

Lastly, when we teach the wise son at the Seder, we end by saying, "אֵין מַפְטִירִין אַחַר הַפֶּסַח אֲפִיקוֹמָן—Not to conclude after the Pesach afikomen." Why does the wisest of sons have to be reminded this?

─────────────── ANSWERS ───────────────

When the Torah says וָחַי בָּהֶם, the lesson is that we are supposed to be "walking Torahs" in the sense that people who see us can clearly identify us as G-d-fearing people of the book. We live "in them" in the sense that we are enveloped within the prism of Torah, rather than merely those who have absorbed the Torah's principles. Unfortunately, when a non-Jew hears the word "Jew" today, the first thing that may enter his mind is Bernie Madoff. The message of וָחַי בָּהֶם is to remind us that our actions will be scrutinized, and we should work at preserving the Torah way. The more we ensconce ourselves with Jewish values, and less with materialistic aspirations, the more we are likely to benefit from this Torah way.

The *Talmud Bavli* explains that the word "afikomen" derives from the Greek word for "dessert," the last thing eaten at a meal. The *Talmud Yerushalmi*, however, derives the word afikomen from *epikomion*, meaning "after-dinner revelry." It was the custom of Romans and Greeks to move from one party or banquet to another. My father, Dr. Larry Ciment, said that when it says, "אֵין מַפְטִירִין אַחַר הַפֶּסַח אֲפִיקוֹמָן," it is saying that after we Jews learn and fulfill a holy familial mitzvah such as the *korban Pesach*, we can't then revert to being a Greek afikomen! Once ensconced in the great Jewish mitzvah of the *korban Pesach*, we should revel in being in the Torah way of life, and not yearn to be goyish! And this is the point of the title above: We should proudly consider ourselves American Jews as opposed to Jewish Americans. The Jew (the faith) is the unchanging essence, the noun, while the nationality is just an adjective that could change over time and place. Although appreciative of our nationality, we take most pride in our Torah essence.

Likewise, when the Mishnah in *Avos* says וּבָהּ תֶּחֱזֵי, he is likewise imploring us to view ourselves as mini-Torahs. When you see us, then "תֶּחֱזֵי—you will see," i.e., you should be able to see the Torah shining through. "And in it," i.e., the Torah, followed by "you will see"—the Torah, so to speak, will be seen and shine through your actions!

────────────── TAKEAWAY MESSAGES ──────────────

A message of וְחַי בָּהֶם is that we should view ourselves as living within the Torah—the *bubble of the Bible*. We are live representations of the Torah and its values, so that when others see us, they should see a Torah way shine through (וּבָה תֶּחֱזֵי). אין מפטירין אחר הפסח אפיקומן—you won't feel the need to live a goyish lifestyle, such as "Greek afterparties (*afikomen*)" after you revel in the classic Jewish family mitzvah, the *korban Pesach*. We need to take pride in our Torah lifestyle. וּבָה תֶּחֱזֵי and וְחַי בָּהֶם and אין מפטירין אחר הפסח אפיקומן—Letting the Torah way shine through unabashedly, and we can call ourselves after all loud and clear…Americans Jews indeed!

IS OUR SOUL IN OUR BLOOD, OR IS THE BLOOD AN EXPRESSION OF OUR SOUL?

מִי שֶׁיֵּשׁ בְּיָדוֹ שְׁלֹשָׁה דְבָרִים הַלָּלוּ מִתַּלְמִידָיו
שֶׁל אַבְרָהָם אָבִינוּ. וּשְׁלֹשָׁה דְבָרִים אֲחֵרִים
מִתַּלְמִידָיו שֶׁל בִּלְעָם הָרָשָׁע. עַיִן טוֹבָה וְרוּחַ
נְמוּכָה וְנֶפֶשׁ שְׁפָלָה מִתַּלְמִידָיו שֶׁל אַבְרָהָם
אָבִינוּ. עַיִן רָעָה וְרוּחַ גְּבוֹהָה וְנֶפֶשׁ רְחָבָה
מִתַּלְמִידָיו שֶׁל בִּלְעָם הָרָשָׁע...

*Whoever possesses the following three traits is of the
disciples of our father Avraham; and whoever possesses the
opposite three traits is of the disciples of the wicked Bilaam.
The disciples of our father Avraham have a good eye, a
meek spirit, and a **humble soul**. The disciples of the wicked
Bilaam have an evil eye, a haughty spirit, and a **gross soul**.*
(Avos 5:19)

QUESTIONS

What is the difference between רוּחַ and נֶפֶשׁ after all? Spirit versus
soul? Bartenura basically classifies "spirit issues" with whether one is
humble or haughty and "soul issues" with temperance versus hedo-
nism/lust. But the specific wording above—"short spirit" by humility,
and "low soul" referring to temperance—needs to be explained.

—— ANSWERS ——

An answer may be derived from analyzing a key *pasuk* in our *parashah*:

כִּי נֶפֶשׁ הַבָּשָׂר בַּדָּם הִוא וַאֲנִי נְתַתִּיו לָכֶם עַל הַמִּזְבֵּחַ לְכַפֵּר עַל
נַפְשֹׁתֵיכֶם כִּי הַדָּם הוּא בַּנֶּפֶשׁ יְכַפֵּר.

*For the **life of the flesh is in the blood**; and I have given it to
you upon the Altar to make atonement for your souls; for it is
the blood that makes atonement by reason of the life.*
(Vayikra 17:11)

There aren't that many *pesukim* directly in the Torah that elucidate
what the crucial element of the life force is. Is it breath, as in, "וַיִּיצֶר ה'
אֱלֹקִים אֶת הָאָדָם עָפָר מִן הָאֲדָמָה וַיִּפַּח בְּאַפָּיו נִשְׁמַת חַיִּים"? Or perhaps it's the blood
(נֶפֶשׁ הַבָּשָׂר בַּדָּם הִוא) as hinted above? Even when a patient is declared
"brain-dead" (where the brain is *completely* not functioning, despite
adequate heartbeat and circulation), which by Florida law is legally
dead, it is quite difficult to say definitively that there is no life force
still in the given person, especially since circulation is still intact! Can
one be dead and yet still have his *nefesh* or *neshamah*? Although there
are several Mishnayos and Gemaras that seemingly hint to what may
determine the end of life (see *Ohalos* 1:6, *Yoma* 85a, *Chullin* 21a), there
is an ongoing debate with interestingly sparse Biblical narrative, save
the above.

So back to our Mishnah: When the Tanna says נֶפֶשׁ שְׁפָלָה and רוּחַ נְמוּכָה,
it is possible that he wasn't trying to get into a hefty discussion about
what life is. רוּחַ simply means "breath," and נֶפֶשׁ means "blood" (as defined in the Torah). Having short breath means that your chin will not
rise up in a haughty manner like that of a רוּחַ גְּבוֹהָה, a high-riding breath.
So on the one hand, your attitude toward others should not be demean-
ing. On the other hand, the way you project yourself to others should
be with a נֶפֶשׁ שְׁפָלָה. When your blood is pooled to one area, it is שְׁפָלָה,
low-down, as determined by gravity. Such is the person who exhibits
modesty—persistently, healthily abashed, fearing sin—he blushes
with pooled blood when he is embarrassed about his missteps! On the
other hand, having a נֶפֶשׁ רְחָבָה is having blood that is widely dispersed

(רְחָבָה is wide); the person is unabashed and unlikely to fear sinful repercussions. The Tanna is artistically saying then that the elements of being a good person revolve around: (1) treating others respectfully; and (2) walking with a sense of healthy abashment and avoiding sin/regression.

So our soul is indeed in our blood—נֶפֶשׁ הַבָּשָׂר בַּדָּם הוּא—either literally, that circulating red blood cells harbor each of our *neshamos*, or figuratively, that our soul is determined by how we "wear" our blood. Is it in a שְׁפָלָה—abashed/fearful manner, or is it as a רְחָבָה—unabashed/stubborn manner?

———————— TAKEAWAY MESSAGES ————————

Where does our soul reside? נֶפֶשׁ הַבָּשָׂר בַּדָּם הוּא may reveal the age-old secret: that the soul is in the blood. Having a נֶפֶשׁ שְׁפָלָה may mean that our blood (now that we know that נֶפֶשׁ = דָּם) is low down (שְׁפָלָה) or pools together when we are appropriately abashed; this is humility. When our blood is too dispersed (נֶפֶשׁ רְחָבָה), we are not acting abashed, and this may lead to haughty/gluttonous behavior. How we wear our blood is the ultimate expression of our individual souls.

Kedoshim

רַבִּי יוֹסֵי אוֹמֵר: יְהִי מָמוֹן חֲבֵרְךָ חָבִיב עָלֶיךָ
כְּשֶׁלָּךְ וְהַתְקֵן עַצְמְךָ לִלְמֹד תּוֹרָה, שֶׁאֵינָהּ
יְרֻשָּׁה לָךְ. וְכָל מַעֲשֶׂיךָ יִהְיוּ לְשֵׁם שָׁמָיִם.

Rabbi Yosi would say: **The property of your fellow should be**
as precious to you as your own. *Perfect yourself for the study*
of Torah, for it is not an inheritance to you. And all your deeds
should be for the sake of heaven. (Avos 2:12)

רַבִּי אֶלְעָזָר בֶּן שַׁמּוּעַ אוֹמֵר: יְהִי כְבוֹד תַּלְמִידְךָ
חָבִיב עָלֶיךָ כְּשֶׁלָּךְ וּכְבוֹד חֲבֵרְךָ כְּמוֹרָא רַבָּךְ
וּמוֹרָא רַבָּךְ כְּמוֹרָא שָׁמָיִם.

Rabbi Elazar ben Shamua said: The honor for your students
should be as dear to you as your own, **the honor for your**
friend as your teacher, *and for your teacher as the fear of*
G-d. (Avos 4:12)

QUESTIONS

In this week's *parashah*, the Torah commands us: "וְאָהַבְתָּ לְרֵעֲךָ כָּמוֹךָ—You shall love your fellow as yourself" (*Vayikra* 19:18). The implication is that you should love your friend like yourself, but not more than yourself! But there is an apparent contradiction between the two Mishnayos (above) from *Pirkei Avos*. The first Mishnah (יְהִי מָמוֹן חֲבֵרְךָ חָבִיב עָלֶיךָ כְּשֶׁלָּךְ) implies that we should afford our friends *the same honor* we afford ourselves, but the Mishnah in the fourth chapter (כְּבוֹד חֲבֵרְךָ כְּמוֹרָא רַבָּךְ) implies a *greater honor* afforded to our friends, such as that we would give to our esteemed rabbis! So in short, are we supposed to honor/respect/love our friends like ourselves or more?

ANSWERS

An answer perhaps reconciling these Mishnayos may be rooted in the following analysis of וְאָהַבְתָּ לְרֵעֲךָ כָּמוֹךָ. The *Maharsha* says that our *pasuk* is the source of Hillel's dictum: "דעלך סני לחברך לא תעביד—That which you abhor, do not do to your friends." This statement sounds like the ethical precept of nonmaleficence par excellence. But wouldn't you expect a more positive ring to our *pasuk*, which Rabbi Akiva proclaimed to be the כלל גדול בתורה—Great principle of the Torah? Should it not say, "Do great things for your friends!" and thus represent beneficence?

In fact, then, our Torah's core value is rooted in nonmaleficence rather than beneficence, which is somewhat unexpected and surprising. Or is it?

I'll explain this best using a medical analogy: When someone has too much acid in their body (say from an infection or the like), the body beautifully attempts to adjust by blowing off carbon dioxide (which is weak acid in the body) vigorously. But the body can never overcompensate: If you have too much acid, your lungs can get you back to less acid or maybe normal levels, but not to base levels! Our spirit is the same: we are created *acidic* in the sense that we have innate selfish tendencies. Notice that little children instinctively grab the things of others. As we grow older and wiser, we become much less acidic, for sure, but are not expected to overcompensate! Nonmaleficence is really

borne from realizing these innate selfish tendencies and trying to limit
how you exercise your right for self-aggrandizement. And so instead of
viewing וְאָהַבְתָּ לְרֵעֲךָ כָּמוֹךָ as an uplifting, sing-song, hunky-dory approach
to going above and beyond for your friends, it is actually probably more
of a limit on our inherent selfish tendencies. For instance, I am not
expected to earnestly desire that someone else has more hair than me,
but at the very least I am expected to want my friend to have the same
amount as me!

But the Torah really applies this nonmaleficent approach when it
comes to physical objects/things, and not to subjective elements of respect and honor. When it comes to respect and honor, the Torah utilizes
the less limited spectrum of beneficence! This is simply because "What
does it cost me to give all the respect in the world to someone else?"
We can naturally overcompensate when it comes to honor and respect,
which doesn't disobey our innate selfishness regarding tangible items!
The Mishnah in *Avos* that warns us to love your neighbor *as yourself*
is talking about money (i.e., tangible physical elements)—יְהִי מָמוֹן חֲבֵרְךָ
חָבִיב עָלֶיךָ כְּשֶׁלָּךְ. The other Mishnah in *Avos* that suggests you love your
neighbor *more than yourself* is talking about honor—כְּבוֹד חֲבֵרְךָ כְּמוֹרָא רַבָּךְ.

──────────── TAKEAWAY MESSAGES ────────────

The interpretation of וְאָהַבְתָּ לְרֵעֲךָ כָּמוֹךָ is purposely given a negative
nonmaleficent tone (דעלך סני לחברך לא תעביד) as opposed to a beneficent
tone to teach us the כלל גדול בתורה that G-d doesn't expect us to overcompensate. He doesn't expect us to want less of tangible items, like
money and things, than our friends. But He wants us to learn how to
want our friends to have at least as much as us. When it comes to the
less material matters, such as honor and respect, however, the sky is the
limit, and a beneficent approach is espoused!

וְאָהַבְתָּ לְרֵעֲךָ כָּמוֹךָ is a lesson of nonmaleficence—one isn't expected to
love one's friends more than oneself, save in the area of respect.

THE CONTRADICTION OF RABBI AKIVA'S TEACHING AND HIS STUDENTS

רַבִּי אֶלְעָזָר הַקַּפָּר אוֹמֵר, הַקִּנְאָה וְהַתַּאֲוָה
וְהַכָּבוֹד, מוֹצִיאִין אֶת הָאָדָם מִן הָעוֹלָם.

*Rabbi Elazar Hakapar says: Jealousy, lust, and **honor** bring a man out of this world. (Avos 4:21)*

How does this relate to our *parashah*?

 QUESTIONS

1. The Torah commands: "וְאָהַבְתָּ לְרֵעֲךָ כָּמוֹךָ—You shall love your fellow as yourself." (*Vayikra* 19:18). *Rashi* comments that Rabbi Akiva says: "This is a fundamental [all-inclusive] principle of the Torah" (*Toras Kohanim* 19:45). It always bothered me that the Gemara in *Yevamos* (62b) explains that Rabbi Akiva's very students died "מפני שלא נהגו כבוד זה לזה—because they didn't show respect to one another." (Hence the time of *sefirah* is nowadays marred by this tragedy that took place.) Did Rabbi Akiva fail to transmit his lesson?

2. Also, since this time period almost always coincides with the *parshiyos* of *Acharei Mos* and *Kedoshim*, is there a connection, specifically to the deaths of Aharon's sons who also purportedly should have "known better," being the sons of the holy Aharon himself?

312

—————————— ANSWERS ——————————

1. The first, simplest answer is that maybe Rabbi Akiva's statement of the importance of "loving your neighbor" was post facto; admittance borne out of the tragedy he saw unfolding.

2. Another answer is that the lesson of personal accountability is so abundantly clear by both the episode of Aharon and Rabbi Akiva: *Even* the sons of Aharon died for their sinning and *even* the students of Rabbi Akiva died despite their unbelievable potential and upbringing. (It is worth mentioning that Rabbi Ari Kahn brings down that in his famous *Igeres*, Rav Sherira Gaon apparently recounts that the students of Rabbi Akiva actually died of "religious persecution," and this time between Pesach and Shavuos is historically a time of blood libels, etc. This is yet another answer that suggests they didn't sin after all, but it doesn't jive well with the Gemara.)

3. A third answer perhaps can be derived from the deaths of Aharon's sons. There is an argument as to why they died. One fascinating opinion derives four sins they committed: "For drawing near," since they entered into the innermost precincts of the Sanctuary; "for offering," since they offered a sacrifice that they had not been commanded to offer; "for the strange fire," they brought in the ordinary flames; "And for not having taken counsel from each other," as it says, "Each of them his censer" (*Vayikra* 10:1), implying that they acted each on his own initiative, not taking counsel from one another (*Vayikra Rabbah* 20:8–10).
    If the sons had just consulted one another, they almost definitely would not have sinned, and so you can argue that sin #4 was their most egregious sin. They lacked כבוד—respect for one another in not consulting with each other. Perhaps the students of Rabbi Akiva also lacked כבוד for one another in the sense of not consulting with each other. This may be hinted by calling them twelve thousand *zugos*, as opposed to twelve thousand students. They didn't act as a team, even if they perhaps loved

each other. In this way, Rabbi Akiva's message of loving your neighbor was present, but alone was not enough. Loving your fellow is not complete when lacking כבוד for one another, as demonstrated by consulting and cavorting with each other! I do not think it is a coincidence that some say the students of Rabbi Akiva were ironically punished with diptheria (some say it was croup)—the hallmark of the disease being a pseudomembrane that blocks the airway—insomuch as they failed to "call" upon one another.

TAKEAWAY MESSAGES

How could the chief proponent for loving your neighbor be the *rebbi* of the students who died from "disrespecting" each other? One answer is that the lesson was post facto. The second answer is that we learn that especially if you have role models as great as Aharon and Rabbi Akiva, you are held accountable for your mistakes! A third answer is that just like the sins of Aharon's sons, which were rooted not in disgust of one another but a mere lack of consultation and desire to communicate, the students of Rabbi Akiva may have loved one another but did not care to consult and thus respect one another. In this way, כבוד indeed does bring one out of this world (*Avos* connection). Loving your neighbors is not enough; you need to consult with one another as well. That is the lesson learned from Rabbi Akiva!

Emor

COUNTING SEFIRAH AND THE TRANSITION FROM THE MATZAH OF PESACH TO THE BREAD OF SHAVUOS

רַבִּי אֶלְעָזָר בֶּן עֲזַרְיָה אוֹמֵר: אִם אֵין קֶמַח
אֵין תּוֹרָה. אִם אֵין תּוֹרָה אֵין קֶמַח.

Rabbi Elazar ben Azariah says…If there is no flour, there is no Torah; if there is no Torah, there is no flour. (Avos 3:21)

רַבִּי יוֹנָתָן אוֹמֵר: כָּל הַמְקַיֵּם אֶת הַתּוֹרָה מֵעוֹנִי
סוֹפוֹ לְקַיְּימָהּ מֵעוֹשֶׁר.

Rabbi Yonasan would say: Whoever fulfills the Torah in poverty, will ultimately fulfill it in wealth. (Avos 4:9)

--- QUESTIONS ---

1. What is the connection between אִם אֵין קֶמַח אֵין תּוֹרָה and our *parashah*?

2. The presumptive understanding of the first Mishnah above is that without food/sustenance, there can be no Torah; but if that is so, shouldn't the Mishnah read, "אִם אֵין אוֹכֵל אֵין תּוֹרָה—If there is no **food**, there is no Torah"? Why does it use the word "flour"?

315

In the second Mishnah, the presumptive understanding is that if one fulfills the Torah when they are impoverished, they will be rewarded with fulfilling the Torah as a wealthy person. But if that is so, shouldn't the Mishnah read: "כָּל הַמְקַיֵּם אֶת הַתּוֹרָה בְּעוֹנִי" ("in poverty"), and not מֵעוֹנִי ("from poverty")?

ANSWERS
---

1. Our *parashah* says: "וּסְפַרְתֶּם לָכֶם מִמָּחֳרַת הַשַּׁבָּת מִיּוֹם הֲבִיאֲכֶם אֶת עֹמֶר הַתְּנוּפָה—Count for yourselves, from the end of the Shabbos, from the day of bringing the *omer*-offering." We count forty-nine days from the day of bringing the barley *omer*-offering until the holiday of accepting the Torah (Shavuos).

2. Rabbi Aharon Greenberg explains that the *Maharal* connects the barley *omer* and Torah acceptance: "הָא בְּהָא תַּלְיָא—This and that depend on each other." In order to have Torah, you need the barley, which represents sustenance: "אִם אֵין קֶמַח אֵין תּוֹרָה. אִם אֵין תּוֹרָה אֵין קֶמַח."

3. As for why it says, "אִם אֵין קֶמַח אֵין תּוֹרָה," as opposed to "אִם אֵין אוֹכֵל אֵין תּוֹרָה," *sefiras ha'omer* is the time between Pesach and Shavuos: On the second day of Pesach, an *omer* (volume) of barley was offered in the Temple, signaling the allowance of the consumption of *chadash* (grains from the new harvest). We count until the fiftieth day, Shavuos, when two loaves made of wheat were offered in the Temple to signal the start of the wheat harvest. The barley flour (made from grinding roasted grains into flour), originating during the holiday of unleavened bread, represents *our realization that we are in an incomplete state* until we accept the Torah and are thus able to achieve the leavened bread, marking Shavuos. And so the *kemach* of the *omer* represents incompleteness.

Now we can better understand our Mishnayos above from *Avos*: If there is no sense of emptiness, there will be no success in achieving Torah observance. But it is also our very study of Torah that perpetuates the appreciation that we are always incomplete and can constantly improve! אִם אֵין קֶמַח אֵין תּוֹרָה—If there is no appreciation of our incompleteness, there will be no Torah achievement. אִם אֵין תּוֹרָה אֵין קֶמַח—If there is no Torah achievement, then we will not appreciate our incompleteness and thus will be unlikely to improve. The concept of *kemach* is not food then, **it is a state of mind!** We need to count the *omer* in order to transition from our unleavened potential (Pesach) to the holiday of the two baked loaves (Shavuos). We must understand that true Torah life is actually constantly being reminded that we are but an incomplete *kemach*, always in need of being leavened. And so the cycle perpetuates.

Rabbi Yonasan in the second Mishnah likewise states, "הַמְקַיֵּם אֶת הַתּוֹרָה מֵעוֹנִי," and not "בְּעוֹנִי," which again means "if you live a Torah life *from viewing yourself as a perpetual,* (מֵעוֹנִי) עוֹנִי poor unleavened state of *kemach*, then you will succeed." (The word בְּעוֹנִי would just mean "in a state of being poor," as opposed to "from being poor.")

─────── TAKEAWAY MESSAGES ───────

In order to reach our "Shavuos moment," leavened with success, we must be motivated by first *understanding our unleavened state.* By counting the *omer* for forty-nine days leading to Shavuos, we remind ourselves forty-nine times that in order to be leavened with success, we must understand our poor, unleavened *kemach* state (אִם אֵין קֶמַח אֵין תּוֹרָה). Ironically, the leavened state will arrive one day and remind us that in order to perpetuate the leavened success, we must view ourselves as needing more (אִם אֵין תּוֹרָה אֵין קֶמַח). Success isn't achieved by living a poor existence, but by viewing ourselves as incomplete (כָּל הַמְקַיֵּם אֶת הַתּוֹרָה מֵעוֹנִי סוֹפוֹ לְקַיְּימָהּ מֵעוֹשֶׁר, and not בְּעוֹנִי).

Counting *sefirah* and transitioning from matzah to bread—only by seeing ourselves as imperfect *kemach* can we become leavened, but only by living a Torah way of life can we perpetually see ourselves as imperfect, renewing the healthy cycle!

SPEAK A LITTLE OR DO A LOT?

שַׁמַּאי אוֹמֵר: עֲשֵׂה תוֹרָתְךָ קֶבַע. אֱמֹר מְעַט
וַעֲשֵׂה הַרְבֵּה, וֶהֱוֵי מְקַבֵּל אֶת כָּל הָאָדָם בְּסֵבֶר
פָּנִים יָפוֹת.

*Shammai would say: Make your Torah study a permanent
fixture of your life. Say little and do much. And receive every
man with a pleasant countenance. (Avos 1:15)*

רַבִּי יִשְׁמָעֵאל אוֹמֵר: וֶהֱוֵי מְקַבֵּל אֶת כָּל
הָאָדָם בְּשִׂמְחָה.

*Rabbi Yishmael says: And receive every man with happiness.
(Avos 3:12)*

QUESTIONS

Hillel the Elder's friendly adversary was Shammai, who was reputed
to be dour, quick-tempered, and impatient. Although admittedly, the
statement's literal interpretation is most likely the right way to understand Shammai's advice above, is there another way to learn it so that it
would be more consistent with his "strict"/insular personality?

---------------- ANSWERS ----------------

וַיִּקֹּב בֶּן הָאִשָּׁה הַיִּשְׂרְאֵלִית אֶת הַשֵּׁם וַיְקַלֵּל וַיָּבִיאוּ אֹתוֹ אֶל מֹשֶׁה וְשֵׁם אִמּוֹ שְׁלֹמִית בַּת דִּבְרִי לְמַטֵּה דָן.

And the son of the Israelite lady cursed Hashem; and they brought him to Moshe. And his mother's name was Shelomis, the daughter of Dibri, of the tribe of Dan. (Vayikra 24:11)

Shelomis, daughter of Dibri of the tribe of Dan, who had a relationship with an Egyptian man, is the only woman mentioned by name in *Vayikra*! She appears in the narrative about her son, a man who pronounces the name of G-d (שם המפורש) in blasphemy during a fight with another Israelite man. Her unnamed son is brought to Moshe and placed in custody until eventually stoned by the congregation.

As *Rashi* points out, one can read something ominous in Shelomis's name: "Shelomis, the daughter of Dibri," implies that she was loquacious; more effusive and outgoing than propriety would dictate. Jwa.org cites that the *Midrash Sechel Tov* relates that Shelomis initially was married to a Jew but would return the taskmaster's greeting; he became acquainted with her, and consequently demanded that she sin with him—a request to which she readily acquiesced (*Sekhel Tov* [ed. Buber], *Shemos* 2:11). The taskmaster knew that Shelomis's husband sensed this, and thus beat the husband. This taskmaster was the very Egyptian whom Moshe saw beating the Jew in *Shemos* 2:11 and whom he smote (since he reckoned that he deserved the death penalty). In an amazing ironic twist, a different midrash (*Tanchuma*; see *Rashi* to *Shemos* 2:14) relates that Moshe killed the Egyptian using the שם המפורש—The Ineffable Name (somehow the pronouncing of G-d's powerful name was miraculously channeled to slay the evil Egyptian).

So in summary, Shelomis set off this tragic sequence of events by essentially just being overly flirtatious! The Egyptian man took advantage of her and was struck by Moshe, who used the Ineffable Name to kill him, but not before leaving over a son who (perhaps out of despair from his life situation) likewise used the Ineffable Name, but inappropriately, and was killed because of it.

What is a lesson from all the sequence of events? Words are powerful. Even one word can kill another person or cause one's death!

Likewise, when Shammai says, "אֱמוֹר מְעַט וַעֲשֵׂה הַרְבֵּה," it may have been more of an exhortation (consistent with his strict personality) rather than a proactive concept: "When you say even a little, you can do a lot [of harm!]." Shammai continues and says that instead of accepting others (primarily of the opposite gender) in an overly joyous and potentially flirtatious way (וֶהֱוֵי מְקַבֵּל אֶת כָּל הָאָדָם בְּשִׂמְחָה), Shammai may have been warning to take a more mild approach: וֶהֱוֵי מְקַבֵּל אֶת כָּל הָאָדָם בְּסֵבֶר פָּנִים יָפוֹת—Be pleasant, but not overly loquacious like Shelomis bas Divri!

─────────── TAKEAWAY MESSAGES ───────────

According to one midrash, Shelomis was loquacious and unwittingly attracted an Egyptian, who sinned with her. He was struck by Moshe who used just one word (G-d's Name) to kill him, and his son was given the death penalty for likewise abusing just one word (G-d's Name). We learn the powerful impact that even just one word can have on our future. Shammai may be exhorting us to watch our words, which may accidentally sound more inviting than intended and which may lead to undesired affairs. אֱמוֹר מְעַט—Even when you just say a little; וַעֲשֵׂה הַרְבֵּה—You can do a lot [of harm], and therefore don't be overly gregarious to those to whom you shouldn't be.

Speaking just a little can do a lot (of harm)!

Behar

THE LESSON OF LO SONU
AND V'AHAVTA L'REI'ACHA K'MOCHA

רַבִּי מֵאִיר אוֹמֵר: הֱוֵי מְמַעֵט בְּעֵסֶק וַעֲסֹק
בַּתּוֹרָה. וֶהֱוֵי שְׁפַל רוּחַ בִּפְנֵי כָל אָדָם...

*Rabbi Meir would say: Engage minimally in business,
and occupy yourself with Torah. Be humble before every
man...(Avos 4:10)*

─── QUESTIONS ───

1. Is the Tanna simply saying that one should minimize one's work so that one will have more time to spend in Torah?
2. What does being humble have to do with engaging minimally in business?
3. Our *parashah* states:

וְלֹא תוֹנוּ אִישׁ אֶת עֲמִיתוֹ וְיָרֵאתָ מֵאֱלֹקֶיךָ כִּי אֲנִי ה' אֱלֹקֵיכֶם.

*And you shall not wrong one another; but you shall
fear your G-d, for **I am Hashem your G-d**.*
(Vayikra 25:17)

This sounds similar to another *pasuk* in *Kedoshim*: "וְאָהַבְתָּ
לְרֵעֲךָ כָּמוֹךָ אֲנִי ה'." The similarity is that each commandment is

noticeably followed by "אֲנִי ה'—I am Hashem." But what does not wronging someone else or loving a friend have to do with "I am Hashem"?

────────────── ANSWERS ──────────────

In our day and age, it seems that levels of religiosity are determined by criteria that are most often rooted in בֵּין אָדָם לַמָּקוֹם or even בֵּין אָדָם לְעַצְמוֹ matters: How many hours does he learn Torah? How black are his tefillin straps? How careful is he with every word of a *berachah*?

Rather, the Torah tells us clearly in our *parashah* that G-dliness (אֲנִי ה') can definitely be achieved by how we deal with others. The best way of showing that we have G-d within us is by holding back the natural tendency to establish our personal supremacy over others and hurting them. Holding back our natural tendencies and giving of ourselves in the context of an interpersonal relationship is the true paradigmatic אֲנִי ה'.

And this is precisely perhaps why אֲנִי ה' also follows the famous *pasuk* of interpersonal relationships: וְאָהַבְתָּ לְרֵעֲךָ כָּמוֹךָ—When the "first" (the "*alef*," i.e., the more fortunate) gives ("הב" means "give" in Aramaic) the "last" (the last letter *tav*), in order for לְרֵעֲךָ כָּמוֹךָ (in order that your friend can be more like you), that is the ultimate expression of "אֲנִי ה'." Again, the giving of yourself, this time proactively, is true religiosity. Living a Torah way of life may not mean simply working on בֵּין אָדָם לַמָּקוֹם or בֵּין אָדָם לְעַצְמוֹ matters in a vacuum. The interpersonal decorum is what decorates "אֲנִי ה'."

And now we can understand *Avos*: הֱוֵי מְמַעֵט בְּעֵסֶק—Look at business success not as an opportunity to get wealthy, but just the opposite: You can use your business success to be able to give up of yourself. You can recognize that your work enables you to become a מְמַעֵט!

In that way, the Mishnah can be understood homiletically as follows: הֱוֵי מְמַעֵט בְּעֵסֶק—Use your business success to then limit yourself (become a מְמַעֵט) and give to others, which is the true definition of וַעֲסֹק בַּתּוֹרָה. By doing so, you will have demonstrated that you are in the same boat with others (וֶהֱוֵי שְׁפַל רוּחַ בִּפְנֵי כָל אָדָם).

———————— TAKEAWAY MESSAGES ————————

אֲנִי ה'—G-dliness and thus religiosity is achieved by holding back the urge to hurt others in an attempt to reign supreme, as well as by proactively helping others to achieve success. וְאָהַבְ-תָּ—when the "first" (the *alef*, the more fortunate) gives the "last" (the last letter *tav*) in order for לְרֵעֲךָ כָּמוֹךָ (that your friend can be more like you), that is the ultimate expression of אֲנִי ה'. Limiting your own work may not be enough for one to be עֵסֶק בַּתּוֹרָה—you may need to limit *yourself by helping others* and become a מְמַעֵט!

The lesson of וְלֹא תוֹנוּ אִישׁ אֶת עֲמִיתוֹ and וְאָהַבְתָּ לְרֵעֲךָ כָּמוֹךָ: Living a Torah way means giving of yourself to/for others.

Bechukosai

THE COVENANT OF YAAKOV AND ITS CONNECTION TO ELIYAHU

נְתַּאי הָאַרְבֵּלִי אוֹמֵר: הַרְחֵק מִשָּׁכֵן רָע וְאַל
תִּתְחַבֵּר לְרָשָׁע וְאַל תִּתְיָאֵשׁ מִן הַפֻּרְעָנוּת.

*Nitai the Arbeli says: Distance yourself from an evil
neighbor, don't attach to an evildoer, and do not despair from
punishment. (Avos 1:7)*

--- QUESTIONS ---

1. The standard interpretation is that if you have bad influences,
   you will not be exempted from being punished. But is there
   another way to learn this?

2. Our *parashah* talks about terrible *yissurim* (hardships) and yet
   it reassures us:

   וְזָכַרְתִּי אֶת בְּרִיתִי יַעֲקוֹב וְאַף אֶת בְּרִיתִי יִצְחָק וְאַף אֶת
   בְּרִיתִי אַבְרָהָם אֶזְכֹּר וְהָאָרֶץ אֶזְכֹּר.

   And I will remember the covenant with
   יַעֲקוֹב—*Yaakov, and even the covenant with Yitzchak,*
   and even the covenant with Avraham...

324

Why is יַעֲקוֹב mentioned before Yitzchak and Avraham? Also why does יַעֲקוֹב have an extra *vav* in his name?

———————— ANSWERS ————————

Rashi brings down that יַעֲקוֹב is spelled with an extra וּ five times, which correspond to the five times that Eliyahu is spelled without a *vav* (אליה). This is symbolic of an agreement of sorts between Yaakov and Eliyahu; in fact, the *Tz'enah U'r'enah* adds that the וּ looks like a finger, and the five times of switching *vavs* looks like one whole hand, akin to a handshake agreement between the two! But what does Yaakov really have to do with Eliyahu?

When going through difficult times, we often think that our *Avos* never had things so bad, and thus we tend to not relate to them. This is far from the truth. The Torah may specifically start with the "Covenant of Yaakov" right after telling us of all the unbelievable tragedies that can befall us to remind us that even though Yaakov had a tough life, he persevered. While Avraham was a respected socialite (אב הֲמוֹן גּוֹיִים), and Yitzchak was the son of a wealthy magnate, Yaakov, however, was born into difficulty. His life is the epitome of "הַרְחֵק מִשָּׁכֵן רָע וְאַל תִּתְחַבֵּר לָרָשָׁע וְאַל תִּתְיָאֵשׁ מִן הַפֻּרְעָנוּת" as he had to distance himself from an evil neighbor (Eisav), then disassociate from an evil "friend" and business associate (Lavan), and by suffering through these difficult life decisions, Yaakov endured and didn't lose hope despite the hardships! וְאַל תִּתְיָאֵשׁ מִן הַפֻּרְעָנוּת does not mean, "Don't assume you will be exempt from punishment," but rather, "Don't give up hope despite your punishments!"

Furthermore, the connection between Yaakov and Eliyahu is evident in that Yaakov represents this idea of always holding out hope despite the harsh realities. When the Gemara says that "Yaakov Avinu did not die" (*Taanis* 5b), it is clearly not referring to his physical body. Rather, perhaps it is reminiscent of his name, "the heel," which reminds us that *he is holding on for dear life*. Yaakov (the heel) represents the attitude of "never die" (as opposed to "Yaakov never dies"). In this sense, Yaakov is very much connected to the ever-floating Eliyahu, who is ready to reappear even in the most difficult of times! In fact, in *Melachim II*

(2:3–9), Eliyahu also never really died but was lifted up in a chariot of fire toward the heavens.

───────────── TAKEAWAY MESSAGES ─────────────

Despite being born next to an evil neighbor (Eisav, הַרְחֵק מִשָּׁכֵן רַע) and being challenged with an evil friend (Lavan, וְאַל תִּתְחַבֵּר לְרָשָׁע), Yaakov was able to not give up hope despite the odds (וְאַל תִּתְיָאֵשׁ מִן הַפֻּרְעָנוּת). Despite the trials, Yaakov always clung on to his laurels for survival (hung on the *heel* to survive—יַעֲקֹב לֹא מֵת). This "never die" attitude is the connection of יַעֲקֹב and the never-dying אֵלִיָּהוּ. Their secret handshake (*Tz'enah U'r'enah*) is about the Jewish survivalist attitude no matter what *yissurim* we endure!

Yaakov and Eliyahu share a *vav* five times: their "handshake" reassures us that we "never die," despite our trials, tribulations, and hard life decisions.

אָמַר רַבִּי יְהוֹשֻׁעַ בֶּן לֵוִי: וְֽאוֹמֵר (שמות לב)
"וְהַלֻּחֹת מַעֲשֵׂה אֱלֹקִים הֵמָּה וְהַמִּכְתָּב מִכְתַּב
אֱלֹקִים הוּא חָרוּת עַל הַלֻּחֹת", אַל תִּקְרָא
חָרוּת אֶלָּא חֵרוּת, שֶׁאֵין לְךָ בֶּן חוֹרִין אֶלָּא מִי
שֶׁעוֹסֵק בְּתַלְמוּד תּוֹרָה.

Rabbi Yehoshua ben Levi says: "And the tablets are the
work of G-d, and the writing is G-d's writing, engraved on
the tablets"; don't read "engraved" (charus), but "liberty"
(cheirus), for there is no free individual except for he who
occupies himself with the study of Torah. (Avos 6:2)

QUESTIONS

Unlike the gospel saying of "the truth will set you free," our gospel
is that Torah involvement is the direct expression of our freedom. Two
questions:

1. As we prepare for Shavuos, which falls just around the time we
   read this *parashah*, are there hints in this *parashah* that this is
   indeed the case?

2. As the transition period from Pesach to Shavuos highlights this
   metamorphosis from slave to Torah-involved freedom, why do
   we start Pesach by saying, "הֻשַּׁתָּא עַבְדֵי לְשָׁנָה הַבָּאָה בְּנֵי חוֹרִין—Now
   I am a slave but next year I'll be free," if indeed the Mishnah

states in *Pesachim* (10:5) that "one is obligated to view himself as though he came out of Egypt"? Shouldn't we say on Pesach night, then, "Now I am a free man" (and not, "Now I am a slave") to better fulfill that precept?

ANSWERS

The answer to these questions can be derived by a beautiful insight I heard from Rabbi Eli Mansour some years ago:

In the beginning of *Parashas Behar*, we read of *yovel*, the fiftieth year after seven *shemittah* cycles. One of the laws of *yovel* is that a Jewish indentured servant (an *eved Ivri*, a situation in which one who was poor or could not repay stolen funds could "sell" himself as a servant, but then elected to stay beyond his initial term of service) had to be set free from his master's home in that year. In presenting this law, the Torah writes, "Each of you shall return to his family" (*Vayikra* 25:10). The Torah places particular emphasis on the fact that the newly freed servant shall "return to his family." Rather than simply stating that he leaves his master, the Torah found it necessary to stress that he must return home, to his wife and children.

As Rabbi Mansour says: "In the world around us, 'freedom' is understood to mean the absence of restraints and limitations, the ability to act as one pleases without restriction. From the Torah's perspective, however, 'freedom' means returning to one's family, to the structured environment and commitments of Jewish family life."

Perhaps a more concise way to say this: A goyish view of freedom is freedom from responsibility, but our approach is that freedom is when we are granted responsibility! The truth thus doesn't "set us free," but the truth is the ultimate expression of our freedom!

And so even though on Pesach night we view ourselves as exiting Egypt and thus should no longer be slaves, we still start off saying "השתא עבדי," because until we received the Torah on Shavuos, we were slaves without responsibilities or goals!

──────── TAKEAWAY MESSAGES ────────

In *Avos*, we learn that the Jewish understanding of true freedom is pursuing Torah (goals/direction/purpose). The concept that "freedom is Torah, freedom is responsibility" may be illustrated by the *eved Ivri* returning to his family at *yovel*, as described by Rabbi Mansour, and may explain why we are still called "slaves" even after we left Egypt, before becoming true free men and women at Har Sinai after we received the Torah. The "Truth" shall not set you free, but the "Truth" is freedom itself!

The Jewish definition of freedom: Not freedom from responsibility, but that freedom *is* responsibility!

REWARD FOR MITZVOS IN THIS WORLD?
A LESSON FROM THE HOLOCAUST

אַרְבַּע מִדוֹת בְּהוֹלְכֵי לְבֵית הַמִּדְרָשׁ: ד–הוֹלֵךְ
וְאֵינוֹ עוֹשֶׂה שְׂכַר– הֲלִיכָה בְּיָדוֹ....

*There are four types of people who attend the study
hall:...Those that go but do not do [anything], [still] get
reward for going. (Avos 5:14)*

בֶּן עַזַּאי אוֹמֵר: שֶׁשְּׂכַר מִצְוָה– מִצְוָה...

*Ben Azzai says: The reward for doing a mitzvah is [getting to
do another] mitzvah. (Avos 4:2)*

--- QUESTIONS ---

1. What does this mean that you get reward for going to do some-thing, even if you don't actually do the mitzvah? When do you get the reward for this "doing"?
2. Also, the simple understanding to שְׂכַר מִצְוָה מִצְוָה is that the re-ward for a mitzvah is getting to do another mitzvah, as there is no earthly reward. Is there another way to understand this?
3. Finally, how can we possibly try to understand how six million Jews died during the Holocaust? What about the reward for all of their mitzvos? How come G-d didn't spare these holy victims who did so many good deeds?

—— ANSWERS ——

One approach is to say that we simply cannot understand and thus it is futile to try. But perhaps we can try and understand a different approach:

Rashi brings a midrash that questions as follows: If it says, "אֶת מִצוֹתַי תִּשְׁמְרוּ—And observe My commandments," what is added by, "אִם בְּחֻקֹּתַי תֵּלֵכוּ—If you follow My statutes"? He answers that the תֵּלֵכוּ—the going, implies that there is *ameilus*, work. And so you must keep the Torah and separately *work* at it. The *Chasam Sofer* reminds us that "שכר מצוה בהאי עלמא ליכא—There is no earthly reward for our good deeds" (courtesy of Rabbi Neuhaus). But he goes further, though, and learns from *Rashi* that *we can expect reward* for the disparate *ameilus* aspect in this very world! Just like we say in *Avos* that "הוֹלֵךְ וְאֵינוֹ עוֹשֶׂה שְׂכַר הֲלִיכָה בְּיָדוֹ—If you go and do not do, you get reward for the going," the *ameilus* is distinct from the mitzvah, and we can expect earthly reward for it.

Even though that sounds more motivating for me in this world, I still have the same problem with this approach as I look at the six million Jews who perished in the Holocaust. Don't you think they also had significant *ameilus* that should have spared them early deaths?

An answer may be that although in some well-defined cases there is reward given in this very world (too deep a topic to list them all), this doesn't preclude the possibility that "there is no heavenly reward for our good deeds" may apply in some fashion to the Holocaust. However, even in that tragedy of tragedies, there is a certain pride and good feeling that we are rewarded with when we are truly *amel* to do good deeds; that itself must be a reward. It's not that we strive and then get reward, but rather that the act itself is actually rewarding as we are doing it. When the Tanna says, "הוֹלֵךְ וְאֵינוֹ עוֹשֶׂה שְׂכַר הֲלִיכָה בְּיָדוֹ," he is saying perhaps that the reward is *in the going itself* (and not a consequence of the going).

And then, why is the *going* so special? Because doing a good deed, knowing that the reward may in fact just be in the next world, shows that you really believe in G-d. In that sense, שְׂכַר מִצְוָה מִצְוָה may also not only mean that a reward for your mitzvah is getting to do another mitzvah, but that simply *believing* in שְׂכַר מִצְוָה is a mitzvah itself! Going to do a mitzvah knowing that we won't get a raise in salary, a lollypop, or a new car is truly commendable. And although the true reward will be in the next world, we get to revel in our *ameilus* in This World and benefit during our limited time.

——————— TAKEAWAY MESSAGES ———————

The six million victims of the Holocaust seem to support the idea that שכר מצוה בהאי עלמה ליכא. The *Chasam Sofer* states that the תֵּלֵכוּ of "אִם בְּחֻקֹּתַי תֵּלֵכוּ" teaches us that if we are הולך to do a mitzvah, we can actually reap reward in this world for that הליכה aspect. Perhaps the likely reward of the הליכה is in the actual going itself; we are rewarded often with the feel-good sensation when we are, in real time, being *amel* in a good deed. Believing in the next-worldly reward of mitzvos (שְׂכַר מִצְוָה) is a mitzvah in and of itself (מִצְוָה). It shows true *emunah* in G-d.

Do we get rewarded in this world for our mitzvos? Maybe yes and maybe no, but a lack of immediate compensation likely adds to our eventual wealth.

IS *SHEMITTAH* FOR THE LAND OR FOR US?

גָּלוּת בָּאָה לָעוֹלָם עַל עוֹבְדֵי עֲבוֹדָה זָרָה,
וְעַל גִּלּוּי עֲרָיוֹת וְעַל שְׁפִיכוּת דָּמִים
וְעַל הַשְׁמָטַת הָאָרֶץ.

Banishment comes to the world because of idol worship,
promiscuity, murder, and not resting the Land. (Avos 5:9)

──── QUESTIONS ────

After reading this statement over a hundred times, a basic obvious question finally popped up: Wouldn't the flow of the Mishnah make more sense if it said, "Idol worship, promiscuity, murder, and *failure* to keep the *shemittah* year"? After all, the exhortation is against promiscuity, against murder and *against* not letting the land lie fallow!

──── ANSWERS ────

The answer is beautifully apparent in our *parashah*:

אָז תִּרְצֶה הָאָרֶץ אֶת שַׁבְּתֹתֶיהָ כֹּל יְמֵי הָשַּׁמָּה וְאַתֶּם בְּאֶרֶץ אֹיְבֵיכֶם אָז
תִּשְׁבַּת הָאָרֶץ וְהִרְצָת אֶת שַׁבְּתֹתֶיהָ.

*Then the **Land will be appeased** regarding its Sabbaticals.*
During all the days that it remains desolate while you are in
the land of your enemies, the land will rest and thus appease
its Sabbaticals. (Vayikra 26:34)

333

Some commentaries say that when Jews fail to observe the Sabbatical year, they show that their work is paramount, and their lack of faith in letting the land lie fallow is punished *middah k'neged middah*, measure for measure, by making them work nonstop in lands outside Israel. Although this approach is popular, another approach (which I personally favor) is more land-centric than people-centric. Let me explain:

The actual Land of Israel (unlike everywhere else) has a legitimate impact on its inhabitants. Beyond mere anthropomorphism, the Land has actionable powers. Like a person who needs Shabbos for some metaphysical and perhaps physical rest, the Land of Israel also needs rest for the Sabbatical year. When not afforded that rest, the Land punishes its inhabitants by kicking them out, with the help of G-d (see similarly in *Vayikra* 20:22: "Keep all my decrees and laws and follow them, so that the Land where I am bringing you to live may not **vomit** you out."). We have a special symbiotic relationship with the land in Israel, but such a miraculous reality also brings basic responsibility.

This second explanation jives perfectly with the Mishnah in *Avos*. The reason that *galus* comes is more a function of the land needing rest than because the people failed to give it rest. The emphasis is not on the people who failed to observe *shemittah*, but on the land itself that needs *shemittah*. Like a person needs to rest or else they will expire, the Land of Israel needs *shemittah* for "survival" (not talking about any crop rotation, but rather just some spiritual need that G-d placed for the land)! In this sense, *galus* comes as a direct result enabling the land to achieve *shemittah* (עַל הַשְׁמָטַת הָאָרֶץ). Just like the Land of Israel kicks out its inhabitants if there is rampant killing, idolatry, or licentiousness, the land will also kick out its inhabitants if it doesn't receive its requisite resting period. So let's say it loud and clear: **The Land of Israel is alive just like you and me**.

Upon closer review of the *pasuk*, perhaps there is a hint in *Rashi* to this idea.

אָז תִּרְצֶה: תפייס את כעס המקום שכעס על שמטותיה.

> **Land will be appeased**: *Appease the anger of HaMakom*
> *(הַמָּקוֹם) who had been angry regarding the Land's shemittah*
> *years.*

At first glance, *Rashi* is refering to G-d by saying *HaMakom*, another one of G-d's names. But it could also be understood as *"ha'makom*—the place," namely the Land of Israel itself, which is mad because it was stripped of its *shemittah* year of rest!

─────────── TAKEAWAY MESSAGES ───────────

The Land of Israel is *appeased* by banishing us out of Israel if we don't allow it (the Land) to rest! The Tanna in *Avos* highlights that the sin of failing to observe *shemittah* may be less of a failed personal endeavor/deed and more of a robbing the "living land" its due rest. Such an approach lends itself to the idea that our Land is very much alive!

We have a symbiotic relationship with this unique Land, which is alive and "kicking," hopefully not kicking us out if we don't treat it with respect!

DADS, GRADS,
AND PARASHAS BECHUKOSAI

וַאֲכַלְתֶּם יָשָׁן נוֹשָׁן וְיָשָׁן מִפְּנֵי חָדָשׁ תּוֹצִיאוּ.

*And you will eat old store long kept, and you shall bring out
the old as you bring in the new. (Vayikra 26:10)*

Rashi asks: "What blessing is it to eat old food?" He answers: "The
Torah means, however, that the produce will be well preserved, growing
mellow with age, so that the very old produce from three years ago will
be better to eat than that of last year!"

And as per bringing in the new grain, *Rashi* continues: "The threshing floors will be full of new grain, which would decay if left there, and
therefore must be stored. The storehouses will be filled with the abundant old produce. Therefore, you will have to remove what was in the
storehouses and take it elsewhere [in your house] in order to put the
new produce into them."

―――――――――― QUESTIONS ――――――――――

So there is a threshing floor, where the produce is formed or put
together, and then a storehouse, where it is stored, and eventually, a
home where it is consumed. Since we have such an abundance of produce, why wouldn't we just take the new (presumably the very best)
produce straight into the home from the threshing floor, rather than
bringing it into the storehouses and mixing it with the older produce?

ANSWERS

My father, Dr. Larry Ciment, once explained to me that there is a *mussar* here: One needs to cherish the aged, but be inviting to the youth.

- **Cherish the aged**: As the first *Rashi* says, the older the better. The aged produce matured longer and was more refined by the time it was consumed than the less-aged. Similarly, we need to respect that time refines, matures, and betters us all.

- **Be inviting to the younger**: Instead of skipping the storehouse and going straight to the house for consumption, the young stalks of wheat need some time in the storehouses. The lesson is that the young need to be invited into the mature crowd of older produce before being sent for their mission. The young need to not only be invited and allowed to intermingle with the more mature and refined produce, but the older produce has to sometimes recognize the need to step out of the storehouse to accommodate the young fledglings. Sometimes, the hardest challenge for older people is to be inviting and recognize that they need to let the younger ones have their time to shine. It is equally as challenging for the younger ones to understand that they need to incubate in the storehouses among the most refined before they are ready for prime time!

TAKEAWAY MESSAGES

Since, when blessed, we will have such an abundance of produce, why not just take the new (presumably the very best) produce straight into the home from the threshing floor, rather than bringing it into the storehouses and mixing it with the older produce? The answer is that the mixing of the young and the old is the ultimate blessing. Recognizing the attributes of those older, the young ones refine themselves and vice versa. *Parashas Bechukosai* falls out near Father's Day and graduation to teach us my father's lesson of וַאֲכַלְתֶּם יָשָׁן נוֹשָׁן וְיָשָׁן מִפְּנֵי חָדָשׁ תּוֹצִיאוּ.

SEFER

Bamidbar

Bamidbar

עֲשָׂרָה נִסִּים נַעֲשׂוּ לַאֲבוֹתֵינוּ בְּבֵית הַמִּקְדָּשׁ. לֹא הִפִּילָה אִשָּׁה מֵרֵיחַ בְּשַׂר הַקֹּדֶשׁ, וְלֹא הִסְרִיחַ בְּשַׂר הַקֹּדֶשׁ מֵעוֹלָם, וְלֹא נִרְאָה זְבוּב בְּבֵית הַמִּטְבָּחַיִם, וְלֹא אֵרַע קֶרִי לְכֹהֵן גָּדוֹל בְּיוֹם הַכִּפּוּרִים, וְלֹא כִבּוּ גְשָׁמִים אֵשׁ שֶׁל עֲצֵי הַמַּעֲרָכָה, וְלֹא נָצְחָה הָרוּחַ אֶת עַמּוּד הֶעָשָׁן, וְלֹא נִמְצָא פְסוּל בָּעֹמֶר וּבִשְׁתֵּי הַלֶּחֶם וּבְלֶחֶם הַפָּנִים, עוֹמְדִים צְפוּפִים וּמִשְׁתַּחֲוִים רְוָחִים, וְלֹא הִזִּיק נָחָשׁ וְעַקְרָב בִּירוּשָׁלַיִם מֵעוֹלָם, וְלֹא אָמַר אָדָם לַחֲבֵרוֹ צַר לִי הַמָּקוֹם שֶׁאָלִין בִּירוּשָׁלָיִם.

Ten miracles were performed for our forefathers in the Holy Temple: No woman ever miscarried because of the smell of the holy meat. The holy meat never spoiled. Never was a fly seen in the slaughterhouse. Never did the High Priest have an accidental seminal discharge on Yom Kippur. The rains did not extinguish the wood-fire burning upon the Altar. The wind did not prevail over the column of smoke [rising from the Altar]. No disqualifying problem was ever discovered in the omer-offering, the Two Loaves, or the Showbread. They stood crowded but had ample space in which to prostrate themselves. **Never did a snake or scorpion cause injury in Yerushalayim. And no man ever said to his fellow, "My lodging in Yerushalayim is too cramped for me."** *(Avos 5:5)*

<hr>

QUESTIONS

1. When reading about the miracles of the Beis Hamikdash, why is it that two out of the ten miracles have to do with Yerushalayim? After all, isn't Yerushalayim just the city in which the Temple happened to stand?
2. Also, what connection does this week's *parashah* have with the opening of the US Embassy there?

ANSWERS

Yerushalayim may harbor an extra special significance to the Jewish People because it is the place where the Beis Hamikdash stood. But this Mishnah in *Avos* makes it clear that even beyond the Beis Hamikdash's walls, Yerushalayim has an inherent holiness. Yerushalayim isn't holy just because the Beis Hamikdash happened to be there, but it is holy and *thus* the Beis Hamikdash was situated there! In fact, the *Tosafos Yom Tov* quotes the *Midrash Shmuel*, which states that this Mishnah affirms that even after the Beis Hamikdash is not present, the holiness of the City prevails.

The opening of the US Embassy in Yerushalayim ironically occurred this week of *Parashas Bamidbar*, where we read the *pasuk*: "And the common man who approaches shall be put to death." The Gemara in *Makkos* (24b) relates that Rabban Gamliel, Rabbi Elazar ben Azariah, Rabbi Yehoshua, and Rabbi Akiva went to Yerushalayim after the destruction of the Temple, and just as they came to Mount Scopus, they saw a fox emerging from the place of the *Kodesh HaKodashim*. The first three rabbis began to cry, but Rabbi Akiva smiled. The three wept because a place so holy of which it was once said, "And the common man who approaches shall be put to death," had become the home to foxes! But Rabbi Akiva replied that he smiled because this fulfilled the prophecy of Uriah the priest that "Tzion shall be plowed as a field, and Yerushalayim shall become heaps, and the mountain of the House as the high places of a forest" (*Michah* 3:12). Rabbi Akiva continued that if Uriah's prophecy came true, then so will Zechariah's, who said: "There shall yet old men and old women sit in the broad places of Yerushalayim" (*Zechariah* 8:4)! Rabbi Akiva comforted the three other rabbis.

How unbelievably apropos that our *parashah* has this famous *pasuk*, "And the stranger who approaches shall be put to death," which is the backbone of the midrash that has given us hope for a revival in Yerushalayim for millennia!

TAKEAWAY MESSAGES

Two out of the ten miracles of the Beis Hamikdash have nothing to do with the Beis Hamikdash, but rather with Yerushalayim, to remind us of the inherent holiness of Yerushalayim that predated and postdates the actual Beis Hamikdash! Our *parashah* ironically harbors the *pasuk*, "And the common man who approaches shall be put to death," behind one of the most powerful midrashim that the Jewish People have clung on to for millennia—the yearning for the restoration of our holy Yerushalayim, the capital of Israel!

DID NADAV AND AVIHU REALLY SIN?

אַבְטַלְיוֹן אוֹמֵר: חֲכָמִים הִזָּהֲרוּ בְדִבְרֵיכֶם... הַתַּלְמִידִים הַבָּאִים אַחֲרֵיכֶם וְיָמוּתוּ וְנִמְצָא שֵׁם שָׁמַיִם מִתְחַלֵּל:

Avtalyon says: Scholars, be careful with your words...The disciples who come after you will then drink of these evil waters and be destroyed, and the name of heaven will be desecrated. (Avos 1:11)

וַיָּמָת נָדָב וַאֲבִיהוּא לִפְנֵי ה' בְּהַקְרִבָם אֵשׁ זָרָה לִפְנֵי ה'.

And Nadav and Avihu died before Hashem when they offered strange fire before Hashem. (Bamidbar 3:4)

QUESTIONS

1. What sin did the sons of Aharon commit? Why was it so egregious? Well, the point of Avtalyon's above ethic is that when you are role models, you have an extra task in "representing"; misrepresentation can have drastic consequences for you and your students who follow you. But if Nadav and Avihu failed to "represent," still what was at the core of their indiscretion?

344

2. What possible lesson/analogy does Avtalyon teach us by addressing *chachamim* specifically (as opposed to *rebbeim*, etc.)?

—————— ANSWERS ——————

חכם מה הוא אומר? מה העדות והחקים והמשפטים אשר
צוה...רשע מה הוא אומר? מה העבדה הזאת לכם?

*What does the chacham say? "What are the testimonies,
statutes and laws that G-d commands…" What does the rasha
say? "What is this service of yours?"*

Shouldn't it say *tzaddik* and *rasha* in the Haggadah? Also, isn't it strange that both the *chacham* and *rasha* are quoting actual *pesukim* verbatim from the Torah, so how can one be evil and one not?

The answer is that the *rasha* starts out by *focusing on the end product* with no focus or attention on the "process." A *chacham* has the tools to succeed (he learns the laws, including all the basic העדות והחקים והמשפטים) but does need the *avodah* to become the *tzaddik* that he can become. When Avtalyon says, "חֲכָמִים הִזָּהֲרוּ בְדִבְרֵיכֶם," he is conjuring up the Haggadah's point that a *rasha* is, unlike a *chacham*, destined for doom because he is focused on the end product without the needed "process." As long as they were offering a fire on the Altar, Aharon's sons figured that would be OK, but they did not heed "the process"! For spiritual completeness, Avtalyon reminds us that "מֶה הָעֲבֹדָה" must be preceded by the process of "מה העדות והחקים והמשפטים."

Similarly, the *ben sorer u'moreh*, wayward son, is the prototype of evil in the Torah and is נידון על שם סופו—judged by his ending, which classically means that he is judged now for the eventuality that he will become a murderer (by eating gluttonously, he will end up murdering for food!). One homily (Rabbi Schreiber) is that he is judged harshly by "his last name," which is *moreh*. Since people may learn bad behavior from the "teacher," he is put to death. I prefer a different homily: "שם סופו" refers to the idea that the *ben sorer u'moreh* is focused only on the end product and is therefore destined to be a *rasha* because that is what a *rasha* is—only focused on the שם סופו without regard to the process. If you lack the raw materials/process and think you can just do the *avodah*, you will inevitably fail; a failure that is destined from the start.

Avtalyon thus explained why Nadav and Avihu sinned: They were not *chachamim* and figured they could do *avodah* without paying heed to the raw materials/process. They were "נידון על שם סופו"—they were "*moreh*" and focused on the סופו, and not on the העדות והחקים והמשפטים.

─────────── TAKEAWAY MESSAGES ───────────

A *chacham* understands that true success is not arrived at without due process. The "מָה הָעֵבֹדָה" must be preceded by the process of "מה העדות והחקים והמשפטים"! Nadav and Avihu did the *avodah* but didn't follow the prescribed regimen, and this disregard of the process was punished by G-d. The *ben sorer u'moreh* is destined for doom from the start because he is only concerned with the end product of things, and without the raw materials to prosper, he is destined for doom and sin.

The difference between a *rasha* and a *chacham* is not in accomplishing tasks per se but in setting up the proper training and adherence to practice so as not to become a *ben sorer u'moreh*. Nadav and Avihu sinned by failing to adhere to the process.

MOSHE RABBEINU'S GRADUATION MESSAGE

רַ־בִּי אֶלְעָזָר בֶּן שַׁמּוּעַ אוֹמֵר: יְהִי כְּבוֹד תַּלְמִידְךָ
חָבִיב עָלֶיךָ כְּשֶׁלָּךְ וּכְבוֹד חֲבֵרְךָ כְּמוֹרָ־א רַבְּךָ
וּמוֹרָ־א רַבְּךָ כְּמוֹרָא שָׁמָיִם.

Rabbi Elazar ben Shamua said: The honor for your students
should be as dear to you as your own, the honor for your
friend as your teacher and for your teacher as the fear of G-d.
(Avos 4:12)

 QUESTIONS

This Mishnah in *Avos* is seemingly saying that you have to raise your
respect a notch, a rung, a level above the expected. The respect accorded
to your student should be raised to that which you accord yourself, etc.
It does seem a bit odd that we should strive to respect our teachers as
much as we fear G-d. But is there another way to understand this?

A related question on our *parashah* that will lend insight on
that question:

וְאֵלֶּה תּוֹלְדֹת אַהֲרֹן וּמֹשֶׁה בְּיוֹם דִּבֶּר ה' אֶת מֹשֶׁה בְּהַר סִינָי...וְאֵלֶּה
שְׁמוֹת בְּנֵי אַהֲרֹן הַבְּכֹר נָדָב וַאֲבִיהוּא אֶלְעָזָר וְאִיתָמָר.

These are the descendants of Moshe and Aharon on the day
that Hashem spoke to Moshe at Mount Sinai...These are the
sons of Aharon, the firstborn Nadav and Avihu, Elazar and
Isamar." (Bamidbar 3:1)

347

Since only the sons of Aharon are enumerated here, why state "these are the descendants of *Moshe* and Aharon"?

─────────────── ANSWERS ───────────────

Rashi answers from *Sanhedrin* (19b): "If you teach your friend's son Torah, the Torah considers it as if you actually gave birth to the child." Therefore, in a sense, Moshe and Aharon were both the fathers of Nadav, Avihu, etc. The *Kli Yakar* actually says that the mention of Moshe here is to highlight that really Elazar and Isamar would also have been killed due to Aharon's involvement with the Golden Calf, but Moshe's merit caused at least two out of the four sons to survive. The obvious problem with this possibly is (especially since Moshe was the most humble man on earth) Moshe would probably not have written himself as the father of Aharon's sons to highlight that he "gave birth to them," or that his merit caused two of the four sons to live. That would not be consistent with Moshe's raison d'être!

Another answer may be that Moshe, in typical humble Moshe fashion, was actually trying to make his brother Aharon feel less responsible for his sons' deaths. Since a *rav* is imbued with the responsibility of guiding the student toward a fear of G-d, Moshe was telling Aharon that he himself partially failed in regard to Nadav and Avihu. He was humbly saying to Aharon that as his children's *rav*, he took equal responsibility for their downfall. This approach is wholly consistent with the holy and humblest human ever.

When the Mishnah says, "וּמוֹרָא רַבְּךָ כְּמוֹרָא שָׁמָיִם," it may not simply be saying that an individual has to respect his *rav* like he respects G-d. Rather, it is speaking to the responsibility of a *rav*, a teacher. The fear of a *rav* is what sets up your fear of G-d. Our rabbis and teachers are burdened with the responsibility to instill that fear of heaven that we cannot really get from books. So "וּמוֹרָא רַבְּךָ כְּמוֹרָא שָׁמָיִם" is not saying that you should fear your *rav* like G-d in heaven (that would be impossible!), but rather that the *rav* should know that he is burdened with injecting the fear of heaven in his constituents.

―――――― TAKEAWAY MESSAGES ――――――

Moshe reminds us that our teachers are burdened with instilling the fear of heaven just as much as the biological parents. Moshe lists himself as a father to Aharon's sons because he was their teacher. Maybe it was to show that if you teach your friend's son Torah, the Torah considers it as if you actually gave birth to the child (*Rashi*) or maybe it was to highlight that Moshe's merit is what saved the other two sons of Aharon (*Kli Yakar*). More consistent with Moshe's humble nature, maybe it was to show remorse to Aharon that Moshe did not properly instill the fear of heaven into Nadav and Avihu that could have averted disaster. "מוֹרָא רַבְּךָ כְּמוֹרָא שָׁמָיִם" is a challenge to the rabbis, and is not necessarily speaking about individuals' respect barometer.

Moshe Rabbeinu's graduation message: We should respect our teachers as we respect heaven, and also recognize that how we fear heaven is a reflection of our rabbis and teachers.

Naso

WHAT'S THE RECIPE FOR
THE PERFECT BLESSING?

יְבָרֶכְךָ ה' וְיִשְׁמְרֶךָ. יָאֵר ה' פָּנָיו אֵלֶיךָ וִיחֻנֶּךָּ.
יִשָּׂא ה' פָּנָיו אֵלֶיךָ וְיָשֵׂם לְךָ שָׁלוֹם.

Hashem will bless you and guard you. Hashem will shine His
face upon you and bestow graciousness upon you. Hashem will
lift His face toward you and give you peace.
(Bamidbar 6:24–26)

QUESTIONS

1. Why are the blessings given in pairs: יְבָרֶכְךָ then וְיִשְׁמְרֶךָ; יָאֵר then וִיחֻנֶּךָּ; and finally יִשָּׂא then וְיָשֵׂם לְךָ שָׁלוֹם? Is there any common thread here?
2. Why does the prayer end in peace (שָׁלוֹם) and not in happiness (שִׂמְחָה)?

ANSWERS

The *Kli Yakar* says that each blessing starts with a *yud* because that letter hints to hidden blessings. How so? He says that when we see a *yud*, all we see is the letter itself (*gematria* of ten) but hidden behind every *yud* is also a *vav* and a *dalet* (which completes the way the letter

350

is pronounced, and which also adds up to the *gematria* of ten). The *Kli Yakar* states that inherent in each blessing is an outward physical manifestation, represented by the *yud*, but also a hidden spiritual blessing equal in magnitude, represented by the hidden and silent *vav* and *dalet*!

Another approach riding this idea of "hidden blessings within the blessings" is the following:

In His signature blessing to us all, G-d is teaching us that every action has a reaction. By giving us blessings of vast possessions (see *Rashi* on יְבָרֶכְךָ), we may have difficulty guarding them both from physical and even spiritual challenges, and therefore G-d has to add a blessing to react to that initial blessing, ensuring that the former remains a blessing! He thus reassures us by telling us He will guard us and protect the blessings He bestows upon us (וְיִשְׁמְרֶךָ).

Likewise, by paying attention to us (יָאֵר ה' פָּנָיו אֵלֶיךָ), we may actually find that it doesn't benefit us to be in G-d's scrutinous limelight! In fact, Dr. (and Kohen!) Jay Reinberg pointed out that similarly in *Bechukosai*, both the blessing and the curse were couched in the idea that G-d will be watching B'nei Yisrael: "ונתתי פני בכם: כמו שנאמר ופניתי אליכם, כך נאמר ברעה ונתתי פני." And so to reassure us, G-d reminds us that despite His scrutiny, He will still grant us grace (וִיחֻנֶּךָּ).

Finally, if G-d indeed shows favoritism (יִשָּׂא ה'), inevitably it will lead to jealousy from another party. The prayer thus ends in *shalom*/peace and not *simchah*/happiness because peace was the blessing that ensures that the blessing of יִשָּׂא ה'—grace remains a blessing!

And there you have it: G-d strategically gave us blessings that would require further blessings to keep them blessings. He teaches us to remember the lesson that every action has a reaction, but also that He wants us to be successful.

────────── TAKEAWAY MESSAGES ──────────

The *Kli Yakar* teaches us that the blessings each start out with the mysterious *yud* to remind us that G-d bestows us external material blessings, represented by the external *yud* (*gematria* of ten), and simultaneously more internal hidden spiritual blessings, represented by the *vav-dalet* of the letter spelled out *yud* (also equals ten!).

G-d's blessings each necessitated a counter blessing to ensure that the blessing remained indeed a blessing! He blesses us with many items, but then will guard us so we don't squander them. He will pay attention to us, but won't over-scrutinize us and still be gracious to us. He will raise us above others, but it won't provoke jealousy and war; it will instead grant us peace!

What's the recipe for the perfect blessing? One that requires more blessings to keep it as a blessing!

SHOULD WE SEPARATE OR BE TOGETHER?

הִלֵּל אוֹמֵר: אַל תִּפְרֹשׁ מִן הַצִּבּוּר.

Hillel says: Don't distance from the congregation. (Avos 2:4)

רַבִּי נְהוֹרַאי אוֹמֵר: הֱוֵי גוֹלֶה לִמְקוֹם תּוֹרָה.

Rabbi Nehorai would say: Exile yourself to a place of Torah.
(Avos 4:13)

QUESTIONS

The obvious question emanating from these seemingly contradictory ethics is: Should we separate ourselves from the rest of the pack or not? Is it really good to "exile" yourself, even if there are holy intentions? After our shul community's *ne'ilas ha'chag*, which brought together people of all stripes, the question is even more pronounced.

ANSWERS

The Torah talks of two separate sin-offerings when it comes to a *nazir*: one when or if he stumbles upon a dead corpse accidentally, and one when or if he finishes his tour of duty.

Since he separates from others by abstaining from haircutting, wine, and impurity (specifically exposure to the dead), the *nazir* brings a sin-offering after he inadvertently comes upon a dead corpse. *Rashi* quotes Rabbi Elazar Hakapar's rationale for his sin: "שצער את עצמו מן היין—since he pained himself from wine"! By abstaining from wine, in

353

effect, the *nazir* is ostracizing himself from everyone else unnecessarily—the implication being that *separating oneself is a bad thing.*

When explaining the rationale for the sin-offering after the *nazir* completes his tour of duty (typical vow of *nazir*-hood would last thirty days), the *Ramban* says: "ראוי היה לו שיזור לעולם—the *nazir* should have continued his separation forever." The implication here is that *not separating oneself is a bad thing.*

And so, at first glance, this looks like a potential rift between *Rashi* and *Ramban*: *Rashi* seemingly holds that the *nazir* is at fault because he shouldn't be separating himself, while the *Ramban* seemingly posits that separating himself is ideal and his coming back to the fold is the actual sin! Neatly put, one may suggest: *Rashi*—not good to be פורש מן הציבור; and *Ramban*—good to be פורש מן הציבור!

Upon closer inspection, there is no rift at all, and they both may hold that it is not good to be פורש מן הציבור. How so? Remember, there are actually two potential sin-offerings the *nazir* may bring: One is brought if he inadvertently violated his vow before he completed his tour of duty, while the other one is brought after he completes it. *Rashi* was commenting on the sin-offering brought if the *nazir* didn't complete his *nazir* tour of duty before contracting impurity. Even if it wasn't his fault, since he never showed that he could really fulfill being a *nazir*, he was unnecessarily separating and thus held accountable for the warning of אַל תִּפְרוֹשׁ מִן הַצִּיבּוּר!

The *Ramban* starts his discussion, however, on the sin-offering brought at the end of the *nazir's* campaign (*Bamidbar* 6:14) when he demonstrated that he, in fact, can be special/committed/durable. Since he thus enters a new realm of holiness, he would actually be separating from his new community of holiness when he reverts back to being a normal person. And so, the *Ramban* may also hold that the sin would be אַל תִּפְרשׁ מִן הַצִּבּוּר, but this time, if the *nazir* comes back!

Similarly in *Avos*, Hillel says that we really shouldn't ostracize ourselves from others (like the *nazir* who really couldn't finish his vow). But Rabbi Nehorai adds that exiling oneself to a מקום התורה is not being פורש מן הציבור, but entering a new community of holiness, which is actually a good thing, akin to the *nazir* who completes his tour of duty.

───────────── TAKEAWAY MESSAGES ─────────────

Separating ourselves from others is generally dissuaded, even for holy intents. But if one demonstrates true holy intent/potential/grit/tenacity/endurance/purpose, the separator is not only allowed to veer off on his individual course, he is dissuaded from separating from his new holy community that he entered. And so, while we espouse Hillel's concept of אַל תִּפְרֹשׁ מִן הַצִּבּוּר, we simultaneously bear in mind Rabbi Nehorai's concept of מעלין בקודש ואין מורידין!

Should we separate or be together? We should separate only in the rarity that we could actually separate.

WHAT DOES CHARITY
HAVE TO DO WITH SOTAH?

יוֹסֵי בֶּן יוֹחָנָן אִישׁ יְרוּשָׁלַיִם אוֹמֵר: יְהִי בֵיתְךָ
פָּתוּחַ לִרְוָחָה וְיִהְיוּ עֲנִיִּים בְּנֵי בֵיתֶךָ וְאַל תַּרְבֶּה
שִׂיחָה עִם הָאִשָּׁה. בְּאִשְׁתּוֹ אָמְרוּ...כָּל הַמַּרְבֶּה
שִׂיחָה עִם הָאִשָּׁה גּוֹרֵם רָעָה לְעַצְמוֹ וּבוֹטֵל
מִדִּבְרֵי תוֹרָה וְסוֹפוֹ יוֹרֵשׁ גֵּיהִנֹּם.

*Yosi ben Yochanan, man of Yerushalayim, says: Let your
home be wide open, and let the poor be members of your
household. And do not engage in excessive conversation with a
woman...One who excessively converses with a woman causes
evil to himself, neglects the study of Torah, and in the end
inherits purgatory. (Avos 1:5)*

QUESTIONS

What does speaking excessively with a woman have to do with having
an open home or being gracious to poor people? What's so bad about
speaking so much to your wife anyway? Wouldn't that be a potentially
good thing?

ANSWERS

Perhaps we can find an answer from the following analysis of our
parashah: The *sotah* story comes after the *parashah* of *terumos* and

356

maaseros, specifically the necessary gifts we must give the Kohanim, as the Gemara in *Berachos* (63a) explains: "Anyone who has *terumos* and *maaseros* and doesn't give them to the Kohen will end up needing the Kohen for his wife!" The *Torah Temimah* asks a great question: If a man commits the bad deed (of not providing the Kohen with his due tzedakah), then why should the wife suffer the fate of the *sotah* process? Shouldn't the man have his own punishment, and why is the wife brought into the punishment?

One approach offered by the *Torah Temimah* (based on *Sotah* 2a) is that "אין מזווגין לו לאדם אשה אלא לפי מעשיו—A man only gets coupled with a woman according to his deeds." If he is a stingy person, then she must also be a bad apple, and thus she herself is deserving of the *sotah* process!

Another approach may be the following: At a *bris*, we bless the young boy that he should grow up "לתורה לחופה ולמעשים טובים." People ask why "good deeds" follow "marriage." The answer is because a purpose of marriage is so that the married couple can do good deeds together! A good wife can be the *enabler* to accomplish a higher level of good deeds than before.

Conversely, if a married person doesn't exhibit the positive trait/ good deed of tzedakah to the Kohen, then it may be a sign that the wife isn't really a good wife; she is destined to be a *sotah*! Since the married man was not *enabled* to do a good deed, the message may be that there must be an inherent problem in their marriage (i.e., the enabler/wife may have been MIA [missing in action])!

And now we can at last understand our Mishnah: Engaging in excessive conversation per se with your wife is not the purpose of marriage. Being able to reach your potential to do good deeds together by opening your home, giving to charity, etc.—those are the higher purposes of marriage. Torah, *chuppah*, and then *maasim tovim*!

─────────── TAKEAWAY MESSAGES ───────────

What does speaking excessively with a woman or one's wife have to do with having an open home or being gracious to poor people? The purpose of marriage is to enable one to do good deeds with that unity. This is why we say that a boy who just entered *bris milah* should grow up

"לתורה לחופה ולמעשים טובים."*Chuppah* precedes *maasim tovim* as that is the purpose of the marriage. If a man doesn't give charity, it may be that his marriage is in trouble (his wife may in fact come to be a *sotah*)!

Lack of charity may predict *Sota*-bility!

IF BEING A NAZIR IS SO GOOD, WHY BRING A SIN-OFFERING?

רַבִּי יְהוֹשֻׁעַ אוֹמֵר: עַיִן הָרָע וְיֵצֶר הָרָע וְשִׂנְאַת
הַבְּרִיּוֹת מוֹצִיאִין אֶת הָאָדָם מִן הָעוֹלָם.

Rabbi Yehoshua says: An evil eye, an evil urge, and hatred of
beings bring a person out of this world. (Avos 2:11)

——— QUESTIONS ———

We can understand that "an evil eye" and "hatred of fellow man,"
which both essentially derive from jealousy, are characteristics that can
be seemingly avoided. But what about the *yetzer hara*, temptations?
These are seemingly more innate/inherent, and so how can that really
be one of the elements that remove one from this world?

The answer to this question will derive from an answer to yet another
classic question on our *parashah*. Is it good or not good to be a *nazir*? On
the one hand, the story of the *nazir* follows that of the *sotah* to teach us
that whoever sees an adulteress in her disgrace would and should vow
to abstain (for the sake of heaven!) from wine, for it leads to adultery
(*Sotah* 2a). On the other hand, *Rashi* reminds us that the Tanna Rabbi
Elazar Hakapar stated that the *nazir* brings a sin-offering because
"שׁצִיעֵר עצמו מן היין," which most commentaries interpret to mean that the
nazir needlessly refrained from a pleasure (wine) that he didn't have to
refrain from. Hence, such refraining from pleasure is actually wrong!

359

So which one is it? Is it good to be a *nazir* in that he is refraining from wine to avoid eventual adultery, or is it not good to be a *nazir* because, after all, he brings a sin-offering for having refrained from wine!

—————— ANSWERS ——————

An answer may be hidden in the language of Rabbi Elazar Hakapar's wording. Notice that he does not say, "פּוֹרֵשׁ מִן הַיַּיִן," which is the usual way we would say "separating" from wine. Rather, he uses the word שֶׁצִּיעֵר—he "pains himself" from [abstaining] from wine. Only someone who harbors a predilection to drinking, or someone who is addicted to wine, would be "pained" by not drinking wine!

The Torah may be telling us that the person who is likely to become a *nazir* is someone who may not be the most stand-up of people to begin with. He could be someone who is already addicted to wine and has an epiphany after witnessing the *sotah* process. The *nazir*, then, is not bringing the sin-offering because he is *bad* in becoming a *nazir* now. But perhaps he is bringing the sin-offering to atone for the fact that it "pains" him to abstain from wine; he must atone for his past lifestyle choices that made him an addict to begin with! So basically the *nazir* process is actually all good, and the sin-offering is just brought because it "pains" the *nazir* to abstain when it should not have been so "painful" if he wasn't so full of vices before his *nazir* choice was made!

A deeper lesson is that we are all brought in this world with certain inherent, innate urges/temptations. But our challenge is to temper these innate urges and be less attached to the vices so that it is not "צִיעֵר" to give that vice up! The lesson of the sin-offering of the *nazir* teaches us that our *yetzer hara* is modifiable. *Yetzer hara* is certainly innate but it can be modified. We can temper/modify/update our urges and temptation to some degree. Therefore, it is one of those elements that can be מוֹצִיאִין אֶת הָאָדָם מִן הָעוֹלָם.

—————— TAKEAWAY MESSAGES ——————

We get punished for our *yetzer hara*, even though it is partially innate and inherent. This is because we are charged with modifying our behaviors to continually improve. The *nazir* brings a sin-offering not because he is separating from wine, but rather because he was שציער עצמו מן היין—it "pained" him so much to refrain from wine. If it pained him so much, he let his inherent addictive personality go unchecked for too long.

The *nazir*'s sin-offering may have been for his past and not for the present. In other words, being a *nazir* is a good thing, but the fact that he wanted to become a *nazir* was because of his previous overindulgence!

Behaalosecha

IS LONG PRAYER BETTER THAN SHORT PRAYER? SHOULD PRAYER BE SET?

רַבִּי שִׁמְעוֹן אוֹמֵר: וּכְשֶׁאַתָּה מִתְפַּלֵּל אַל
תַּעַשׂ תְּפִלָּתְךָ קֶבַע אֶלָּא רַחֲמִים וְתַחֲנוּנִים
לִפְנֵי הַמָּקוֹם בָּרוּךְ הוּא.

Rabbi Shimon says: When you pray, do not make your prayers
routine, but [an entreaty of] mercy and a supplication before
the Almighty." (Avos 2:13)

QUESTIONS

What does it mean not to make your prayers routine? Don't we strive to have set times for *Shacharis*, *Minchah*, and *Maariv*? (And BTW, kudos to all those who get to minyan on time!)

An answer can be derived from the quintessential *tefillah* found in this week's *parashah* after Miriam spoke *lashon hara* and was smitten with leprosy. Moshe screamed out: "אֵל נָא רְפָא נָא לָהּ." Rashi brings down two midrashim:

1. Why did Moshe not pray at length? So that the Israelites should not say, "His sister is in distress, yet he stands and prolongs his prayer." (*Sifrei, Behaalosecha* 1:42:13; *Tanchuma, Tzav* 13)

362

2. So that Israel should not say, "For his sister he prays at length, but for our sake he does not pray at length." (*Midrash Aggadah*; *Yalkut Shimoni*; *Midrash Lekach Tov*)

According to the first midrash *Rashi* brings, the implication seems to be that long prayer is **undesirable**; after all, why would the Israelites find fault with Moshe praying at length unless there was something wrong with doing that! Conversely, the second midrash implies that long prayer is actually **desirable**; after all, B'nei Yisrael would desire a long prayer just like the one given to his sister! So, to reiterate the above question, is long prayer good or not?

──────── ANSWERS ────────

Long prayer is indeed praiseworthy. The Gemara in *Berachos* (32b) highlights the benefit of long prayer: "If one prays long, his prayer does not pass unheeded!" So then the midrash that needs explanation is the one implying that long prayer is undesirable when it says that the Israelites claim against Moshe would have been: "His sister is in distress, yet he stands and prolongs his prayer."

Instead of looking at this midrash as a knock on long prayer, there is another way to look at it: Moshe knew that if he would prolong his prayer, people might actually think that Miriam was so nefarious that she needed such extensive help, which would have been passive *avak lashon hara*, leading people to needlessly think badly of Miriam. Moshe so internalized the dangers of even the fringes of *lashon hara* that he did not want to lead the people astray in their thoughts! Thus, the midrash's meaning is this: "Why did Moshe not pray long? So that the Israelites [wouldn't misconstrue that] 'His sister is in distress [as evidenced by] his standing and prolonging his prayer!'"

When the Tanna in *Avos* says that *tefillah* should not be **set**, this is classically understood to be saying that *tefillah* should not be rote; it shouldn't be a fixed passage devoid of fluidity. But **set** can also refer to the actual people praying as well: that the *tefillah* should be done in a way that it *changes the one praying* so that he or she demonstrates they are not **set** but rather "moved" by whatever they are praying about. Moshe so internalized the dangers of *lashon hara* he saw afflicting his very sister Miriam, that in response, his prayer for her recovery was done with sensitivity, so as not to smell of *lashon hara* in and of itself! Moshe thus, perhaps, didn't limit the length of his prayer because people might think he should have been tending to Miriam instead; rather, he limited the prayer's length so that people wouldn't err and think that she was so bad that she needed a lengthy prayer to recover!

──────────── TAKEAWAY MESSAGES ────────────

Moshe's paradigmatic short but sweet prayer for the healing of his leprous sister showed that he was not קֶבַע, set, when he davened. He was so moved by the horrific repercussions of her sin that he did not want to potentially sin with his very *tefillah* by misleading the people into thinking she needed lots of *tefillah* to heal her!

Long prayer is thus generally preferred over short prayer. Prayers should be set, but the one who prays needs to be "moved" and not set! Don't make your prayer "set"; change something to make it efficacious!

THE PROBLEM OF CALLING
THE UGLY BEAUTIFUL

הַמְהַלֵּךְ בַּדֶּרֶךְ וְשׁוֹנֶה וּמַפְסִיק מִמִּשְׁנָתוֹ
וְאוֹמֵר, מַה נָּאֶה אִילָן זֶה וּמַה נָּאֶה נִיר זֶה,
מַעֲלֶה עָלָיו הַכָּתוּב כְּאִלּוּ מִתְחַיֵּב בְּנַפְשׁוֹ.

*One who is walking on a path and learning and stops from his
learning and says, "How beautiful is this tree and how nice is
the plowed field," then the Torah considers him culpable with
his life. (Avos 3:7)*

——— QUESTIONS ———

This makes no sense! If a person appreciates G-d's creation, whether
a tree or a plowed field, why would that be a bad thing? The standard
answer given is that the person is being מַפְסִיק מִמִּשְׁנָתוֹ—he is stopping his
learning; he fails to see the tree or the plowed field as a "continuation"
of his learning, insomuch as they are really a continuation of the goal
of learning, which is to be more in tune with G-d and His creations. But
that nice idea can be made by just saying that the man said, "How pretty
is the tree?" or "How pretty is the field" alone! Why both?

Another answer may be derived from yet another question, this time
on our *parashah* at the episode of the complainers:

זָכַרְנוּ אֶת הַדָּגָה אֲשֶׁר נֹאכַל בְּמִצְרַיִם חִנָּם אֵת הַקִּשֻּׁאִים וְאֵת
הָאֲבַטִּחִים וְאֵת הֶחָצִיר וְאֶת הַבְּצָלִים וְאֶת הַשּׁוּמִים.

We remember the fish, which we were wont to eat in Egypt for
free; the cucumbers, and the melons, and the leeks, and the
onions, and the garlic. (Bamidbar 11:5)

It is understandable that the complainers would pine for the fish of
Egypt. It seems equally reasonable to pine for the sumptuous and wa-
ter-filled vegetables, especially in a desert. But what about cucumbers?
These vegetables were thought (at the time) to be constipation-produc-
ing, as well as harmful to pregnant ladies! Why would the complainers
include cucumbers in their complaints, which seems to water down
their otherwise valid complaints regarding the watermelons and fish?

─────────────── ANSWERS ───────────────

When the Jewish complainers complained, their lack of differ-
entiation between the delicacies of fish and watermelon versus the
potentially harmful cucumbers perhaps showed Moshe that they were
just boors, just complaining for the sake of...complaining. Maybe if
they legitimately complained about the delicacies they missed, they
wouldn't have been punished. By showing a lack of true discernment,
they showed a lack of the appreciation and attention to detail that
G-d wanted to see in the Jewish People as they were to enter the Land
of Israel. Perhaps the Jewish complainers were punished because by
complaining about the foods with such a discrepant value, they were
showing they neither appreciated nor cared to appreciate G-d's gifts;
they were just complaining in order to complain!

As for the Mishnah in *Avos*: The purpose of learning and Torah is
to apply it to our lives and give us perspective to live by. The Torah
shows us that things/objects are all to be appreciated but do have relative value. A beautiful tree is quite different than a plowed, dirt-ridden
field! When one is not able to see the difference between a beautiful
tree and a plowed field, he is showing that his learning has not got him
anywhere. A point of the Mishnah may be that learning Torah is meant
to help give relative value to things/ideas, and is not meant only to be
learned for learning sake alone!

The Jewish complainers complained about the delicacies of fish and watermelon. They also complained about missing the potentially injurious cucumbers, showing that they complained just to complain! They lacked an appreciation between the true value of a delicacy and a non-delicacy. This lack of depth perception showed their boorish nature. When one is truly learned, the Torah is supposed to show that person the relative value of things in our lives. A tree is more beautiful than a dirty field if your Torah got through to you!

Everything is not equally beautiful per the Torah. Things have relative value, and the Torah should help us appreciate both the ugly and the beautiful.

HOW IS MOSHE THE "MOST HUMBLE MAN"? ISN'T THAT A HAUGHTY STATEMENT?

וְהַתּוֹרָה נִקְנֵית בְּאַרְבָּעִים וּשְׁמֹנָה
דְבָרִים...בַּעֲנָוָה.

The Torah is aquired in forty-eight ways...humility, etc.
(Avos 6:6)

אֵיזֶהוּ חָכָם, הַלּוֹמֵד מִכָּל אָדָם.

Who is wise? One who learns from every man. (Avos 4:1)

Kehati on *Avos* defines "humility" as שפל—lowly (as per *Taanis* 7a). In the *parashah*, we are told, "וְהָאִישׁ מֹשֶׁה עָנָו מְאֹד מִכֹּל הָאָדָם אֲשֶׁר עַל פְּנֵי הָאֲדָמָה—Now the man Moshe was very meek, more than all the men upon the face of the earth." *Rashi* defines עָנָו also as "שפל וסבלן—lowly and tolerant."

─── QUESTIONS ───

1. First, the age-old question: If Moshe was so humble, why is he writing about how humble he is? As Timothy Keller once said: "Humility is so shy; if you begin talking about it, it leaves."
2. עָנָו in this *pasuk* is perhaps the most unusual *kri-ksiv* in the Torah. The word is written עָנָו but is supposed to be read as עָנָיו; not that much of a difference! Usually the reading of the word

368

(קְרִי) is verbalized differently than the כְּתִיב form, and so this seems bizarre!

3. At first glance, one may think that humility means acting lowly (as *Rashi* hints) without self-determination. But does being humble really preclude individual creativity, pride, and self-confidence?

4. Rabbi Avraham Lieberman beautifully asks: Why does the above Mishnah in *Avos* say, "Who is wise? One who 'learns' [i.e., in the present tense]"? It should say, "who has learned [i.e., in the past tense]"!

ANSWERS

There is an *esnachta*, pause, by the word עָנָו, which changes the reading of the *pasuk*: "Moshe was humble—PAUSE—[humble being defined as] believing he was just like everyone else on earth!" In other words, Moshe was defining עָנָו as "מִכֹּל הָאָדָם אֲשֶׁר עַל פְּנֵי הָאֲדָמָה." Thus, humility is to *believe in humanity*. Moshe was the ultimate believer in "מִכֹּל הָאָדָם אֲשֶׁר עַל פְּנֵי הָאֲדָמָה." He was certainly glowing with pride, self-determination, and individual creativity, but this confidence was predicated on his belief that everyone else was similarly bestowed G-d-given gifts and potential to achieve greatness!

Another *kri-ksiv* to note is when the Torah refers to the *nesi'im* as "קְרִיאֵי הָעֵדָה" (the *ksiv*), although it is supposed to be read as "קְרוּאֵי הָעֵדָה." Rabbi Bixon points out that the *yud* denotes self, because when added to almost any word it connotes possession. For instance, my כְּסֵא is simply כְּסְאִי. He beautifully posits that the *yud* perhaps signified that the *nesi'im* were naturally self-absorbed, and their challenge (the calling of the *kri*!) was to "shed the *yud*" of self-absorption and be more people-centric. Perhaps likewise here (in an opposite sense), the only way to achieve self-worthiness signified by the *yud* in עָנָיו is to first live a life as an עָנָו, believing in the rest of humanity. The prerequisite to succeed in life and enjoy your own confidence, self-determination, and individual creativity (עָנָיו) is to first and foremost believe in others (עָנָו)!

Revisiting our questions:

1. Moshe wasn't boasting about being humble insomuch as he was defining what humility is!

2. The עָנָו/עָנָיו unusual *kri-ksiv* may hint to how one may achieve self-worthiness—by first focusing on appreciating others. Thus, the *kri-ksiv* is not bizarre after all!

3. Humility doesn't exclude confidence but is rather the prerequisite for confidence!

4. Rabbi Lieberman answers his question differently, but another answer can be: "Who is wise? One who 'learns' (present tense)" is correct because it should be read as follows: "אֵיזֶהוּ חָכָם, הַלּוֹמֵד מִכָּל אָדָם—Who is wise? One who learns from the concept that Moshe taught us, i.e., the belief of מִכֹּל הָאָדָם—the concept that **hum**ility is a belief in **hum**anity!

─────────── TAKEAWAY MESSAGES ───────────

The *kri-ksiv* of עָנָו/עָנָיו and the *esnachta* splitting the famous *pasuk* teach us what humility really means. **Hum**ility is a belief in **hum**anity! Only by being an עָנָו and recognizing the strengths and potential of others as we work together can one ultimately enjoy personal success as an עָנָיו.

Moshe Rabbeinu was humble in recognizing that he was the ultimate team player.

Shelach

IS THERE A DOWNSIDE TO
TOO MANY MIRACLES?

עֲשָׂרָה נִסִּים נַעֲשׂוּ לַאֲבוֹתֵינוּ בְמִצְרַיִם וַעֲשָׂרָה
עַל הַיָּם. עֶשֶׂר מַכּוֹת הֵבִיא הַקָּדוֹשׁ בָּרוּךְ הוּא
עַל הַמִּצְרִיִּים בְּמִצְרַיִם וְעֶשֶׂר עַל הַיָּם. עֲשָׂרָה
נִסְיוֹנוֹת נִסּוּ אֲבוֹתֵינוּ אֶת הַמָּקוֹם בָּרוּךְ הוּא
בַּמִּדְבָּר, שֶׁנֶּאֱמַר (במדבר יד) וַיְנַסּוּ אֹתִי זֶה עֶשֶׂר
פְּעָמִים וְלֹא שָׁמְעוּ בְּקוֹלִי.

*Ten miracles were performed for our forefathers in Egypt,
and another ten at the sea. Ten afflictions were wrought by
G-d upon the Egyptians in Egypt, and another ten at the
sea...With ten trials our forefathers tested G-d in the desert,
as is stated: "**They tested Me these ten times and did not
listen to My voice**" (Bamidbar 14:22). (Avos 5:4)*

QUESTIONS

1. In the fifth *perek* of *Avos*, the Mishnayos about numbers are
    divided up into separate sentences. For instance, "there are
    four types of personalities" is on a separate line away from

371

"four types of students," etc. Why here are these "tens" lumped together? I can understand why the miracles and the plagues are put together, as they seem to be one and the same, but why throw in the "tests" that we tested G-d with? Why doesn't the Tanna separate these points out?

2. Why does the verse quoted in the ethic above, which also appears in this *parashah*, utilize the word וַיְנַסּוּ to mean "test"? This word וַיְנַסּוּ as it is punctuated only comes up three other times, all of which are in *sefer Tehillim*. Furthermore, why does G-d say אֹתִי as opposed to לִי (me), which would seem more fluent here?

3. Why repeat "and they didn't listen to My voice," which is obvious by the first part of the *pasuk*? The Torah in general is not redundant!

─────── ANSWERS ───────

One approach is that "וַיְנַסּוּ אֹתִי" is reminiscent of "אֹתִי וַיָּנַסּוּ," which actually would read well: "The Jews fled from me (אֹתִי) these ten times and didn't listen to me." I'll admit, though, that this is a stretch.

Rather, the word וַיְנַסּוּ contains the word נֵס—miracle. Perhaps G-d purposely used this word "test" here because He is, in a sense, taking responsibility for the undeveloped spiritual strength of His people. By giving B'nei Yisrael the "easy way out" with miracle upon miracle, we inevitably didn't develop true long-lasting *emunah* or deep-rooted belief. Hence, אֹתִי substitutes for לִי, as G-d is saying, "This one is on Me, i.e., by giving you so many miracles, you have consequently lacked *emunah*, and have thus challenged Me these ten times and not listened to Me."

One may appropriately question this: Why wouldn't roughly forty years of seeing Hashem on a real level drive it into us that He is there, cares for us, and has a plan? All of that can be missed and forgotten when going through the mundane everyday world, where He isn't apparent; but they were in the desert, living on miracles! The answer is that miracles, in fact, did fortify the indelible connection of G-d to B'nei Yisrael, but continuous miracles or gifts can naturally spoil us. This is likely because continuous miracles are expected, irrespective of our behavior. But it is also because we fail to appreciate the natural, which is equally miraculous! The greatest proof that the continually miraculous connection was not the panacea, was seeing how B'nei Yisrael managed to sin despite such awesome miracles.

Revisiting the questions:

1. The miracles are indeed connected to the eventual betrayal tests of B'nei Yisrael because we did not develop the proper *emunah* by virtue of all the supernatural gifts. This explains why the "tests" are mentioned in the same Mishnah as the miracles and plagues.

2. וַיְנַסּוּ was used here to show the connection of our betrayal to the miracles! אֹתִי is used as if to say G-d *admitted* some responsibility for our shortcomings.

3. "וְלֹא שָׁמְעוּ בְּקוֹלִי" is not redundant then, but is the consequence of וַיְנַסּוּ, which was the over-miraculization, leading to the betrayals!

———— TAKEAWAY MESSAGES ————

Miracles in abundance can actually have a negative impact on the development of our deep-rooted *emunah*. Our relationship with G-d is a microcosm of a parent-child relationship, and G-d is teaching us the dangers of spoiling our children (אֹתִי וַיְנַסּוּ), while simultaneously hinting that taking parental ownership (אֹתִי וַיְנַסּוּ) of our miscues can lead to a possible resolution. Miracles can hinder developing lasting *emunah*!

CAN YISRAEL REALLY SUCCEED?

דַ-הַכֹּל צָפוּי וְהָרְשׁוּת נְתוּנָה.

*[Rabbi Akiva says:] Everything is expected and yet permission
is granted. (Avos 3:15)*

QUESTIONS

At first glance, this is the philosophic conundrum: How can we have
free choice with G-d knowing what will happen? How are we to really
understand this?

ANSWERS

To answer this question, let's analyze a statement of *Rashi* from this
week's *parashah*. We are told that the *meraglim*, spies, who eventually
spoke ill of the Land of Israel, initially took forty days to scout the Land,
even though it was a very wide expanse that should've taken them
more time. G-d miraculously shortened their journey because, as *Rashi*
points out:

גלוי לפני הקב"ה שיגזור עליהם יום לשנה קצר לפניהם את הדרך.

*Since it was revealed before the Holy One Blessed Be He
that He would sentence them with a year for every day, He
shortened the way [so they covered ground more rapidly].*

The obvious question is similar to the question of Rabbi Akiva: If G-d knew that the spies were going to sin (even though they only later delivered their evil report), where is their free choice?

The answer is in the very next words in the Torah (after "forty days"): "וַיֵּלְכוּ וַיָּבֹאוּ." *Rashi* explains the need for the unusual double language of "they went and they came." It was "to compare their going with their coming; just as their return was with evil intent, so was their departure [on the journey] with evil intent." When the spies started their journey, they became evil. Their mission wasn't to prove to the people that the Land was good, but rather that the Land was naturally harmful and dangerous, and that it was filled with hostile enemies. Their failed attitude doomed their mission to failure from the very beginning!

Rabbi Avi Bossewitch taught us, in the name of the Rav, that when Rabbi Akiva says, "הַכֹּל צָפוּי וְהָרְשׁוּת נְתוּנָה," he may in fact be talking less about the philosophical conundrum and more about the reality of any given potential. He explained: "הַכֹּל צָפוּי"—Everything is expected of you," and "הָרְשׁוּת נְתוּנָה"—we are given dominion/power" (רשות doesn't only mean "choice" but also "domain" or "power") to execute our wills. As long as we genuinely believe in ourselves, we can be successful, but our expectations are inexorably linked to our attitude and belief that we have the power to execute.

Now it makes perfect sense. When G-d shortened the spies' trip to forty days before they sinned, He did so knowing that each day would be punished for one year, and He didn't want them to suffer too much. But He wasn't punishing them per se for their *future* evil, but rather because G-d saw **now** that their attitude was doomed, and they had no chance for success. The negative application of "הַכֹּל צָפוּי וְהָרְשׁוּת נְתוּנָה" here is that G-d recognized the evil intent of the spies and wasn't punishing them knowing that they will sin later, as much as providing them some discount on what He saw as inevitable, emanating from an evil, uncorrectable, bad approach! If you start off anything with a poor attitude or don't believe you have control of a situation, then the outcome is inevitably poor.

In 2019, when we look at our Israel, we shouldn't fear the Hezbollah to our north, Hamas to our south, and Iran/Syria to our east, as much as recognizing our unyielding great strength in being able to stand up strong to these bullies. הַכֹּל צָפוּי only works when we understand that רְשׁוּת נְתוּנָה.

───────────── TAKEAWAY MESSAGES ─────────────

When G-d shortened the spies' travel in Israel before they actually delivered their evil report, *Rashi* explains that G-d knew they were going to sin. But as the next two words clarify (וַיֵּלְכוּ וַיָּבֹאוּ), G-d wasn't challenging their free will as much as He was teaching us that with such a poor attitude and lack of *emunah*, the spies in fact had no chance to be good from the outset. They were focusing only on the formidable enemies and not on their own inherent strengths. Rabbi Bossewitch reminds us of the Rav's lesson on Rabbi Akiva: "הַכֹּל צָפוּי וְהָרְשׁוּת נְתוּנָה"—G-d expects everything from us as He gives us the power to execute, even the unthinkable.

Israel will continue to succeed as we focus on our strengths and worry less about our surrounding enemies!

SHOULD WE TARGET THE BULLY OR THE BULLIED?

רְהָיָה אוֹמֵר: אַל תְּהִי בָז לְכָל אָדָם וְאַל תְּהִי
מַפְלִיג לְכָל דָּבָר שֶׁאֵין לְךָ אָדָם שֶׁאֵין לוֹ שָׁעָה
וְאֵין לְךָ דָבָר שֶׁאֵין לוֹ מָקוֹם.

*He [Ben Azzai] would say: Do not scorn any man, and do not
disrespect anything.* **For there is no man who has not his
hour, and no thing that has not its place.** *(Avos 4:3)*

QUESTIONS

1. This Mishnah is confusing! So I should not be despicable to
   someone else because that person may have his moment of
   fame? I should not neglect an object because it may prove
   useful one day? Were we not taught by our mothers not to be
   disrespectful to anyone or anything because *it is just wrong*, disparate from the fact that the "disrespected" are perhaps worthy!
2. What is with this unusual and passive sounding verbiage here
   of אַל תְּהִי בָז? It sounds more proper to write "אל תבוז—Don't be
   despicable to…"! What does this Mishnah mean?

ANSWERS

So Moshe tells the spies to report about the Land and its inhabitants,
and the spies come back. Despite being rather pessimistic, their report
seems to be somewhat true at first glance.

וְשָׁם רָאִינוּ אֶת הַנְּפִילִים בְּנֵי עֲנָק מִן הַנְּפִלִים וַנְּהִי בְעֵינֵינוּ כַּחֲגָבִים וְכֵן
הָיִינוּ בְּעֵינֵיהֶם.

There we saw the giants, the sons of Anak, descended from
the giants. In our eyes, we seemed like grasshoppers, and so
we were in their eyes. (Bamidbar 13:33)

Wouldn't you expect the *pasuk* to read: "And they viewed us as grass-hoppers, and so then did we"? The problem with the spies was that they viewed themselves pessimistically rather than with pride. If you play the part of a grasshopper, no wonder the Canaanites will dwarf you. One of the sins of the spies, perhaps, was that they viewed themselves so negatively. If you are "וַנְּהִי בְעֵינֵינוּ כַּחֲגָבִים," then you are certainly weak "בְּעֵינֵיהֶם"!

Being victorious in anything you do first requires building yourself up. Bullies will be bullies, but the bullied need not be the bullied.

The Mishnah in *Avos* may not be speaking to a potential bully but rather to the bullied! "אַל תְּהִי בָז לְכָל אָדָם"—You, the potential bullied, **must not feel despicable** (hence the passive לשׁון) to all, or any person, because everyone (namely, you!) has his time and place!

────── TAKEAWAY MESSAGES ──────

When the Mishnah in *Avos* says, "אַל תְּהִי בָז לְכָל אָדָם," he may not be speaking to a potential bully but rather to the bullied. Once a bully is usually always a bully, and the trick is for the bullied to realize that "אֵין לְךָ אָדָם שֶׁאֵין לוֹ שָׁעָה וְאֵין לְךָ דָּבָר שֶׁאֵין לוֹ מָקוֹם"—that he has strength and power. This should enable him to stand up for himself when he needs to. Cowardly acts, such as those demonstrated by the spies, are borne of people viewing themselves as nothing but weak grasshoppers.

Should we target the bully or the bullied? The bullied are more likely to be modifiable.

Korach

IN A DISPUTE, IS IT BETTER
TO BE RIGHT OR...

כָּל מַחֲלֹקֶת שֶׁהִיא לְשֵׁם שָׁמַיִם סוֹפָה
לְהִתְקַיֵּם וְשֶׁאֵינָהּ לְשֵׁם שָׁמַיִם אֵין סוֹפָה
לְהִתְקַיֵּם. אֵיזוֹ הִיא מַחֲלֹקֶת שֶׁהִיא לְשֵׁם
שָׁמַיִם זוֹ מַחֲלֹקֶת הִלֵּל וְשַׁמַּאי. וְשֶׁאֵינָהּ לְשֵׁם
שָׁמַיִם, זוֹ מַחֲלֹקֶת קֹרַח וְכָל עֲדָתוֹ.

Any dispute that is for the sake of heaven is destined to
endure; one that is not for the sake of heaven is not destined
to endure. Which is a dispute that is for the sake of heaven?
The dispute[s] between Hillel and Shammai. Which is a
dispute that is not for the sake of heaven? The dispute of
Korach and all his company. (Avos 5:17)

QUESTIONS

The classic question on this statement in *Avos* is that just like the
"good" dispute was between Hillel and Shammai, the "bad" dispute
really should be Korach and Moshe, and not "all his company." Korach,
after all, was not fighting his company, and the parallel structure should
list Moshe, especially since he was the protagonist in that dispute!

379

One classic answer is that Korach actually did fight with his whole company, and this fragmented infighting is thus a classic example of a "dispute not for the sake of heaven." But perhaps there's another answer...

After Korach directly challenges Moshe, Moshe responds:

וַיְדַבֵּר אֶל קֹרַח וְאֶל כָּל עֲדָתוֹ לֵאמֹר בֹּקֶר וְיֹדַע ה' אֶת אֲשֶׁר לוֹ וְאֶת הַקָּדוֹשׁ וְהִקְרִיב אֵלָיו וְאֵת אֲשֶׁר יִבְחַר בּוֹ יַקְרִיב אֵלָיו.

And he spoke to Korach and all his company, saying: In the morning, Hashem will make known who is His, and who is holy, and He will draw [them] near to Him, and the one He chooses, He will draw near to Him." (Bamidbar 16:5)

Then Moshe complains to G-d a few *pesukim* later:

לֹא חֲמוֹר אֶחָד מֵהֶם נָשָׂאתִי וְלֹא הֲרֵעֹתִי אֶת אַחַד מֵהֶם.

Do not accept their offering. I have not taken a donkey from a single one of them, and I have not harmed a single one of them. (Ibid., v. 15)

Why didn't Moshe respond to Korach directly, saying, "I have not taken a donkey from you!" Why did he direct his frustration to G-d?

ANSWERS

A profound lesson may be that Moshe realized that Korach's attacks were not directed to him per se. They were not borne out of a real complaint or problem with Moshe but rather a personal ambition of Korach—a selfish jealousy not based on reality. To engage Korach head-on would be admitting that his complaints had merit and warranted defense. Moshe saw this as outrageous and wanted to make clear that this was all about Korach and his ambition.

A dispute that is not for the sake of heaven is likewise never a real dispute between one that is right and one that is wrong. It is most often about one who is misguided and another who is an innocent bystander. The innocent bystander, though, is often successfully drudged into a battle, making the antagonists succeed in creating the false impression of a real battle. Moshe teaches us how to battle those with nefarious agendas: stay clear and avoid direct dialogue!

Even when you are right, there is a negativity about being involved in any real dispute, and by demonstrating to the nation that Moshe wasn't disputing Korach but that Korach was just "disputing himself," Moshe was ex post facto able to avoid being involved or dragged into a מַחֲלֹקֶת שֶׁאֵינָה לְשֵׁם שָׁמַיִם. Who wants to be "right" and yet be associated with a מַחֲלֹקֶת שֶׁאֵינָה לְשֵׁם שָׁמַיִם?

─── TAKEAWAY MESSAGES ───

A dispute that is not for the sake of heaven is most often not a dispute, but is one that arises from someone's quest for fame/infamy. The challenge is for the attacked to avoid being dragged into battle. By avoiding battle, one may be able to stay out of being included in the same sentence as the attacker in a מַחֲלֹקֶת שֶׁאֵינָה לְשֵׁם שָׁמַיִם. Moshe is not mentioned in our Mishnah as being involved against Korach in a מַחֲלֹקֶת שֶׁאֵינָה לְשֵׁם שָׁמַיִם because he simply wasn't!

In a dispute, what's better than being right? Not being in the dispute to begin with.

IS IT WORTH ARGUING FOR ARGUMENT'S SAKE? THE LESSON OF KORACH

כָּל מַחֲלֹקֶת שֶׁהִיא לְשֵׁם שָׁמַיִם סוֹפָהּ
לְהִתְקַיֵּם וְשֶׁאֵינָהּ לְשֵׁם שָׁמַיִם אֵין סוֹפָהּ
לְהִתְקַיֵּם. אֵיזוֹ הִיא מַחֲלֹקֶת שֶׁהִיא לְשֵׁם
שָׁמַיִם זוֹ מַחֲלֹקֶת הִלֵּל וְשַׁמַאי. וְשֶׁאֵינָהּ לְשֵׁם
שָׁמַיִם, זוֹ מַחֲלֹקֶת קֹרַח וְכָל עֲדָתוֹ.

*Any dispute that is for the sake of heaven is destined to
endure; one that is not for the sake of heaven is not destined
to endure. (Avos 5:17)*

The examples in the Mishnah of arguments that will remain standing are the disputes between Hillel and Shammai. The arguments that did not last...are most notably from our *parashah* about Korach and his congregation.

―――――――――――― QUESTIONS ――――――――――――

What does it mean, "סוֹפָהּ לְהִתְקַיֵּם"? If you have an argument that is לְשֵׁם שָׁמַיִם, in the end it will be standing! What? Why would we want an argument to be "left standing"? Don't we want our arguments to *sit down* after they are duked out? I would have expected "סוֹפָהּ לְהִיבָּטֵל—It will be neglected and/or resolved"!

382

―――――――――― ANSWERS ――――――――――

My father, Dr. Larry Ciment, explained to me the following: When we say in the Talmud, תיקו, which implies that something is left unresolved (not surprisingly, tie games in Israel are called תיקו!), we are taught that it is an acronym: "תשבי יתרץ קושיות ואיבעיות"—[Eliyahu] Tishbi will answer problems and questions [in the future]." In other words, תיקו is thought to be saying that we are leaving this dispute for Eliyahu Hanavi to show us which is the right/actual way to go as only one answer is right! However, per Wiktionary, the word תיקו actually derives from the third-person singular feminine future tense of קם, which means "to rise/stand." When we are saying תיקו, we are really not implying or suggesting that one answer will eventually beat out the other, but rather *that very argument itself will stand the test of time.* Since each point has sound logic and basis, one way is not necessarily right and one wrong, although we clearly will practice only one way. In Judaism, we value sound Torah arguments, which is what propelled us to succeed all these years. Healthy arguments with sound logic will stand the test of time, irrespective of which is ultimately practiced.

Likewise, when Hillel and Shammai argued based on halachic truisms and facts, and their arguments can stand the test of time. "אֵלּוּ וְאֵלּוּ דִּבְרֵי אֱלֹקִים חַיִּים"—their arguments are **alive** today in the sense that their אמת nature makes each respective side of the argument a valid Torah point.

Korach's arguments directed at Moshe, however, did not have any halachic truism that would stand the test of time. He argued for the sake of arguing, and such arguments aren't everlasting. Yeshivos all over the world aren't learning about the *machlokes* between Korach and Moshe except during this week of *Parashas Korach* because his arguments were devoid of true meaning and life.

――――――――― TAKEAWAY MESSAGES ―――――――――

When the Tanna in *Avos* says that arguments for the sake of heaven are סוֹפָהּ לְהִתְקַיֵּם, he is likely saying that even when there are no clear winners (תיקו), the honesty/faithfulness/sincerity/truism behind each side will cause that argument to stand the test of time and be living as if the discussion was happening today; אלו ואלו דברי אלקים חיים. Arguing just for the sake of arguing and showmanship, like Korach against Moshe, will not be סוֹפָה לְהִתְקַיֵּם; i.e., they will not ever end up in a תיקו situation and will be forgotten the second they end.

A lesson of Korach is not to argue just for the sake of arguing. His arguments with Moshe were not left as תיקו because they were not סוֹפָה לְהִתְקַיֵּם! Arguments without any credibility will not stand the test of time.

THE ARGUMENT BETWEEN
KORACH AND MOSHE

רַבִּי אוֹמֵר: דַּע מַה לְמַעְלָה מִמְּךָ, עַיִן רוֹאָה
וְאֹזֶן שׁוֹמַעַת, וְכָל מַעֲשֶׂיךָ בַּסֵּפֶר נִכְתָּבִין.

*Rebbi says: Know what is above you: a seeing eye, a hearing
ear, and all of your deeds will be written in a book.*
(Avos 2:1)

הִלֵּל אוֹמֵר: הֱוֵי מִתַּלְמִידָיו שֶׁל אַהֲרֹן,
אוֹהֵב שָׁלוֹם וְרוֹדֵף שָׁלוֹם, אוֹהֵב אֶת הַבְּרִיּוֹת
וּמְקָרְבָן לַתּוֹרָה.

*Hillel says: Be of the disciples of Aharon—a lover of peace, a
pursuer of peace, one who loves the creatures and draws them
close to Torah. (Avos 1:12)*

QUESTIONS

1. What is the connection between these two great ethics?
2. What is the root of the argument between Korach and Aharon/
   Moshe? What is the significance of Moshe's plea with Korach and
   sons: לָכֵן אַתָּה וְכָל עֲדָתְךָ...וְאַהֲרֹן מַה הוּא כִּי תלּוֹנוּ (תַלִּינוּ) עָלָיו"—Therefore
   you and your company...and Aharon, what is he that you all
   complain against him?" *(Bamidbar* 16:11)

385

─────────── ANSWERS ───────────

The simple understanding of the above ethic is: "דַּע מַה לְמַעְלָה מִמְּךָ"—Know that He (G-d) is above you, watching and writing down your deeds from which you will be judged.

Homiletically, though, it can be read: "דַּע מַה לְמַעְלָה מִמְּךָ"—You should know that מַה—what (as in what you do) is greater than מִמְּךָ—who you are (born as).

You accumulate wisdom and knowledge by seeing and hearing (עַיִן רוֹאָה וְאֹזֶן שׁוֹמַעַת), but ultimately, only the things you actually do are written down for eternity. Ultimately, you are what you do—וְכָל מַעֲשֶׂיךָ בַּסֵּפֶר נִכְתָּבִין. The מַה aspect of your existence, represented by your accomplishments, is more important than your mere physical presence alone—מִמְּךָ.

Korach argues with Moshe, thinking that since he was also a Levi, why should Moshe and Aharon be granted favored status if in fact they were all born to the spiritually elite tribe? Moshe answered: "לָכֵן אַתָּה וְכָל עֲדָתְךָ...וְאַהֲרֹן מַה הוּא כִּי תַלּוֹנוּ (תַלִּינוּ) עָלָיו"—Therefore you and your company...and Aharon, **what is he** that you all complain against him?" The simple interpretation is that Moshe is downplaying Aharon's greatness to placate Korach. But notice the *kri-ksiv* here of תַלּוֹנוּ (*ksiv*, written, which denotes "complain") and תַלִּינוּ (*kri*, read, which denotes "complain" but also can mean "to rely on"). And so homiletically: "And Aharon is a מַה הוּא [his focus is on the what and not on the where-from], and we therefore *rely* on him—תַלִּינוּ עָלָיו." As the ultimate "אוֹהֵב שָׁלוֹם וְרוֹדֵף שָׁלוֹם," Aharon embodied the concept of מַה being even more important than מִמְּךָ! Perhaps Aharon could have had a peaceful existence resting on his laurels as the holy man of Kohanic stature, but as the paradigmatic "מַה הוּא," he understood that you are what you do!

So in answering the above questions:

1. In light of his communal virtues, Aharon represented the concept of מַה—what you do, superseding מִמְּךָ (לְמַעְלָה)—who you are born.

2. Korach and Moshe/Aharon argued this concept, and Moshe reminded Korach that we relied on Aharon as he was a מַה הוּא!

———————— TAKEAWAY MESSAGES ————————

The classic Korach and Moshe/Aharon argument may have partially been predicated on birth status versus life accomplishment. Moshe reminded Korach that what one strives to accomplish in his life (אוֹהֵב שָׁלוֹם וְרוֹדֵף שָׁלוֹם אוֹהֵב אֶת הַבְּרִיוֹת וּמְקָרְבָן לַתּוֹרָה) is more important than merely acquiring holy status by virtue of birth station. Moshe reminded Korach that דַּע מַה לְמַעְלָה מִמְּךָ, that the concept embodied by מַה is more important than מִמְּךָ. Am I a מַה הוּא or a מִמְּךָ? It's not about the wisdom we learn from seeing or hearing (עַיִן רוֹאָה וְאֹזֶן שׁוֹמַעַת) but rather our deeds reign supreme (וְכָל מַעֲשֶׂיךָ בַּסֵּפֶר נִכְתָּבִין)...

The argument between Korach and Moshe: Be a מַה הוּא or a מִמְּךָ?

Chukas

LESSON OF THE DESERT

אָמַר רַבִּי יְהוֹשֻׁעַ בֶּן לֵוִי: וְכָל מִי שֶׁעוֹסֵק
[בְּתַלְמוּד תּוֹרָה / שֶׁעוֹסֵק בַּתּוֹרָה תָּדִיר]
הֲרֵי זֶה מִתְעַלֶּה, שֶׁנֶּאֱמַר (במדבר כא) וּמִמַּתָּנָה
נַחֲלִיאֵל וּמִנַּחֲלִיאֵל בָּמוֹת.

*Rabbi Yehoshua ben Levi says: And whoever occupies himself
with the [teaching of Torah / with learning regularly] is
elevated, as is stated: "And from Matanah to Nachaliel, and
from Nachaliel to Bamos" (Bamidbar 21:19). (Avos 6:2)*

Rashi, on the cryptic *pasuk* from our *parashah* quoted in the above
ethic, guides us to *Targum Onkelos*, who translates these apparent places
homiletically: "A gift becomes an inheritance, which then enables you
to become elevated."

--- QUESTIONS ---

Regarding the aforementioned Mishnah in *Avos*, there are actually
two versions: One says, "וכל מי שֶׁעוֹסֵק בְּתַלְמוּד תּוֹרָה," and the other says,
"וכל מי שֶׁעוֹסֵק בַּתּוֹרָה תָּדִיר." Why not just say "וכל מי שֶׁעוֹסֵק בַּתּוֹרָה" without any
additions?

ANSWERS

The Talmud *Nedarim* (55a) and *Eruvin* (54a) actually expands on the homily derived from the *pasuk*, explaining that the aforementioned *literal homily* actually starts with the *pasuk* before, which says, "וּמִמִּדְבָּר מַתָּנָה." And so, why start with "וּמִמִּדְבָּר—from the desert"?

The first Gemara (*Nedarim* 55a) essentially explains that when one makes himself as the wilderness (וּמִמִּדְבָּר), which is free and expansive, representing an open-mindedness teaching approach, only then can the gifts of Torah be inherited and perpetuated.

The second Gemara (*Eruvin* 54a) essentially explains that when one makes himself as the wilderness (וּמִמִּדְבָּר), in the sense of being like sand that is trodden upon over and over again, only then can the gifts of Torah be inherited and perpetuated.

And so, the first Gemara (*Nedarim* 55a) aligns with the version "וכל מִי שֶׁעוֹסֵק בְּתַלְמוּד תּוֹרָה," because the focus is on how we need to teach others in an open fashion.

And the second Gemara (*Eruvin* 54a) aligns with the version "וכל מִי שֶׁעוֹסֵק בַּתוֹרָה תָּדִיר," as it is highlighting the concept of treading over and over again!

Regardless of which version you read of this Mishnah, the key that enables the flow from **inheritance** to **heights** (מִמַּתָּנָה נַחֲלִיאֵל וּמִנַּחֲלִיאֵל בָּמוֹת) is thus not the gift itself but the *mode of transmission*, i.e., the *midbar* is the key—whether by repeating things over and over (*Eruvin* 54a) or by being open-minded (*Nedarim* 55a) and inclusive in your teaching. It is very possible that the two versions of the Mishnah in *Avos* (תָּדִיר or the בְּתַלְמוּד version) derive from the two Gemaras trying to explain how the process of aquiring Torah begins.

TAKEAWAY MESSAGES

The only time a gift can become inherited and then perpetuated to great heights is if the transmission starts off with a מִדְבָּר. By both enriching our tradition by constant repetition (תָּדִיר) and by teaching with an open, accepting mind (בְּתַלְמוּד), we can ensure that the unique optimistic *literal homily* is not homilized in any other way. וּמִמִּדְבָּר מַתָּנָה is the hidden key to the homily!

Make yourself into a desert to transmit your teachings effectively.

THE LESSON OF THE CONTAMINATED EARTHENWARE

וְהַתּוֹרָה נִקְנֵית בְּאַרְבָּעִים וּשְׁמֹנָה דְבָרִים.
וְאֵלוּ הֵן: בְּתַלְמוּד בִּשְׁמִיעַת הָאֹזֶן בַּעֲרִיכַת
שְׂפָתַיִם...

The Torah is acquired in forty-eight ways. These are: study,
listening, verbalizing...(*Avos 6:6*)

QUESTIONS

1. So being a good listener (בִּשְׁמִיעַת הָאֹזֶן) and a prepared speaker (עֲרִיכַת שְׂפָתַיִם) are important traits of a Torah-observant Jew. But why is שְׁמִיעַת הָאֹזֶן in the singular tense (as opposed to שְׁמִיעַת הָאָזְנַיִם)?

2. Also, the term עֲרִיכַת שְׂפָתַיִם—literally "organization of lips," to denote "verbalizing" is unusual.

ANSWERS

The answer may be hidden in the following:

וְכֹל כְּלִי פָתוּחַ אֲשֶׁר אֵין צָמִיד פָּתִיל עָלָיו טָמֵא הוּא.

Any open vessel which has no seal fastened around it becomes
unclean. (Bamidbar 19:15)

Rashi says: "Scripture refers to an **earthenware** vessel, whose exterior does not accept contamination, only its interior. Thus, if the seal around its top is not securely fastened, it becomes contaminated. But if there is a securely fastened seal, it remains clean (*Sifrei*, *Chukas* 50; *Chullin* 25a)."

Besides teaching us about impurity, *Rashi* may be hinting to a practical lesson. After all, **earthenware** is made from clay and water, conjuring up the imagery of G-d creating mankind.

Essentially, the lesson is for humankind: "**Keep your lids closed!**" The more you keep your lid (i.e., your mouth) open, the more likely you are to say or do something stupid. Even if well-intended, if the vessel does not have the seal fastened, ultimately something *tamei* will result. It is probably not a coincidence that the mitzvah of avoiding *lashon hara* is derived from "לֹא תֵלֵךְ רָכִיל בְּעַמֶּיךָ." But being a *rachil*, according to the *Rambam*, is someone who is just a blabbermouth who isn't saying anything per se to hurt anyone else and is not technically speaking *lashon hara*. The point may be that a blabbermouth will eventually get into trouble by virtue of being…a blabbermouth, and so the laws of *lashon hara* appropriately start there!

But the open vessel (כְּלִי פָתוּחַ) may not only refer to our mouths. The כְּלִי פָתוּחַ may also refer to our hearing receptacles as well: If you listen to everything and everyone around you at all times, you are destined to be influenced negatively and become impure. You have to know when to keep your ears open and when to close them! Similarly, in *Kesuvos* (5b): "Why is the entire ear formed from firm matter while only the lobe is soft? So that if one hears something improper, they can fold the lobe into the ear and block out the sound." Again, any receptacle, whether your mouth or ear, that is left open at all times, is destined to become impure. Perhaps the lesson of כְּלִי פָתוּחַ is that we need to be selective of what we say and of what we hear.

And so now we can understand *Avos* as well. The עֲרִיכַת of the lips is to be differentiated from the similar sounding word, אֲרִיכוּת. "אֲרִיכוּת שְׂפָתַיִם" would connote long-winded speech, which makes us prone to error! Better it is to be short, organized, and concise, because אֲרִיכוּת—lengthiness of speech can lead to becoming *tamei*, much like the concept of a seemingly innocent *rachil* destined to speak *lashon hara*! Likewise, our ears should be "the hearing of one ear"—in order to remain pure, you have to know when to shut one ear and when to close one ear, i.e., to have selective reception!

———————— TAKEAWAY MESSAGES ————————

Perhaps the hidden lesson of the earthenware vessel that becomes contaminated on its inside when open is a lesson in "selective reception." It is better to have עֲרִיכַת שְׂפָתַיִם and not אֲרִיכוּת שְׂפָתַיִם; we also need to have שְׁמִיעַת הָאֹזֶן and not שְׁמִיעַת הָאָזְנַיִם!

The lesson of the contaminated earthenware: Know when to talk and when to hear.

WHICH LETTER CAUSED MOSHE THE MOST HEARTACHE?

רַ־בִּי אֶלְעָזָר אוֹמֵר: הֱוֵי שָׁקוּד ...וְנֶאֱמָן דהוּא
בַּעַל מְלַאכְתְּךָ שֶׁיְשַׁלֶּם לְךָ שְׂכַר פְּעֻלָתֶךָ.

*Rabbi Elazar would say: Be diligent in the study of
Torah...**and believe that He** is the Master of your work
[i.e., employer] who will repay you the reward of your labors.
(Avos 2:16)*

 QUESTIONS

Isn't this an unusual way to make the point that G-d will pay you
for your toil? Why not just say, "דע שהוא בעל—Know that He is Master,"
rather than this whole convoluted "Believe that he is the Master of
your work..."

An answer is derived from asking a few questions on our *parashah*:

וַיֹּאמֶר לָהֶם שִׁמְעוּ נָא הַמֹּרִים הֲמִן הַסֶּלַע הַזֶּה נוֹצִיא לָכֶם מָיִם.

*And he [Moshe] said to them: "Now listen, you rebels, can we
draw water for you from this rock?" (Bamidbar 20:10)*

G-d is then mad at Moshe for presumably not acting appropriately
and then says:

יַעַן לֹא הֶאֱמַנְתֶּם בִּי לְהַקְדִּישֵׁנִי לְעֵינֵי בְּנֵי יִשְׂרָאֵל לָכֵן לֹא תָבִיאוּ אֶת
הַקָּהָל הַזֶּה אֶל הָאָרֶץ אֲשֶׁר נָתַתִּי לָהֶם...וַיִּקָּדֵשׁ בָּם.

394

*"Since you did not have faith in Me to sanctify Me in the eyes
of the Children of Israel, therefore you shall not bring this
assembly to the Land which I have given them"...and He was
sanctified through them. (Bamidbar 20:12)*

What did Moshe do wrong? The word לָכֵן has the same *gematria* as
"מידה במידה—measure for measure" (*Baal Haturim*), implying that Moshe
and Aharon were barred from entering Israel because, measure for measure, they failed by the rock. But what is the measure for measure here,
and why is the action enough to spoil his legacy so much that he would
be barred from entering Israel? Did Moshe not "believe" in G-d (יַעַן לֹא
הֶאֱמַנְתֶּם בִּי)?

―――――――― ANSWERS ――――――――

The *Baalei Tosafos* beautifully say that, simply put, Moshe and
Aharon's mistake was that they said, "הֲמִן הַסֶּלַע הַזֶּה **נוֹצִיא** לָכֶם מָיִם—Can
we draw water for you from this rock?" Rather, they should have said,
"הֲמִן הַסֶּלַע הַזֶּה **יוֹצִיא** לָכֶם מָיִם—Can **He** draw water for you from this rock?"
Worded that way, they would have highlighted that only G-d Himself
can do such a miracle.

Perhaps true *emunah* may be a belief that everything we do is actually
G-d's doing, and that we are just going through His motions, for better
or for worse. Moshe, of course, knew this but failed in this moment to
teach B'nei Yisrael that G-d was separate (קדוש) from him and Aharon in
leading the Jews. "יַעַן לֹא הֶאֱמַנְתֶּם בִּי" may be read "יַעַן לֹא הֶאֱמַנְתֶּם בְּ"י," because
Moshe didn't teach this lesson of *emunah* (that G-d is separately/קדוש/
alone acting) because of the *yud*; in other words, they didn't highlight
or emphasize to B'nei Yisrael their obvious *emunah* by writing the *yud*
(instead of the *nun* when they said נוֹצִיא instead of יוֹצִיא)! In this sense,
Moshe wasn't punished per se by not going into Eretz Yisrael, but this
was the only final avenue for G-d to teach B'nei Yisrael the lesson of
emunah; namely that G-d is really working alone and that we are just in
it for the ride! "וַיִּקָּדֵשׁ בָּם" means that by Moshe and Aharon dying before
entering the Land, they showed that they are separate (קדוש) from G-d,
and that G-d is קדוש.

The Mishnah in *Avos* likely also reads homiletically:

- וְנֶאֱמָן—And who/what is a believer?
- הוּא בַעַל מְלַאכְתֶּךָ—The One who knows that He is doing all of your work (not that He is your employer, but rather that He is behind all of your work)!
- שֶׁיְּשַׁלֶּם לְךָ שְׂכַר פְּעֻלָּתֶךָ—And who [nevertheless] still pays you for your work (even though He is behind it all)!

Emunah is believing that G-d is running the show, with or without us.

———————————— TAKEAWAY MESSAGES ————————————

Moshe may have lost Eretz Yisrael, not as a punishment, but as measure for measure, because he was unable to teach B'nei Yisrael the lesson of *emunah* by the rock when he said "נוֹצִיא" when he should have said "יוֹצִיא." Because he didn't show the lesson of *emunah* by saying יוֹצִיא (יַעַן לֹא הֶאֱמַנְתֶּם בִּ"י), Moshe and Aharon were given another opportunity to show that G-d really runs alone separate from us (*kadosh*) by not going into Israel (וַיְּקַדֶּשׁ בָּם).

Which letter caused Moshe the most heartache? The *yud* that kept him out of Eretz Yisrael.

Balak

THE TIP-OF-THE-TONGUE BILAAM TEST

אָמַר רַבִּי יוֹסֵי בֶּן קִסְמָא: פַּעַם אַחַת הָיִיתִי
מְהַלֵּךְ בַּדֶּרֶךְ וּפָגַע בִּי אָדָם אֶחָד וְנָתַן לִי שָׁלוֹם
וְהֶחֱזַרְתִּי לוֹ שָׁלוֹם. אָמַר לִי רַבִּי מֵאֵיזֶה מָקוֹם
אַתָּה. אָמַרְתִּי לוֹ מֵעִיר גְּדוֹלָה שֶׁל חֲכָמִים
וְשֶׁל סוֹפְרִים אָנִי. אָמַר לִי רַבִּי רְצוֹנְךָ שֶׁתָּדוּר
עִמָּנוּ בִּמְקוֹמֵנוּ וַאֲנִי אֶתֵּן לְךָ אֶלֶף אֲלָפִים דִּינְרֵי
זָהָב וַאֲבָנִים טוֹבוֹת וּמַרְגָּלִיּוֹת. אָמַרְתִּי לוֹ בְּנִי
אִם אַתָּה נוֹתֵן לִי כָּל כֶּסֶף וְזָהָב וַאֲבָנִים טוֹבוֹת
וּמַרְגָּלִיּוֹת שֶׁבָּעוֹלָם, אֵינִי דָר אֶלָּא בִּמְקוֹם
תּוֹרָה...

*Said Rabbi Yosi ben Kisma: Once, I was traveling and
I encountered a man. He greeted me and I returned his
greetings. He said to me: "Rabbi, where are you from?" I said
to him: "From a great city of sages and scholars." He said to
me: "Rabbi, would you like to dwell with us in our place?* **I
will give you a million dinars of gold, precious stones and
pearls."** *I said to him:* **"If you were to give me all the silver,**

*gold, precious stones, and pearls in the world, I would not
dwell anywhere but in a place of Torah!" (Avos 6:9)*

QUESTIONS

I always wondered the following: Why does this Mishnah in ethics
go over the whole give-and-take here? It seems redundant and frankly
overstated!

Also, in this week's *parashah*, Bilaam initially staves off Balak's ser-
vants by saying, "Even if Balak gives me a house full of silver and gold, I
cannot do anything small or great that would transgress the word of the
Lord, my G-d." *Rashi* says the following on that *pasuk*:

> *A house full of silver and gold*—This shows us that he was
> greedy and coveted other people's money. He said, "He ought to
> give me all his silver and gold, since he has to hire many armies,
> and even then, it is questionable whether he will be victorious
> or not, whereas I will certainly succeed." (Midrash Tanchuma,
> Balak; Bamidbar Rabbah 20:10)

I don't get it! When Rabbi Yosi from *Avos* says, "If you were to give
me all the silver, gold etc.," we don't question him and assume that he's
full-on sincere; with Bilaam, though, *Rashi* informs us that his statement of "even if Balak gives me a house full of silver and gold" shows
that he is satiated with greed and insincerity!

ANSWERS

The reason why the whole give-and-take is mentioned in the Mishnah
in *Avos* is to show that the utmost priority of a community leader/*rav*,
or even a layman, really should not be money/materialism/wealth.
"Silver, gold, precious stones" should only be discussed if you are asked
a question directly about them, *but shouldn't be at the tip of your tongue.*
Rabbi Yosi thus only said, "If you were to give me all the silver, gold,
precious stones and pearls," because he was asked if he would take them
to leave his place.

Bilaam, however, was not asked about silver and gold but brought it up on his own, showing his materialistic nature. If we become engrossed in money talk, we will talk about money. It is human nature to talk about things that we value, and clearly silver and gold were on the tip of Bilaam's tongue—unusual for a prophet of G-d!

TAKEAWAY MESSAGES

We are what we speak. If unsolicited talk begins with gross materialism, perhaps it is time to reset. The whole give-and-take of Rabbi Yosi's story was to show this lesson: that unsolicited talk should not be replete with the mundane. Unsolicited, Bilaam revealed what his brain was imagining, i.e., silver and gold; his mundane nature was revealed! If you think holy, you speak holy and vice versa.

The tip-of-the-tongue Bilaam test can be used to assess someone's underlying nature. Would we pass the tip-of-the-tongue Bilaam test?

THE KEY TO JEWISH SURVIVAL—BILAAM AND THE LESSON FROM "HEN HEN"

רַבִּי אֱלִיעֶזֶר בֶּן חִסְמָא אוֹמֵר: קִנִּין וּפִתְחֵי
נִדָּה הֵן הֵן גּוּפֵי הֲלָכוֹת. תְּקוּפוֹת וְגִימַטְרִיָאוֹת
פַּרְפְּרָאוֹת לַחָכְמָה.

Bird-nest issues and the openings of a menstrual period, these and these are major halachos. Timings of seasons and word counts are just seasoning for wisdom. (Avos 3:18)

QUESTIONS

Presumably a point is to differentiate bird-nest issues, which entails bringing a certain *number* of bird-offerings, and *opening* of menstrual periods, which also entails numerical acumen, both of which represent a complicated type of counting, from the less-complicated *counting* of just knowing the seasons and *gematrias*! But what is meant by "הֵן הֵן—these, these"? Why is he specifically referring to these very obscure halachos of bird-offerings and openings of menstrual periods? Is there another deeper, veiled message here? An answer may be derived from our *parashah*:

ANSWERS

כִּי מֵראשׁ צֻרִים אֶרְאֶנּוּ וּמִגְּבָעוֹת אֲשׁוּרֶנּוּ הֶן עָם לְבָדָד יִשְׁכֹּן וּבַגּוֹיִם
לֹא יִתְחַשָּׁב.

For from their beginning, I see them as mountain peaks, and
I behold them as hills; it is a nation that will dwell alone and
will not be reckoned among the nations. (Bamidbar 23:9)

Bilaam's "blessing" was meant to show Balak how to attack B'nei Yisrael. The Jewish key to survival has always been in their ability to stay insular. If you can integrate them into society, Bilaam advised Balak, then the Jews may lose their Jewishness, and that is the best way to attack them. The midrash states that the letters ה and ו of הֵן are unique in the following way: When you have two numbers that need to add up to ten, every number will need a different number to get to the number ten. For instance, a 2 (ב) will need an 8 (ח), and a 3 (ג) will need a 7 (ז). However, the 5 (ה) is unique because it simply needs "itself" (another ה!) to make up the rest to ten. The same is true by the נ (50) when it comes to 100. Two of the same 50s (נ) will make up 100, while every other number will need to be combined with different numbers. The point is that the word הֵן represents the concept that we don't seek outside influences to "complete" us. We are happy joining with more of ourselves rather than complementing with an "outside number"! The danger with trying hard to complement ourselves with those outside our faith is that we risk diluting, and often straying from, our faith.

Interestingly, Rabbi Berel Wein beautifully explains that in 1812, Rabbi Shneur Zalman rebuffed Napoleon's surge for precisely that reason. "All of the physical benefits for the Jews that may have come in the wake of Napoleon's victory would be canceled by the loss of Jewish identity, purpose, and religious beliefs and practices." Similarly, Rabbi Shimshon Raphael Hirsch established an *Austritts Gemeinde* to break away from the Reform movement's strong push at assimilation in the 1870s. Both Rabbi Shneur Zalman and Rabbi Hirsch embodied the concept of הֵן and saw the positives of our insularity and homogeneity!

And as for the Mishnah in *Avos*, the obscure laws and halachos of bird-offerings and menstrual periods, which have so many permutations and difficult computations, are purposely obscure halachos that are precisely ways in which we can become insular—halachos like those guarantee our insularity. "הֵן—These are the ways to be, הֵן—insular and homogenous!" הֵן הֵן!

──────────── TAKEAWAY MESSAGES ────────────

When Bilaam blessed B'nei Yisrael, saying, "הֶן עָם לְבָדָד יִשְׁכֹּן—It is a nation that will dwell alone," he was actually pointing out B'nei Yisrael's strength in the ה and ן of הֵן—as a nation that keeps with themselves. He was thus cursing them by showing Balak how to attack them—attack their insularity!

The key to Jewish survival—avoiding assimilation by cherishing our insularity. Difficult Jewish ideas/concepts/traditions are the הֵן that keep us together and immortal.

BILAAM OR BALAK—WHO WAS WORSE?

כָּל מִי שֶׁיֵּשׁ בְּיָד וֹ...עַיִן רָעָה וְרוּחַ גְּבוֹהָה וְנֶפֶשׁ
רְחָבָה מִתַּלְמִידָיו שֶׁל בִּלְעָם הָרָשָׁע.

*All who have...an **evil eye**, a haughty spirit, and a gross soul*
are of the students of Bilaam the wicked. (Avos 5:19)

וַיִּשָּׂא מְשָׁלוֹ וַיֹּאמַר: נְאֻם בִּלְעָם בְּנוֹ בְעֹר וּנְאֻם
הַגֶּבֶר שְׁתֻם הָעָיִן.

And he took up his parable, and said: "The saying of Bilaam
the son of Beor, and the saying of the man whose eye is
opened." (Bamidbar 24:3)

Rashi explains שְׁתֻם הָעָיִן to means that Bilaam's eye had been gouged out and its socket appeared open. He was a classic one-eyed pirate prophet!

QUESTIONS

1. How is the one-eyed Bilaam the poster child of *ayin hara*?
2. Why is Bilaam the bad guy in this story, while his employer, King Balak, seems to get a free pass (actually, David HaMelech is a descendant of Balak!)?
3. What is the significance of the vast seeing imagery in this *parashah*? We start out "וַיַּרְא בָּלָק בֶּן צִפּוֹר אֵת כָּל אֲשֶׁר עָשָׂה יִשְׂרָאֵל לָאֱמֹרִי—And Balak **saw** all that Israel had done to the Amorites,"

403

and we end with "וַיַּרְא פִּינְחָס...וַיִּקַּח רֹמַח בְּיָדוֹ"—And when Pinchas **saw** it, he rose up...and took a spear in his hand"!

———————— ANSWERS ————————

From elsewhere in *Avos*, it seems that an *ayin hara*, evil eye, may actually be synonymous with *kinah*, jealousy. (Interestingly, "evil eye" in Arabic is *ayn al-hasud*, eye of the envious.)

But what makes an *ayin hara* an **evil** eye is that it is **one** eye (singular). Simply put, we generally have two eyes: one eye to "look" out for *ourselves*, and one eye to "look" out for *others*. The advantage of having two eyes versus one is in "stereopsis"—binocular vision delivers us the perception of depth.

Perhaps "being of two eyes" represents the idea that one should not be self-infatuated and should rather appreciate the depth/meaning to their surrounding environment. Perhaps it is no coincidence that words רַע—evil, and רֵעַ—friend, share the same letters, but that the transition from "evil" to "friend" simply requires having *two* eyes (the *two* dots of the *tzereh* beneath the *resh*!). By avoiding singular emphasis and opening your eyes to others, someone who is רַע turns into a רֵעַ.

Balak may have had evil intent, but *he was looking* (without qualification, referring to binocular vision) for himself and to protect his nation (וַיַּרְא בָּלָק מוֹאָב מִפְּנֵי בְּנֵי יִשְׂרָאֵל). Pinchas likewise *was looking* out without qualification, not only with regard to his own piety but for the benefit of his nation. One-eyed Bilaam, however, was solely focused on himself, and for that he garners eternal disdain of Biblical proportions.

Questions answered:

1. "One eye" represents jealousy; *ayin hara* is perhaps defined by its singularity (not *einayim*). *Ayin hara* is being completely absorbed with oneself with disregard for others. The "שְׁתֻם הָעָיִן"—one-eyed Bilaam, is the paradigm of *ayin hara*.

2. Unlike Bilaam (commentators say homiletically בְּלִי עַם), Balak was acting on his own behalf as well as his nation, and was therefore not as bad.

3. Both Balak and Pinchas, respectively, וַיַּרְא—saw (using two eyes), both for themselves and for their nations, in contradistinction to the nation-less, haughty, and jealous one-eyed Bilaam.

──────────── TAKEAWAY MESSAGES ────────────

The evil that belies an *ayin hara* is reflected by the word's singular tense—only one eye for oneself with no regard for others. Bilaam's jealousy and self-infatuation is contrasted with Pinchas's zealotry in the same *parashah* to highlight their difference. We must keep both eyes open at all times so that we don't fall into the trap of Bilaam. Enjoy this *vort*, בלי עין הרע!

One-eyed Bilaam is worse than Balak because he has the evil eye.

Pinchas

PINCHAS AND THE LESSON OF CHASING AWAY PEACE

הִלֵּל אוֹמֵר: הֱוֵי מִתַּלְמִידָיו שֶׁל אַהֲרֹן, אוֹהֵב
שָׁלוֹם וְרוֹדֵף שָׁלוֹם, אוֹהֵב אֶת הַבְּרִיּוֹת
וּמְקָרְבָן לַתּוֹרָה.

*Hillel says: Be of the disciples of Aharon—a lover of peace, a
pursuer of peace, one who loves the creatures and draws them
close to Torah. (Avos 1:12)*

לָכֵן אֱמֹר הִנְנִי נֹתֵן לוֹ אֶת בְּרִיתִי שָׁלוֹם.

*Therefore say: Behold, I give unto him My covenant of peace.
(Bamidbar 25:12)*

When Zimri ben Salu publicly brought a Midianite woman, Kazbi bas
Tzur, over to his companions, Pinchas ben Elazar ben Aharon HaKohen
took a spear, followed Zimri and Kazbi and then stabbed them through
the belly. The context of this seemingly gruesome killing was that
Zimri was rebellious (*Sanhedrin* 82a), and his outward licentiousness
had endangered all of Israel at that time. But imagine the *New York
Times* (the *Desert Times* back then, of course) headlines in 1272 BCE:
Would it have read, "Pinchas Heroically Slays Two," or would it have

406

read, "Pinchas Violently Slays Two"? Even if you think the headlines would have deemed it "heroic," it seems unimaginable that Pinchas would be granted "the covenant of peace," which indeed he receives in the beginning of this week's *parashah*!

QUESTIONS

1. What's the significance of reminding us that Pinchas was the grandson of Aharon?
2. Why does Pinchas get the covenant of peace?

ANSWERS

Rabbi Yaakov Frand says in the name of the *Kesav Sofer* that the connection of Pinchas to Aharon is to remind us that Pinchas was well aware of his grandfather's creed of אוֹהֵב שָׁלוֹם וְרוֹדֵף שָׁלוֹם (see above statement from *Avos*), and he still did what he did. He explains that if רוֹדֵף שָׁלוֹם meant "run after peace," then it would be written "רוֹדֵף אַחַר הַשָׁלוֹם," and if "רוֹדֵף שָׁלוֹם" meant "go for peace," then אוֹהֵב שָׁלוֹם would be redundant. Instead, the *Kesav Sofer* explains that sometimes we have to love peace and sometimes you have to רוֹדֵף שָׁלוֹם—run peace out of town!

Pinchas thus perhaps received the covenant of peace because he knew exactly when to invoke peace and when to chase it away; he was a רוֹדֵף שָׁלוֹם when he needed to avoid peace just as he sought peace when it was worthwhile! "Pinchas Heroically Slays Two" because Pinchas heroically understood that preserving the peace at that juncture would actually be deleterious to our nation.

TAKEAWAY MESSAGES

Aharon's creed of אוֹהֵב שָׁלוֹם וְרוֹדֵף שָׁלוֹם may not mean "preserve peace at all cost." Sometimes pursuing the ultimate peace is best achieved by not only avoiding a peaceful-yet-poor alternative, but to actually chase that poor alternative away—רוֹדֵף שָׁלוֹם. Pinchas thus gives meaningful value to peace as he delineates exactly when it should or should not be applied; he is thus granted the covenant of peace. May it be G-d's will that Israel and our USA likewise know when to seek peace and when to chase peace away, but all for the sake of a truer lasting peace! Chasing away peace can be a key to true peace.

HOW A *MECHALLEL SHABBOS* EARNED FIVE RIGHTEOUS DAUGHERS

וְכָל דֹֹ־הַמַּחֲטִיא אֶת הָרַבִּים אֵֹ־ין מַסְפִּיקִין בְּיָדוֹ
לַעֲשׂוֹרֹ תְּשׁוּבָה...יָרְבְעָם חָטָא וְהֶחֱטִיֹא
אֶת הָרַבִּים חֵטְאֹ הָרַבִּים תָּלוּי בּוֹ, שֶׁנֶּאֱמַר
(מלכים א טו) עַל חַטֹּאות יָרְבְעָם אֲשֶׁר חָטָא
וַאֲֹ־אֲשֶׁר הֶחֱטִיֹא אֶת יִשְׂרָאֵל.

*One who causes the community to sin is not given the
opportunity to repent...Yeravam ben Nevat sinned and caused
the community to sin, so the community's sin is attributed to
him; as is stated, "For the sins of Yeravam, which he sinned
and caused Israel to sin" (Melachim I 15:30). (Avos 5:18)*

—————————— QUESTIONS ——————————

Doesn't G-d afford everyone the possibility of *teshuvah*? What is the
specific lesson of "אֵין מַסְפִּיקִין בְּיָדוֹ לַעֲשׂוֹת תְּשׁוּבָה"?

————————— ANSWERS/ANALYIS —————————

Tzelafchad had five righteous daughters who famously plead and win
a historic case in our *parashah*. They reference their father as the *one
who died in the desert*. Rabbi Akiva famously learns a *gezeirah shavah* here
that indicates that he in fact was the *mekoshesh eitzim* who desecrated
Shabbos and was put to death:

409

אָבִינוּ מֵת בַּמִּדְבָּר וְהוּא לֹא הָיָה בְּתוֹךְ הָעֵדָה הַנּוֹעָדִים עַל ה' בַּעֲדַת
קֹרַח כִּי בְחֶטְאוֹ מֵת וּבָנִים לֹא הָיוּ לוֹ.

*Our father died in the desert, but he was not in the
assembly that banded together against Hashem in Korach's
assembly, **but he died for his own sin**, and he had no sons.*
(Bamidbar 27:3)

Rashi says here:

> *Since they were going to say that "he died for his own sin," they
> had to say that it was not for the sin of those who grumbled,
> and [that he was] not in Korach's company who incited [the
> people] against the Holy One Blessed Be He, but he died for his
> own sin alone, and **he did not cause others to sin with him**
> (Bava Basra 18b; Sifrei, Pinchas 13). Rabbi Akiva says: He was
> the wood gatherer [see Bamidbar 15:32], and Rabbi Shimon
> says: He was among those who ascended [the mountain] defi-
> antly [see ibid., 14:44]. (Shabbos 96b)*

Investigating the Gemara in *Shabbos* (96b), there is great effort to
show that Tzelafchad was in fact a righteous person. That being said,
he was killed for overtly desecrating Shabbos (meaning he must have
been warned and witnessed desecrating Shabbos!). What lesson can
we take away from that? What good did Tzelafchad possess that gave
him the merit of having such great children? (One answer, based on
a midrash quoted in *Tosafos* on *Bava Basra* (119b), is that he actually
sinned purposely, *l'shem Shamayim*, to show B'nei Yisrael the gravity of
desecrating Shabbos!)

A point may be as follows: We all sin. "כִּי אָדָם אֵין צַדִּיק בָּאָרֶץ אֲשֶׁר יַעֲשֶׂה
טּוֹב וְלֹא יֶחֱטָא—For [regarding] man, there's no *tzaddik* in the land that
does good and doesn't sin" (*Koheles* 7:20). Also, the *Seforno* famously
points out that it says, "אֲשֶׁר נָשִׂיא יֶחֱטָא—When a *nasi* sins" (*Vayikra* 4:22),
because inevitably someone with any sort of power is naturally going
to sin. Once found guilty of sin, however, it is quite natural to try and
get others to sin along with you as a defensive mechanism, á la "misery

loves company." There is a certain מעלה, goodness, in being able to say, "The sin stops with me or with my wrong act." Even though Tzelafchad was indeed convicted of a crime, of which he actually received the death penalty, he still did not try to influence others to sin! In that way, a sinner can actually accomplish *teshuvah* by merely accepting the punishment and not trying to sway others to sin. Tzelafchad's daughters precisely point out that their father's greatness in sinning was that he showed that the "buck stopped with his sin." He did not stubbornly cause others to sin with him. A hint to this may be in Tzelafchad's name itself (צְלָפְחָד). A צלף is a sniper, an assassin. He only, so to speak, assassinated one person, namely himself, *not dragging down anyone else with his sin!*

The Mishnah in *Avos* above similarly highlights the very important difference between a personal sin and a sin that causes others to stray as well. Although, of course, Yeravam can do *teshuvah* for himself, but this alone is not enough because the sinners he influenced also need to do *teshuvah*! It is not that he doesn't have a chance to do personal *teshuvah*, but rather that it is not מַסְפִּיקִין בְּיָדוֹ—it's not enough for his hands alone; he needs to find all those he influenced to do bad and try to change them, which is a herculean/impossible task. The difference between a Tzelafchad and a Yeravam is it is possible to repent for a sin that stays local (the Tzelafchad variety), while it is quite difficult to repent for the sin that blossoms and drags others down (the Yeravam variety).

TAKEAWAY MESSAGES

Tzelafchad had five righteous daughters, despite the fact that he was the *mekoshesh eitzim* who desecrated Shabbos. It was a true greatness of his that he died alone for the sin he committed, and did not drag down others by causing them to sin as well. There is a powerful lesson in Tzelafchad—that of **taking personal responsibility for error** while not letting the error turn into an unrepentable situation, as was the case by Yeravam ben Nevat. The desecrator of Shabbos did not drag others into sin—he was a צלף—assassin of only חד—one person, and successfully did not drag others into error! Perhaps for this he merited such righteous daughters.

WHY IS THE DAILY OFFERING BROUGHT TWICE A DAY?

כָּךְ הִיא דַרְכָּה שֶׁל תּוֹרָה: פַּת בְּמֶלַח תּאֹכַל
וּמַיִם בִּמְשׂוּרָה תִשְׁתֶּה וְעַל הָאָרֶץ תִּישַׁן וְחַיֵּי
צַעַר תִּחְיֶה וּבַתּוֹרָה אַתָּה עָמֵל אִם אַתָּה עֹשֶׂה
כֵן (תהלים קכח) אַשְׁרֶיךָ וְטוֹב לָךְ. אַשְׁרֶיךָ בָּעוֹלָם
הַזֶּה וְטוֹב לָךְ לָעוֹלָם הַבָּא.

Such is the way of Torah: Bread with salt you shall eat, water
in small measure you shall drink, and upon the ground you
shall sleep; live a life of deprivation and toil in Torah. If so you
do, "Fortunate are you, and good is to you" (Tehillim 128:2):
Fortunate you are in this world, and it is good for you in the
World to Come. (Avos 6:4)

QUESTIONS

Why the prologue and epilogue to the Mishnah here? "כָּךְ הִיא דַרְכָּה
שֶׁל תּוֹרָה—And this is the way of the Torah"; it all sounds redundant!
The idea is seemingly that if you suffer, i.e., by having bread with salt
alone or actually living a life of pain, then that is the key to living a successful Torah life. But is that really true? Does Judaism really espouse
asceticism?

—————— ANSWERS ——————

The answer may be found in this *parashah* regarding the *korban tamid*:

אֶת הַכֶּבֶשׂ אֶחָד תַּעֲשֶׂה בַבֹּקֶר וְאֵת הַכֶּבֶשׂ הַשֵּׁנִי תַּעֲשֶׂה בֵּין הָעַרְבָּיִם.

The one lamb you shall offer up in the morning, and the other lamb you shall offer up in the afternoon. (Bamidbar 28:4)

The nation was commanded to offer two lambs each day as a *korban olah* (burnt-offering), one in the morning and one in the afternoon. The "daily, perpetual" sacrifices were intended to draw us closer to G-d, but what is the point of having to do this in the morning and as the night is coming (בֵּין הָעַרְבָּיִם—afternoon)? Wouldn't the "perpetual" conditioning of the Jewish People be satisfied by just bringing this *korban* every morning?

It may be that G-d is teaching us that sometimes sacrifices and devotion will be in good and easy times, represented by the *tamid* brought in the morning, but we are also expected to show that very same sacrifice and devotion when times get rougher as well, represented by the afternoon *tamid* (literally, בֵּין הָעַרְבָּיִם means "between the evenings")! One step further, it is the *tamid* brought in the morning (i.e., sacrificing during the good times) that enables us to make sacrifices in the late afternoon (i.e., sacrificing even during hardships!).

The Mishnah in *Avos* may be saying similarly. The כּ of the word כַּךְ has a *dagesh* in it, and is the hard form of this letter כ, while the softer sounding ך of the word כַּךְ is the softer form of the letter כ. When the Mishnah says, "כַּךְ הִיא דַּרְכָּהּ שֶׁל תּוֹרָה," it may be saying that in order for us to be able to sacrifice and remain devoted Jews during the כ times, the harder times, we need to sacrifice during the ך times, the softer times. כ-ך is the message of the Mishnah. It isn't that we necessarily have to be ascetics and purposely live a difficult life. Rather, if we practice our devotion during the good times and become so accustomed to sacrificing of ourselves then, it will become natural for us. Once engrained, we are more likely to act the same during difficult times.

──────────── TAKEAWAY MESSAGES ────────────

כָּךְ הִיא דַּרְכָּהּ שֶׁל תּוֹרָה is a message that in order to be able to deal with difficult times that come our way (the hard כ), we should be diligent and practice during the easier times (the softer-sounding ךְ). כְּ-ךְ is the way a Torah life would be viewed. We bring a daily offering in the morning when it is light and comfortable outside so that we know how to make the necessary sacrifices when it gets dark as well, in the afternoon.

The daily offering is brought twice in one day, perhaps to highlight how and when we need to be willing to sacrifice of ourselves—in light periods and in the darker ones.

Mattos

ROLE MODELS AND FIRE

רַבִּי אֱלִיעֶזֶר אוֹמֵר: וֶהֱוֵי מִתְחַמֵּם כְּנֶגֶד
אוּרָן שֶׁל חֲכָמִים וֶהֱוֵי זָהִיר בְּגַחַלְתָּן שֶׁלֹּא
תִכָּוֶה...וְכָל דִּבְרֵיהֶם כְּגַחֲלֵי אֵשׁ.

*Rabbi Eliezer would say: Warm yourself by the **fire** of the*
*sages, but be beware lest you be burned by its **embers**...and*
*all their words are like **fiery** coals. (Avos 2:10)*

QUESTIONS

What is with the fire imagery anyway? Specifically, why are the wise
sages/teachers of Torah discussed in fiery terms?

ANSWERS

כָּל דָּבָר אֲשֶׁר יָבֹא בָאֵשׁ תַּעֲבִירוּ בָאֵשׁ וְטָהֵר...וְכֹל אֲשֶׁר לֹא יָבֹא בָּאֵשׁ
תַּעֲבִירוּ בַמָּיִם.

*Every thing that came through **fire**, you shall make to go*
*through the **fire**, and it shall be clean...and all that did not*
*come through **fire**, you shall pass through **water**.*
(Bamidbar 31:23)

After attacking Midian, Elazar told the troops to take any article that could withstand fire—gold, silver, copper, iron, tin, and lead—and pass them through fire to clean them, and to clean everything with the water of purification.

Literally this is talking about immersing utensils that have been ritually impure, but this passage literally begs to be homilized—specifically its references to fire and water!

Both fire and water are frequently compared/syllogized with Torah. For example: "מִימִינוֹ אֵשׁ דָּת לָמוֹ—From His right hand was a fiery law unto them" (*Devarim* 33:2); "מה מים חיים לעולם כך תורה חיים לעולם—Just like water brings life to the world, so does Torah (*Shir Hashirim Rabbah* 1:19). But these elemental qualities represent different facets of acquiring Torah.

Fire represents the teachers of Torah that can be fiery, enthusiastic, catchy, and inspiring. One small flame can light up thousands of wicks. The very *passing over* element of fire may be why the *pasuk* highlights transmittance: "*From His right hand* was a fiery law unto them." The sages above in the Mishnah in *Avos* are thus aptly described in **fiery** terms because they can be inspirational, causing many others to be lit up by their enthusiasm and vigor: "אוּרָן שֶׁל חֲכָמִים...וְכָל דִּבְרֵיהֶם כְּגַחֲלֵי אֵשׁ."

Water, on the other hand, represents the actual bulk/responsibility/yoke of the Torah. To feel the water, one must really immerse oneself. There is no real "catchy/passing-over" element of water as there is by fire, and thus the water really represents the actual potential of Torah itself.

So when we each try to grow spiritually, we basically have two possible approaches: Should we try to study the Torah by our own reading/learning or is the ideal to find some teacher, inspirational leader, or role model to follow in the quest to study? Truthfully, this applies to virtually any quest for knowledge as well: Should I focus my energy on the immersing in the material myself or should I expend significant energy in seeking a role model?

The answer from our *parashah* is the latter—if you are fortunate to have such people readily available! "כָּל דָּבָר אֲשֶׁר יָבֹא בָאֵשׁ תַּעֲבִירוּ בָאֵשׁ וְטָהֵר"—Anytime you have an opportunity to be with an אֵשׁ—fire, you must let yourself be inspired/guided/affected by that אֵשׁ who can bring you to an entirely different level—וְטָהֵר. If, heaven forbid, you don't have the opportunity to have that inspirational leader you wish for (וְכֹל אֲשֶׁר לֹא יָבֹא בָּאֵשׁ...), do not despair, as you can still succeed but you must ensconce/surround/envelop yourself in the water (תַּעֲבִירוּ בַמָּיִם)!

─────── TAKEAWAY MESSAGES ───────

The Mishnah in *Avos* compares Torah scholars with fire. Our rabbis are imbued with fire, an ability to spark and inspire. Our *parashah* tells us "כָּל דָּבָר אֲשֶׁר יָבֹא בָאֵשׁ תַּעֲבִירוּ בָאֵשׁ וְטָהֵר"—It is our duty to take advantage of these inspirational figures that can take us to greater heights than we can on our own. If we can't, we can always fall back on trying to learn on our own, but then we have to immerse ourselves wholeheartedly. "וְכֹל אֲשֶׁר לֹא יָבֹא בָּאֵשׁ...תַּעֲבִירוּ בַמָּיִם."

"Fiery" inspirational role models give us the best chance of more easily achieving our goals, but if you cannot find those role models, take on and immerse yourself in the challenges.

Masei

הַרְחֵק מִשָּׁכֵן רָע, וְאַל תִּתְחַבֵּר לָרָשָׁע,
וְאַל תִּתְיָאֵשׁ מִן הַפֻּרְעָנוּת.

*Distance yourself from an evil neighbor, don't attach to an
evildoer, and **do not despair from punishment**. (Avos 1:7)*

QUESTIONS

How do we understand the connection between avoiding an evil
neighbor and despairing from "punishment"?

ANSWERS

There may be two ways to understand this ethic:

1. You should avoid an evil neighbor, or someone with poor character attributes, because otherwise you may end up sinning
   ("don't despair in punishment" thus means, "don't be surprised
   if you get punished").

2. Another approach can be: You should distance yourself from
   calling your neighbor "a bad neighbor" in the sense of ascribing
   him "an evil person," despite his clear problems, so that he or

418

she does not despair (or lose hope) in lieu of their other punishments. In other words, הַרְחֵק מִשָּׁכֵן "רָע", וְאַל תִּתְחַבֵּר "לְרָשָׁע", וְאַל תִּתְיָאֵשׁ מִן הַפֻּרְעָנוּת.

These two ways of interpreting this Mishnah are best elucidated by analyzing two key elements by the "cities of refuge" in our *parashah*.

When a *shogeg* (accidental sinner) with partial negligence kills another, the Gemara in *Makkos* (7b) details that

1. Two learned men escort him (the Gemara clearly points out the main reason is to warn the גואל הדם—the avenger, not to kill this man who only accidentally killed).

2. Signs were set up to guide the killer to his safe haven in the עיר מקלט.

Why are two men needed and why are signs set up? We do not hang signs for the travelers all across Israel when they travel to Yerushalayim for the *shalosh regalim*, so why for the unintentional murderer?

One way to understand the need for the two men and for the signs is as follows: Since the killer has poor characteristics, in his being a *shogeg* with at least partial negligence (as opposed to an *oness*, where the killing was due to circumstances completely out of his control), perhaps two men (as opposed to one man!) are sent with him so as to avoid the need of any of these assigned "גואל הדם warners" to have to spend alone time with the killer. This relates to "הַרְחֵק מִשָּׁכֵן רָע" in that it is best to avoid evil vis-à-vis the negligence factor here.

Signs are likewise set up so as to avoid the possibility of the *shogeg* having to communicate with commonfolk in asking directions to the cities of refuge. As opposed to the journey to Yerushalayim for the *shalosh regalim*, when signs were specifically not set up so commonfolk would purposely be asked for directions to enjoin all with common spirit, here the goal would be to limit chances of poor qualities to "rub off" on the commonfolk!

This approach very much aligns with our first rendition of "הַרְחֵק מִשָּׁכֵן רָע, וְאַל תִּתְחַבֵּר לְרָשָׁע," namely to avoid any meaningful contact with someone who may "pass" on his evil traits to you by mere exposure.

A second way to understand the need for two men and the signs is as follows: Since he is merely a *shogeg* and not completely at fault, we really do not wish for him to abandon ship, and we go to great lengths to make sure he is not תִּתְיָאֵשׁ מִן הַפֻּרְעָנוּת—we don't want him to despair because of his punishment. All too often, sin begets sin because the one who sins feels abandoned, castigated without guidance. Perhaps two learned men accompany the inadvertent sinner to lend some *chizuk*, and we go out of our way to put up signs to help this man so that he doesn't descend into the abyss of depravity.

This aligns best with our second version of "הַרְחֵק מִשְּׁכֵן רַע וְאַל תִּתְחַבֵּר לְרָשָׁע," namely to avoid calling one "an evil neighbor" or "an evil person," as this will inevitably result in him despairing from his sins and self-castigation! This second approach is certainly a more positive approach.

TAKEAWAY MESSAGES

When dealing with people with known evil or poor attributes, intrinsic or extrinsic, we are reminded that too much exposure can inevitably make us vulnerable to their possible pitfalls. "וְאַל תִּתְיָאֵשׁ מִן הַפֻּרְעָנוּת" thus means, "Don't think you can easily escape their influence and so beware!" The first explanation as to why the castigated sinner has two escorts is so that the two did not have to cavort with and be influenced by this negligent man; the first explanation that the castigated sinner (albeit nondeliberate) had signs directing him to the refuge city was so that he didn't talk to commonfolk on the way and thus did not negatively impact them.

However, we are simultaneously reminded that we should go out of our way, perhaps obliquely and with a guarded eye, to point the way toward safety and improvement so that the sinner doesn't feel abandoned and fall deeper into a free-falling abyss. "וְאַל תִּתְיָאֵשׁ מִן הַפֻּרְעָנוּת" thus hints that we should do things to help others not feel despair over their troubled past! The second explanation for why the castigated sinner had two escorts was to give the man extra attention and love; the second explanation for why the castigated sinner had signs directing him was so that he would see the love afforded to a negligent man to help him find refuge.

The two escorts and the signs may have highlighted to what lengths we go to show that even the castigated among us are deeply loved and cared for!

HOW TO FIGHT ADDICTIONS—
CUT DOWN OR COLD TURKEY?

רַבִּי נְ—וֹרַאי אוֹמֵר: הֱוֵי גוֹלֶה לִמְקוֹם תּוֹרָ—ה...

*Rabbi Nehorai says: Exile yourself to a place of
Torah...(Avos 4:14)*

─────── QUESTIONS ───────

Why doesn't this ethic simply state, "Take up residence" in a place of
Torah? Why say "Exile yourself" to a place of Torah?

─────── ANSWERS ───────

An answer may be derived from our *parashah's* recounting of the
forty-two stops along the way from Egypt to Israel in the desert. Since
we know that the Torah is not a storybook, it is not surprising that the
names of the places that B'nei Yisrael travel through have some repre-
sentational significance. A great example is, "וּמִמַּתָּנָה נַחֲלִיאֵל וּמִנַּחֲלִיאֵל בָּמוֹת"
(*Bamidbar* 21:19), which is brought down in *Avos*. The homily suggests
that Torah is first given as a gift (וּמִמַּתָּנָה), then it is inherited (וּמִנַּחֲלִיאֵל),
and then it elevates you (בָּמוֹת)! In fact, apparently, the Chozeh of Lublin
had all but one destination figured out (see *sefer Iturei Torah* for a few
nice examples).

"וַיִּסְעוּ מִקִּבְרֹת הַתַּאֲוָה וַיַּחֲנוּ בַּחֲצֵרֹת"—And they journeyed from Kivros-
Hataavah and pitched in Chatzeros." Rabbi Yitzchak of Vorki states
beautifully that this may be homiletic: The best way to escape materialism (מִקִּבְרֹת הַתַּאֲוָה—burial of lusts) is to understand that we are

living now only in חֲצֵרֹת (front yards), and that the real home is in the next world.

Perhaps we can take this a step further: A חצר represents going outside the home, leaving the house. Sometimes, the best way to change oneself from the risks and effects of materialism and lusts is to realize the toxic environment that is causing the problems. Some problems just can't be fixed and must be avoided. For instance, the best way to stop smoking is not by cutting down smoking but by stopping it cold turkey. The best way to stop drinking alcohol is not by cutting down the amount of whiskey one drinks but by eliminating it entirely (admittedly both addictions are very tough to beat). The Torah may be hinting that the best way to disinfect from a toxic environment (מִקִּבְרֹת הַתַּאֲוָה—literally, the "burial of lusts") is by taking the one-time plunge and leaving (וַיַּחֲנוּ בַּחֲצֵרֹת—go "outside in the yard!"). The best way to tackle addiction is not to "cut down," but rather to "cut out."

When the Tanna in *Avos* says, "Banish yourself to a place of Torah," he is also espousing the concept that having bad influences around is a recipe for failure. To truly succeed, you have to sometimes make a clean cut from some of the negativity of the past. "Banish" yourself and remain in the חֲצֵרֹת, i.e., far away from the distractions that pull you down!

─────────────── TAKEAWAY MESSAGES ───────────────

The travels of B'nei Yisrael are listed to teach us lessons. "וַיִּסְעוּ מִקִּבְרֹת הַתַּאֲוָה וַיַּחֲנוּ בַּחֲצֵרֹת"—The message here may be that in order to really bury your lust/addiction/תַּאֲוָה, you must go to חֲצֵרֹת—remove yourself from the "house of addiction" and go outside! The best way to stop drinking, smoking, or doing drugs is not to cut down but rather to stop cold turkey. Similarly, when it comes to trying to better ourselves in whatever religious pursuit we have, it is best to make some clean break from the distractions rather than cutting them down—הֱוֵי גוֹלֶה לִמְקוֹם תּוֹרָה.

Fighting addiction? Better to stop cold turkey.

SEFER

Devarim

Devarim

FOR WHOM IS TESHUVAH NOT SO EASY?
THE LESSON FROM THE MERAGLIM

יָרָבְעָם חָטָא וְהֶחֱטִיא אֶת הָרַבִּים חֵטְא
הָרַבִּים תָּלוּי בּוֹ, שֶׁנֶּאֱמַר (מלכים א טו) עַל
חַטֹּאות יָרָבְעָם (בֶּן נְבָט) אֲשֶׁר חָטָא וַאֲשֶׁר
הֶחֱטִיא אֶת יִשְׂרָאֵל.

Yeravam sinned and made others sin; the sin of the others was
attributed to him, as it is said, "And on the sins of Yeravam
that he sinned and he caused Israel to sin"
(Melachim I 15:26). (Avos 5:18)

—————— QUESTIONS ——————

Isn't it a central tenet in Judaism that one can always repent? Why is
Yeravam different?

The answer can be derived by first positing a few more questions
on our *parashah*: When discussing the initial sinning of the spies when
they bad-mouthed the Land of Israel, it says:

וַיִּשְׁמַע ה' אֶת קוֹל דִּבְרֵיכֶם וַיִּקְצֹף וַיִּשָּׁבַע לֵאמֹר ...וַתָּשֻׁבוּ וַתִּבְכּוּ לִפְנֵי
ה' וְלֹא שָׁמַע ה' בְּקֹלְכֶם וְלֹא הֶאֱזִין אֲלֵיכֶם.

G-d heard their complaints and got mad and swore [that they would not enter Israel]…They returned and cried before G-d, and He didn't hear their cries, and He didn't listen to them.
(Devarim 1:34, 45)

If G-d didn't hear them (וְלֹא שָׁמַע), why does it repeat and say, "He didn't listen to them" (וְלֹא הֶאֱזִין)? Clearly listening to them (הֶאֱזִין אֲלֵיכֶם) and hearing their voices/cries (שָׁמַע ה' בְּקֹלְכֶם) do not mean the same thing. Also, what is the significance of the word קוֹל in this episode? There seems to be a connection between the קוֹל by the spies' complaining (וַיִּשְׁמַע ה' אֶת קוֹל דִּבְרֵיכֶם) and the קוֹל that they cried in seeming repentance (וְלֹא שָׁמַע ה' בְּקֹלְכֶם) in the end. Finally, the B'nei Yisrael who were influenced by the spies are repenting, and so why is the subsequent repentant faction of B'nei Yisrael rejected?

ANSWERS

The word קוֹל actually is a code word for *teshuvah*. In the *U'Nesaneh Tokef* of Rosh Hashanah, nearly every *machzor* has the word קוֹל printed above the word תשובה for that reason (at the part when everyone declares: "תשובה תפלה וצדקה מעברין את רע הגזירה").

When are we implored to do *teshuvah*? "הַקֹּל קוֹל יַעֲקֹב וְהַיָּדַיִם יְדֵי עֵשָׂו—The voice is that of Yaakov and the hands are Eisav's." When it comes to the *teshuvah* process for us Yaakov-ites, the appropriate course when our hands are those of Eisav's, i.e., when we act nefariously like Eisav, is in our voice. "When can Yaakov do *teshuvah* (הַקֹּל קוֹל יַעֲקֹב)? When you sin like Eisav (וְהַיָּדַיִם יְדֵי עֵשָׂו). But one cannot do *teshuvah*, however, when he causes others to sin! If your hands get dirty from wrongdoing, that is one thing, but if you cause others to sin, things are rougher.

This is precisely how the *Seforno* explains why the spies and their posse were not entitled to *teshuvah* (וְלֹא שָׁמַע ה' בְּקֹלְכֶם) because their initial קוֹל created a *chillul Hashem* in which they caused others to sin. The *Seforno* connected the first and the second קוֹל: the first קוֹל of the spies that caused others to sin led to Hashem not listening to their second קוֹל of *teshuvah*!

The same way the spies were not granted the opportunity for קוֹל (i.e., repentance) because of their ill-advised קוֹל of causing others to sin, so too Yeravam ben Nevat, as mentioned in *Avos*, caused others to sin, and thus he was not granted the ability to do *teshuvah* in this world.

──── TAKEAWAY MESSAGES ────

Sins that lead others to fall as well are the least repent-able! The spies, like Yeravam ben Nevat later on, were not afforded the chance to do *teshuvah* in this world because the קוֹל that preceded their קוֹל was one that caused many others to stumble! הַקֹּל קוֹל יַעֲקֹב וְהַיָּדַיִם יְדֵי עֵשָׂו—When can we have a קוֹל or do *teshuvah*? Only when our hands are personally like those of Eisav, but not when we cause others to be like Eisav!

When we sin, we should try to sin by ourselves and leave others out of it!

DEVARIM'S LESSON IN HOW TO SHOW OFF OUR "THINGS"

רַ־בִּי יוֹנָתָן אוֹמֵר: כָּל הַמְקַיֵּם אֶת הַ־תּוֹרָה
מֵעֹנִי סוֹפוֹ לְ־קַיְּמָהּ מֵעשֶׁר... וְכָל הַמְבַטֵּל אֶ־ת
הַ־תּוֹרָה מֵעשֶׁר סוֹפוֹ לְ־בַטְּלָהּ מֵעֹנִי.

Rabbi Yonasan would say: Whoever fulfills the Torah in poverty, will ultimately fulfill it in wealth...and whoever neglects the Torah in wealth, will ultimately neglect it in poverty. (Avos 4:9)

The classic understanding is that if you fulfill the Torah when poor, you will be rewarded with fulfilling the Torah with wealth; conversely, if you neglect the Torah way when wealthy, you will neglect the Torah way in destitution. The classic understanding then speaks of two scenarios and highlights the challenge of fulfilling a Torah life against the odds, specifically when destitute (either monetarily or devoid of opportunity).

─── QUESTIONS ───

Why does it say מֵעֹנִי and מֵעשֶׁר, which means *from* destitution and *from* wealth, as opposed to בְּעֹנִי and בְּעשֶׁר, *in* poverty/wealth?

─── ANSWERS ───

It may very well be that the ethic is talking about a frame of mind and not a financial status, e.g., poverty or wealth. This explanation is derived from this *parashah*:

G-d instructs B'nei Yisrael to move from the mountain they were on: "רַב לָכֶם סֹב אֶת הָהָר הַזֶּה פְּנוּ לָכֶם צָפֹנָה—You have compassed this mountain long enough; turn **northward**" (*Devarim* 2:3).

The *Gelilei Yosef* says that the word צָפֹנָה also means "hidden," and the homiletic lesson here is that when one achieves success, he needs to avoid being ostentatious; hide your wealth/success/fame and be modest! He further homilized that when the Talmud says (*Bava Basra* 25), "הרוצה שיעשיר יצפין—Whoever wants to be wealthy, turn to the **north direction**," it can be read, "Whoever wants to remain wealthy, he should **hide**/not show off this wealth!" A reason posited is to avoid generating *ayin hara* from others! The bottom-line message is that if you want your wealth to sustain, you must "hide" it, in a sense.

It is not a coincidence that people descending from Yosef HaTzaddik are spared the deleterious effects from the *ayin hara*. Yosef learned that his good looks and ostentatious behavior led him to many difficulties (e.g., being sold as a slave by his brothers, and later being framed by Potifar's wife when he resisted her advances). He adapted, and eventually became the ultimate disguiser, hiding his appearance so well that even his very brothers didn't recognize him. Clearly there is value in hiding our gifts so as not to provoke the "evil eye," whatever that may be.

With this, we can now reexamine the Mishnah in *Avos*: When one fulfills the Torah מֵעֹנִי—*from* a state of destitution, as opposed to *in* a state of destitution (בְּעֹנִי), the Tanna is likewise reminding us that in spiritual pursuits as well, we shouldn't flaunt and be ostentatious. The only way to really become successful (מֵעֹשֶׁר) is by pursuing spirituality with a non-flaunting, non-conceited nature—מֵעֹנִי. The lesson is not saying that you have to be literally poor (בְּעֹנִי) to be a *talmid chacham* or holy person; rather, you just simply need to be unassuming despite your great spirituality.

——— TAKEAWAY MESSAGES ———

When G-d tells B'nei Yisrael when they are high on the mountaintop to go צָפוֹן—northward, perhaps the message is to remind us that in order to succeed, we need to keep things צָפוֹן—hidden to some extent (*Gelilei*

Yosef). Being showy in our materialistic as well as spiritual endeavors (we should be הַמְקַיֵּם אֶת הַתּוֹרָה מֵעֹנִי) can bring upon *ayin hara*!

The lesson from *Devarim*: Keep your things "hidden" if you want to keep them!

WHY JEWS ARE COMPARED TO STARS AND THE LESSON OF "HAYOM"

הַיּוֹם קָצֵר וְהַמְּלָאכָה מְרֻבָּה, וְהַפּוֹעֲלִים עֲצֵלִים, וְהַשָּׂכָר הַרְבֵּה, וּבַעַל הַבַּיִת דּוֹחֵק.

The day is short, the work is much, the workers are lazy, the reward is great, and the Master is pressing. (Avos 2:15)

--- QUESTIONS ---

Why does the author in *Avos* say, "The day is short"? Shouldn't it say, "Life is short"?

Let us analyze the following from our *parashah*:

וְהִנְּכֶם הַיּוֹם כְּכוֹכְבֵי הַשָּׁמַיִם לָרֹב.

*Behold, you are **this day** as the stars of heaven for multitude.*
(Devarim 1:10)

As Moshe begins his discourse to us, he starts out by apparently stating a fact that the Jews have burgeoned into a large multitude.

Were the Jews on **that day** as many as the stars of the heavens? Weren't they only six hundred thousand? What does "**that day**" add? Furthermore, why are the Jews often compared to the stars in the sky [and the sand of the earth]?

———— ANSWERS ————

Rashi answers from the *Sifri*: "[It means:] Behold, you are compared to the sun, [signifying that you will] exist forever as the sun, the moon, and the stars do." In other words, just as **the day** is a naturally reliable entity, so is our eternal survival! This answers the meaning behind "the day," but what about the analogy to the stars?

My father, Dr. Larry Ciment, always says that Jews are compared to the stars of the sky and the sand of the sea because "just like you don't see the stars during the day but you know they will come out again, and just like the sand seemingly disappears during high tide, inevitably, the stars show up again and the sand reappears in due time. We Jews likewise have our historic lows (i.e., Crusades, Nazi Germany) but always find a way to seemingly miraculously reappear." *Parashas Devarim* is often read during the month of Av when unfortunately we need the reminder from Moshe that despite being down and out, G-d never abandons us.

I would like to add two points in addition to the *Sifri* and my father:

Moshe Rabbeinu may specifically be pointing out that the Jewish People are like the stars in the sky *during the day*. During the day, one cannot normally appreciate the multitude of stars because the light blurs out the image (on a moonless night, you can actually count up to three thousand to four thousand stars after eye adaptation). Moshe may be saying that the Jews' existence is as miraculous as seeing a multitude of stars during the day! Further, Moshe may even more likely be *prescribing* how we should act as a nation: It is easy to appreciate a multitude of stars during the night. Our role is to realize that we are a multitude of stars even during the day. According to this, Moshe is saying: Don't only realize our stardom during the "nighttime hours," i.e., times of distress and pain, but even during the happy days, we must recognize that we are a bunch of stars! Moshe is thus not giving a description but a prescription!

Whether you view Moshe's "וְהִנְּכֶם הַיּוֹם...." as a description (Jewish existence is miraculous) or as a prescription (Jewish uniqueness should be recognized even during happy times), it is "*the day*" that evokes this sense of positivity. This is likewise why the author in *Avos* uses the term "the *day* is short" and not "*life* is short" because "the day" evokes a positive mindset. No matter how hard our life is, our existence is miraculous, and we should strive to recognize each other's stardom even in good times.

───────── TAKEAWAY MESSAGES ─────────

Moshe compares us to "today, to the multitude of stars in the sky" to remind us of our national immortality (*Sifri*). Like stars, we should take solace during Tishah b'Av in knowing that we will be visible again, even though there are times when we can't be seen (my father, Dr. Larry Ciment). Our immortality is as unlikely as stars being visible during the day, and our challenge is to appreciate our nations' uniqueness even during the happy, quiet times! Don't only be a star-gazer at night!

Jews are compared to stars during the day because we must know our greatness is there, even when it isn't clearly visible!

...BUT WORDS WILL NEVER HURT ME?

הוּא הָיָה אוֹמֵר: וְאַל תֹּאמַר דָּבָר שֶׁאִי אֶפְשָׁר לִשְׁמֹעַ שֶׁסּוֹפוֹ לְהִישָּׁמַע.

He [Hillel] would say: And don't say something that's impossible to hear because in the end it can be heard.
(Avos 2:4)

QUESTIONS

What does this cryptic Mishnah mean? There are many possibilities, but one answer is related to our *parashah* and explains why *Parashas Devarim* is always read on the Shabbos before Tishah b'Av.

ANSWERS

Hillel may be simply referring to *lashon hara*. You should not think that what you say or what you listen to bear no consequence. We need to pay particular attention and understand that every action has a re-action. "Don't say 'something that no one will hear' because in the end 'it will be heard'" means that we need to take responsibility for what we say and even what we listen to.

When the spies gave their bad report, the Jews "murmured in [their] tents and said, 'Because the Lord hates us, He took us out of the land of Egypt to deliver us into the hand[s] of the Amorites to exterminate us'" (*Devarim* 1:27). The Jews perhaps figured they wouldn't be punished for merely expressing their words/opinions, but G-d reminds us that He indeed "heard their complaints and got mad and swore [that they would not enter Israel]." Tishah b'Av is a time when we learn that our words are just as powerful as our deeds!

Here is a list of the tragedies that occurred on Tishah b'Av (from Aish.com):

1. During the time of Moshe, Jews in the desert accepted the slanderous report of the ten spies, and the decree was issued forbidding them from entering the Land of Israel. (1312 BCE)
2. The First Temple was destroyed by the Babylonians, led by Nebuchadnetzar. One hundred thousand Jews were slaughtered and millions more exiled. (586 BCE)
3. The Second Temple was destroyed by the Romans, led by Titus. Some two million Jews died, and another one million were exiled. (70 CE)
4. The Bar Kochba revolt was crushed by Roman emperor Hadrian. The city of Betar, the Jews' last stand against the Romans, was captured and liquidated. Over one hundred Jews were slaughtered. (135 CE)
5. The Temple area and its surroundings were plowed under by the Roman general Turnus Rufus. Jerusalem was rebuilt as a pagan city—renamed Aelia Capitolina—and access was forbidden to Jews.

Other grave misfortunes throughout Jewish history occurred on Tishah b'Av, including:

1. The Spanish Inquisition culminated with the expulsion of Jews from Spain on Tishah b'Av in 1492.
2. World War I broke out on the eve of Tishah b'Av in 1914 when Germany declared war on Russia. German resentment from the war set the stage for the Holocaust.
3. On the eve of Tishah b'Av, 1942, the mass deportation of Jews from the Warsaw Ghetto en route to Treblinka began.

It is no coincidence that Tishah b'Av always falls out the week of *Parashas Devarim* ("These are the words (*devarim*) that Moshe spoke to all of Israel." The lesson is that even words can impact our lives, and in fact, they changed the course of Jewish history.

———————— TAKEAWAY MESSAGES ————————

When Hillel says, "Don't say something that no one will hear because in the end it will be heard," he is reminding us that words are just as powerful as physical actions. The negativity surrounding Tishah b'Av emanated from our initial misstep, which was under-appreciation of the power in our words and thoughts.

Tishah b'Av and *Parashas Devarim*—Sticks and stones may break my bones when words are ill-advised and ill-considered!

Va'eschanan

SHABBOS AND BEING A GOOD JEW

בֶּן עַזַּאי אוֹמֵר: הֱוֵי רָץ לְמִצְוָה קַלָּה כְּבַחֲמוּרָה, וּבוֹרֵחַ מִן הָעֲבֵרה...

Ben Azzai says: Run to to do a small mitzvah like a hard one and run from a sin... (Avos 4:2)

The quintessential ethical Jew is not merely defined by avoiding transgressions but also by actively seeking to do good deeds. The "וּבוֹרֵחַ מִן הָעֲבֵרה" (nonmaleficence) must be combined with "הֱוֵי רָץ לְמִצְוָה" (beneficence). Shabbos is the mitzvah in the Torah that is set as our training tool to become such an ethical Jew. How so? Let's find out by first analyzing a different question:

— QUESTIONS —

Gavriel Mendelsohn observed that the nighttime *Shemoneh Esreh* (מעריב) of שבת says: "וינוחו בה ישראל מקדשי שמך"—And Yisrael will rest in it, the sanctifiers of Your name." By the daytime *Shemoneh Esreh* (שחרית), we change to בו, and in the afternoon *Shemoneh Esreh* (מנחה) it changes to בם. Why switch from feminine to masculine to plural by this very same statement in each successive *Shemoneh Esreh*?

It says in our *parashah*: "שָׁמוֹר אֶת יוֹם הַשַּׁבָּת לְקַדְּשׁוֹ." On the spot, *Rashi* reminds us of the other directive vis-a-vis fulfilling the precept of Shabbos, namely זָכוֹר. And so, there are essentially two different aspects of Shabbos: the *zachor* and the *shamor*.

The *shamor* aspect is "Don't do *melachah*," which is in fact spelled out in the *pesukim* in our *parashah*. The *zachor* aspect has to do with things that make Shabbos special (see the end of *Rashi* to *Shemos* 20:8). The primary *zachor* obligation is Kiddush on Friday night, as Shabbos enters.

When you look at the nighttime *tefillah/Maariv* of Shabbos, the concept of "וַיְכֻלּוּ הַשָּׁמַיִם" is highlighted—remembering that G-d *completed* the creation on the seventh day. This aspect of Shabbos is more "feminine" in that it shows how B'nei Yisrael were "*mekabel*" i.e., passively endowed (women are generally considered as being "*mekabel*") the gift from G-d of Shabbos. This "passivity" goes well with the relatively passive literal concept of *zachor*, "remembering" the Shabbos. On Friday night, it is toward the end of the day, when we are no longer at work, that Shabbos is expressed and experienced by "passively" sitting at the Shabbos table at a Shabbos *seudah*, etc.

But come Shabbos morning, we take a more active, decisive step of **not** going to work. This now satisfies the *shamor* aspect.

Finally, at *Minchah* time, we see a culmination of both—spending a day away from work, together with living a Shabbos experience with *seudos*, family, going to shul, Shabbos schedule, etc. Thus, we see a culmination of *zachor* and *shamor*!

And so now we can understand why our *Shemoneh Esreh* first says בה by *Maariv*, highlighting the feminine aspect of remembering (through Kiddush and "passively" sitting at the table!), how we were endowed and completed with this holy gift of Shabbos (i.e., the *zachor* element). Then the next *Shemoneh Esreh* says, בו, highlighting the more masculine, positive actions in keeping Shabbos (i.e., the *shamor* aspect of not going to work). Then by *Minchah*, we say בם, which represents the culmination of the feminine and masculine aspects of keeping Shabbos.

Shabbos is the quintessential mitzvah that harbors both the concepts of:

1. וּבוֹרֵחַ מִן הָעֲבֵרָה, as we not only avoid work/*muktzeh* items but also actively pursue actionable deeds
2. הֱוֵי רָץ לְמִצְוָה, as we accomplish the *mitzvos ha'yom*!

We repeat Shabbos week in and week out to inculcate this approach into our ethical DNA.

TAKEAWAY MESSAGES

Shabbos is our weekly training course in our quest to become an ethical Jew: avoiding sin and pursuing good—nonmaleficence and beneficence. The *zachor* (passive/feminine qualities) and the *shamor* (more masculine, go-getter aspects) components are equally important. וינוחו בו and וינוחו בה...

How does Shabbos train us to be good Jews? By avoiding sin and doing good—nonmaleficence and beneficence.

HOW IS PRAYER STRONGER
THAN GOOD DEEDS?

רַ—בִּי שִׁמְעוֹן אוֹמֵר: הֱוֵי זָהִיר בִּקְרִיַ—ﬨ שְׁמַע
וּבַﬨְּפִלָּ—ה. וּכְשֶׁאַתָּה מִתְפַּלֵּל, אַל־תַּעַשׂ
תְּפִלָּ—ﬨְךָ קֶבַע, אֶלָּא רַחֲמִים וְﬨַחֲנוּנִים לִפְנֵי
הַמָּקוֹם בָּר—וּךְ הוּא, שֶׁנֶּאֱמַר—(יואל ב) כִּי חַנּוּן
וְרַחוּ—ם הוּא אֶרֶךְ אַפַּיִם וְרַב חֶסֶד—וְנִחָם עַל
הָרָעָ—ה.

*Rabbi Shimon says: Be meticulous with the reading of Shema
and with prayer. When you pray, do not make your prayers
routine, but [an entreaty of] mercy and a supplication before
the Almighty, as is stated, "For He is benevolent and merciful,
slow to anger and abundant in loving kindness, and **relenting
of the evil decree**" (Yoel 2:13). (Avos 2:13)*

In *Parashas Va'eschanan*, prayer is one of the central themes. Besides being the *parashah* that contains *Shema*, it starts out with the word "*va'eschanan*," which *Rashi* reminds us is another word for prayer. In fact, many halachos of prayer are derived from Moshe's supplication to G-d. One key aspect of prayer (*Shema/tefillah*) as highlighted above in *Avos* is that our supplications can actually influence G-d to change His decree for our sake.

440

The following *pesukim* hold the key to the unbelievable power of prayer (Moshe was praying to be allowed entrance into Israel after being told he would not enter):

וַיֹּאמֶר ה' אֵלַי רַב לָךְ אַל תּוֹסֶף דַּבֵּר אֵלַי עוֹד בַּדָּבָר הַזֶּה.

And Hashem said to me: "Enough for you! Speak no more to Me of this matter."

עֲלֵה רֹאשׁ הַפִּסְגָּה וְשָׂא עֵינֶיךָ יָמָּה וְצָפֹנָה וְתֵימָנָה וּמִזְרָחָה וּרְאֵה בְעֵינֶיךָ כִּי לֹא תַעֲבֹר אֶת הַיַּרְדֵּן הַזֶּה.

Go to the top of Pisgah, and lift up your eyes westward, northward, southward, and eastward, and behold with your eyes; for you will not go over this Jordan. (Devarim 3:27)

The Gemara in *Berachos* (32b) says that "prayer is even better than good deeds (גדולה תפלה יותר ממעשים טובים), for there was no one greater in good deeds than Moshe Rabbeinu, and yet he was answered only after prayer, as it says, 'Speak no more to Me' and immediately afterward, 'Go to the top of Pisgah.'" Apparently, his good deeds did not succeed in procuring for him permission to enter the Land, but his prayer granted him the vision of Pisgah (to at least see Israel).

QUESTIONS

1. How do these *pesukim* show that Moshe's prayer (to the exclusion of his deeds) helped him see Israel?
2. In this paradigmatic lesson of prayer, isn't it ironic that Moshe's prayer/request wasn't even fulfilled, because after all, he was only granted a vision of Israel and not admittance into the Land?
3. Is prayer really better than good deeds?

ANSWERS

The *Torah Temimah* states that the *pesukim* (*Devarim* 3:26–27 above) should actually be read together (בַּדָּבָר הַזֶּה עֲלֵה רֹאשׁ הַפִּסְגָּה), and thus the flow would be: "Moshe, don't speak to me more...because of **this** (הַזֶּה)

thing [i.e., prayer and not necessarily your good deeds!], you are able to see Israel"!

If the *Torah Temimah* was really right, though, the *Gemara* above from *Berachos* should have written: "Yet he was answered only after prayer, as it says, 'Speak no more to Me **of this matter,**'" and immediately afterward, "Go up to the top of Pisgah." But the Gemara conspicuously leaves the part of the *pasuk* out that the *Torah Temimah* used for his lesson. Left out from the Gemara are the words "on this matter," which is the thrust of the *Torah Temimah's* proof! The point may be that the key is not "on this matter," but on "**Speak no more to Me.**" G-d was telling Moshe to stop excessively praying because that extra *speaking* (i.e., prayer) would force Hashem to have to acquiesce in some way! G-d was pleading with Moshe to stop.

Prayer is greater than good deeds in the sense that it can be done in excess; good deeds can only be done when the time or place present themselves, but we can always indulge and excessively pray! Perhaps Moshe wasn't satisfied and his prayer was only answered with permission to see Israel from a distance, but not because his prayer wasn't efficacious. It was because G-d pleaded with him not to pray excessively, which would have led to the likely rescinding of the decree!

Thus, the answers to the questions posed earlier:

1. *Torah Temimah* says, "In this matter he ascended Pisgah," teaches us that Moshe's prayer alone helped him at least see Israel from afar.

2. The power of Moshe's prayer isn't that Moshe got his way but that he likely would have gained entry into Israel if G-d had allowed him to pray more! Hence, the key was G-d saying, "**Speak no more to Me** (אַל תּוֹסֶף דַּבֵּר אֵלַי)."

3. Prayer is better than good deeds in the sense that we can easily overindulge and pray all the time, while good deeds need specific times/places! אַל תַּעַשׂ תְּפִלָּתְךָ קֶבַע—G-d gives us the powerful tool of prayer that is not limited by time/place.

—————— TAKEAWAY MESSAGES ——————

We are reminded in *Avos* that prayer has the ability to change our fate for the better. Prayer actually has a leg up over good deeds in that we can do it anytime and all the time—אַל תַּעַשׂ תְּפִלָּתְךָ קֶבַע! G-d gives us the powerful tool of prayer that is not limited by time/place. Perhaps if Moshe would have been given the opportunity to continue praying, G-d may have given in to his request allowing him full entry! Powerful lesson of prayer from the *parashah* of prayer that is named *va'eschanan*, prayer.

Prayer is stronger than good deeds in the sense that it can be done in excess.

Eikev

TRUE LOVE—WHAT YOU DO FOR ANOTHER

רַבִּי יִשְׁמָעֵאל בְּנוֹ אוֹמֵר: הַלּוֹמֵד תּוֹרָה עַל
מְנָת לְלַמֵּד מַסְפִּיקִין בְּיָדוֹ לִלְמֹד וּלְלַמֵּד
וְהַלּוֹמֵד עַל מְנָת לַעֲשׂוֹת מַסְפִּיקִין בְּיָדוֹ לִלְמֹד
וּלְלַמֵּד לִשְׁמֹר וְלַעֲשׂוֹת.

*Rabbi Yishmael his son says: If you learn [only] in order to
teach, you will be given enough to learn and teach, but if you
learn in order to do, you will be given enough to learn, teach,*
keep, *and do! (Avos 4:5)*

--- QUESTIONS ---

If I learn in order to "do," why am I also granted the extra ability
לִשְׁמֹר—to keep the mitzvos as well? What does that "keeping" mean
anyway? (Interestingly, *nusach Eretz Yisrael* omits this word.)

--- ANSWERS ---

The answer is a profound insight into true love, derived from analyzing our *parashah*:

כִּי אִם שָׁמֹר תִּשְׁמְרוּן אֶת כָּל הַמִּצְוָה הַזֹּאת אֲשֶׁר אָנֹכִי מְצַוֶּה אֶתְכֶם
לַעֲשֹׂתָהּ לְאַהֲבָה אֶת ה' אֱלֹקֵיכֶם לָלֶכֶת בְּכָל דְּרָכָיו וּלְדָבְקָה בוֹ.

*For if you **keep** all these commandments that I command you
to do them, to love Hashem, your G-d, to walk in all His ways,
and to cleave to Him." (Devarim 11:22)*

Just one *parashah* earlier (וְאָהַבְתָּ אֵת ה' אֱלֹקֶיךָ), we learn that we have an obligation to love G-d. Rabbi Ozer Alport asks how G-d can command us to love Him if, after all, love is a feeling that can't be forced upon us. He beautifully answers that since it is natural to love those who love us, we should naturally love G-d, who undeniably loves us wholeheartedly. He adds that this is why we preface both the morning and nighttime *Shema*, which has וְאָהַבְתָּ אֵת ה' אֱלֹקֶיךָ, with the statement that G-d loves us ("*Ha'bocher b'amo Yisrael **b'ahavah**" and "**ohev** amo Yisrael*").

Unlike Rabbi Alport's beautiful idea, though, I do think you can command to love. Love can be created, and Hashem is showing us the blueprint in *Parashas Eikev*. The first step in the development of love is: וְהָיָה אִם שָׁמֹעַ תִּשְׁמְעוּ אֶל מִצְוֹתַי אֲשֶׁר אָנֹכִי מְצַוֶּה אֶתְכֶם הַיּוֹם לְאַהֲבָה, which is simply listening to G-d.

The next step is just as crucial, though, and is based on obviating your will for the sake of the other. *Shemirah* essentially refers to keeping the "negative" commandments, meaning not doing something I would otherwise want to do. G-d may be telling us that in order to develop love for Him (and love for each other, no less), you must obviate your desires and sacrifice for Him. Most noticeably, G-d doesn't say that He will shower us with gifts and do great things for us, and then we will love Him, but rather that we "listen" and then "keep" His mitzvos, which will leave an indelible love. Since G-d's relationship with us is supposed to mimic our own relationships, perhaps it is possible to learn how to love by "listening" and "sacrificing" to/for another!

The Tanna in *Avos* likewise did not mistakenly add the word לִשְׁמֹר when describing the meritorious path toward becoming someone who is successful (לִלְמֹד וּלְלַמֵּד לִשְׁמֹר וְלַעֲשׂוֹת); the "keeping" (avoidance of negative aspects, and thus sacrificing oneself for the Torah) is needed to be a perpetual "do-er"; doing positive things alone does not suffice, but rather you must abstain from the negatives as well.

——————— TAKEAWAY MESSAGES ———————

How can G-d command us to love Him? Rabbi Ozer Alport says because it is natural to love someone who loves you, and thus we should naturally love G-d. But perhaps love can be "commanded" and forced upon us. Love can be derived from "listening" (וְהָיָה אִם שָׁמֹעַ תִּשְׁמְעוּ...לְאַהֲבָה) and also by adhering to the negative commandments, i.e., sacrificing yourself for Him (כִּי אִם שָׁמֹר תִּשְׁמְרוּן...לְאַהֲבָה).

True love can be learned, perhaps derived from listening and sacrificing oneself.

BE HEARD BY YOUR HEEL,
NOT BY YOUR HEART

אָמַר לָהֶם: צְאוּ וּרְאוּ אֵיזוֹהִי דֶרֶךְ יְשָׁרָה,
שֶׁיִּדְבַּק בָּהּ הָאָדָם...רַבִּי אֶלְעָזָר [בֶּן עֲרָךְ]
אוֹמֵר, לֵב טוֹב. אָמַר לָהֶם: רוֹאֶה אֲנִי אֶת
דִּבְרֵי אֶלְעָזָר בֶּן עֲרָךְ מִדִּבְרֵיכֶם שֶׁבִּכְלָל דְּבָרָיו
דִּבְרֵיכֶם.

*[Rabbi Yochanan] said to them: Go and see which is the
best trait for a person to acquire...**Said Rabbi Elazar [ben
Arach]: A good heart**. He said to them: I prefer the words of
Elazar ben Arach to yours, for his words include all of yours.*
(Avos 2:9)

Rabbi Yochanan posed the question we have all wondered about
to his five favorite students: What characteristic should we yearn for
most? It seems pretty clear that he concludes that Rabbi Elazar ben
Arach's answer, to have a good heart, is the most important quality
to acquire.

———————————— QUESTIONS ————————————

1. Is it really true that "having a good heart" is the most desirable quality?
2. What is the significance of the words that start out this
   parashah: "וְהָיָה עֵקֶב תִּשְׁמְעוּן"—It will be because you listen..."?

447

ANSWERS

There is a story in *Avos D'Rebbi Nasan* (14) that states that after Rabbi Yochanan died, Rabbi Elazar ben Arach (one of his five main students) chose not to learn in Yavneh with his colleagues, but went out on his own to a different town, far away from Torah scholars. The Gemara (*Shabbos* 147b) states that in time, Rabbi Elazar forgot how to even read the Torah, and when he got to the *pasuk* of "הַחֹדֶשׁ הַזֶּה לָכֶם—This month shall be for you" (*Shemos* 12:2), he read it erroneously, saying, "החרש היה לבם—Silent became their hearts."

A point may be that this Gemara is giving commentary on the afore-mentioned question we posed in *Avos*: The very same Rabbi Elazar, who said that having a good heart is the most important element, forgot all of his precious learning when he tried to go out on his own. (This is why the Gemara specifically used the line "החרש היה לבם," which not only shows that he had lost simple reading skills but simultaneously reminds us that it was ironically *he* who said that yearning for a good heart was the most important). Perhaps Rabbi Elazar's "heart became silent" because he relied too heavily on his own heart rather than on community participation/actions!

It is worth noting that although Rabbi Yochanan originally agreed (see above) with Rabbi Elazar ben Arach's suggestion that having a good heart is the best trait to aquire, this story clarifies that Rabbi Yochanan likely felt that to be the case as long as one remains steadafast in one's religious observance and practice!

The word עֵקֶב is another word for "heel." Homiletically, "וְהָיָה עֵקֶב תִּשְׁמְעוּן" may hint that you should "be heard" (תִּשְׁמְעוּן) with your heel as opposed to your heart. Of course, it is great to have a good heart, but ultimately, it is not how you feel (the Torah does not say, "וְהָיָה לֵב תִּשְׁמְעוּן") that will ultimately be heard, but it is your actions!

TAKEAWAY MESSAGES

"וְהָיָה עֵקֶב תִּשְׁמְעוּן" may teach us that we should be *heard by our heel* in the sense that ultimately it is our actions that actually supersede how we feel inside. Having a good heart is great, but it is only as a prelude to what you do with this good heart. Rabbi Elazar ben Arach said that having a good heart was the most important character trait, but he himself was a living example of how the heart can be silenced if not complemented by fortifying actions.

Being heard by your heel reminds us that we are what we do.

A HEEL SUPPORTS THE SOLE MUCH LIKE...

הוּא הָיָה אוֹמֵר: נְגַד שְׁמָא אֲבַד
שְׁמֵהּ וּדְלֹא מוֹסִיף יָסֵף...וּדְלֹא יָלֵיף קְטָלָא
חַיָּב. וּדְאִשְׁתַּמֵּשׁ בְּתַגָּא חָלֵף.

*He [Hillel] would also say: One who advances his name,
destroys his name. One who does not increase, diminishes.
One who does not learn is deserving of death. And one
who makes personal use of the crown of Torah **shall
perish**...(Avos 1:13)*

QUESTIONS

1. It seems a bit odd that the "peace-loving" Hillel had such vitriol for those "who make personal use of the crown of Torah" or for those who don't learn. It seems out of character for sure.
2. Also, חָלֵף is a very unusual term, even in Aramaic. Does it really mean "shall perish"?

ANSWERS

An answer may be found in the first *pasuk* of our *parashah*:

וְהָיָה **עֵקֶב** תִּשְׁמְעוּן אֵת הַמִּשְׁפָּטִים הָאֵלֶּה וּשְׁמַרְתֶּם וַעֲשִׂיתֶם אֹתָם
וְשָׁמַר ה' אֱלֹקֶיךָ לְךָ אֶת הַבְּרִית וְאֶת הַחֶסֶד אֲשֶׁר נִשְׁבַּע לַאֲבֹתֶיךָ.

*And it will be, **because you** will heed these ordinances and
keep them and perform, that the Lord, your G-d, will keep*

> *for you the covenant and the kindness that He swore to your forefathers. (Devarim 7:12)*

Rashi picks up on the unusual word עֵקֶב here and points out that it is teaching us: "...אָם הַמִּצְוֹת הַקַּלּוֹת שֶׁאָדָם דָּשׁ **בַּעֲקֵבָיו** תִּשְׁמָעוּן—If you will heed the minor commandments that one [usually] tramples with **his heels** (עֲקֵב meaning heel i.e., which a person treats as being of minor importance)," then G-d will bestow הַחֶסֶד upon you...

Interestingly, however, *Onkelos* actually translates the uncommon עֵקֶב here as "reward": "וִיהֵי חֳלַף דִּי תְקַבְּלוּן יָת דִּינַיָּא הָאִלֵּין." The *Stone Chumash* actually adopts this rendition: "And it will be, **reward** will be given if you heed these ordinances and keep them and perform, as the Lord, your G-d, will keep for you the covenant and the kindness that He swore to your forefathers."

Where does *Onkelos* get this definition of "reward" from a word that typically means "heel"? It is quite possible that since the function of the heel is to both act as a shock absorber and stabilizer of the sole, it is a perfect bodily example of "balance." In order for us all to have balance, we need laws that keep us in check. In this way, our "reward" is our "balance," which is predicated on our Torah observance. As a Libra, I can tell you that there is no greater satisfaction than feeling a sense of balance; and so it makes sense that "heel" is synonymous with "reward"!

We often think that we must obey laws/Torah so that we can reap reward, but the lesson here is that **the keeping of the laws in and of itself** is actually a reward to some degree, as it grants us balance!

That, perhaps, explains Hillel's dictum perfectly: He may not be saying that if you take the teachings of Torah for granted, you will perish; but rather that the learning itself can bring reward and satisfaction. Being ensconced in Torah (דְּאִשְׁתַּמֵּשׁ בְּתָגָא) will be itself a reward. חֳלַף may not mean *perish*, as most interpret there, but actually *reward*, as *Onkelos* interprets it here in *Parashas Eikev*!

To review: Homiletically, "וְהָיָה עֵקֶב"—And your reward will be, "תִּשְׁמָעוּן אֵת הַמִּשְׁפָּטִים הָאֵלֶּה וּשְׁמַרְתֶּם וַעֲשִׂיתֶם אֹתָם"—the fact that you are given the chance to keep all the laws.

We need to start looking at our laws as gifts and opportunities, rather than simply conduits to eventual reward! This is the lesson of *Eikev*, our balancing heel, and this is the lesson of חֵלֶף!

──────── TAKEAWAY MESSAGES ────────

Involving ourselves in the pursuit of more Torah-abiding/focused lives is actually חֵלֶף—reward in and of itself! דְּאִשְׁתַּמֵּשׁ בְּתָגָא חָלֵף may be a positive lesson and not negative! עֵקֶב—the heel that balances is the same as חֵלֶף—reward, because balance is our ultimate gift. "וְהָיָה עֵקֶב—And your reward will be" the ability to be involved in a Torah way of life. To some degree, the reward for obeying Torah laws is having the Torah laws in the first place that give us balance.

A heel supports the sole much like our laws balance our souls...

FEARING G-D AND KNOWING TO ASK "WHAT"

רַבִּי אֶלְעָזָר אוֹמֵר: וְדַע מַה שֶׁתָּשִׁיב לְאֶפִּיקוֹרוֹס.

*Rabbi Elazar says: Know **what** to answer a heretic.*
(Avos 2:14)

QUESTIONS

Would you not expect *Avos* to explain what the "what" is, rather than simply tell us that we should know *what* to respond?

An answer will be derived from asking a few more questions on our *parashah*:

וְעַתָּה יִשְׂרָאֵל מָה ה' אֱלֹקֶיךָ שֹׁאֵל מֵעִמָּךְ כִּי אִם לְיִרְאָה אֶת ה' אֱלֹקֶיךָ לָלֶכֶת בְּכָל דְּרָכָיו וּלְאַהֲבָה אֹתוֹ וְלַעֲבֹד אֶת ה' אֱלֹקֶיךָ בְּכָל לְבָבְךָ וּבְכָל נַפְשֶׁךָ.

And now, Israel, what does Hashem your G-d require of you,
but to fear Hashem your G-d, to walk in all His ways, and to
love Him, and to serve Hashem your G-d with all your heart
and with all your soul. (Devarim 10:12)

The Torah seems to imply that this task of fearing G-d is no big deal. G-d is seemingly saying, "What do I ask from you? Just fear Me!" as if fearing G-d is a small and easy task! What really is *yiras Hashem* anyway?

453

The famous line found in the Gemara (*Berachos* 33b) that says, "Everything is in the hands of heaven, except for fear of heaven," derives from this very *pasuk*. The Kotzker Rebbe explains that this cryptic statement actually applies to the realm of prayer. The Kotzker Rebbe says that unlike any other specific requests that we beseech G-d for, if we sincerely ask Hashem for *yiras Hashem*, then He guarantees that our wish will be granted. In that sense, when G-d says, "What do I ask from you? Just fear Me," He is not saying that fear of G-d is an easy thing, but rather that it is the *only* request that he expects us to ask Him and expect a definite "yes" in return!

Using the Kotzker approach as a springboard, perhaps we can take a small leap that can answer our questions: "מָה ה' אֱלֹקֶיךָ שֹׁאֵל מֵעִמָּךְ" may not mean, "What does Hashem request from you?" but rather: "**What** is what G-d is asking from us!"

In other words, G-d wants us to challenge Him. Not to believe "*que será, será*—whatever will be, will be," but rather that we should ask G-d to help us achieve.

Furthering the homily, "כִּי אִם לְיִרְאָה אֶת ה' אֱלֹקֶיךָ לָלֶכֶת בְּכָל דְּרָכָיו" may not be saying that G-d is only asking us to fear Him, but that כִּי אִם לְיִרְאָה—the way to achieve *yiras Hashem* is through the כִּי and the אִם! How so? The Hebrew word כִּי has seven meanings (because, if, when, rather, question, that, and perhaps), which depend on the context. The word אִם also is unique because depending on the context, it also has several (five to seven different meanings!). In order to get or have *yiras Hashem*, we have to feel that our actions change the celestial machinations. The context that we provide (the כִּי and the אִם) is the way we challenge G-d (מָה ה' אֱלֹקֶיךָ שֹׁאֵל מֵעִמָּךְ).

When we say, "דַע מַה שֶׁתָּשִׁיב לְאֶפִּיקוֹרוֹס—Know **what** to respond to an *apikorus*," we are possibly also saying: "Know that the best way to respond to an *apikorus* is to tell him or her that G-d wants us to challenge Him (מָה ה' אֱלֹקֶיךָ שֹׁאֵל מֵעִמָּךְ)." G-d hopes that we challenge His natural course by demonstrating that we understand things are effected by the context we provide.

——————— TAKEAWAY MESSAGES ———————

According to the Kotzker Rebbe, "מָה ה' אֱלֹקֶיךָ שֹׁאֵל מֵעִמָּךְ" is saying that if we ask Hashem to give us *yiras Hashem*, He won't say no! Homiletically, the *pasuk* may be read: "G-d wants us to ask מָה," i.e., to challenge Him. כִּי אִם לְיִרְאָה—The words כִּי and אִם may reflect the ability of G-d to change His decrees based on our actions (just like the meaning of these words depends on their context). The challenging of G-d is what differentiates us from the *apikorus*.

Fearing G-d and knowing to ask "what."

Re' eh

RABBI AKIVA'S PRESCRIPTION FOR DESTROYING AVODAH ZARAH NOWADAYS

רַבִּי יִשְׁמָעֵאל אוֹמֵר: וֶהֱוֵי מְקַבֵּל אֶת כָּל
הָאָדָם בְּשִׂמְחָה...רַבִּי עֲקִיבָא אוֹמֵר, שְׂחוֹק
וְקַלּוּת רֹאשׁ, מַרְגִּילִין לְעֶרְוָה.

Rabbi Yishmael says: Receive all people with a smile...Rabbi
Akiva said: Happiness and lightheadedness leads to
promiscuity. (Avos 3:12–13)

אַבֵּד תְּאַבְּדוּן אֶת כָּל הַמְּקֹמוֹת אֲשֶׁר
עָבְדוּ שָׁם הַגּוֹיִם אֲשֶׁר אַתֶּם יֹרְשִׁים אֹתָם
אֶת אֱלֹהֵיהֶם: עַל הֶהָרִים הָרָמִים וְעַל הַגְּבָעוֹת
וְתַחַת כָּל עֵץ רַעֲנָן.

*You will **surely destroy all the places**, where the nations*
*that you will dispossess served their gods, **upon the high***
***mountains, and upon the hills, and under every leafy tree**.*
(Devarim 12:2)

456

The *Mechilta* (*Shemos* 22:19) explains that B'nei Yisrael knew how to search out the places of idolatry and destroy them from the hints given in this *pasuk*. The latter part of the *pasuk*, "on the high mountains and under the leafy trees," was a hint as to where they could find the idols they had to destroy. Taking that lead, Rabbi Akiva expounds: "כל מקום שאתה מוצא הר גבוה וגבעה נשאה ועץ רענן דע שיש שם עבודה זרה—Wherever you find a high mountain or an elevated hill or a green tree, know that an idolatrous object is there" (*Avodah Zarah* 45b).

At first glance, Rabbi Akiva is seemingly telling us how to seek out and destroy idols.

QUESTIONS

1. What's the relevance of idolatry to us today—do you know of any local *asherahs*? It would seem rather unusual to go around now searching for idols to destroy.
2. What is a possible connection of the aforementioned ethic in *Avos* of Rabbi Akiva with his statement on our *parashah*?

ANSWERS

Rabbi Akiva's statement that laughter/frivolity may lead to promiscuity comes right after Rabbi Yishmael's ethic to accept all people with happiness. It seems obvious that Rabbi Akiva is putting limits on the happiness that Rabbi Yishmael prescribes. Rabbi Akiva is warning us about the dangers of being too comfortable, as it makes us vulnerable. Comforts in excess that are not tempered inevitably lead to *ervah*, promiscuity, as we end up wasting time in frivolous activities that ultimately leave us empty inside.

Just as in *Avos*, where Rabbi Akiva warns us of the dangers of too much laughter, it is Rabbi Akiva in our *parashah* who teaches us that *avodah zarah* can be found specifically "in the high beautiful mountains and trees," i.e., challenges (represented as *avodah zarah*) always accompany beautiful gifts and pleasantries, so beware! *Avodah zarah* nowadays is probably less about a Buddha-sized idol and more about being caught up in spending all of our energies running after/worshipping the latest fad, instead of allocating time/resources toward meaningful spiritual endeavors. *Avodah zarah* is in all of our own backyards, so to speak. Wherever you find niceties, you will find the challenge of *avodah zarah*, which is the vulnerability of being swept away by the vagaries of the comforts achieved!

But Rabbi Akiva and the *Mechilta* are not just giving us a warning of the dangers of comfort. They remind us that the *pasuk* actually states: "אַבֵּד תְּאַבְּדוּן אֶת כָּל הַמְּקֹמוֹת"; we need to proactively prepare in advance to wipe out these places. Knowing that certain comforts can be deleterious to our spirituality, we need to proactively search them out and prepare to deal with them.

—— TAKEAWAY MESSAGES ——

Though of course we should be happy as prescribed by Rabbi Yishmael, Rabbi Akiva reminds us to temper our comforts so as not to become promiscuous or vulnerable to destruction. *Avodah zarah* is not only about stones and literal idols, but rather is anything that takes us away from our holy essence. Rabbi Akiva reminds us in our *parashah* that *avodah zarah* is found beneath the most pleasant of niceties, consistent with his warning in *Avos* about the dangers "beneath" too much comfort. The *Mechilta* reminds us to "אַבֵּד תְּאַבְּדוּן אֶת כָּל הַמְּקֹמוֹת"; we have to **proactively** come up with a game-plan as we arrive in comfortable situations to search out and destroy the *avodah zarah* elements that lurk beneath…

Destroying *avodah zarah* nowadays, as prescribed by Rabbi Akiva, is about recognizing that *avodah zarah* may be camouflaged behind niceties and amenities, so beware!

CAN YOU GIVE CHARITY/TITHES
IN ORDER TO GET WEALTHY?

אַנְטִיגְנוֹס אִישׁ סוֹכוֹ קִבֵּל מִשִּׁמְעוֹן הַצַּדִּיק.
הוּא הָיָה אוֹמֵר: אַל תִּהְיוּ כַּעֲבָדִים הַמְשַׁמְּשִׁין
אֶת הָרַב עַל מְנָת לְקַבֵּל פְּרָס אֶלָּא הֱווּ
כַעֲבָדִים הַמְשַׁמְּשִׁין אֶת הָרַב שֶׁלֹּא עַל מְנָת
לְקַבֵּל פְּרָס וִיהִי מוֹרָא שָׁמַיִם עֲלֵיכֶם.

*Antiginos of Socho received the tradition from Shimon the
Righteous. He would say: Do not be as slaves, who serve their
master for the sake of reward. Rather, be as slaves who serve
their master **not for the sake of reward**. And the fear of
heaven should be upon you. (Avos 1:3)*

--- QUESTIONS ---

The Gemara (*Taanis* 9a and *Shabbos* 119a) brings up the famous
explanation of why the double language is present of עַשֵּׂר תְּעַשֵּׂר in the
pasuk in this *parashah*:

עַשֵּׂר תְּעַשֵּׂר אֵת כָּל תְּבוּאַת זַרְעֶךָ הַיֹּצֵא הַשָּׂדֶה שָׁנָה שָׁנָה.
*You shall surely tithe all the increase of your seed which is
brought forth in the field year by year. (Devarim 14:22)*

The explanation is "עשר בשביל שתתעשר—Give your tithe in order for you to become wealthy"! In other words, עַשֵּׂר תְּעַשֵּׂר is homiletically read עשר תעשר (a *shin* in תעשר, meaning "wealthy")—if you give *maaser*, then you will indeed get wealthy. But wait a second, doesn't the Mishnah say above in *Avos* that we should not serve G-d for the sake of reward?

<hr/>

ANSWERS

There are three possible reasons.

1. One approach is per the Gemara in *Taanis* (9a), which says that although you can't really test G-d in general and cannot expect reward in this world for doing mitzvos, giving *maaser* is actually an exception to this rule! (In general, this is referring only to tithing lands in Israel alone, however the *Tosafos* brings a *Sifri* that says the extra word כָּל in "אֶת כָּל תְּבוּאַת זַרְעֶךָ" actually includes tithes given to poor people as well!) And so one answer is quite plain: Tzedakah (or at least tithing of lands in Israel) is an exception to the rule of striving "not to serve the Master for the sake of reward" because there is this special homily of עַשֵּׂר תְּעַשֵּׂר/ עַשֵּׂר תעשר!

2. Another approach from the *Maharsha* is that the *limud* of עַשֵּׂר תְּעַשֵּׂר is that if you give *maaser*, you will be rewarded with giving *maaser* again in the future! Perhaps you can read a bit into the *Maharsha* and say that it is not so much that you are rewarded with becoming rich as an endpoint. The wealth is actually just the means to enable you to do more of the mitzvah of *maaser* in the future! "עשר בשביל שתתעשר" in this context means that you are doing *maaser* in order for you to gain wealth not for the sake of the wealth itself, per se, but for the merit of being able to give future tithes down the road (it so happens that you need to become rich in order to give *maaser*)! And so another answer to the above question: In fact, there are no exceptions to the rule of striving "not to serve the Master for the sake of reward," but rather the שתתעשר here is merely the *means* (not the end-goal itself) for you to be able to perpetuate the great mitzvah over and over, year in and year out.

3. *Rashi* brings on our *pasuk*: "If you do not tithe your produce properly, when it is near ripening I will bring forth an easterly wind, which will blast them." Wouldn't you expect the positively phrased, "tithe so that you become *wealthy*," as opposed to the concept here of "if you don't tithe you will become poor"? I think *Rashi* is echoing the *Midrash Tanchuma*'s alternative and lesser-known homily of "עַשֵּׂר תְּעַשֵּׂר," namely that the words תתחסר and תְּעַשֵּׂר sound very alike, and so the midrash says, "עשר שלא תתחסר—Tithe so you **don't lose out!**" And so thirdly, as per *Rashi* and the midrash, it does sound like that even by *maaser*, you can't really serve in order to get earthly reward per se, but rather can just prevent yourself from losing out!

— TAKEAWAY MESSAGES —

In general, we cannot ask G-d to give us earthly reward for doing mitzvos in this world. And yet the *limud* from the double language of עַשֵּׂר תְּעַשֵּׂר, being עשר בשביל שתתעשר, can be reconciled in three possible ways:

1. Tithing is the exception!
2. We aren't tithing to become wealthy insomuch as we are tithing just to be able to perform the mitzvah of tithing again in the future! The wealth is thus the means and not the ends.
3. Based on the midrash and *Rashi*, עשר שלא תתחסר—it's not that you are tithing so that you become wealthy, but rather tithing so that you don't lose your wealth!

You can tithe for wealth, so that you can tithe again, or so that you don't lose your wealth. The bottom line is that tithing sounds wise!

Addendum: Arthur Litwin says in the name of a rabbi from Har Nof: עַשֵּׂר תְּעַשֵּׂר can mean you take a tenth of תְּעַשֵּׂר: The *gematria* of *tav* is 400, and so one tenth is 40. The *gematria* of *ayin* is 70, and one tenth of that is 7. The *gematria* of *sin* is 300, and so one tenth is 30. The *gematria* of *reish* is 200 and so one tenth is 20. The total is 97, which is identical to the *gematria* of מזלך—your luck; it's entirely dependent on your charity!

PARASHAS RE'EH, VEGETARIANISM, AND THE BAND POISON?

עַיִן רָ־עָה וְרוּחַ גְּבוֹהָה וְנֶפֶשׁ רְחָבָ־ה מִתַּלְמִידָיו
שֶׁל בִּלְעָם הָרָ־שָׁע.

*An evil eye, a haughty spirit, and a **gross soul** [characterize]
the students of Bilaam the wicked. (Avos 5:19)*

QUESTIONS

What is meant by a "widened" soul? The term *nefesh rachavah* apparently denotes lust; what does widening have to do with lustfulness? What is the specific lesson of the adjective *rechavah*?

ANSWERS

An answer may be from our *parashah*:

כִּי יַרְחִיב ה' אֱלֹקֶיךָ אֶת גְּבֻלְךָ כַּאֲשֶׁר דִּבֶּר לָךְ וְאָמַרְתָּ אֹכְלָה בָשָׂר כִּי
תְאַוֶּה נַפְשְׁךָ לֶאֱכֹל בָּשָׂר בְּכָל אַוַּת נַפְשְׁךָ תֹּאכַל בָּשָׂר.

*When Hashem **enlarges** your territory, as (G-d) has promised
you, and you will say, "I will eat flesh [meat]," for you have
the urge to eat meat, you may eat meat whenever you wish.
(Devarim 12:20)*

This verse above seemingly does not command but rather permits the consumption of meat. Some notable vegetarianism advocates, such as Dr. Richard Schwartz, remind us that this *pasuk* highlights that if

462

not for our inability to quench our תאוה—lust, we would ideally all be vegetarians. The Gemara in *Chullin* (84a) reinforces this:

> *Our Rabbis taught: When Hashem, your G-d shall enlarge your border, as He has promised you, and you will say: "I will eat flesh." The Torah here teaches a rule of conduct, that a person should not eat meat unless he has a special appetite for it.*

The Gemara seems to clarify this cryptic statement by continuing that as a person gets wealthier and wealthier, he may have more meat and eat the meat more frequently ("If he has fifty *maneh* he may buy for his stew a liter of meat; if he has a hundred *maneh*, he may have a pot set on for him every day"). In other words, the dispensation to eat meat comes from a natural need to have something more filling to satiate the natural growth in lustfulness as one gets wealthier. So when the Gemara says, "A person should not eat meat unless he has a special appetite for it," this is referring to those who are so wealthy that they need the meat to quench their lust.

The lesson in this apparent grudging dispensation to eat meat is really couched in the very word יַרְחִיב—enlarges, which refers to when G-d gives us more territory/wealth. As we enlarge with material wealth, we naturally become wider but consequently further away from our home base! We become more distanced from our spirit when we expand our materialism, and we simultaneously become bigger with more empty space to fill. The new void mirrors the challenges that one has when he gets wealth; it is only natural that they will become needier to satiate this new expanse. It is not a question of right or wrong, but just a reality and just nature.

The *mussar* from this *pasuk* is less an attack on meat-eating and more of a lesson in the **reality** of the inherent challenges of becoming successful. The challenge is in the word יַרְחִיב: Wealth will widen you and leave you with a void that you will need to fill. Before you get wealthy, G-d is warning us that feeling a natural void comes with every *berachah*. The students of Bilaam allow their wealth to affect their souls; they fail to counteract this natural course because they aren't prepared for this void. They have a נֶפֶשׁ רְחָבָה as they allow their wealth to naturally distance them from spirituality. The sons of Avraham Avinu, armed with this *pasuk*, are expected to understand the risks of wealth—that making larger makes one wider—and thus we must strike the balance.

—————————— TAKEAWAY MESSAGES ——————————

The students of Bilaam have "widened souls" as they let their wealth naturally distance themselves from their spirit. We are tasked with understanding that meat will naturally become needed as we get larger and wider with wealth. We should strive to counteract the natural distancing from our spiritual core that wealth inevitably brings. Merely understanding that expanding (יַרְחִיב) is by definition widening and thus distancing us (יַרְחִיב) is the very first step in preventing a spiritual downfall on account of our largess. The lesson of כִּי יַרְחִיב is to know that along with wealth comes a natural void.

Parashas Re'eh has a meaty lesson, and teaches that the *berachah* of wealth naturally creates a spiritual void that needs attention. Poison: every rose has its thorn!

Shoftim

רַ־בִּי חֲנִינָא בֶן חֲכִינַאי אוֹמֵר: ד־הַנֵּעוֹר בַּלַּיְלָה
וְהַמְהַ־לֵּךְ בַּדֶּרֶךְ יְחִידִי וְהַמְפַנֶּה לִ־בּוֹ לְבַטָּלָה הֲרֵי
זֶה מִתְ־חַיֵּב בְּנַפְשׁוֹ.

*Rabbi Chanina the son of Chachina'i would say: One who
stays awake at night, **travels alone on the road**, and turns
his heart to idleness, has forfeited his life. (Avos 3:4)*

QUESTIONS

What is meant by he who "**travels alone on the road**...has forfeited his life"?

By analyzing the *eglah arufah* episode (the decapitated calf) at the end of our *parashah*, we can perhaps understand better the message of Rabbi Chanina ben Chachinai.

The cryptic *eglah arufah* story is summarized as such: If a dead corpse is found between cities, an elaborate procedure is done whereby the elders of both places would measure from the place where the corpse was found to the various cities in the area to see which one was the closest. Once that was determined, the elders of that closest city would do the *eglah arufah* procedure and thus proclaim that they were not responsible for the death of this unfortunate individual. The *pasuk* details:

וְעָנוּ וְאָמְרוּ יָדֵינוּ לֹא שפכה (שָׁפְכוּ) אֶת הַדָּם הַזֶּה וְעֵינֵינוּ לֹא רָאוּ.

And they (the Elders) shall speak and say: "Our hands have not shed this blood, neither have our eyes seen it."
(Devarim 21:7)

Reference to this unusual halachah is made back in *Bereishis* (45:27) when Yosef sends wagons (heifers pulled the wagons) to his father Yaakov to remind him that despite being Pharaoh's right-hand man in Egypt, and despite having been away from his Jewish family for over twenty years, he still remembered the last halachah he had learned with his father, which was the halachah of the *eglah arufah* (see *Rashi* there; *Bereishis Rabbah* 94:3)!

Even if Yosef wanted to show Yaakov that he still remembered the Torah that he had taught him, what is the significance of his very last lesson having been specifically about the esoteric *eglah arufah*?

ANSWERS

One of the key reasons why the elders of the town closest to the murdered corpse bore guilt is because they should have escorted the man safely out of their city limits (see *Rashi*). In other words, people really should never be traveling alone, and they should be escorted in some fashion by the municipality they are leaving.

The *Meiri* beautifully explains that "traveling alone" or וְהַמְהַלֵּךְ בַּדֶּרֶךְ יְחִידִי refers to someone who doesn't work with others and only looks out for himself (his comments on *Avos* above). Such a person is מִתְחַיֵּב בְּנַפְשׁוֹ, destined to not survive as he is bereft of the security that his community would afford him.

Consider then the following line of reasoning: It may be possible that after so many years of solitude, Yosef finally understood that he had created his unfortunate destiny (being sold a slave and almost killed!) because he in fact isolated himself from his family by his grandiose dreams. He may have understood that like "the individual not escorted by the city's elders," he had cut the connection between him and his family and thus was, in a sense, guilty for his own fate! By showing his father that he remembered the *eglah arufah* lesson, he thus assuaged the possible guilt his father would feel: "Dad, don't feel bad about my disappearance years ago; the very lesson of the *eglah arufah* you taught me was about the symbiotic relationship between individual and community. Because I broke off from my family/community (by virtue of my early grandiosity), I am responsible for the fate that fell my way!"

———————————— TAKEAWAY MESSAGES ————————————

The problem with traveling life by oneself, bereft of community, is that one loses the safety and security that the community affords (*Meiri*). Yosef best illustrates the transformation of someone who at first was a הַמְהַלֵּךְ בַּדֶּרֶךְ יְחִידִי, but after internalizing the lesson of the *eglah arufah*, he realized the importance of connecting back to the family/community, which gave him the ultimate security. The *eglah arufah* is about our symbiotic relationship with our community. No individual, even a Yosef HaTzaddik, is safe without relying on the merits of his community.

Connecting Yosef with the decapitated calf and traveling alone, we can say that even Yosef the *tzaddik* needed to be part of a team!

WHY SHOULDN'T WE CUT
THE TREES DOWN?

הִלֵּל אוֹמֵר: וְאַל תֹּאמַר דָּבָר שֶׁאֲי אֶפְשָׁר
לִשְׁמֹעַ שֶׁסּוֹפוֹ לְ־־הִשָּׁמַע.

Hillel would say: And don't say something that's impossible to
hear because in the end it can be heard. (Avos 2:4)

QUESTIONS

This is an unusual ethic, which is perhaps why there are so many
different versions of what it means. One might expect the ethic to say,
"Do not say, 'This is something that is not understandable,' because
in the end that will lead you to not understand it." Who really cares if
one says, "This is something that is not understandable," if they end up
"understanding it" in the end?

ANSWERS

כִּי תָצוּר אֶל עִיר יָמִים רַבִּים לְהִלָּחֵם עָלֶיהָ לְתָפְשָׂהּ **לֹא תַשְׁחִית אֶת**
עֵצָהּ לִנְדֹּחַ עָלָיו גַּרְזֶן כִּי מִמֶּנּוּ תֹאכֵל וְאֹתוֹ לֹא תִכְרֹת: כִּי הָאָדָם עֵץ
הַשָּׂדֶה לָבֹא מִפָּנֶיךָ בַּמָּצוֹר.

When you will besiege a city a long time, in making war
*against it to take it, **you may not destroy the trees thereof***
by wielding an axe against them; for you may eat of them,

468

*but you may not cut them down; for is the tree of the field
man, that it should be besieged by you?" (Devarim 20:19)*

When attacking our enemies, the Torah tells us in our *parashah* that
we should preserve the trees so we can make use of their fruits thereafter. Alex Friedman said in the name of the *Seforno* [paraphrasing]
that although typical marauding nations will destroy everything in
their path, a truly optimistic nation will preserve the trees because they
know they are going to win and inherit the fruit of those trees. In other
words, by not cutting down the trees as you attack the nation, you are
demonstrating that you know you are going to win and will thus benefit
from those fruit trees in the end!

Perhaps, though, we can take it one step further: the literal transla-
tion of "לֹא תַשְׁחִית אֶת עֵצָהּ...כִּי מִמֶּנּוּ תֹאכֵל" is "Don't wipe out the trees because
you can eat the fruits from them." Homiletically, it may read: "Don't
cut down the trees [because from that act of positive confidence], you
will eat [you will reap reward from that very optimistic approach]!" And
herein lies a great message: In Judaism, the *ends* are not the only thing
that matters. The *process* is very important. The approach to winning
a battle is not only a path to winning the battle but can be a win itself.
Better to lose some battles with a winning approach than to win them
with a losing approach, because ultimately the approach shines through.
Similarly, Rabbi Simchah Bunim of Peshischa famously answers why
the *pasuk* says "צֶדֶק צֶדֶק תִּרְדֹּף," rather than just "צֶדֶק תִּרְדֹּף": It's not enough
to achieve "justice"; you need to accomplish justice by pursuing it with
a wholesome, positive approach! צֶדֶק—righteous justice, i.e., tzedakah,
i.e., a society in which helping others is a part of the very framework,
and isn't just a nice sometimes-extra; צֶדֶק תִּרְדֹּף—has to be pursued with
a just approach.

When the Mishnah in *Avos* says, "Do not say, 'This is something that
is not understandable,' because in the end it will be readily understood,"
Hillel is saying that even though you will be successful in the end, don't
approach your quest in a negative fashion. The approach is just as important as the end result. Even if you achieve your goal, your process
has to be refined.

———————— TAKEAWAY MESSAGES ————————

By not cutting the trees as we attack our enemies, we are demonstrating our positive, confident approach and trust in G-d as we battle. This approach is beneficial even on its own. לֹא תַשְׁחִית אֶת עֵצָה...כִּי מִמֶּנּוּ תֹאכֵל—We will "eat," i.e., benefit from such a positive confident outlook. The end result is important, but we must accomplish justice through just means: "צֶדֶק צֶדֶק תִּרְדֹּף."

Why shouldn't we cut the trees down? So that our belief in victory will lead us to victory!

IS SIXTY REALLY OLD AGE?
THE LESSON OF SIXTY

הוּא הָיָה אוֹמֵר: בֶּן שִׁשִּׁים לַזִּקְנָה.

He [Rabbi Yehudah ben Teima] would say: The number sixty?
For old age. (Avos 5:21)

QUESTIONS

1. The obvious way to understand this is that the number sixty represents old age. When you are sixty, you have achieved older age. But what does the number sixty really have to do with old age?
2. Regarding another "sixty," the midrash says that when you visit the sick, you can take away one sixtieth of their illness. Where does this one sixtieth come from?

ANSWERS

רֵאשִׁית דְּגָנְךָ תִּירשְׁךָ וְיִצְהָרֶךָ וְרֵאשִׁית גֵּז צֹאנְךָ תִּתֶּן לוֹ.

The first of your grain, your wine, and your oil, and the first of
the fleece of your sheep, you shall give him. (Devarim 18:4)

Rashi relates the *Talmud Yerushalmi* on this *pasuk*, which says that our rabbis set an amount as to how much of the "first" of one's produce he must give: "A generous [person] gives one fortieth of the crop, a miserly [person] one sixtieth, and [a person of] average generosity one fiftieth."

471

Of note, this miserly person who gives only one sixtieth is described as having *ayin hara*, an evil eye.

From here, we can see that this number of one sixtieth (actually further derived from a *pasuk* in *Yechezkel* 45:13) is the minimum amount; anything less is negligible. Let's call this number then, the "negligible limit." Interestingly, we also know of the concept of *batel b'shishim*, whereby if one part meat gets lost in sixty parts milk, then the mixture is still kosher; again, this is presumably because this one sixtieth is considered negligible!

Perhaps, then, this could explain why this number is mentioned by visiting the sick. When you visit the sick, you remove "one sixtieth" of their illness in the sense that when it comes to doing such good deeds, the number "one sixtieth" is actually mentioned because it is not negligible. G-d counts even the one sixtieth when it comes to doing good deeds. If one sixtieth was negligible by the mitzvah of *bikur cholim*, then the statement should read, "being *mevaker cholim* is useless." Instead, the midrash specifically says this amount to show that even a seemingly negligible amount of one sixtieth really does count when you are trying in any way to help one another.

Wanting to stretch this idea even further, there is another very cryptic *Yerushalmi* that states that Rav visited the cemetery and concluded that 99 percent of all people die because of *ayin hara*. It is worth noting that this *ayin hara* seems to be a different form of *ayin hara* than the former, in that this one entails receiving an evil eye from a jealous neighbor, whereas the former evil eye is merely being miserly and "evil-eyeing" his own property. Be that as it may, perhaps the act of visiting the sick is such a selfless act on the part of the visitor that it is supposed to remove the "one sixtieth," that very number that we see elsewhere is associated with an *ayin hara*. By graciously giving up of your time and effort to visit the sick, G-d sees the very opposite of the miserly (who only gives away one sixtieth of his produce) and that perhaps is *metaken*, fixes, the *ayin hara* that is ailing someone else.

When it says "*ben shishim l'ziknah*," it may likewise be hinting that if we inculcate this concept of sixty, that "when it comes to doing good deeds for others, even one sixtieth is not negligible," then we hope and pray we can somehow be granted to extend our own and others' lives *l'ziknah* (to older age)!

─────────── TAKEAWAY MESSAGES ───────────

The miserly person who only gives one sixtieth of his crop is described as having an *ayin hara*, evil eye. One part of sixty parts is generally considered negligible (i.e., *batel b'shishim*). Nevertheless, when it comes to doing *gemilus chassadim*, even one sixtieth may actually be considered meaningful, and that is why we say "visiting the sick alleviates one sixtieth of their illness," because even the smallest token helps! Alternatively, the one sixtieth is associated with *ayin hara* (the miserly), and in order to help *metaken* the *ayin hara* that befalls the infirmed, we can remove the one sixtieth (*ayin hara*) of someone's illness by doing the good deed of visiting them!

The lesson of "sixty"—that even one sixtieth counts when doing a good deed—is a lesson that hopefully can carry us *l'ziknah*!

Ki Seitzei

AMALEK AND REMEMBERING
THE POWER OF BA'DERECH

הַמְהַלֵּךְ בַּדֶּרֶךְ וְשׁוֹנֶה וּמַפְסִיק מִמִּשְׁנָתוֹ
וְאוֹמֵר, מַה נָּאֶה אִילָן זֶה וּמַה נָּאֶה נִיר זֶה,
מַעֲלֶה עָלָיו הַכָּתוּב כְּאִלּוּ מִתְחַיֵּב בְּנַפְשׁוֹ.

*One who is **walking on a path** and learning and stops from*
his learning and says, "How beautiful is this tree and how nice
is the plowed field," then the Torah considers him culpable
with his life. (Avos 3:7)

QUESTIONS

What is wrong with saying how beautiful a tree is after all?

ANSWERS

The classic explanation is that the person should realize that the tree
and field are part of his learning, and because he doesn't appreciate
G-d's nature as part of the context of Torah, he is missing the point. But
there may be another way to understand this Mishnah; this alternate
approach derives from analyzing the following from our *parashah*:

זָכוֹר אֵת אֲשֶׁר עָשָׂה לְךָ עֲמָלֵק בַּדֶּרֶךְ בְּצֵאתְכֶם מִמִּצְרָיִם. אֲשֶׁר קָרְךָ
בַּדֶּרֶךְ וַיְזַנֵּב בְּךָ כָּל הַנֶּחֱשָׁלִים אַחֲרֶיךָ וְאַתָּה עָיֵף וְיָגֵעַ וְלֹא יָרֵא אֱלֹקִים.

Remember what Amalek did to you by the way as you came
forth out of Egypt; how he met you by the way, and smote
those behind you, all who were enfeebled in the rear, when
your were faint and weary; and he feared not G-d.
(Devarim 25:17)

Rashi brings down that "וְלֹא יָרֵא אֱלֹקִים" refers to Amalek, i.e., Amalek attacked us because they didn't fear G-d. However, the Gemara records an opinion that "וְלֹא יָרֵא אֱלֹקִים" actually refers to B'nei Yisrael, and furthermore that "כָּל הַנֶּחֱשָׁלִים אַחֲרֶיךָ" refers to the Jewish People being lackadaisical with their Torah observance, i.e., Amalek was able to attack us because *we* were not G-d-fearing and/or observant at that moment in time. But if we weren't G-d-fearing at the time, and if we were נחשל בדרך, then what did Amalek do that was so wrong by attacking us?

The answer and theme here is that we were בדרך. Although we were in fact lowly at that very moment in time, we were heading in the right direction with potential, complemented by a positive trajectory!

Back to our question of what could be wrong with saying how beautiful a tree is, perhaps the answer is that just like Amalek attacked us by trying to block our path to improvement, any other person or thing that *blocks our path* is akin to Amalek for us. If someone else comes along and is מַפְסִיק מִמִּשְׁנָתוֹ—interrupts our learning, so to speak, even if they say something seemingly nice such as, "What a beautiful tree that is!," we have to be wary that such interruptions may sway us, redirecting us from our general holy mission. Modern-day Amalek may not only be Hamas, Hezbollah, ISIS, and Iran; they may be someone seemingly nice showing us pleasant trees and fields (מָה נָּאֶה אִילָן זֶה, מָה נָּאֶה נִיר), but who wishes to take us off our path toward Yiddishkeit and *menschlichkeit*. Beware the pleasant terrorists!

And so the Mishnah can be read: "One who walks **on the way** and studies, and [someone else comes and] interrupts his studying [saying], 'How beautiful is this tree! How beautiful is this plowed field!' the Torah considers [that person like Amalek] as if he had forfeited his life."

―――――――― TAKEAWAY MESSAGES ――――――――

Modern-day Amalek may refer to anything that takes us away from בדרך—away from the path toward Yiddishkeit and *menschlichkeit*. We are concerned with how we can better ourselves, and anything that hinders us or potentially blocks our path must be attacked! Amalek nowadays certainly may refer to the terrorists that threaten to kill us, but it may also refer to more subtle elements that try to thwart our בדרך as well. Remembering Amalek is remembering the lesson of בדרך.

HOW TO CONQUER ALL YOUR PROBLEMS

שִׁבְעָה דְבָרִים בַּגּוֹלֶם וְשִׁבְעָה בֶחָכָם:
חָכָם...אוֹמֵר עַל רִאשׁוֹן רִאשׁוֹן וְעַל אַחֲרוֹן
אַחֲרוֹן...וְחִלּוּפֵיהֶן בַּגּוֹלֶם.

*There are seven things that characterize a boor, and seven
that characterize a wise man: A wise man...**responds to
first things first**...With the boor, the reverse...is the case.*
(Avos 5:7)

QUESTIONS

This sounds super ironic and somewhat self-deprecating. If the sign
of wisdom is to be organized and discuss things in the order they were
introduced, then since the ignoramus was introduced first ("Seven
things differentiate an unlearned *ignoramus* from a wise man"), it would
have made more sense to proceed with the ignoramus (and not the wise
man) first: "The ignoramus does not discuss that which he introduced
first" (i.e., he is not orderly!). And so, unless the Tanna was purposely
trying to say that he himself is not a wise man, this cannot be what is
meant by "אוֹמֵר עַל רִאשׁוֹן רִאשׁוֹן"!

ANSWERS

An alternative way to understand "אוֹמֵר עַל רִאשׁוֹן רִאשׁוֹן" then may be
found in a beautiful *Kesav Sofer* on this *parashah*!
The Torah says:

כִּי תֵצֵא לַמִּלְחָמָה עַל אֹיְבֶיךָ וּנְתָנוֹ ה' אֱלֹקֶיךָ בְּיָדֶךָ וְשָׁבִיתָ שִׁבְיוֹ.

*When you go against your enemies (plural tense), and G-d will
give over your enemy (singular tense)..."*

The *Kesav Sofer* ponders why there is this obvious change from plural
to singular and says that "כִּי תֵצֵא לַמִּלְחָמָה עַל אֹיְבֶיךָ" can be homiletically
learned to relate to each of our fights with our own inherent evil nature
(*yetzer hara*). In order to win the war, we need to be our best advocate
(אִם אֵין אֲנִי לִי מִי לִי), realize we are not alone in the fight (וּכְשֶׁאֲנִי לְעַצְמִי מָה אֲנִי),
and fight while we have our most strength (וְאִם לֹא עַכְשָׁיו אֵימָתַי)! But he
continues in this homily and says that the best way to fight the multi-
faceted *yetzer hara* is not to try to overcome all the battles at once but
to take each fight one at a time! That is hinted in the *pasuk* as it shifts
from plural (עַל אֹיְבֶיךָ—your enemies) to singular (וּנְתָנוֹ—he will deliver
your **enemy**!). When you are attacked by your multifaceted evil nature,
take the fight methodically, one aspect at a time!

In a 2009 study, Stanford researcher Clifford Nass challenged 262
college students to complete experiments that involved switching
among tasks, filtering irrelevant information, and using working
memory. They expected that frequent multitaskers would outperform
non-multitaskers on at least some of these tasks, but actually found
that chronic multitaskers were abysmal at all three tasks! As a result
of the study, Nass suggested what he called the "twenty-minute rule."
Rather than switching tasks from minute to minute, dedicate a twenty-minute chunk of time to a single task and then switch to the next
one. This same concept can be applied to how we may best contend
with our spiritual struggles, which unfortunately are always multiple
and often fight us on several fronts.

The "אוֹמֵר עַל רִאשׁוֹן רִאשׁוֹן" may not necessarily be about prioritizing or
organizing speech but rather about tackling one task at a time! The lesson may be not to try to be Hercules and win everything at once. A wise
man takes one challenge at a time. This now fits better with the flow in
Avos, as the Tanna no longer is making himself look inconsistent!

—————— TAKEAWAY MESSAGES ——————

The *Kesav Sofer* says that "כִּי תֵצֵא לַמִּלְחָמָה עַל אֹיְבֶיךָ" relates to each of our fights with our own inherent evil nature: In order to win, we need to be our own best advocate (אִם אֵין אֲנִי לִי מִי לִי), realize we are not alone in the fight (וּכְשֶׁאֲנִי לְעַצְמִי מָה אֲנִי) and fight while we have our most strength (וְאִם לֹא עַכְשָׁיו אֵימָתָי)! He continued that the best way to fight the multi-faceted *yetzer hara* is not to try to overcome all the battles at once but to rather take each fight one at a time! That is hinted at in the *pasuk* as it shifts from plural (עַל אֹיְבֶיךָ—your enemies) to singular (וּנְתָנוֹ—he will deliver your **enemy**). The "אוֹמֵר עַל רִאשׁוֹן רִאשׁוֹן" may not necessarily be about prioritizing/organizing speech but rather about tackling one task at a time...

How to conquer all your problems? The *Kesav Sofer* recommends focusing on one problem at a time.

SHOULD WE NOT JUDGE OTHERS?

הַלֵּל אוֹמֵר: וְאַל תָּדִין אֶת חֲבֵרְךָ עַד שֶׁתַּגִּיעַ
לִמְקוֹמוֹ.

*Hillel says: Do not judge your fellow until **you have stood in his place**! (Avos 2:4)*

QUESTIONS

The classic understanding of this ethic is "Do not judge others until you can see their position/vantage point." But why specifically couch this idea with the concept of *makom*, space? There is perhaps another way to understand this ethic, though, and both ways are greatly illustrated in our *parashah*.

ANSWERS

לֹא תְתַעֵב אֲדֹמִי כִּי אָחִיךָ הוּא לֹא תְתַעֵב מִצְרִי כִּי גֵר הָיִיתָ בְאַרְצוֹ.

You shall not abhor an Edomite, for he is your brother; you shall not abhor an Egyptian, because you were a stranger in his land. (Devarim 23:8)

There are two ways to understand this:

The first is to say that it means: Do not be too unwelcoming to the Edomites, because after all, we are related (Eisav/Edom being Yaakov's brother). Also, don't be unwelcoming to the Egyptians, because after all, we were strangers in their land (and at least they fed/sustained us as strangers). But this version, albeit the most accepted one, seems some-what unrealistic and could invite some cynicism. Are we really supposed to be thankful for the courtesy of the Egyptians while enslaving us in their land?

Another version, utilizing the above ethic of "אַל תָּדִין אֶת חֲבֵרְךָ עַד שֶׁתַּגִּיעַ לִמְקוֹמוֹ—Do not judge others until you can see their position/vantage point," may read as follows: Don't be unwelcoming to the Edomite, *because as your brother, he had reason to be harsh to you!* Familiarity breeds contempt. We say, "הִנֵּה מַה טּוֹב וּמַה נָּעִים שֶׁבֶת אַחִים גַּם יָחַד" (*Tehillim* 133:1). What is so special and unique (מַה טּוֹב וּמַה נָּעִים) about brothers sitting next to each other? The answer is that brothers unfortunately tend to fight; it is sometimes miraculous to see older siblings actually get along so nicely. The Edomites were unkind to us, but the Torah may be telling us to give them a pass: it was natural for them to dislike us because after all, they were our brothers (who tend to squabble!).

The Torah continues: Don't be unwelcoming to the Egyptians as well but rather "see their position/vantage point." We were strangers in their land, and it is natural to try to be wary of strangers. They also had a reason to abhor us, and so we have to at least try to sympathize on some level with them. And so, by the Edomites and the Egyptians, our due and expected animosity should be tempered by this concept of "אַל תָּדִין אֶת חֲבֵרְךָ עַד שֶׁתַּגִּיעַ לִמְקוֹמוֹ," that we should not judge others until we can see their position/vantage point!

But there is yet a second beautiful way to understand this ethic from our *parashah*: We are adjured not to allow Ammon and Moav into our community for ten generations (i.e., forever, as ten generations is a figure of speech) because they did not give us food and water once we entered into their boundary. The commentators struggle to un-derstand why the Ammonites and Moavites are denied entry for ten generations while the aforementioned Egyptians/Edomites are denied until the third generation. An answer may be that the Ammonites and Moavites looked good from afar, but once we got into their territory, they betrayed us: "עַל דְּבַר אֲשֶׁר לֹא קִדְּמוּ אֶתְכֶם בַּלֶּחֶם וּבַמַּיִם בַּדֶּרֶךְ." This is a second understanding of "אַל תָּדִין אֶת חֲבֵרְךָ עַד שֶׁתַּגִּיעַ לִמְקוֹמוֹ"—*You can't really judge a person until you reach their actual physical place!* The true characteristics of a person or nation are sometimes only evident when you get up close and personal. The lesson of the ethic then may also be that true character can best be determined by how people conduct themselves in their place, i.e., in their home base! *You can't really judge a person until you reach their actual physical place* is then not a hunky-dory positive message, but rather a warning to be wary of seemingly nice folks who seem inviting until you enter their airspace!

───────────── TAKEAWAY MESSAGES ─────────────

"אַל תָּדִין אֶת חֲבֵרְךָ עַד שֶׁתַּגִּיעַ לִמְקוֹמוֹ" may mean that you shouldn't judge others until you fully understand their motives/vantage point: Perhaps the Edomites (brothers that have natural squabbles) and the Egyptians (strangers are often looked upon suspiciously) had reason to treat us poorly, and so we should be a bit less vengeful to them. "אַל תָּדִין אֶת חֲבֵרְךָ עַד שֶׁתַּגִּיעַ לִמְקוֹמוֹ" may also mean that you can't fully judge someone until you get into their personal space; the true evil and inhospitality of the Ammonites and Moavites was only discovered once we were entrenched בִּמְקוֹמוֹ. The best way to fully appreciate someone's character is to look at his "place": how he or she treats you in their home base!

Should we not judge others? Perhaps we can, but we have to understand their place (viewpoint) and not fully judge until we see how they act with us in their place!

DOES ORECH YAMIM REALLY MEAN LONG LIFE?

גְּדוֹלָה תוֹרָה שֶׁהִיא נוֹתֶנֶת חַיִּים לְעוֹשֶׂיהָ
בָּעוֹלָם הַזֶּה וּבָעוֹלָם הַבָּא, שֶׁנֶּאֱמַר (משלי ד, ג)
אֹרֶךְ יָמִים בִּימִינָהּ בִּשְׂמֹאולָהּ עֹשֶׁר וְכָבוֹד.

*Torah is great because it gives life in this world and the next,
as it says (Mishlei 4:3), **"Long life** in the right [hand] and in
the left [hand] is wealth and honor" (Avos 6:7).*

QUESTION

What really is meant by *orech yamim*, long life?

ANSWER

We see two out of the three mitzvos in the Torah that are rewarded with long life in our *parashah*: (1) sending out the mother bird before taking its eggs, and (2) having accurate weights (not cheating in business!).

Here they are as related by the *pesukim*:

שַׁלֵּחַ תְּשַׁלַּח אֶת הָאֵם וְאֶת הַבָּנִים תִּקַּח לָךְ לְמַעַן יִיטַב לָךְ
וְהַאֲרַכְתָּ יָמִים.

*Send off the mother before taking the young [egg or bird], so
that your days will be **lengthened**! (Devarim 22:7)*

אֶבֶן שְׁלֵמָה וָצֶדֶק יִהְיֶה לָךְ אֵיפָה שְׁלֵמָה וָצֶדֶק יִהְיֶה לָךְ לְמַעַן יַאֲרִיכוּ
יָמֶיךָ עַל הָאֲדָמָה אֲשֶׁר ה' אֱלֹקֶיךָ נֹתֵן לָךְ.

*A perfect and just weight you should have; a perfect and just
measure you should have; in order that your days should be
lengthened! (Devarim 25:14)*

The only other time we see this reward of long life for doing a mitzvah is in *parashas Yisro*:

כַּבֵּד אֶת אָבִיךָ וְאֶת אִמֶּךָ לְמַעַן יַאֲרִכוּן יָמֶיךָ עַל הָאֲדָמָה אֲשֶׁר ה'
אֱלֹקֶיךָ נֹתֵן לָךְ.

*Honor your mother and father in order for your days to be
lengthened upon the land which Hashem gives you.
(Shemos 20:11)*

QUESTIONS

Why are these three mitzvos rewarded with long life? What is the
connection between them?

ANSWERS

Dr. Larry Ciment explained to me that these three mitzvos aren't
necessarily connected but rather are **complementary**! In order to live
a fulfilled life, one must show respect for their mother and father (כַּבֵּד
אֶת אָבִיךָ וְאֶת אִמֶּךָ), must exhibit proper compassion for one another (שַׁלֵּחַ
תְּשַׁלַּח אֶת הָאֵם), and must be honest in their personal business dealings
(אֶבֶן שְׁלֵמָה וָצֶדֶק יִהְיֶה לָךְ).

To further bolster Dr. Ciment's analysis, note that the Ramban clearly
states that one reason we are instructed to send off the mother before
taking her eggs is that this act has an element of *rachamim* (mercy) that
we must try to instill in ourselves.

Also, it is worth noting that all these instances are not marked by
orech shanim but rather by *orech yamim*, as if to say that we aren't necessarily talking about long years or long life per se but a more *fulfilling*

life—making the most of every day! This may partly explain how righteous people pass on "before their time."

And finally, the emphasis may not be on the *orech shanim* or the *orech yamim* but rather on the word *orech* (אֹרֶךְ) itself. Let me explain. The word אֹרֶךְ can be viewed as an acronym: the letter א is for אב and אם (father and mother)—one must constantly recognize and appreciate where they come from; the letter ר is for רחמים (mercy)—one must have mercy and compassion for animals and *kal v'chomer* for humans; and the letter כ (ך) is for כיסך (*kischa*, your pocket, referring to monetary dealings)—one must be honest in business (לֹא יִהְיֶה לְךָ בְּכִיסְךָ אֶבֶן וָאָבֶן). Alternatively, the כ is for כף מאזנים (a scale), signifying fair weights and measures.

"Long life" is really "fulfilling life," and fulfillment is three-pronged, as explained above!

───────── TAKEAWAY MESSAGES ─────────

The three mitzvos of honoring your parents, sending off the motherbird before taking its eggs, and having fair weights and measures are complementary to one another—every day we have a challenge to earn *orech yamim*, simply by recognizing our roots, being compassionate, and exhibiting honesty in business, and these are the components in living a fulfilled life.

Does *orech yamim* really mean long life? Maybe not; maybe it means more fulfilling days!

Ki Savo

הוּא הָיָה אוֹמֵר: יָפָה שָׁעָה אַחַת בִּתְשׁוּבָה
וּמַעֲשִׂים טוֹבִים בָּעוֹלָם הַזֶּה מִכָּל חַיֵּי הָעוֹלָם
הַבָּא. וְיָפָה שָׁעָה אַחַת שֶׁל קוֹרַת רוּחַ בָּעוֹלָם
הַבָּא מִכָּל חַיֵּי הָעוֹלָם הַזֶּה.

*He would also say: A single moment of repentance and good
deeds in this world is greater than all the World to Come. And
a single moment of bliss in the World to Come is greater than
all of the present world. (Avos 4:17)*

QUESTIONS

This statement in *Avos* is confusing! Where is it better to be—in this world or the next? עוֹלָם הַבָּא is presumably the only other world, and so if not born, one's spirit would de facto be in עוֹלָם הַבָּא. So the question rephrased: Is it better to be born in this world or never born at all? Also, why does it say, "יָפָה שָׁעָה אַחַת בִּתְשׁוּבָה וּמַעֲשִׂים טוֹבִים בָּעוֹלָם הַזֶּה," i.e., "repentance" and then "good deeds"? It would seem to flow better if the Mishnah just said "good deeds" alone; after all, if one has good deeds, he will never need to do *teshuvah* anyway!

486

—— ANSWERS ——

Rabbi Yaakov Greenberg says in the name of the *Chasam Sofer* that the answer to Hamlet's classic question ("To be or not to be?") is rooted in the *pasuk* from our *parashah*: "בָּרוּךְ אַתָּה בְּבֹאֶךָ וּבָרוּךְ אַתָּה בְּצֵאתֶךָ—You will be blessed in your coming, and you will be blessed in your leaving" (*Devarim* 28:6). How does this verse express this? The Gemara in *Eruvin* (13b) says: Is it better to ever be brought into this world or not? The Gemara there says:

> *Our Rabbis taught: For two and a half years, Beis Shammai and Beis Hillel were in dispute, the former asserting that it were better for man not to have been created than to have been created, and the latter maintaining that it is better for man to have been created than not to have been created. They finally took a vote and decided that it would be better for man not to have been created than to have been created, but now that he has been created, let him investigate his past deeds or, as others say, let him examine his future actions.*

On this note, the *Chasam Sofer* homiletically says, the only way one can be "blessed as he comes in" is if he or she demonstrates good deeds that would lead to being "blessed as he comes out" (righteous in death!). Indeed, it is better not to be created at all, and in most cases a moment of serenity in the next world outweighs this whole world. However, *once created in this world*, we have a duty to make it worthwhile by being involved in positive spiritual endeavors that can, in effect, make our existence here superior to the next world! Perhaps when the Mishnah in *Avos* thus says, "A single moment of bliss in the World to Come is greater than all of the present world," this refers to the concept that it is indeed better not to be created at all in most cases. But when it says, "A single moment of repentance and good deeds in this world is greater than all of the World to Come," that is referring to when one lives a life full of *teshuvah* and good deeds.

Perhaps this aforementioned Gemara in *Eruvin* (13b) fits in nicely with the Mishnah in *Avos*. The Gemara stated: "עכשיו שנברא **יפשפש**

במעשיו ואמרי לה: **ימשמש במעשיו**—But now that he has been created, let him **investigate his past deeds** or, as others say, let him **examine his future actions**." Although technically, someone born in this world can potentially never sin and thus earn עוֹלָם הַבָּא by getting straight "A"s all along, the reality is that we all sin. Thus, before even mentioning, "Let him examine his future actions" with a focus on the future good deeds, the Amora in the Gemara posits, "Let him investigate his past deeds!" Similarly, our Mishnah in *Avos* realistically precedes *teshuvah* before good deeds to reassure us that we can still be a "בָּרוּךְ אַתָּה בְּצֵאתֶךָ" even if we sin, which is inevitable and expected!

———— TAKEAWAY MESSAGES ————

In general, the next world is better than this world, and it actually is better never to have been born into this tough world. But by living a life of *teshuvah* and good deeds, where we are constantly יפשפש במעשיו and ימשמש במעשיו, we can earn a reputation bless-worthy in death (בָּרוּךְ אַתָּה בְּצֵאתֶךָ), which will make our existence in this world potentially even better than the next! Our Tanna in *Avos* further reassures us that sinning is expected, and thus doing *teshuvah* actually precedes good deeds!

What greater solace in Elul is the point that we still have a chance to be a בָּרוּךְ אַתָּה בְּצֵאתֶךָ, even if we perform imperfectly in an imperfect world. *Teshuvah* precedes good deeds because we are not expected to be perfect!

To be or not to be? The answer is "to be," as long as we apply the *Chasam Sofer*'s lesson of בָּרוּךְ אַתָּה בְּבֹאֶךָ וּבָרוּךְ אַתָּה בְּצֵאתֶךָ.

NOT FULFILLING THE TORAH LEADS TO DEMENTIA?

רַבִּי דוֹסְתָּאִי בְּרַבִּי יַנַּאי מִשׁוּם רַבִּי מֵאִיר
אוֹמֵר: כָּל הַשׁוֹכֵחַ דָּבָר אֶחָד מִמִּשְׁנָתוֹ מַעֲלֶה
עָלָיו הַכָּתוּב כְּאִלוּ מִתְחַיֵּב בְּנַפְשׁוֹ, שֶׁנֶּאֱמַר
(דברים ד) רַק הִשָּׁמֶר לְךָ וּשְׁמֹר נַפְשְׁךָ מְאֹד פֶּן
תִּשְׁכַּח אֶת הַדְּבָרִים אֲשֶׁר רָאוּ עֵינֶיךָ.

Rabbi Dustai the son of Rabbi Yannai would say in the name
of Rabbi Meir: Anyone who forgets even a single word of this
learning, the Torah considers it as if he had forfeited his life.
As is stated, "Just be careful, and verily guard your soul, lest
you forget the things that your eyes have seen" (Devarim 4:9).
(Avos 3:8)

QUESTIONS

If you forget your learning, why is it so terrible?

ANSWERS

One answer I forgot. Another answer is simply homiletical: If you forget "דָּבָר אֶחָד מִמִּשְׁנָתוֹ"—that our learning is all "one thing," i.e., that all of our learning is to be directed for one purpose, namely לשמה, in which case our learning is worthwhile.

Another approach/idea may be derived from our *parashah*, where it says: "לֹא עָבַרְתִּי מִמִּצְוֹתֶיךָ וְלֹא שָׁכָחְתִּי—I have not transgressed any of Your commandments, neither have I forgotten them" (*Devarim* 26:13). Shouldn't the *pasuk* read: "I did not forget the laws, and hence I have not transgressed your commandments"? The order seems wrong.

The *Arvei Nachal*, quoted in the *Ma'ynah Shel Torah*, beautifully reminds us that one Gemara states that if you fail to separate your tithes, the punishment is that a mouse will eat your food. A different Gemara says that if you eat food that was partially eaten by a mouse, you will forget your learning. Therefore, the *pasuk* is saying: Since I did not transgress tithing, no mice ate my food, and I therefore did not forget my learning!

But perhaps there is a deeper lesson that is sparked by this nice message: We generally think that forgetting is a *just cause* for neglecting to do something, e.g, I forgot my homework at school, therefore I cannot be expected to complete my homework. However, from the Torah's perspective, forgetting is not a *just cause* but rather a *symptom* of disobedience, e.g., I did not bring *maaser*, and so I am punished with forgetting! In other words, I didn't forget the laws and thereby missed *maaser*, but rather I was lackadaisical about the laws and thereby forgot them!

The Mishnah in *Avos* now makes sense! "כָּל הַשּׁוֹכֵחַ דָּבָר אֶחָד מִמִּשְׁנָתוֹ מַעֲלֶה עָלָיו הַכָּתוּב כְּאִלּוּ מִתְחַיֵּב בְּנַפְשׁוֹ" is not saying, "If you forget your learning, that forgetfulness will *lead you* down to punishment," but rather, "if you forget your learning, it is only because that was a symptom of your carelessness and lack of attentiveness!" I forgot my homework at school because I did not think it was important; such recklessness is no excuse and I should be expected to complete my tasks!

─────── TAKEAWAY MESSAGES ───────

Forgetfulness is not a just cause for failing to do a task. Rather it is a *symptom* of not caring enough to pay the due energy requisite to complete the commandments properly. "כָּל הַשּׁוֹכֵחַ דָּבָר אֶחָד מִמִּשְׁנָתוֹ, מַעֲלֶה עָלָיו הַכָּתוּב כְּאִלּוּ מִתְחַיֵּב בְּנַפְשׁוֹ" is telling us that if we forget our learning, it is because we neglected to see such spirituality as a priority—the symptom of forgetting is the punishment itself! Conversely, if I do not transgress the laws, I will not forget: "לֹא עָבַרְתִּי מִמִּצְוֹתֶיךָ וְלֹא שָׁכָחְתִּי."

Not learning enough Torah *can* be a potential risk factor for being forgetful. This is one *d'var Torah* you should never forget!

WHAT'S BETTER: HAVING LITTLE BUT THINKING ONE HAS MUCH, OR VICE VERSA?

מַרְבֶּה נְכָסִים מַרְבֶּה דְּאָגָה.

The greater the assets, the more worry one has. (Avos 2:7)

---- QUESTIONS ----

At the end of our *parashah*, the verse states:

וּשְׁמַרְתֶּם אֶת דִּבְרֵי הַבְּרִית הַזֹּאת וַעֲשִׂיתֶם אֹתָם לְמַעַן תַּשְׂכִּילוּ אֵת
כָּל אֲשֶׁר תַּעֲשׂוּן.

*And you should keep the words of the covenant, and you
should do them, in order to understand all that was done.
(Devarim 29:8)*

The Gemara learns out from here that "כל העוסק בתורה נכסיו מצליחין
לו—Anyone who involves themselves in Torah, their belongings will be
successful" (*Avodah Zarah* 19b).

But didn't we just say from *Avos* that those with many belongings will
likely have more worry? What is the proper understanding here?

To understand this question, we must first really understand this last
pasuk of our *parashah*. What does "in order to understand all that was
done" actually mean?

492

────────── ANSWERS ──────────

Taskilu, understand, has the root of *sechel*, which means "sensical." Yet, *Onkelos* and *Targum Yonasan* both translate *taskilu* as "succeed," as if to say, "You should keep the Torah so that you'll succeed." Since *Onkelos* actually predated the Talmud (roughly 110 CE), it is likely that our very Gemara above derived from *Onkelos*'s translation. Since *Targum Yonasan* was written by a Tanna (Yonasan ben Uziel), it could be that the tradition derived from him as well. Interestingly, the *Targum Yerushalmi* (probably composed in the eighth-century CE) has *taskilu* meaning "understanding," as we ourselves would have probably translated it.

OK, then, but why do *Onkelos*, *Targum Yonasan*, and the Gemara translate *taskilu* as "succeed"? The answer may be very simple: Success has nothing to do with how much one has but rather how much one thinks he has!

Success is a state of mind, not a state of wealth. Two people can each have a million dollars, and one of them can be perfectly happy and the other can be perfectly miserable. When the Torah tells us to keep its laws and do them in order to "succeed," this success is achieved by the mindset and framework that the Torah gives us.

But it gets even better...

The Gemara from *Avodah Zarah* that we quoted above, "All those who involve themselves in Torah, their possessions are successful for them," is giving a super clear message: If you involve yourself in Torah, you yourself will consider "successful" what you have or get. You will be granted the mindset to appreciate all the gifts you have! The key is in the language of the Gemara: "מצליחין לו."

Putting it all together, in general, the more property or possessions we get, the more worry they will entail. But if you keep the Torah, G-d grants us the mindset to appreciate all of our possessions so that they become מצליחין לו, so that they are viewed only positively. The biggest *berachah* we can have is not wealth itself, but the *sechel* in which to see our possessions as wealth!

—————— TAKEAWAY MESSAGES ——————

The more you get, the more worry you will have. But if we strive to keep the Torah and do good deeds, G-d guarantees us *sechel*, which is "success" according to *Onkelos* and *Targum Yonasan*, likely because it is the G-d-given reward to view any or all our posessions as gifts/wealth. *Sechel* is one and the same as success.

What's better? Having little and thinking you have a lot. Success in Torah is *sechel*; wealth is a state of mind.

Nitzavim

DOES JUDAISM FROWN ON INDIVIDUALISM?

וְד־יְּמְהַלֵּךְ בַּדֶּרֶךְ יְחִידִי...הֲרֵי זֶה מִר־יְתְחַיֵּיב בְּנַפְשׁוֹ.

If you walk on a path alone, you are responsible for your life.
(Avos 3:4)

— QUESTIONS —

What is meant by this cryptic statement in *Avos*? Shouldn't we espouse individualism?

— ANSWERS —

An answer from a question on our *parashah*:

מִשָּׁם יְקַבֶּצְךָ ה' אֱלֹקֶיךָ וּמִשָּׁם יִקָּחֶךָ.

From there G-d will gather you and from there He will take you. (Devarim 30:4)

This *pasuk*, included in the weekly *tefillah shel ha'medinah*, seems wordy and redundant. Why say "*mi'sham*—from there" twice when the *pasuk* could simply read, "From there G-d will gather you and take you"?

495

My cousin, Rabbi Elchanan Ciment, answered my question by saying that the *pasuk* is another example of *areivus*, togetherness. He continued by homilizing the following *pasuk* in *Devarim*:

וַיְהִי בִישֻׁרוּן מֶלֶךְ בְּהִתְאַסֵּף רָאשֵׁי עָם יַחַד שִׁבְטֵי יִשְׂרָאֵל.

*He became King over Yeshurun, when the leaders
of the people **gathered**, the tribes of Israel in unity.*
(Devarim 33:5)

When is G-d's kingship most evident? Only when his people unify. Similarly, in order to attain the dream of coming back to our land, we must do it in steps. First, we need to unify, and then once we show our *areivus*, the gathering in to our land becomes easier.

This concept of *kibutz* prior to *kichah* (gathering prior to taking) is not only relevant to the coming into Israel (that we should all be *zocheh* to!), but also to our individual goals. In order to be successful at anything, we must first earnestly gather in our ideas/philosophies/strengths, and only then expect to be brought forward to the next level. We need to first have a *kibutz* before *kichah* can take place.

Perhaps a proof to this idea can be in analyzing the *trop* on this *pasuk*. The first *mi'sham* (מִשָּׁם) has a diamond-shaped *revi'i*, which is placed above the letter, but the second *mi'sham* (וּמִשָּׁם) has a *tipcha*. When we embark on such glorious yet difficult journeys in life (such as making aliyah!), the journey will look like it is a hard-to-achieve diamond (*revi'i*) that hovers above us in the distance far away. But once we collect ourselves and join others, the next *mi'sham* has a plain-looking *tipcha* (which is usually a second leg or stopping sound following the *mercha*), which is beneath the word, intimating that "we can do this without problem!" The trick in morphing from a difficult, hard-to-fathom "diamond above the sky" challenge into something attainable au naturel is by coming together and working with others to achieve our goal.

Likewise, in *Avos*, we aren't knocking individualism as much as we are pointing out that only true success comes from unifying and banding together!

———————— TAKEAWAY MESSAGES ————————

Pirkei Avos says that one who embarks on his own journey is liable for his life, perhaps because he should be banding with others! The Torah tells us that G-d will take us into the "Promised Land" once we first band together. The *kibutz* must not only precede but also create the reality of *kichah*. "He became King over Yeshurun, when the leaders of the people **gathered**, the tribes of Israel in unity"! At first, things look like hard-to-achieve diamonds in the sky (מְשֻׁם) before the treading makes it natural (וּמְשֻׁם).

Does Judaism frown on individualism? Not as much as it values collectivity!

DON'T DO GOOD IN ORDER
TO GET A PRIZE

אַנְטִיגְנוֹס אִישׁ סוֹכוֹ...הָיָה אוֹמֵר: אַל תִּהְיוּ
כַּעֲבָדִים הַמְשַׁמְּשִׁין אֶת הָרַב עַל מְנָת לְקַבֵּל
פְּרָס אֶלָּא הֱווּ כַּעֲבָדִים הַמְשַׁמְּשִׁין אֶת הָרַב
שֶׁלֹּא עַל מְנָת לְקַבֵּל פְּרָס וִיהִי מוֹרָא שָׁמַיִם
עֲלֵיכֶם.

Antignos of Socho…would say: Do not be as slaves, who serve
their master for the sake of reward. Rather, be as slaves who
serve their master not for the sake of reward. And the fear of
heaven should be upon you. (Avos 1:3)

שְׂכַר מִצְוָה מִצְוָה.

For the reward of a mitzvah is a mitzvah. (Avos 4:2)

QUESTIONS

1. Regarding the first Mishnah above: Why use the word *pras*,
   portion, and not *schar*, reward? Is there any lesson to be learned
   from this less-common term being used here?

2. Regarding the second Mishnah: The classic understanding of
   "שְׂכַר מִצְוָה מִצְוָה" is that if you do one mitzvah, you are rewarded
   with the ability to do more mitzvos, and that this will eventually

498

compound your ultimate reward. Is there a connection to the first Mishnah above about reward?

——————— ANSWERS ———————

The answer is clear from our *parashah*:

אֲשֶׁר אָנֹכִי מְצַוְּךָ הַיּוֹם לְאַהֲבָה אֶת ה' אֱלֹקֶיךָ לָלֶכֶת בִּדְרָכָיו וְלִשְׁמֹר מִצְוֹתָיו וְחֻקֹּתָיו וּמִשְׁפָּטָיו; וְחָיִיתָ וְרָבִיתָ וּבֵרַכְךָ ה' אֱלֹקֶיךָ **בָּאָרֶץ אֲשֶׁר** אַתָּה בָא שָׁמָּה לְרִשְׁתָּהּ.

In that I command you this day to love Hashem your G-d, to walk in His ways, and to keep His commandments and His statutes and His ordinances; then you will live and multiply, and Hashem your G-d shall bless you **in the Land** *where you go to possess it. (Devarim 30:19)*

Why juxtapose the reward that G-d will bestow upon us if we listen to Him with the added "בָּאָרֶץ אֲשֶׁר אַתָּה בָא שָׁמָּה"? Isn't the reward of "וְחָיִיתָ וְרָבִיתָ—You will live and multiply" enough? Why do I need the "in the Land" part?

There is a difference between a prize and a reward. A prize is a trophy that you showcase on your shelf in celebration of an achievement. A reward is a deeper payback that creates a bond between the Master and servant. When G-d tells the Jews that they will live and thrive **in the Land**, He is saying that true reward is enabling a further closeness/bond to develop. As the Jews will be **in the Land**, they will have further opportunity to establish a further closeness with G-d!

In general, when you get a prize/trophy, it is usually a culmination of a success and a time to *break away* and move on to new endeavors. In fact, the word meaning prize actually has פ-ר-ס as its root, and the word actually means to "divide/cut"! The Mishnah can read homiletically: "Don't be like a servant who wants to slice/cut away." Don't view the reward as a be-all and end-all. The reward itself is simply a way for us not to divide away like a servant yearning for freedom from his master but rather an opportunity to get closer to the Master! The וְחָיִיתָ וְרָבִיתָ וּבֵרַכְךָ

leads us not away from G-d, celebrating that we earned a reward but rather בָּאָרֶץ אֲשֶׁר אַתָּה בָא שָׁמָּה, in the place closest to G-d in Eretz Yisrael.

Finally, since the reward itself is a mitzvah, in the sense that it is supposed to bring you closer to G-d and not an excuse to cut away from Him, we can likewise understand שְׂכַר מִצְוָה מִצְוָה in this way: the reward for a mitzvah is a mitzvah itself. The rewards for hard work/achievements should be seen as a celebration to get closer to G-d, and not farther away. This is not saying like many others say, namely, that a reward for a mitzvah is getting to do another mitzvah, but rather that the reward of a mitzvah is a **mitzvah itself** (שְׂכַר מִצְוָה מִצְוָה), the recognition that it isn't a chance to cut loose but rather to bind closer!

─────────── TAKEAWAY MESSAGES ───────────

When we do good, G-dly rewards are not health and prosperity alone. The rewards are also opportunities to get closer to G-d—an opportunity to dwell בָּאָרֶץ אֲשֶׁר אַתָּה בָא שָׁמָּה. The reward for doing good deeds is actually a mitzvah itself, as it is an opportunity to get close to G-d.

We don't work for a פְּרָס, a prize that *separates* us from the benefactor. We strive for a reward in which we can embellish our holy relationships. I'll trade in my פְּרָס for שְׂכַר any day of the week.

So yes, perhaps we shouldn't do good in order to get a "prize," but we should do good in order to get "reward."

HOW TO ENTER ROSH HASHANAH— UPRIGHT AND CONFIDENT OR BOWING IN FEAR?

יְהוּדָה בֶּן טַבַּאי אוֹמֵר ...וּכְשֶׁיִּהְיוּ בַעֲלֵי
דִינִין עוֹמְדִים לְפָנֶיךָ, יִהְיוּ בְעֵינֶיךָ כִּרְשָׁעִים.
וּכְשֶׁנִּפְטָרִים מִלְּפָנֶיךָ, יִהְיוּ בְעֵינֶיךָ כְּזַכָּאִין,
כְּשֶׁקִּבְּלוּ עֲלֵיהֶם אֶת הַדִּין.

Yehudah ben Tabai says: When the litigants stand before you, consider them both guilty; and when they leave your courtroom, having accepted the judgment, regard them as equally righteous. (Avos 1:8)

Yehudah ben Tabai is talking to judges, saying that when they see litigants "fighting" their cases before them, they should presume each party is guilty until the case is figured out.

--- QUESTIONS ---

1. Most of the commentaries on *Avos* observe that by establishing a "leveled playing field" (i.e., both parties are considered guilty at first, כִּרְשָׁעִים), this guarantees that neither party will be given any sort of preferential consideration due to his background, reputation, or social status. But still, why does the "level playing field" espoused by the Tanna in *Avos* start out as guilty?

501

What about the tenet of "innocent until proven guilty" (see *Bava Kama* 46b)?

2.   In this week's *parashah*, it says:

רְאֵה נָתַתִּי לְפָנֶיךָ הַיּוֹם אֶת הַחַיִּים וְאֶת הַטּוֹב וְאֶת הַמָּוֶת וְאֶת הָרָע.

Behold, I have set before you today life and good, and death and evil. (Devarim 30:15)

Rashi points out that the *pasuk* is saying: "Each one [life or death,] is dependent upon the other: if you do good, then you get *chayim*, life, and if one does bad, one gets *maves*, death." But then shouldn't the *pasuk* say, "If you do good, then you get life, and if you do bad, then death" (אֶת הַטּוֹב וְאֶת הַחַיִּים)? The order seems redundant and odd!

———————————— ANSWERS ————————————

The answer may be derived from looking at how judges of flesh and blood differ from the ultimate Judge, Hashem. Our *parashah* starts:

אַתֶּם נִצָּבִים הַיּוֹם כֻּלְּכֶם לִפְנֵי ה' אֱלֹקֵיכֶם.

You are all standing this day before the Lord, your G-d. (Devarim 29:9)

The Lubavitcher Rebbe beautifully said that הַיּוֹם refers to Rosh Hashanah, and G-d always puts this *parashah* before Rosh Hashanah to lift our spirits up going in to the High Holidays by calling us all נִצָּבִים, which can mean "standing" but can also mean "upright individuals." In fact, the Rebbe posits that this assurance of vindication in the up-coming Rosh Hashanah judgment contained in the opening words of *Nitzavim* is G-d's blessing of Tishrei (hence we need not do a formal *Birkas Ha'chodesh*!) which is embodied in the Torah-reading!

Pointedly, perhaps the word נִצָּבִים purposely precedes הַיּוֹם to further show that when G-d judges us, He will consider us litigants as upstanding, giving us the benefit of the doubt coming into Rosh Hashanah. Unlike a judge of flesh and blood, who needs to establish a "level playing field of guilty" at first glance so that he will be forced to be extra meticulous before adjudicating to set someone free from guilt, G-d establishes for us a "level playing field of *nitzavim*/upright" at first glance because He is not *forced* to find anyone guilty and is happy if He can get us off the hook!

And this explains why it says, "אֶת הַחַיִּים וְאֶת הַטּוֹב," even though *Rashi* points out that really it would make sense to say "אֶת הַטּוֹב וְאֶת הַחַיִּים." G-d is *reassuring* us in telling us that **we will get life** because we will do good. It's not that we will do good, and if we do good then we will earn/get life, but rather that we will get life because we will certainly do good!

—————— TAKEAWAY MESSAGES ——————

Judges of flesh and blood differ from G-d in that G-d wants to be less meticulous with us and is looking for ways to find us upright. What better advocate to have before Rosh Hashanah than the Almighty Himself who teaches us that even before הַיּוֹם, we are נִצָּבִים, and that even before הַטּוֹב—doing good, we have אֶת הַחַיִּים—assured life!

Go into Rosh Hashanah standing upright in confidence!

Vayeilech

YOU ARE WHAT YOU DO

בֶּן בַּג בַּג אוֹמֵר: הֲפֹךְ בָּה וַהֲפֹךְ בָּה דְּכֹלָא בָה.
וּבָהּ תֶּחֱזֵי וְסִיב וּבְלֵה בָּהּ, מִנַּהּ לֹא תָזוּעַ שֶׁאֵין
לְךְ מִדָּה טוֹבָה הֵימֶנָּה.

*Ben Bag Bag says: Delve and delve into it; and **in it you shall
see**, and be mindful of it, and never leave it, for there is no
greater thing than it [Torah life]. (Avos 5:22)*

--- QUESTIONS ---

This statement in *Avos* is said by Ben Bag Bag, who is widely considered to be a convert. Why is his statement in Aramaic, the colloquial language of the time, rather than Hebrew like the other Mishnayos?

The answer to this question should also answer another puzzling question: When the converting gentile in the Gemara in *Shabbos* (31a) asked for the Torah to be explained to him while he stood on one foot, Hillel said to that man in Aramaic, "דעלך סני לחברך לא תעביד זו היא כל התורה כולה—'That which you abhor, do not do to your friends,' that is the whole Torah." Again, why is his response in Aramaic when the rest of that Gemara is in Hebrew? Furthermore, why is it that he picks this seemingly natural ethic as opposed to any or every other precept? Also, why does Hillel call that ethic, "כל התורה—the whole Torah"?

504

────────────── ANSWERS ──────────────

The answer is in our *parashah*. The Torah says that when bad things happen to someone because he went astray, he may say, "הֲלֹא עַל כִּי אֵין אֱלֹקַי בְּקִרְבִּי מְצָאוּנִי הָרָעוֹת הָאֵלֶּה—Are not these evils coming upon me because G-d is not with me?" (*Devarim* 31:17). At first glance this seems to be the sinner realizing his sin and starting the *teshuvah* process, but the very next *pasuk* states: "וְאָנֹכִי הַסְתֵּר אַסְתִּיר פָּנַי בַּיּוֹם הַהוּא עַל כָּל הָרָעָה אֲשֶׁר עָשָׂה כִּי פָנָה אֶל אֱלֹהִים אֲחֵרִים—And I will surely hide My face in that day for all the evil which they shall have wrought, in that they are turned unto other gods." Now if the man was repenting, why would G-d continue and accelerate the punishment?

Rabbi Simchah Bunim of Peschischa says that the first verse isn't showing that the man is repenting; it is rather revisiting the inherent problem that the man does not realize he has G-d within him! (Not that "G-d isn't with me," but that he actually does not see himself possessing G-dliness!)

The purpose of learning Torah over and over again (הֲפֹךְ בָּהּ וַהֲפֹךְ בָּהּ) is so that you and others can see that Torah is within you, not just with you—וּבָהּ תֶּחֱזֵי. You and the Torah become indistinguishable. וּבָהּ תֶּחֱזֵי thus doesn't mean that you will see it, but that it will be seen in you!

Ben Bag Bag the convert specifically says this lesson, and specifically in Aramaic, to highlight that Torah is not merely genetically transmitted via family trees. Rather, the precepts can be practiced and practiced, reviewed and reviewed, until they become miraculously part of even a convert's genetic build! When Hillel says to the convert the seemingly obvious ethic, he is demonstrating that if you study and perform the Torah precepts over and over, it will become part and parcel of your very being. The Torah will become as natural as the simple ethic: "What is hateful to you, do not do to your fellow." You are what you do.

────────────── TAKEAWAY MESSAGES ──────────────

Rabbi Simchah Bunim explains that bad things can happen not so much because G-d is not *with* (i.e., disparate entities) us, but rather when we fail to realize the G-dliness *within* us! By reviewing and performing Torah precepts regularly, it becomes evident to all that G-d is within us (וּבָהּ תֶּחֱזֵי). Hillel reminds us that "G-dliness" is not some esoteric, hard-to-achieve characteristic but rather is attained by practicing rather simple Torah ethics regularly, enabling the Torah to be a natural part of our being, as natural as the concept of, "What is hateful to you, do not do to your fellow."

By doing and doing (הֲפֹךְ בָּהּ וַהֲפֹךְ בָּהּ), we become it (וּבָהּ תֶּחֱזֵי)!

Addendum: Also, the epilogue of the Gemara in *Shabbos* (31b), where Hillel famously says to treat others as you wish to be treated, ends by saying *"Zil gemor."* If you learn and learn, then Torah becomes a natural part of you. Finally, since *"Anochi hastir astir panai"* is the *remez* in the Torah for Esther, you can positively spin this *pasuk* as highlighting the beginning of the *teshuvah* process—G-d is reminding us that He is there, albeit hiding. This is because at least G-d admits to being around in the background, and this is a perfect response to הֲלֹא עַל כִּי אֵין אֱלֹקַי בְּקִרְבִּי.

DID MOSHE WALK THE WALK
OR TALK THE TALK?

הִלֵּל אוֹמֵר: וְאַל תָּדִין אֶת חֲבֵרְךָ עַד שֶׁתַּגִּיעַ
לִמְקוֹמוֹ וְאַל תֹּאמַר דָּבָר שֶׁאִי אֶפְשָׁר לִשְׁמעַ
שֶׁסּוֹפוֹ לְהִשָּׁמַע.

Hillel says: Do not judge your fellow until you have stood in
*his place, and **don't say something that's impossible to hear***
***because in the end it can be heard.** (Avos 2:4)*

QUESTIONS

1. The classic interpretation of Hillel's message of אַל תֹּאמַר דָּבָר שֶׁאִי
   אֶפְשָׁר לִשְׁמעַ is to not say something that should not be heard,
   i.e., should not be made public, should not be said, rationalizing
   that it will not get around and will stay a secret, for it will inevitably be revealed and made public. But is there another possible
   idea here? After all, the wording itself is not too concise and,
   frankly, the message is unclear.

2. Also, is there any possible connection to the immediately
   preceding statement of "judging your fellow friend"? Is there a
   lesson in criticism here?

ANSWERS

The answer may be found in the first *pasuk* of our *parashah*:

507

וַיֵּלֶךְ מֹשֶׁה וַיְדַבֵּר אֶת הַדְּבָרִים הָאֵלֶּה אֶל כָּל יִשְׂרָאֵל.

And Moshe went and spoke these words unto all Israel.
(Devarim 31:1)

Ziv Mendelsohn showed me the following awesome idea of Rabbi Rudinsky: The *Midrash Tanchuma* explains the word *vayeilech* as: "אין וילך אלא לשון תוכחה—The word *vayeilech* is language of rebuke." The *Ibn Ezra* says on this *pasuk* that "Moshe went to each and every tribe to tell him he was going to die." Is there was any connection between the idea that Moshe went to every tribe individually and that he rebuked them?

The answer paraphrased is that this was a classic דוגמא אישית—personalized example. Moshe didn't have to verbalize any rebuke to the nation, he was able to merely visit each tribe, and his very presence was itself an example or rebuke/lesson for the tribes. Leading by example is much stronger than merely leading with a forceful tongue!

On the heels of that nice idea, perhaps we can add that the Gemara in *Yevamos* (65b) says that you should not give rebuke to those who will not heed your rebuke. The terminology used in the Gemara is: "מצוה שלא לומר **דבר שאינו נשמע**." A reason why you should not rebuke those who will not heed your advice is that if they ignore you, they are more punish-worthy. (מוטב שיהיו שוגגין ואל יהיו מזידין—see *Tosafos, Shabbos* 65b). But notice the language here is exactly the same as our Mishnah in *Avos:* דָּבָר שֶׁאֵינוֹ נִשְׁמָע is very similar to דְּבָר שֶׁאִי אֶפְשָׁר לִשְׁמֹעַ! A point may be that our Mishnah in *Avos* may be talking about how to rebuke or give criticism to others: אַל תֹּאמַר דָּבָר שֶׁאִי אֶפְשָׁר לִשְׁמֹעַ שֶׁסּוֹפוֹ לְהִשָּׁמַע may mean, "Don't criticize your fellow with words that are too hard for them to hear if they can hear the same lesson in some other way!" Moshe perhaps didn't rebuke each and every tribe with words because they would not accept the words, but his very presence was effective *mussar* in and of itself—שֶׁסּוֹפוֹ לְהִשָּׁמַע. This can also explain the proximity of this statement to the other line referring to giving *mussar* to others: "אַל תָּדִין אֶת חֲבֵרְךָ עַד שֶׁתַּגִּיעַ לִמְקוֹמוֹ," because they both deal with how to counsel others.

────────── TAKEAWAY MESSAGES ──────────

אַל תֹּאמַר דָּבָר שֶׁאִי אֶפְשָׁר לִשְׁמֹעַ may not merely be about publicizing some-thing that should not be publicized, but may rather be a lesson on how we impart messages to those around us, and how we rebuke/counsel others. It may mean, "Do not say a thing that is too difficult to hear" to others as they are less likely to listen to you. It may be better to walk the walk rather than talk the talk. The rebuke will then be more self-ev-ident. Moshe went to each tribe and his mere visit was enough of a תוכחה—rebuke/counsel. "וַיֵּלֶךְ מֹשֶׁה וַיְדַבֵּר אֶת הַדְּבָרִים הָאֵלֶּה"—By *going*, Moshe was speaking many *words* indeed, and his "walk the walk" lessons were certainly סוֹפוֹ לְהִשָּׁמַע!

Moshe taught us that walking the walk is better than talking the talk.

VAYEILECH, "L'DAVID HASHEM ORI," AND SHABBOS SHUVAH

Rabbi Bixon gave a fascinating talk about why we say Psalm 27, לְדָוִד ה' אוֹרִי, between Elul and Shemini Atzeres. He pointed out a midrash highlighting the words in the very *pasuk*: "אוֹרִי—my light" is associated with Rosh Hashanah, and "וְיִשְׁעִי—my salvation" is associated with Yom Kippur. The *Mateh Ephraim* added that "כִּי יִצְפְּנֵנִי בְּסֻכֹּה בְּיוֹם רָעָה—For He conceals me in His pavilion in the day of evil" is associated with Sukkos.

Another connection of לְדָוִד ה' אוֹרִי to this period of *teshuvah* was: G-d's name (the *Yud Kei Vav Kei*) is mentioned thirteen times in this psalm, which conjures up the "Thirteen Attributes of Mercy" that pepper our *Selichos* prayers, and which are derived from when Moshe beseeched forgiveness for B'nei Yisrael from G-d. Rabbi Bixon then went through an entertaining and thorough discussion of the earliest customs surrounding the adoption of לְדָוִד ה' אוֹרִי into our prayer during this season, including *sefer Shem Tov Katan*, published in 1706, where the Kabbalist Rabbi Binyamin Benish Cohen writes essentially that one who recites this psalm will have his prayers almost magically answered! But I was fixated on his great question and wondering if any other connections existed...

As *Nitzavim* always precedes Rosh Hashanah, *Parashas Vayeilech* naturally always falls out during this *Selichos* time of repentance as well. Is there any theme of repentance in *Vayeilech*?

וַיֹּאמֶר אֵלָיו לְעֵינֵי כָל יִשְׂרָאֵל חֲזַק וֶאֱמָץ.

Moshe called [to Yehoshua], and said unto him in the sight of all Israel: "Be strong and of good courage." (Devarim 31:23)

The *Kli Yakar* has a beautiful approach to this in his consideration of why Moshe had to say to Yehoshua, "Be strong" in front of *all the eyes of B'nei Yisrael*. Essentially, the *Kli Yakar* says that the *pasuk* really should be read: "Be strong and courageous to all the eyes of Israel." When Moshe was faulted for hitting the rock, it was really because he wasn't being mindful of the "less religious" among the Jews who would misinterpret his actions and think that the rock was actually bringing forth water. Moshe learned that Hashem wanted the actions of a leader to be done in a way that *all* of Israel would understand and not misinterpret. So Moshe felt the need, while passing on the mantle, to teach Yehoshua the lesson that led to his own downfall. He thus tells Yehoshua, "To all of Yisrael [i.e., not just to some], be strong and courageous." חֲזַק וֶאֱמָץ, according to the *Kli Yakar*, must thus be the epitome of *teshuvah* because it represents changing an approach that was clearly deemed by G-d to be a sinning approach.

And where else do we see the words חֲזַק וֶאֱמָץ? The very last *pasuk* of Psalm 27: "קַוֵּה אֶל ה' חֲזַק וְיַאֲמֵץ לִבֶּךְ וְקַוֵּה אֶל ה'." Again, the words חֲזַק וֶאֱמָץ, which epitomize *teshuvah*, are the very words that end לְדָוִד ה' אוֹרִי. This may be another reason why we say לְדָוִד ה' אוֹרִי during this time! And to strengthen this idea—that the words חֲזַק וֶאֱמָץ epitomize *teshuvah*—it says that four aspects need strengthening: Torah, *maasim tovim*, *tefillah*, and *derech eretz*. Then it brings two *pesukim* that include the words חֲזַק וֶאֱמָץ, which the Gemara says is referring to these four aspects! This is the epitome of what we try to improve upon during our *teshuvah* process!

—————————— TAKEAWAY MESSAGES ——————————

לְדָוִד ה' אוֹרִי is said between Elul and Shemini Atzeres. It may be said because the *pesukim* have words that relate to Rosh Hashanah and Sukkos. It may be said because G-d's name is mentioned thirteen times, reminding us of the Thirteen Attributes of Mercy. *Parashas Vayeilech* has the ultimate message of *teshuvah* in the words חֲזַק וֶאֱמָץ. The *Kli Yakar* shows that Moshe's words to Yehoshua were actually sent to repent for and simultaneously prevent the misstep that Moshe had done years before. The message inherent in the words חֲזַק וֶאֱמָץ, according to the Gemara in *Berachos*, applies to "strengthening" Torah, *maasim tovim*, *tefillah*, and *derech eretz* (all aspects of *teshuvah* par excellence). Another reason why לְדָוִד ה' אוֹרִי may be said every year during the *teshuvah* season is because it ends with the message of חֲזַק וְאֱמָץ: "קַוֵּה אֶל ה' חֲזַק וְיַאֲמֵץ לִבֶּךָ וְקַוֵּה אֶל ה'". The connection of Vayeilech and לְדָוִד ה' אוֹרִי to Shabbos Shuvah? חֲזַק וְאֱמָץ.

Haazinu

"ASPIRATION OF MANKIND IS A WORM"—DEPRESSING OR UPLIFTING?

רַבִּי לְוִיטָס אִישׁ יַבְנֶה אוֹמֵר: מְאֹד מְאֹד הֱוֵי שְׁפַל רוּחַ שֶׁתִּקְוַת אֱנוֹשׁ רִמָּה.

Rabbi Levitas of Yavneh says: You should be exceedingly humble, because the hope/aspiration of mankind is a worm.
(Avos 4:4)

The simple understanding of this Mishnah is that we should all be humble, because in the end, we all unfortunately die and end up being engulfed by worms. The "hope/aspiration" of mankind is a worm in the sense that we all get to "look forward" to that depressing end.

————————— QUESTIONS —————————

Reviewing our *parashah* carefully, though, perhaps we can conjure up a less depressing reading of this famous Mishnah. Let's analyze by asking three separate questions that will be answered as one:

1. Why does this Mishnah in *Avos* say "hope/aspiration," as opposed to "the end will be"? Is there "hope" to be engulfed by worms?

2. The Gemara in *Taanis* (5b) says, "יעקב אבינו לא מת—Yaakov never died." Is the Gemara really telling us that Yaakov Avinu is still alive and well at 3,600-plus years? The Gemara itself answers

513

that the statement of יעקב אבינו לא מת means that he remains alive in or by virtue of his progeny, the Jewish People. But can there be any alternative meaning?

3. "כִּי חֵלֶק ה׳ עַמּוֹ יַעֲקֹב חֶבֶל נַחֲלָתוֹ"—For the portion of Hashem is His People, Yaakov the lot of His inheritance." This *pasuk* in our very *parashah* simply read means: we are a portion of G-d's vast existence, and as descendants of Yaakov Avinu, we are the steadfast rope of His inheritance. This *pasuk* does seem rather unusually wordy/repetitive, and what's with this rope imagery?

--- ANSWERS ---

The Tanna in *Avos* may have used the word "hope/aspiration" because the Mishnah should, in fact, be understood as follows: "You should be exceedingly humble because the *hope* of mankind is akin [to the very existence of a] worm." Just like a worm that has no nose, eyes, ears, or hands to gather sensory information about their environment, somehow survives, we must humbly appreciate even the "smallest" of gifts that we have (certainly more than a worm!) and a fortiori survive (and excel)! Humility will lead to an appreciation of our strengths no matter what the challenge.

The very nascence of our existence is as we came out of the womb, as Yaakov demonstrates this lesson. *Yaakov* means "heel," and Yaakov had to hold on to Eisav's heel for his dear life to "miraculously" exit the womb. Our nation's existence is predicated on narrowly escaping. Homiletically, the Gemara in *Taanis* (5b) can be read: "יעקב אבינו—pause—לא מת." In other words, what does יעקב אבינו really signify? The answer is לא מת, i.e., a never-die attitude. The very name Yaakov means "heel," which reminds us of our perseverance and our "never-die" (לא מת) attitude!

Finally, in our *parashah* (question #3), by the Torah saying "כִּי חֵלֶק ה׳ עַמּוֹ," G-d is assuring us that just as G-d is הָיָה הֹוֶה וְיִהְיֶה, our nation is also assured a past, present, and future. But Hashem further reassures us: "Yaakov, the 'rope,' is your inheritance." The rope represents our eternal ability to "hold on to the rope for survival"; we are guaranteed to survive because we always believe in "the rope" of survival. Only by being

humble and appreciating every single gift/ability that we have do we
ultimately survive the hardships (and atrocities) that have befallen us.

———————————— TAKEAWAY MESSAGES ————————————

The *pasuk* in our *parashah*: "כִּי חֵלֶק ה' עַמּוֹ יַעֲקֹב חֶבֶל נַחֲלָתוֹ," may be a lesson
in hope for us all. We are reminded that the rope is our inheritance in
the sense that we never give up and will hold on to survival no matter
the odds. The Tanna in *Avos* reminds us that this indefatigable attitude
is predicated on our humility and being able to appreciate whatever
small gifts each and every one of us possesses.

Yaakov thus never died because "the rope" is our inheritance, and
with humility, we can survive the odds much like a worm! שֶׁתִּקְוַת אֱנוֹשׁ רִמָּה
is no longer depressing but uplifting!

RESURRECTION—GOOD THING
OR BAD THING?

הוּא הָיָה אוֹמֵר: הַיִּלוֹדִים לָמוּת וְהַמֵּתִים
לְהַחֲיוֹת וְהַחַיִּים לִדּוֹן...וְאַל יַבְטִיחֲךָ יִצְרְךָ
שֶׁהַשְּׁאוֹל בֵּית מָנוֹס לָךְ שֶׁעַל כָּרְחֲךָ אַתָּה נוֹצָר
וְעַל כָּרְחֲךָ אַתָּה נוֹלָד וְעַל כָּרְחֲךָ אַתָּה חַי וְעַל
כָּרְחֲךָ אַתָּה מֵת וְעַל כָּרְחֲךָ אַתָּה עָתִיד לִתֵּן
דִּין וְחֶשְׁבּוֹן לִפְנֵי מֶלֶךְ מַלְכֵי הַמְּלָכִים הַקָּדוֹשׁ
בָּרוּךְ הוּא.

*He would also say: Those who are born will die, and the dead
will live...Let not your heart convince you **that the grave is
your escape**; for **against your will** you are formed, **against
your will** you are born, against your will you live, **against
your will** you die, and **against your will** you are destined to
give a judgment and accounting before the King, King of all
kings, the Holy One Blessed Be He. (Avos 4:22)*

QUESTIONS

In *Avos*, we are told that G-d will revive us from the dead. Wouldn't
you expect such a revelation (הַמֵּתִים לְהַחֲיוֹת) to reverberate in a message of
solace, comfort, and hope? Instead, the wording is quite pejorative, specifically, "אַל יַבְטִיחֲךָ יִצְרְךָ שֶׁהַשְּׁאוֹל בֵּית מָנוֹס לָךְ"—Your grave is not an escape!"

Also, "against your will you are formed and die!" Why does the Tanna in *Avos* paint such a picture?

The answer to our question will actually answer a bigger fundamental question: Where did all these "ethics of the fathers" come from anyway? Are these just natural moral feelings said by great rabbis, or did the rabbis say messages that are based in the Torah?

───── ANSWERS ─────

Our *parashah* states:

אֲנִי אָמִית וַאֲחַיֶּה מָחַצְתִּי וַאֲנִי אֶרְפָּא וְאֵין מִיָּדִי מַצִּיל.

I kill, and I make alive; I have wounded, and I heal; and there is none that can deliver out of My hand. (Devarim 32:39)

What is meant by "וְאֵין מִיָּדִי מַצִּיל"—There is none that can deliver out of My hand"? At first glance, you may think that it is just heaping on more praise of G-d, showing how dominant He is over everyone, including our enemies. But the Gemara beautifully says that this *pasuk* is the source of *techias hameisim*, resurrection of the dead: Just like "מָחַצְתִּי וַאֲנִי אֶרְפָּא—I have wounded and I heal" is talking about one person, so too "אֲנִי אָמִית וַאֲחַיֶּה—I kill and I make alive" is referring to one person. Being able to kill a person and then bringing them back to life again is resurrection indeed! If that is the case, the words "אֵין מִיָּדִי מַצִּיל" make perfect sense as well: Don't think that we can escape G-d by dying because He resurrects us as well. Contrary to our hunky-dory, enthusiastic picture of resurrection, the classic Jewish etiology is admittedly more dark: G-d will resurrect you, and so don't think you can escape Him ever! (Contributing to this dark version of *techias hameisim* is the *limud* of מָחַצְתִּי וַאֲנִי אֶרְפָּא, which means that people are resurrected in their death state and then healed back to form!)

Is it not fascinating, then, that *Avos* above presents *techias hameisim* in a rather dark fashion as well: "אַל יַבְטִיחֲךָ יִצְרְךָ שֶׁהַשְּׁאוֹל בֵּית מָנוֹס לָךְ—Don't think your grave will be an escape route"? Also fascinating is how "הַמֵּתִים לְהֵחָיוֹת," the idea in *Avos* of resurrection perfectly mirrors the "אֵין מִיָּדִי מַצִּיל—none out of My hand," which comes right after the source of resurrection in the Torah! Besides showing beautiful syllogism, this idea also shows that the ethics in *Pirkei Avos* were not just ideas morally fancied by great rabbis, but rather were based on actual *mesorah*. Now the question for you to ask is why resurrection is painted negatively. Although some will posit (with this as a proof) that being in this world is not good in the first place, and hence resurrection is likewise not a *berachah*, perhaps knowing that we are cogs in G-d's wheel actually relieves us of the stresses about trying to figure out the mysteries of yonder...

———————— TAKEAWAY MESSAGES ————————

Surprisingly, the Jewish version of *techias hameisim* is quite pejorative! The negative tone in *Avos* of "אַל יַבְטִיחֲךָ יִצְרְךָ שֶׁהַשְּׁאוֹל בֵּית מָנוֹס לְךָ"—Don't think your grave will be an escape route" may be rooted in "אֵין מִיָּדִי מַצִּיל—No one can escape Me," which is the source of *techias hameisim* in the Torah! This *vort* demonstrates that *Pirkei Avos* were most likely rooted in analysis of Torah *pesukim*, rather than personal moral whims.

Is resurrection a good thing or a bad thing? There is no escaping.

THE ONLY PREDICTABLE THING
ABOUT A STORM

אֵין בְּיָדֵינוּ לֹא מִשַּׁלְוַת הָרְשָׁעִים וְאַף לֹא
מִיִּסוּרֵי הַצַּדִּיקִים.

*It is not in our hands [for us to understand]; neither the
reward given to evildoers or the punishment for the righteous.
(Avos 4:15)*

דֶּבֶר בָּא לָעוֹלָם עַל מִיתוֹת הָאֲמוּרוֹת בַּתּוֹרָה
שֶׁלֹא נִמְסְרוּ לְבֵית דִּין, וְעַל פֵּרוֹת שְׁבִיעִית.
חֶרֶב בָּאָה לָעוֹלָם עַל עִנּוּי הַדִּין, וְעַל עִוּוּת
הַדִּין, וְעַל הַמּוֹרִים בַּתּוֹרָה שֶׁלֹא כַהֲלָכָה: חַיָּה
רָעָה בָּאָה לָעוֹלָם עַל שְׁבוּעַת שָׁוְא, וְעַל חִלּוּל
הַשֵּׁם. גָּלוּת בָּאָה לָעוֹלָם עַל עוֹבְדֵי עֲבוֹדָה
זָרָה, וְעַל גִּלּוּי עֲרָיוֹת, וְעַל שְׁפִיכוּת דָּמִים,
וְעַל הַשְׁמָטַת הָאָרֶץ.

*Plagues come to the world for those capital crimes mentioned
in the Torah that have not been given over to the court, and
for desecrating the produce of the Sabbatical year. The sword
comes to the world for the procrastination of justice, the
corruption of justice, and because of those who misinterpret*

the Torah. Carnage by wild beasts comes to the world for false
oaths and the desecration of G-d's name. Exile comes to the
world for idol worship, sexual promiscuity, murder, and the
failure to leave the land fallow on the Sabbatical year.
(Avos 5:8–9)

QUESTIONS

1. When reading in *Avos* about the naturally wrought "plagues,
wild beasts, and exile," as opposed to the human-executed
"sword," one begins to wonder how heavenly wrought natural
disasters differ from human-executed ones. (One cannot really
make an argument that a natural one is "worse" off when you
consider the tragedy of the Holocaust and the countless other
massacres we endured in our history.)

2. On one hand, we have a tradition above that "it is not in our
hands" to understand G-d's reward/punishment, but in the
same book of ethics, we are told that "banishment comes because of…" implying there is a simple cause-and-effect relationship. Do we have a hand in the development or ending of these
almost-supernatural storms?

ANSWERS

An insight from our *parashah*:

הַאֲזִינוּ הַשָּׁמַיִם וַאֲדַבֵּרָה וְתִשְׁמַע הָאָרֶץ אִמְרֵי פִי.

*Listen heavens and I will speak, land, listen to the words of
my mouth. (Devarim 32:1)*

The *Ohr Hachaim Hakadosh* points out the obvious question: Why
does Moshe call out "וַאֲדַבֵּרָה," which is more of a harsh terminology, and
has to get the heavens to have to lend an ear (הַאֲזִינוּ) in order to listen
(implying that it is harder to get the heavens' attention), while the earth
easily listens up (וְתִשְׁמַע), and the wording regarding the land listening to
him is much smoother (אִמְרֵי פִי is a lighter way of saying "words").

He posits one answer, but in light of Hurricanes Harvey, Irma, and Maria, perhaps we can suggest: When it comes to the heavens, the only thing that is predictable is that it all is unpredictable. Even the most advanced weather experts frankly were wrong when Irma skirted up the West and not the East Coast as it ravaged Florida. Just one week earlier, the storm—which in just a day or two left the majority of the twenty million residents of Florida without power, caused six million to evacuate (into exile!), and cost roughly $100–150 billion in damage—was not even in existence! Terrible man-executed tragedies are generally predictable (which admittedly doesn't make them any more pleasant). Consider Hitler and Nazi Germany: The world saw Hitler at his Beer Hall Putsch in 1923, saw him come to power in 1933, saw him begin to massively rearm, saw him annex Austria in 1938, saw Chamberlain ignore the threat and proudly return the news to England that everything is under control, and so on and so forth. Jews could have easily left Europe (until 1937 at least), and it was only after so many missed opportunities that the Holocaust happened. However, natural disasters are marked by הַאֲזִינוּ הַשָּׁמַיִם וַאֲדַבֵּרָה—even if we somehow get the heavens to hone in on our voices, we would still have to scream out (talk loud), because we are so far removed and ineffectual against the heavens. Nevertheless, Moshe and we (today) must speak up, as the heavens will hear us if we speak strongly enough (וַאֲדַבֵּרָה).

Rashi brings down the midrash that Moshe is, so to speak, calling the heavens and earth as witnesses to the covenant of G-d and Israel. If B'nei Yisrael fail to abide, they are to be held accountable by these mighty witnesses. And so there you have it: the answer to question #2 is that the heavens can be unleashed against us if we are not worthy. In fact, *Rashi* continues and reminds us that the *Shema* we recite twice a day confirms that actually, first G-d brings down the "natural" disasters to wake us up before he unleashes the man-executed ones (וְעָצַר אֶת הַשָּׁמַיִם וְלֹא יִהְיֶה מָטָר וְהָאֲדָמָה לֹא תִתֵּן אֶת יְבוּלָהּ...[ואחר כך] וַאֲבַדְתֶּם מְהֵרָה מֵעַל הָאָרֶץ [על יְדֵי האומות]).

——————— TAKEAWAY MESSAGES ———————

Although we certainly do not know why we were punished with Irma ("it is not in our hands"), it is not sacrilegious to suspect that we have some impact on the storm ("exile comes to the world for idol worship…"). The very first *pasuk* in our *parashah* warns us that the Heavens (nature via G-d) are unleashed against us if we do not abide by the covenant, but it also gives us solace that despite being so detached and seemingly ineffectual, the Heavens do hear our cries if we speak hard enough (וָאֲדַבְּרָה). Unlike man-executed, large-scale disasters/persecution, which are typically somewhat predictable (וְתִשְׁמַע and אִמְרֵי פִי), natural disasters are almost always marked by their relative unpredictability, which leaves us running for cover.

The only thing predictable about storms: unpredictability.

Vezos Haberachah

REMEDY FOR BAD DREAMS/CURSES?

וְאַל־ תִּתְיָאֵשׁ מִן הַפֻּרְעָנוּת.

Do not despair from punishment. (Avos 1:7)

When Moshe gives the final blessings in this *parashah*, Shimon is not even mentioned, while Levi is blessed:

הָאֹמֵר לְאָבִיו וּלְאִמּוֹ לֹא רְאִיתִיו וְאֶת אֶחָיו לֹא הִכִּיר וְאֶת בָּנָו לֹא
יָדָע. כִּי שָׁמְרוּ אִמְרָתֶךָ וּבְרִיתְךָ יִנְצֹרוּ. יוֹרוּ מִשְׁפָּטֶיךָ לְיַעֲקֹב וְתוֹרָתְךָ
לְיִשְׂרָאֵל יָשִׂימוּ קְטוֹרָה בְּאַפֶּךָ וְכָלִיל עַל מִזְבְּחֶךָ. בָּרֵךְ ה' חֵילוֹ וּפֹעַל
יָדָיו תִּרְצֶה מְחַץ מָתְנַיִם קָמָיו וּמְשַׂנְאָיו מִן יְקוּמוּן.

*Who said of his father and his mother, "I do not see him";
neither did he recognize his brothers, nor did he know his
children, for they observed Your word and kept Your covenant.
They shall teach Your ordinances to Yaakov, and Your Torah to
Israel; they shall place incense before You, and burnt offerings
upon Your Altar. May Hashem bless his army and favorably
accept the work of his hands; strike the loins of those who rise
up against him and his enemies, so that they will not recover.*
(Devarim 33: 9–11)

Back in *Bereishis*, though, Yaakov cursed both Shimon and Levi, being upset about how they went about the slaughter of the inhabitants

523

of Shechem (some say it was the fact that they took the spoils of the victory): "אָרוּר אַפָּם כִּי עָז וְעֶבְרָתָם כִּי קָשָׁתָה...‎"—Cursed be their anger, so fierce, and their fury, so cruel! I will scatter them in Yaakov and disperse them in Israel" (*Bereishis* 49:7).

— QUESTIONS —

1. Why is Shimon left out here, and Levi not only reinstated but given a large blessing by Moshe?
2. Why is it that the tribe of Levi, which Yaakov cursed, is the tribe we eagerly receive blessings from?
3. Why do some have the custom of trying to hear *Birkas Kohanim* to reverse a bad dream?
4. And what does all this have to do with the introductory ethic above of not despairing from retribution?

— ANSWERS —

In the *midbar*, the Shimonites dwindled from 59,300 to 22,200 men (compare *Bamidbar* 1:23 and 26:14) and eventually their inheritance was absorbed into the land of Yehudah (*Yehoshua* 19:9). Given their small numbers, Moshe may have left them out (this is consistent with the *Ramban*'s approach). But why is Levi's curse reversed if, after all, their lot is also absorbed into the other tribes as well?

The answer is as Moshe himself stated: "Who said of his father and his mother, 'I do not see him.'" This is referring to B'nei Yisrael's actions after the Golden Calf, where specifically the Leviim killed the perpetrators of the sin, even their own relatives. They used their innate "impetuosity trait" for the sake of heaven and prevented a national calamity. A lesson is that Divine reward and punishment, even when specified in prophecy, are nevertheless conditional upon human conduct. Instead of the Leviim giving up hope after receiving a curse from Yaakov, they rose up and actually were able to change that curse into a blessing! *They did not lose hope despite their curse*, fulfilling the ethic of "Don't despair because of punishment"!

In Rabbi Jonathan Sacks's beautiful essay about turning curses into blessings, he says:

It is well-known that the Chinese ideogram for "crisis" also means "opportunity"...Hebrew goes one better. The word for crisis, mashber, also means "a child-birth chair." Written into the semantics of Jewish consciousness is the idea that the pain of hard times is a collective form of the contractions of a woman giving birth. Something new is being born. That is the mindset of a people of whom it can be said that "the more they were oppressed, the more they increased and the more they spread."

Now this perhaps may partly explain why the priestly blessing is used to ward off bad dreams. After all, the Gemara in *Berachos* (55b) prescribes the following conclusory statements of the *yehi ratzon* that we say: "Just as You changed the curse of Bilaam to a blessing, so, too, change all my dreams for the good." Just like we receive blessings from the tribe who showed us firsthand that curses can be changed into blessings, we should not be nervous when our dreams show an apparent curse, which can also be transformed into a blessing!

───────────── TAKEAWAY MESSAGES ─────────────

The Leviim are the ultimate examples of "Don't give up because of punishment." They were able to reverse the curse and channel it to a blessing. The ultimate curse-to-blessing examples are thus instilled with blessing power to remind us that all blessings/curses depend, to some degree, on how we act. We can all change curses into blessing.

The remedy for bad dreams/curses? Ask a Levi to bless you, as they showed that curses can turn into blessings!

Moadim

Rosh Hashanah

ROSH HASHANAH AND DUST

עֲקַבְיָא בֶּן מַהֲלַלְאֵל אוֹמֵר, הִסְתַּכֵּל בִּשְׁלֹשָׁה
דְּבָרִים וְאִי אַתָּה בָא לִידֵי עֲבֵרָה...מֵאַיִן בָּאתָ,
מִטִּפָּה סְרוּחָה, וּלְאָן אַתָּה הוֹלֵךְ, לִמְקוֹם עָפָר
רִמָּה וְתוֹלֵעָה. וְלִפְנֵי מִי אַתָּה עָתִיד לִתֵּן דִּין
וְחֶשְׁבּוֹן, לִפְנֵי מֶלֶךְ מַלְכֵי הַמְּלָכִים הַקָּדוֹשׁ
בָּרוּךְ הוּא.

Akavia the son of Mahalalel would say: Reflect upon
three things and you will not come to the hands of
transgression…From where you come—from a putrid drop;
where you are going—to a place of dust, maggots, and worms;
and before whom you are destined to give a judgment and
accounting—before the supreme King of kings, the Holy One
Blessed Be He. (Avos 3:1)

--- QUESTIONS ---

1. If you start out as a putrid drop and end up in a place of *dust*,
   then is it such a bad progression after all?
2. How does seeing these three things motivate one not to sin?

3. Why does it say, "וּלְאָן אַתָּה הוֹלֵךְ—where you are going," as opposed to "תהיה—end up"?

———————— ANSWERS ————————

The answer may lurk in our Rosh Hashanah *tefillah*:

אדם יסודו מעפר וסופו לעפר.

Man is created from dust and ends up in dust. (Based on Koheles 3:20)

Rabbi Matis Blum asked a similar question in the name of the *Chiddushei HaRim*: If man starts out as dust and ends up as dust, then how does this motivate us to do *teshuvah*? After all, if we start out as dust, then it isn't so bad that we end up as dust! He answers that really man is created from dust, but through living a productive life, he is supposed to metamorphosize into something greater. The fact that we often remain as mere dust and nothing greater is a depressing reality that is supposed to motivate us to try and improve ourselves!

There may be another (perhaps more optimistic) approach: *yesod* can mean "created," but can also mean "foundation." The *pasuk* can be read: "**אדם יסודו מעפר**"—if man has a foundation that is but dust, then "**סופו לעפר**"—his end will likewise inevitably be of dust! We can only be as good as the potential/opportunities we give ourselves. For instance, I cannot just wake up one morning and be a great tennis player. First, I have to work on my forehand, then the backhand, then the serve, then the return of serve, and then learn how to throw down my racquet during a perfectly timed temper tantrum to baffle my opponent...If you just rely on the basic skills or the dust as your foundation, you can't expect to be anything but dust in the end.

When the Mishnah in *Avos* says to look at these three things and you won't sin, it may likewise be saying (homiletic reading): "מֵאַיִן בָּאתָ, מִטִּפָּה סְרוּחָה"—yes, you started out as a putrid drop. But your challenge is a *present* one: "וּלְאָן אַתָּה הוֹלֵךְ?"—though you started as a putrid drop, you still are *presently* (i.e., you can actively change that foundation) a place of dust—לְמָקוֹם עָפָר רִמָּה וְתוֹלֵעָה. Thus, your challenge is *here and now* to realize that we are going to judgment day soon and thus need to pick up our game so that we don't merely remain a putrid fleck of dust! We are what we do, and we can only accomplish things if we set up the opportunities/potential for ourselves to grow.

TAKEAWAY MESSAGES

Man is born from dust and sometimes doesn't improve him or herself through life and merely remains dust (*Chiddushei HaRim*). We must realize that we can only accomplish things in this world if we set up the priorities/opportunities and put ourselves in position to grow from our inauspicious beginnings. If we retain the foundation of dust, how can we expect to not end up as dust? If our *yesod* is dust and is not actively improved upon then we cannot expect great things! The good news is that we are still "going" and have the opportunity to create opportunities.

Time to dust off then...we start out as dust, but don't need to end up as dust.

PRAYING FOR WEALTH ON ROSH HASHANAH? THE MESSAGE FROM U'NESANEH TOKEF

ר־בִּי מֵאִיר אוֹמֵר־: הֱוֵי מְמַעֵט בְּעֵסֶק, וַעֲסֹק בַּתּוֹרָה. וֶהֱוֵי שְׁפַל רוּחַ בִּפְנֵי כָל אָדָם...

Rabbi Meir says: Engage minimally in business, and occupy yourself with Torah. Be humble before every man..."
(Avos 4:10)

QUESTIONS

What is the connection between limiting your work and being humble before man? The answer is found in perhaps the most memorable part of Rosh Hashanah prayer, the *U'Nesaneh Tokef*:

מי ינוח ומי ינוע מי ישקט ומי יטרף מי ישלו ומי יתיסר מי יעני ומי יעשר מי ישפל ומי ירום.

Who will rest and who will run/flee, who will have quiet and who will be harried, who will be be given reward and who will be persecuted; who will be poor and who will be rich; who will be lowered and who will rise!

The prayer *U'Nesaneh Tokef* is recorded in the thirteenth-century commentary *Ohr Zarua* by Rabbi Isaac Ben Moshe, who attributes the writing to Rabbi Ephraim of Bonn. Ben Moshe claimed that *U'Nesaneh*

Tokef was composed by an eleventh-century sage named Rabbi Amnon of Mainz who, apart from this one story, is utterly unknown to history.

There seems to be parallel structure near the end with something good/desirable followed by the bad. The good מי ינוח, meaning "who will rest," is followed by the bad מי ינוע, meaning "who will flee." Then מי ישקט, meaning "who will have silence," is followed by מי יטרף, meaning "who will be harried." Then מי ישלו, meaning "who will have success," is followed by מי יתיסר, meaning "who will suffer." But then the flip occurs: מי יעני, meaning "who will be poor," is followed by מי יעשר, meaning "who will be rich"; מי ישפל, meaning "who will be lowly," is followed by מי ירום, meaning "who will be raised." And since seemingly being poor or lowly are not desirable traits, why are they in the "desirable" slots of this otherwise flowing parallel structure?

ANSWERS

The answer will also answer our question on *Avos*: Our society often values being wealthy with success, but sometimes wealth is abused or mismanaged. Likewise, being "elevated" may not always be good. Although exciting at first, imagine living life constantly heckled by the paparazzi. Having wealth and being elevated can leave one little room/time/space to do the things he or she wants to do. The author of this *piyut* is likely echoing the sentiment laid forth by the Tanna in *Avos*: Minimize your work so that you can be lowly/humble. If you work so hard, you will either have no time for anything else or become so successful that your time will be sucked up by other endeavors. By limiting your work to some degree and setting your priorities straight at the get-go, the Tanna is saying that you can strive to be lowly (not elevated) so that you can grow spiritually. Being poor/lowly may not always be so bad, just like being wealthy/elevated may not always be so good.

TAKEAWAY MESSAGES

The prayer *U'Nesaneh Tokef* has an apparent glitch in the flowing parallel structure as מי יעני and מי ישפל seem to be flipped, making it seem that being poor or lowly is desirable. The reality is that it may not be a glitch at all. As it says in *Avos*, we should limit our tendencies to strive for immense wealth/fame so that we can be less absorbed with ourselves. Rosh Hashanah is an opportunity for us all to examine our priorities!

Praying for wealth on Rosh Hashanah? Wealth is a state of mind.

Yom Kippur

YOUR BEST ADVOCATE

רַ־בִּי שִׁמְעוֹן אוֹמֵר, הֱוֵי זָהִיר בִּקְרִיאַת שְׁמַע
וּבַתְּפִלָּה. וּכְשֶׁאַתָּה מִתְפַּלֵּל, אַל תַּעַשׂ
תְּפִלָּתְךָ קֶבַע, אֶלָּא רַחֲמִים וְתַחֲנוּנִים לִפְנֵי
הַמָּקוֹם בָּרוּךְ הוּא, שֶׁנֶּאֱמַר (יואל ב) כִּי חַנּוּן
וְרַחוּם הוּא אֶרֶךְ אַפַּיִם וְרַב חֶסֶד וְנִחָם עַל
הָרָעָה. וְאַל תְּהִי רָשָׁע בִּפְנֵי עַצְמֶךָ.

*Rabbi Shimon says: Be **careful** with the k'rias Shema and
tefillah…When you pray, do not make your prayers routine
but [an entreaty of] mercy and a supplication before the
Almighty…And don't be **a wicked person** in front of yourself.*
(Avos 2:13)

QUESTIONS
---

1. Why specifically the word זָהִיר, beware?
2. What is meant by "don't be a wicked person in front of yourself"?

535

—— ANSWERS ——

The standard answer is that you should be זָהִיר, careful, how you pray as it can affect your life; and by not viewing yourself negatively as a רָשָׁע, you can more effectively advocate on your own behalf.

Another approach may be taken that is related to our Yom Kippur *vidui* confession:

שאין אנו עזי פנים וקשי ערף לומר לפניך ה' אלקנו ואלקי אבותנו צדקים אנחנו ולא חטאנו, אבל אנחנו ואבותנו חטאנו.

*We aren't emboldened to say to G-d that we are **righteous tzaddikim** and haven't sinned but rather we and our fathers sinned!*

The standard understanding is that we are simply saying that we acknowledge that we aren't *tzaddikim* but rather sinners. Notice, however, that the second part of that line doesn't say that we are not *tzaddikim*. In other words, it should say: "We and are fathers are not *tzaddikim* and sinned!"

From the fact that the *nusach* does *not* say this, it seems that we have to offer a different approach in what we *are* saying. We are saying to G-d, "We aren't brazen enough to say we are *tzaddikim* and haven't sinned, but rather we believe that we **are** *tzaddikim* despite our collective [selves and fathers] sinning." This reading better aligns with our practice of trying to be extra-special Jews during the time leading to Yom Kippur (i.e., some only drink *chalav Yisrael*, some only speak *lashon hara* about really distant cousins [kidding!]). It's not that we are tricking G-d into thinking we are something that we are not, but rather highlighting the fact that we can be better and know how to be better. If we cannot advocate for ourselves, no one will. The Tanna in *Avos* used *zahir* specifically, which means "be careful," but also has the *shoresh* of *zohar*, which means "light." When beseeching G-d for mercy, although we need to admit and confess our wrongdoings, we also have to be *zohar*—shed a positive image of ourselves for Him so that He is more readily merciful to us.

Finally, by saying "אנחנו ואבותנו חטאנו—We and our fathers sinned," we aren't just blaming our fathers for our sinning, which seems even more brazen than not saying we sinned in the first place! Rather, we are re-minding G-d about the collectivity of our congregation in our sinning, which makes us each individually less culpable. Notice we don't say, "עַל חֵטְא שֶׁחָטָאתִי," but rather "עַל חֵטְא שֶׁחָטָאנוּ." And so the Tanna in *Avos* reminds us: "וְאַל תְּהִי רָשָׁע בִּפְנֵי עַצְמְךָ"—Don't highlight your wrongdoings in a singular fashion to G-d so that you can benefit from G-d's even greater collective compassion." You can only be "רָשָׁע," so to speak, if/when you invoke others along with you to mitigate the punishment. But, in gen-eral, be *zahir* in the sense of "show yourself in a positive vein."

─────── TAKEAWAY MESSAGES ───────

As we pray before G-d on Yom Kippur, we remember the exhortation to *zahir*, concentrate on *Shema* and *tefillah* while simultaneously trying to show ourselves (זָהִיר/זוֹהַר) in a positive light. We remind G-d that although we sinned, we still can be *tzaddikim*, and so have mercy on us! We should never despair and consider ourselves individually *reshaim* (אַל תְּהִי רָשָׁע בִּפְנֵי עַצְמְךָ), and when we do *vidui*, our individual sins are thus shrouded in a communal undertone (עַל חֵטְא שֶׁחָטָאנוּ and אֲנַחְנוּ וַאֲבוֹתֵינוּ חָטָאנוּ)! אִם אֵין אֲנִי לִי מִי לִי—with plenty of people of around to highlight your faults, Yom Kippur reminds us that **you are your best is…yourself!**

GEMATRIA OF *HASATAN* = 364?
YOM KIPPUR IS THE HINT

וְדַע לִֿפְנֵי מִי אַתָּ֫ה עָמֵל.

Know in front of whom you are toiling. (Avos 2:14)

The quintessential day that we must know that we are standing before G-d is on Yom Kippur…

כִּי בַיּוֹם הַזֶּה יְכַפֵּר עֲלֵיכֶם לְטַהֵר אֶתְכֶם מִכֹּל חַטֹּאתֵיכֶם
לִפְנֵי ה' תִּטְהָרוּ.

*For on this day [Yom Kippur] He shall effect atonement for
you to cleanse you. **From all of your sins, before Hashem,
you shall be cleansed.** (Vayikra 16:30)*

—————————— QUESTIONS ——————————

1. The word מִכֹּל seems redundant. It could have simply read "לְטַהֵר
   אֶתְכֶם מֵחַטֹּאתֵיכֶם"? Why מִכֹּל?
2. Also, the *esnachta*, which is the cantillation equivalent of a stop
   sign, is on אֶתְכֶם, which is saying that "מִכֹּל חַטֹּאתֵיכֶם לִפְנֵי ה' תִּטְהָרוּ"
   is a separate idea. What then is meant by "From all your sins,
   before G-d, you will be pure!" I would expect the *pasuk* to read,
   "Before G-d, you will be pure from all your sins!" The bottom
   line is that the מִכֹּל חַטֹּאתֵיכֶם is conspicuously either redundant
   or misplaced!

―――― ANSWERS ――――

1. One idea is that Hashem wants to remind us that "מִכּל
חַטֹּאתֵיכֶם—From all your sins" (but not all your sins!) is a *miyut*,
exclusion, as in the case of Rabbi Elazar ben Azaryah, who holds
that only those sins *between man and G-d* are absolved by Yom
Kippur (man-to-man sins need personal entreaties).

2. A second possibility is that "from" implies a station and destination (i.e., travel *from* Miami *going* to New York). Reish Lakish
famously says that sins miraculously go from sins to merits if
one does genuine repentance. This could also explain the usage
of "*from* all your sins"; this idea of מִכּל hints to this miraculous
transformation.

3. My favorite and third explanation is from my father, Dr. Larry
Ciment: G-d is reminding us that on Yom Kippur, we need to
unabashedly confess our sins. The very "admitting that we
sin" will make us pure. From our sins, we become pure! Only
by admitting that we have issues/problems can we really ever
begin to get better and ultimately become pure. By starting
out the day as מִכּל חַטֹּאתֵיכֶם, saying we are from sin (and doing
wholehearted *vidui*), we can then sequentially become לִפְנֵי ה'!

The *Meiri* likewise states that Yom Kippur isn't some miraculous
day that just wipes away our sins as much as it is the blueprint to
inspire the rest of the year, because on this day we are honest with
our shortcomings unabashedly! The *Michtav M'Eliyahu* notes that the
gematria of השטן is 364, implying that on one day of the year, namely
Yom Kippur, the Satan takes the day off and we're thus *sans* "טמטום
הלב—a deceiving of ourselves" (see *Yoma* 85b, Schottenstein *Talmud
Bavli*). We are able to honestly assess our foibles, confess our sins, and
thus know how to be better. The true challenge in life is not really in
doing *teshuvah*, but rather admitting that we need to do *teshuvah*. עַד
מִכּל חַטֹּאתֵיכֶם לִפְנֵי מִי אַתָּה עָמֵל begins by recognizing our shortcomings.
precedes לִפְנֵי ה' because in order to really stand before G-d, we have to
be honest with ourselves.

———————— TAKEAWAY MESSAGES ————————

"From all of your sins, before the Lord, you shall be cleansed" may mean that only some sins get wiped away by Yom Kippur, namely those between man and G-d (like Rabbi Elazar ben Azaryah), or it may hint that sins go from being sins to merits on this miraculous day (like Reish Lakish). It may even be consistent with the ideas of the *Meiri* and *Michtav M'Eliyahu*, namely that only by admitting our foibles can we expect to ever get close to G-d. דַּע לִפְנֵי מִי אַתָּה עָמֵל becomes most evident on Yom Kippur when we are *sans* our טמטום הלב. מִכֹּל חַטֹּאתֵיכֶם precedes לִפְנֵי ה' because in order to really stand before G-d, we have to be honest with ourselves, at least on Yom Kippur! Why is the *gematria* of *haSatan* 364? He takes off on Yom Kippur to allow us to do *vidui*/soul searching.

Sukkos

THE THIRTEEN ATTRIBUTES OF MERCY AND SUKKOS—WHY NOW?

On Shabbos Chol Hamoed of Sukkos, the Torah reading includes the Thirteen Attributes of Mercy:

ה' ה' אֵ-ל רַחוּם וְחַנּוּן אֶרֶךְ אַפַּיִם וְרַב חֶסֶד וֶאֱמֶת. נֹצֵר חֶסֶד לָאֲלָפִים נֹשֵׂא עָוֹן וָפֶשַׁע וְחַטָּאָה וְנַקֵּה לֹא יְנַקֶּה פֹּקֵד עֲוֹן אָבוֹת עַל בָּנִים וְעַל בְּנֵי בָנִים עַל שִׁלֵּשִׁים וְעַל רִבֵּעִים.

Hashem, Hashem, G-d, merciful and gracious, long-suffering,
and abundant in goodness and truth keeping mercy unto the
thousandth generation, forgiving iniquity and transgression
and sin; and that will by no means clear the guilty.
(Shemos 34:6–7)

According to most, the Thirteen Attributes begin with the first "Hashem" in verse 6, and end with the word "*v'nakeh*" in verse 7. The single attributes are contained in the verses as follows:

1. *Hashem*—compassion before a person sins
2. *Hashem*—compassion after a person has sinned
3. *El*—mighty in compassion to give all creatures according to their need
4. *Rachum*—merciful, that humankind may not be distressed
5. *V'chanun*—and gracious if humankind is already in distress
6. *Erech apayim*—slow to anger
7. *V'rav chessed*—and plenteous in kindness

8. *V'emes*—and truth
9. *Notzer chessed l'alafim*—keeping kindness unto thousands
10. *Noseh avon*—forgiving iniquity
11. *V'feshah*—and transgression
12. *V'chata'ah*—and sin
13. *V'nakeh v'lo yenakeh*—and pardoning (and He doesn't pardon)

QUESTIONS

1. Everything sounds OK until you get to the last attribute! We usually read "*v'nakeh*—and He pardons," but the *Rambam* includes "*v'lo yenakeh*—but He doesn't pardon," as part of this thirteenth *middah* as well (*Rambam, Pe'er HaDor*, p. 19b)! Isn't it odd that the *Rambam* includes *v'lo yenakeh*? This is how it sounds: G-d is so nice to us that He is compassionate and merciful, gracious, pardons, and doesn't pardon! What's merciful and kind about not pardoning us? And even if you hold like most do that the thirteenth attribute is just read as *v'nakeh*, isn't it odd that the very next words in the Torah are *v'lo yenakeh*?
2. Isn't it odd that right before we read the *vidui* during *Selichos* and Yom Kippur, we said the following words: "*Aval anachnu v'avoseinu chatanu*—But we and our fathers have sinned." Why bring our fathers into our mess?
3. Why are we reading this on Sukkos?

ANSWERS

To understand *v'nakeh v'lo yenakeh*, we need to see the next words in that *pasuk* of "*Poked avon avos al banim*—He remembers the sins of the fathers on the sons." At first glance, it seems very gloomy: The sons will be punished for their fathers' sins! But, my father, Dr. Larry Ciment, says that it could very well mean that the sons are absolved of many sins in light of the fact that they were indeed caused in some part by their fathers!

Poked avon avos al banim can thus potentially mean not that the sins of the fathers are placed on the sons, but rather that G-d remembers that the sins of the sons are really the result of the fathers (i.e., the fathers take some of the blame). Likewise, when we say, "*Aval anachnu v'avoseinu chatanu*," we are reminding G-d that we are not totally at fault because we just didn't know any better and perhaps can be considered *shogegim* or absent-minded (and thus less culpable).

And so back to our main question: *V'lo yenakeh* may in fact refer to those responsible for our sins (the fathers!); shirking some of the blame onto our fathers can make G-d go easier on us by making us less guilty. Of course, this puts extra pressure on all us parents to make sure we lead our children on the right path!

And so why do we read this on Sukkos? The answer may be related to a beautiful *Nesivos Shalom*, which essentially says that Sukkos is a culmination of our *teshuvah* process: First we do *teshuvah* from fear (on Yom Kippur), and now we are doing *teshuvah* from love (through the *simchah* of Sukkos). When G-d says, "*B'sukkos hoshavti es B'nei Yisrael*" (*Vayikra* 23:43) the word *hoshavti* may refer to G-d allowing us to do *teshuvah* in our sukkos!

——————— TAKEAWAY MESSAGES ———————

V'lo yenakeh actually may be from G-d's graciousness to us in the sense that he displaces our burden on those who put us in the position of sinning in the first place. Although this may seem harsh to our parents, it is actually just a reminder to parents to be extra vigilant in how to guide their children. "*Aval anachnu v'avoseinu chatanu*"! Sukkos is the ultimate time of *teshuvah* from love—*B'Sukkos hoshavti es B'nei Yisrael*!

Since Sukkos is the time of "*teshuvah* from love," how appropriate is it to review G-d's attributes of mercy!

WHAT'S SO BEAUTIFUL ABOUT
A DIMPLY ESROG ANYWAY?

דַּע מֵאַיִן בָּאתָ וּלְאָן אַתָּה הוֹלֵךְ.

*Know from where you come and to where you are **going**.*
(Avos 3:1)

QUESTIONS

1. What does the esrog have to do with this classic ethic?
2.

> וּלְקַחְתֶּם לָכֶם בַּיּוֹם הָרִאשׁוֹן פְּרִי עֵץ הָדָר ...
>
> *You shall take for yourselves on the first day the fruit*
> *of an esrog tree [lit., a beautiful tree]...*
> *(Vayikra 23:40)*

What is so beautiful about the esrog tree after all?

ANSWERS

Rabbi Moshe Bogomilsky beautifully points out that a uniqueness of the esrog is that on the bottom it has an *uketz*, the stem by which it is connected to the tree, and on the top a *pitom*, stem, topped with a *shoshanta*, rosette blossom. Should one of these fall off, the esrog is no longer considered to be beautiful (*Shulchan Aruch Harav* 648:17, 649:18). He eloquently continues: "The lesson of the esrog tree is that a beautiful person is one who is connected with the past, and who also has accomplishments of his own. A descendant of a fine family, who

544

continues the family tradition, and who does not rest contented with the family's past glories but goes forth to blossom on his own, is indeed a *hadar*, a very beautiful person."

This is very consistent with the message in *Avos*: "דַּע מֵאַיִן בָּאתָ וּלְאָן אַתָּה הוֹלֵךְ—Know from where you came from and to where you are going." The lesson of the esrog's *uketz* and *pitom* is to not only connect to the past but to focus on improving the present!

Consistent with this theme of connecting parent to child, which is really a hallmark of the *simchah* of Sukkos, Rabbi Bogomilsky quotes the Gemara in *Sukkah* (35a): The esrog tree is one where "*ta'am eitzo u'pirio shaveh*—the wood of the tree and the fruit have the same flavor." In Rabbi Moshe's own words again: "Similarly, true splendor for a Jew is achieved when the taste of the tree (parent) and the fruit (child) is the same. It is the greatest source of pride and feeling of achievement for parents when the children do not merely represent a physical resemblance, but are inspired to carry on in the image of the parents spiritually as well."

Perhaps I can add to this theme of developing connectivity: The Gemara (ibid.) says that an esrog is "*dar b'ilano mi'shanah l'shanah*—It dwells on its tree from one year to the next year" (i.e., it can be left on the tree for more than one season and remain fresh). The simple understanding of this statement is that *hadar* doesn't mean beautiful at all, but rather that it "returns," as in it "stays on the tree and returns despite a change in season." **But it may very well be that this concept of *endurance* is precisely the *beautiful* nature of the fruit.** Consistency and endurance, especially when you see legacies passed down from one generation to the next, is the most beautiful thing to behold!

—————— TAKEAWAY MESSAGES ——————

What makes the esrog beautiful? Rabbi Moshe Bogomilsky points out that there is a lesson of connectivity that is most beautiful:

1. An esrog is only *hadar* if it has an *uketz* and a *pitom*; you must know where you came from and where you are going (דַּע מֵאַיִן בָּאתָ וּלְאָן אַתָּה הוֹלֵךְ).

2. The esrog tree is one whose "*ta'am eitzo u'pirio shaveh*—The wood of the tree and the fruit have the same flavor." Children carrying out their parents' legacy is indeed beauty.

3. **My addendum**: "*Dar b'ilano mi'shanah l'shanah*—It dwells on its tree from one year to the next year." Beauty is defined by endurance and consistency; being able to transmit your *mesorah* despite the odds is beauty. *Hadar* means returning, signifying an endurance that is beautiful indeed!

The esrog's beauty is about connectivity and endurance.

SUKKOS, A HERNIATED DISK, AND A GRASSHOPPER

1. Rabbi Tzadok HaKohen says that the first time a word in the Torah is used sets the precedent for what the word will mean or represent thereafter. What then does סֻכֹּת mean or represent, since the first time it is said is by Yaakov when he made *suk-kos*—shelters for animals?
2. Why is the shaking of the lulav on Sukkos (so-called *na'anuim shel simchah*) the cornerstone act demonstrating our happiness during the *chag*?

ANSWERS

After I herniated a disk recently in my lumbar spine, I couldn't walk on my right leg. Finally cleared to swim on Sukkos, I did quasi-yoga exercises in the pool, and with my eyes closed in the water, I felt something hit my leg. Lo and behold it was a grasshopper that I thought was possibly dead from the chlorinated water. As I created waves to usher the motionless grasshopper to the side of the pool, I realized that the hopper was missing his right leg. As he neared the edge of the pool, he incredibly grabbed the side, and with one leg climbed up the most insane incline, finally escaping the pool after thirty minutes! The fact that he was missing his right leg and I was in the pool rehabilitating my right leg only reinforced the key lesson that I took away from this *bashert* encounter on Sukkos: that mobility is *simchah*; freedom to roam about is happiness.

Our *Shemoneh Esreh* starts out: "מלך עוזר ומושע ומגן." Elie Ciment says that מלך represents Rosh Hashanah (G-d is King); עוזר represents the Ten Days of Repentance (הבא ליטהר מסיען); ומושע represents Yom Kippur (we get salvation then); and ומגן represents Sukkos, which is a step beyond salvation where G-d protects us on our journey of life after being saved! When Sam Weintraub was liberated from Auschwitz, he was relieved (his Yom Kippur moment), but he undoubtedly only started to have true *simchah* when he was liberated from his DP camp, protected (ומגן, his Sukkos moment) from danger in being allowed to roam freely to America. The *Ohr Hachaim Hakadosh* says that Yaakov made *sukkos*, shelters for animals and was the first person in history to do so. Perhaps consistent with the ומגן theme of Sukkos, Yaakov wasn't content enough that his animals survived alone but wanted to protect them so they could roam freely and comfortably. His compassion (with his *sukkos*) undoubtedly set the stage à la *maaseh avos siman l'banim* for G-d's compassion toward us, granting us *sukkos* that represent compassionate freedom to roam in after being saved on Yom Kippur!

Finally, consistent with this theme, the lulav represents the *shidrah*, spine. True *simchah* is not when we merely stand tall after salvation, but rather when we are given the freedom to move around unabashedly. Shaking the spine in all directions represents moving on from our Yom Kippur moment of salvation. Again, true happiness is mobility!

─────────── TAKEAWAY MESSAGES ───────────

The first mention of *sukkos* in the Torah is by Yaakov, who compassionately made shelters for his animals. Their sustenance was already provided for, but he gave them extra care in making these *sukkos*, highlighting that mere survival is not enough. מלך עוזר ומושע ומגן may symbolize Rosh Hashanah through Sukkos, and the Yom Kippur moment of salvation must be followed up with the ומגן moment of Sukkos where G-d enables us to "move" on safely after being saved. The shaking of the lulav is true *simchah* as it reminds us of the spine moving gracefully, which is needed for movement. Mobility is true *simchah*; just ask the guy with a herniated disk in his lumbar spine.

The grasshopper reminds us that mobility trumps mere survival; the *simchah* of Sukkos is in the "moving on" (the *na'anuim shel simchah*) from standing tall after our salvation of Yom Kippur.

Pesach

IF YOU EAT THE TOIL OF YOUR HANDS, FORTUNATE YOU ARE?

אֵיזֶהוּ עָשִׁיר, הַשָּׂמֵחַ בְּחֶלְקוֹ, שֶׁנֶּאֱמַר
(תהלים קכח) יְגִיעַ כַּפֶּיךָ כִּי תֹאכֵל אַשְׁרֶיךָ וְטוֹב לָךְ.
אַשְׁרֶיךָ, בָּעוֹלָם הַזֶּה. וְטוֹב לָךְ, לָעוֹלָם הַבָּא.

Who is rich? One who is satisfied with his lot. As is stated: "If you eat of toil of your hands, fortunate are you, and good is to you" (Tehillim 128); "fortunate are you" in this world, "and good is to you" in the World to Come. (Avos 4:1)

--- QUESTIONS ---

How is it that complacency ("satisfied/happy with his lot") is really seen from that *pasuk* in *Tehillim*? All it seemingly says is that if you eat of the toil of your hands, it is good for you; I would have expected the word "happy" in the *pasuk* at the very least? The answer is found upon analyzing the key elements of Pesach:

--- ANSWERS ---

"עַל מַצּוֹת וּמְרֹרִים יֹאכְלֻהוּ"—On matzos and maror we shall eat it" (*Bamidbar* 9:11). Although every Jewish holiday seems to be predicated on the notion of "They tried to kill us; we survived; let's eat," *Chag Hamatzos* is really an *eating-based* holiday from its very inception. Why is this?

Out of all human activities, eating most evidently is taking something from outside and internalizing it. The act of eating itself represents the figurative processing of information received. We have a plethora of laws/customs to do actions that symbolize or represent ideas and/or historic events, and so this concept is not far-fetched. Examples include sitting surrounded in a sukkah or holding a lulav next to *hadasim*. Similarly, we eat matzah and maror on Pesach to highlight that we must internalize the concepts bequeathed therein!

Being able to internalize and thus gain insight is not the way of a slave. A slave works for work's sake and doesn't quite understand or get to understand the fruits of his labor. Matzah is *lechem oni*, poor man's bread, because it represents the hard work done for no clear goal during our servitude in Egypt. Our miraculous transformation recognizing salvation through G-d enabled us to be עשירים in that we could now understood that our subsequent work has meaning and purpose.

The very word שמח hints to this enlightenment via internalization. The ש is open on the top at first, but then the מ eats up and encloses that taken above the ש, before the ח expels the refuse below it.

And so now let's study again: "אֵיזֶהוּ עָשִׁיר הַשָּׂמֵחַ בְּחֶלְקוֹ"—Who is happy? The person who *comprehends/internalizes* his hard work and appreciates the purpose whatever it may be. "יְגִיעַ כַּפֶּיךָ כִּי תֹאכֵל" perhaps should not be read, "If you eat of toil of your hands," but rather "יְגִיעַ כַּפֶּיךָ," the work of your hands should be, "כִּי תֹאכֵל" like the act of *eating*!

Your toil should be *digested* or internalized (like the act of eating!) every step of the way, with clear goals in sight; this is true עשירות. (This goes well with the concept of אין שמחה אלא בבשר ויין). Happiness is thus essentially defined as כִּי תֹאכֵל—being given the blessing of internalization/comprehension!

TAKEAWAY MESSAGES

We lean on Pesach night like the *wealthiest* of kings because we drink and eat the wine, matzos and maror, **internalizing** the respective concepts inherent in each. It is not "they tried to kill us; we survived; let's eat," but rather, "We eat to show that we *digest* the concepts embedded in the matzos and maror." The bread is poor and herbs are bitter when we work aimlessly, but once on the *derech* of Hashem we can experience true עשירות.

You are fortunate by being able to eat, i.e., comprehend your purpose and happiness. The toil of our hands should be like eating!

HALF-HEARTED *HALLEL* OUT OF SYMPATHY FOR OUR ENEMIES? REALLY?

בִּנְפֹל אוֹיִבְךָ אַל תִּשְׂמָח...פֶּן יִרְאֶה ה' וְרַע
בְּעֵינָיו וְהֵשִׁיב מֵעָלָיו אַפּוֹ.

***Don't be happy when your enemy falls...for G-d may find
this evil and remove from him His wrath. (Avos 4:24)***

--- QUESTIONS ---

Some quote the above *pasuk* from *Avos* (which is actually from *Mishlei* 24) to highlight the idea that "we shouldn't revel too much in the pain of even our oppressors!"

In fact, one reason (מדרש הרנינו) given as to why we likewise say only half-*Hallel* on the latter part of Pesach is based on the midrash that the *malachei ha'shareis* asked Hashem to sing during the engulfing of the Egyptians, but Hashem responded, "מעשה ידי טובעים בים ואתם אומרים שירה—My creations are drowning and you are singing!" The implication at first glance is that it is simply inappropriate to revel in the downfall of G-d's creations!

Yet another possible support for this pacifist notion is an idea begot by analyzing a Gemara in *Shabbos* (118b):

כל הקורא הלל בכל יום הרי זה מחרף ומגדף.

*Saying Hallel every day is blasphemy [i.e., for miracles of
Exodus and splitting of the sea. The first opinion, that you*

553

could say Hallel every day, is because one is saying it over the
routine miracles of life].”

Seemingly, the idea is that we should not constantly root for the destruction of our enemies because, after all, they are creations of G-d as well. And we certainly shouldn't revel over such defeats.

So we have at least three proofs that support the notion of a tempered half-*Hallel* on the second days.

But is it really true that we shouldn't revel in our success over our enemies? It seems very unrealistic.

ANSWERS

To answer this, we must focus on the second part of that *pasuk* brought down in *Avos*: "Don't be happy when your enemy falls…for G-d may **find this evil** (ורע בעיניו) and remove from him his wrath." The "evil" is commonly thought to be the reveling in others' suffering. But if that was the case, then it wouldn't make sense that the end of the *pasuk* says, "I will be [forced to] remove from them my wrath," which implies that G-d really would like to punish them!

The "evil" thus is the fact that if we revel too much and focus on the reveling, without spending time doing the more important good deeds that distinguish us from our enemies, such misfocus is *our evil* that G-d will not excuse. During such auspicious times when G-d chose us over our enemies, we need to focus more on being good and doing good and less with merely praising G-d! "Saying *Hallel* [for miracles of Exodus and the splitting of the sea] every day is blasphemy" in the sense that we need to spend less time saying *Hallel* and more time doing productive things. "My creations are drowning and you are singing!" can be understood as meaning, "Why are you *only* singing? You need to also show Me why I chose you over them!"

We say half-*Hallel* now because we are showing G-d that we understand that He needs our praise less and that the He wants us to spend the other "half" focusing on showing Him why we were in fact chosen to survive over others!

—————— TAKEAWAY MESSAGES ——————

"When your enemies fall, don't be gladdened...lest G-d see you and it is evil in their eyes and He removes anger from them"—the focus is more of a concern of השיב מעליו אפו than on us being too happy when our oppressors are destroyed. We hope G-d doesn't focus on our missteps if we are demonstrably ecstatic when our oppressors are destroyed. By reciting only half-*Hallel*, we demonstrate that we understand that G-d wants us to spend at least half-the-other-time showing us why we were deserving to be spared. "Saying *Hallel* [for miracles of Exodus and the splitting of the sea] every day is blasphemy" because we should be spending our time doing productive things instead to distinguish ourselves from our enemies!

Half-hearted *Hallel* out of enmity for our enemies! We should just spend the other half showing why were were chosen over our enemies!

WHY REPEAT THE PLAGUES WHEN THEY ARE THE MIRACLES?

עֲשָׂרָה נִסִּים נַעֲשׂוּ לַאֲבוֹתֵינוּ בְמִצְרַיִם וַעֲשָׂרָה
עַל הַיָּם. עֶשֶׂר מַכּוֹת הֵבִיא הַקָּדוֹשׁ בָּרוּךְ הוּא
עַל הַמִּצְרִיִּים בְּמִצְרַיִם וְעֶשֶׂר עַל הַיָּם.

Ten miracles were performed for our forefathers in Egypt,
and another ten at the sea. Ten afflictions were wrought by
G-d upon the Egyptians in Egypt, and another ten at the
sea...(Avos 5:4)

QUESTIONS

Why does the Mishnah in *Avos* repeat the point? The miracles in Egypt and on the Sea performed for the Jews were in fact one and the same as the afflictions wrought on the evil Egyptians, and so why the wordiness?

ANSWERS

We humans cannot be expected to view our evil enemies as *ma'asei yadav*, Hashem's handiwork, but we need to be cognizant of a celestial reckoning to effectuate a complete victory over our enemies! By focusing on the positive aspects of our own salvation, rather than celebrating our enemies' downfall, we can better assure that our enemies will actually be punished more!

And that is why the Mishnah in *Avos* is repeated twice, because the first line focuses on our own salvation: "עֲשָׂרָה נִסִּים נַעֲשׂוּ לַאֲבוֹתֵינוּ בְמִצְרַיִם וַעֲשָׂרָה עַל הַיָּם." Only after recognizing that the *makkos* were actually a manifestation of miracles for us does the Mishnah record that "עֶשֶׂר מַכּוֹת הֵבִיא הַקָּדוֹשׁ בָּרוּךְ הוּא עַל הַמִּצְרִיִּים." Our enemies can be punished only as we view them from the vantage point of miracles for us.

─────────── TAKEAWAY MESSAGES ───────────

In order to punish our enemies, we must recognize the miracles bestowed upon us.

WHY IS PASSOVER CALLED "PASSOVER"? AN ANSWER FROM UTAF GAZA

עֲשָׂרָה נִסִּים נַעֲשׂוּ לַאֲבוֹתֵינוּ בְמִצְרַיִם וַעֲשָׂרָה
עַל הַיָּם. עֶשֶׂר מַכּוֹת הֵבִיא הַקָּדוֹשׁ בָּרוּךְ הוּא
עַל הַמִּצְרִיִּים בְּמִצְרַיִם וְעֶשֶׂר עַל הַיָּם.

Ten miracles were performed for our forefathers in Egypt,
and another ten at the sea. Ten afflictions were wrought by
G-d upon the Egyptians in Egypt, and another ten at the sea.
(Avos 5:4)

QUESTIONS

Why do we call Passover "Passover"? Given the plethora of clearly identifiable miracles (i.e., each of the visible plagues), why does the name of our holiday stem from the "hidden" miracle of G-d passing over the Jews and targeting only the firstborn Egyptians?

ANSWERS

Twenty minutes before a UN-brokered ceasefire in the Gaza-Israeli war in 2014, the Gazans rained down 120 missiles, which in retrospect were sent to disguise their first terror tunnel infiltration set to cross from Palestinian Gaza into an Israeli wheat field in Utaf Gaza. Thirteen terrorists were sent on this mission, and such a surprise attack would have killed many.

Just two days before this, two students from B'nei Brak, who were looking for a good field to purchase for *shemurah matzah* production, finally got the OK on a sale of that very field to start clearing the dense sheaves of wheat that covered this precious Land. To the thirteen terrorists' surprise, their disguise and shade had vanished as they emerged from this secretive tunnel. A courageous Israeli soldier easily spotted these infiltrators, all because the two students from B'nei Brak purchased that very field and, unbeknown to the Arab infiltrators, had chopped the wheat stalks down, exposing the land. Half the terrorists were annihilated, and the other half forced back into Gaza. At the time of this event, Israelis thanked G-d for the miracle of getting these Arab terrorists in such a timely fashion. Only later were we able to see the miracles behind the miracle: the fact that these two students from B'nei Brak were able to purchase the field and clear it just in time, as well as the fact that an Israeli soldier was able to spot such an unexpected surprise!

The reason why we specifically celebrate Passover as "Passover" is because we are sophisticated enough to acknowledge that there are miracles that are hidden to our eyes that set the stage for the "evident" miracles, such as the wondrous plagues. The smiting of the firstborn Egyptian is certainly miraculous, but the "hidden" passing over of the B'nei Yisrael is the crux of that miracle and the backdrop of every other plague as well.

Perhaps we can add to the question posed in the previous chapter regarding the Tanna in *Avos* repeating the same miracles and plagues wrought on the Egyptians. The Tanna in *Avos* is precise when he reminds us that the miracles and plagues were in fact not necessarily the same. There is little doubt that each of the wondrous plagues that G-d brought to smite the Egyptians was accompanied by its own inherent Jewish miraculous stories, much like the story of Utaf Gaza.

——— TAKEAWAY MESSAGES ———

Hidden miraculous stories in Egypt went side by side with the glorious wondrous open miraculous plagues. The holiday is specifically called "Passover" to remind us of the hidden miracles that provided the backdrop of our miraculous redemption. The two students of B'nei Brak performing the mitzvah of *shemurah matzah* saved our nation in the ultimate "Passover" type of way.

Passover is called "Passover" to remind us of the hidden miracles essential for our survival. Utaf Gaza reminds us of the power of "Passover"—the hidden miracle behind the exposed one.

THE LESSON OF KAR"PAS" AND "PASS"OVER

QUESTIONS

1. First, Avraham Ciment asks why Rabban Gamliel encapsulated the Seder by reminding us to highlight "Pesach, matzah, and maror" in that order. Didn't the maror precede our freedom, represented by the *korban Pesach*? The order should be matzah, maror and then *Pesach*!

2. Why is it that on Seder night we make the *Borei Pri Ha'adamah* on the *karpas*, having in mind the eventual maror? What's the significance of that unusual *kavanah*, coupled with the unusual *minhag* of some to use sweet fruits, like Rabbi Bixon's banana *minhag* for *karpas*?

3. What does it mean when we say "כשם שמברכים על הטובה כך מברכים על הרעה—Just like we make a blessing over the good, we also make a blessing over a curse"? It seems to imply that apparent curses may have some inherent good as well? Is there another way to understand it?

ANSWERS

One answer as to why Pesach precedes maror is simply because we often don't recognize how bitter we actually have it until we have some reprieve!

"וַיְהִי בַיָּמִים הָרַבִּים הָהֵם וַיָּמָת מֶלֶךְ מִצְרַיִם וַיֵּאָנְחוּ בְנֵי יִשְׂרָאֵל מִן הָעֲבֹדָה וַיִּזְעָקוּ"—only after the king of Egypt died and they had some reprieve did B'nei Yisrael start to realize their bitterness (*Shemos* 2:23). Similarly, only after they experienced freedom did they realize just how bitter their lives were! We are slaves

561

to certain lifestyles or situations and only when the shackles are loosened are we able to realize the bitterness we didn't even see.

But yet a better answer as to why Pesach may indeed purposely come before the maror is an answer to our *karpas* question. The word *karpas* is first mentioned by the כְּתֹנֶת פַּסִים, where *Rashi* reminds us that פַּס is wool, as in כַּרְפַּס תְּכֵלֶת—the blue wool mentioned in the *megillah* as Mordechai's tunic. The *karpas* is thus a reference to the wool of the beautiful coat given by Yaakov to Yosef, which of course caused the whole Egyptian slavery! At first, Yaakov figured that he was giving a total blessing to his favorite son by giving this beautiful coat, but inherent in the blessing was actually a much larger curse. Whenever faced with a *karpas*, we must have in mind the potential maror that lurks beneath even the most evident of blessings. Who would think that a beautiful multicolored coat could lead eventually to a nation enslaved! By making a *berachah* of ha'adamah on the "sweet" *karpas*, we must have in mind the maror. This reminds us to be careful even with blessings, because even blessings can bring on challenges and potential curses!

We say "כשם שמברכים על הטובה כך מברכים על הרעה"—Just like we make a blessing over the good, we also make a blessing over a curse!" This may actually mean, "When you make a blessing over a blessing [i.e., the *karpas* of the beautiful coat], you must understand the potential curse that lurks behind the blessing [i.e., the maror of jealousy that led to slavery]." In other words, every rose has its thorn.

Pesach may have come before maror to remind us that maror did not only exist before our redemption, but also because of our redemption. Just like the matzos have an inherent duality, being the matzos of affliction and of redemption, the maror also has a duality: The maror of slavery and also the maror of freedom. With the blessing of our redemption, symbolized by the Pesach, we had new maror to contend with! We can all relate to this nowadays, as our freedoms often lead us astray.

─────────── TAKEAWAY MESSAGES ───────────

One answer as to why Pesach precedes maror is simply because we often don't recognize how bitter we indeed have it until we have some reprieve. Another answer is that with the blessing of our redemption, symbolized by the Pesach, we had new maror to contend with! "כשם שמברכים על הטובה כך מברכים על הרעה—When you make a blessing over something apparently great [i.e., the *karpas* of the beautiful coat], you must understand the potential curse that lurks because of this blessing [i.e., the maror of jealousy that led to slavery]." The lesson is that we should beware of the pitfalls in even blessings. Matzah and maror both have dual implications on Pesach; there is a maror of redemption and hence maror comes after Pesach! Why is the holiday called "Pass"over? Because it is all over the pieces of "*pas*" that Yaakov gave to Yosef!

THE MYSTERIOUS SEDER OF
PESACH—SECRET PEP TALK?

קַדֵּשׁ. וּרְחַץ. כַּרְפַּס. יַחַץ. מַגִּיד. רָחְצָה.
מוֹצִיא. מַצָּה. מָרוֹר. כּוֹרֵךְ. שֻׁלְחָן עוֹרֵךְ. צָפוּן.
בָּרֵךְ. הַלֵּל. נִרְצָה.

QUESTIONS

My favorite part of the Seder is actually singing this order of the Seder. We introduce the night by reminding everyone that there is an order to the evening. As free people celebrating our national redemption from slavery, this order is reminiscent of our national freedom, as now we can finally count on some order for a change! But somehow, Pesach is not just a holiday for the righteous. Out of all the holidays, it is the most inclusive. Case in point, we talk about what the *rasha* says, and include the simpleton and ignorant among us; it's not only about the educated Jews. But then how does the concept of the *seder*/order relate to everyone at the Seder? The tatooed brother-in-law and the open *apikorus* cousin at the table feels an almost miraculous personal and individual connection on this very night. What about this Seder is the hidden individual message that relates to all of us?

ANSWERS

- קַדֵּשׁ וּרְחַץ—Before embarking on any new challenge or important maneuver in life, you cannot just jump in without due preparation. *Kadesh* hints that you need to sanctify, i.e., dedicate yourself wholeheartedly to your fateful step. Once you made up your mind, you must take the plunge and not look back. *Urechatz* means "to wash," but symbolically means to "jump in the water" and get your feet wet; you need to commit your full energy to the challenge you chose to pursue.

- כַּרְפַּס יַחַץ—The etymology of this unusual word *karpas* is found in the Bible, most recently read in *Megillas Esther*. Mordechai was wearing a coat of *karpas*, which is fine cotton! The idea may be that once you are committed wholeheartedly and dive into your new challenge, you can *yachatz*, break away from your prior situation or possible missteps as easily as dividing soft cotton balls!

- מַגִּיד רָחְצָה—In order to solidify your place in this new environment, the Haggadah reminds us that you will have to recount (*maggid*) how you were able to impressively sacrifice and dive into this new challenge (*rachtzah*). This will give you the due strength to stay fortified in whatever challenge you are pursuing, while not being sucked back into prior precarious predicaments.

- מוֹצִיא מַצָּה—As you embark on your newfound mission, you cannot expect leavened bread at first. Things will be immature and unleavened. You can't hit the stars before you enter space.

- מָרוֹר—Natural for any change will be hardships, bitterness, and unfamiliarity.

- כּוֹרֵךְ—The bitter herbs and matzah are mixed together to show the person that actually the aforementioned bitterness is really part and parcel of the immaturity of fledgling individual freedom and the new challenge that simply has not had the time to ripen.

- שֻׁלְחָן עוֹרֵךְ—Once you mature some more and go through this evolution, though, at last your table is set and you are ready to start seeing the profits you hoped for.

- צָפוּן בֵּרֵךְ—The word *tzafun* means "hidden," and once you start coasting in your newfound more positive environment, "hidden" benefits beyond even those that you dreamed of become realized (*barech*).

- הַלֵּל נִרְצָה—After persevering through the hardships of your nascent newfound freedom and challenge, and after discovering the greatness in your new stead, you will give *hallel*, thanks to G-d for helping you make those right difficult choices, and then you will finally *nirtzah*, accept that all your efforts and sacrifices were indeed worth it!

─────────── TAKEAWAY MESSAGES ───────────

The actual Seder of the night is a microcosm of our national evolution, but also of our individual evolution: First we must make up our mind before jumping in (*kadesh urchatz*). Then we will see it is easy to break from a less than ideal past (*karpas yachatz*). Then we must remember our sacrifices and not get sucked back (*maggid rachtzah*). Knowing that we will struggle with immaturity (*motzi matzah*) and bitterness (*maror*), which often are one and the same (*korech*), we will finally be set on a positive path (*shulchan orech*), which will open up some great surprises (*tzafun barech*) along the way. Then when we look back, we will indeed praise G-d (*hallel*) for helping us make the hard choices and finally accept (*nirtzah*) ourselves for taking them!

The mysterious Seder of Pesach is a pep-talk for all of us ready to embark on any journey!

HAGGADAH PEARLS

Biblical sources of the Haggadah—emphasis on today or tomorrow?

The answer for the *chacham*, which emphasizes *tomorrow*, is: "כִּי יִשְׁאָלְךָ בִנְךָ מָחָר לֵאמֹר מָה הָעֵדֹת וְהַחֻקִּים וְהַמִּשְׁפָּטִים—When your son asks you tomorrow saying what are the testimonies, decrees, and laws" (*Devarim* 6:20). However, the answer for the *she'eino yodei'a lishol* emphasizes *today*: "וְהִגַּדְתָּ לְבִנְךָ בַּיּוֹם הַהוּא—And you should tell your son on this day" (*Shemos* 13:8).

So what's the significance between the tomorrow/today imagery? The only way to ensure that your son will ask questions tomorrow is to work with him or her in the present. You can only guarantee a "יִשְׁאָלְךָ בִנְךָ מָחָר" if you are a "וְהִגַּדְתָּ לְבִנְךָ בַּיּוֹם הַהוּא"! (Rabbi Aron Blech)

Why does Kadesh precede Urchatz?

Though throughout the year, cleansing ourselves from sin must precede *Kadesh*, sanctifying through mitzvos à la סוּר מֵרָע וַעֲשֵׂה טוֹב, Pesach is different in that we are sanctified before we cleanse ourselves. These special holy days remind us how we were spared from Egypt despite essentially still being rogue! (Rabbi Asher Weiss)

What is Karpas, and why do we have Maror in mind when we make the berachah on it?

The letters of כַּרְפַּס can be rearranged to spell "פרך ס'." *Perach* means backbreaking labor, and the letter *samech* is numerically worth sixty, referring to the sixty myriads of Jewish males who left Egypt in the exodus. But why the inverted message? The *Midrash Rabbah* (*Shemos* 1:11) explains פרך to mean that men were given women's work and vice versa (see David Holzer, *The Medieval Illuminated Haggadah*), where he explains that by maror, some actually had the custom to point at their

567

spouses to remind of this lesson!). Perhaps the inversion of *karpas* is also to teach this inverted lesson. Hard work is really defined by doing things that we are not accustomed to! (AC)

Why does Yachatz come after Karpas?

Here is a play on words: How can you break the cycle of bitterness? If you do good deeds (*Kadesh*) and cleanse yourself of sin (*Urchatz*), then the bitterness (*Karpas*—since we have the maror in mind when making the blessing on the *karpas*) will be broken (*Yachatz*)! (AC)

Maggid—Why is Ha Lachma Anya in Aramaic?

Shibolei Haleket gives two reasons why *Ha Lachma Anya* is in Aramaic:

1. Destructive angels do not understand Aramaic.
2. Uneducated masses do understand Aramaic.

Rabbi Asher Weiss opines that this was actually said *before* the Seder back in the Temple times before the *korban Pesach* was slaughtered. After all, you don't invite guests once you are seated at your meal already! Clearly this is a commemorative statement. (Rabbi Asher Weiss)

מה נשתנה הלילה הזה מכל הלילות?

How is this night different from all other nights?

Is Mah Nishtanah a question after all?

The Vilna Gaon explains that *laylah* is actually feminine (i.e., its plural is *leilos*), as it is usually a time associated with few mitzvos (*yom* is masculine, conversely, because of the abundance of mitzvos that must be performed by day). מה has the same *gematria* as אדם—man, and it is what is different about this night! The night of Passover changes from a feminine time, i.e., devoid of mitzvos, to a לילה הזה (and not לילה הזאת!); it is a masculine night now in the sense that it is packed with mitzvos! (Rabbi Asher Weiss)

וכל המרבה לספר ביציאת מצרים הרי זה משבח.

And all those who prolong discussion of the Exodus from Egypt are praiseworthy.

Why does it specifically say "Kol ha'marbeh…harei zeh meshubach" at the end of Avadim Hayinu?

The *Kesav Sofer* quotes the Gemara in *Shabbos* (118b): "הקורא הלל בכל יום הרי זה מחרף ומגדף—Saying *Hallel* every day is blasphemy." He explains that normally by glorifying the supernatural deeds too much, you neglect to appreciate the natural miracles. But on the night of Pesach, the glorification of the supernatural is praiseworthy; we show this distinction on this night in which we glorify the miraculous! (Rabbi Meyers/ *Kesav Sofer*)

מעשה ברבי אליעזר ורבי יהושע ורבי אלעזר...רבותינו הגיע זמן קריאת שמע של שחרית.

There was an instance of Rabbi Eliezer and Rabbi Yehoshua and Rabbi Elazar…"Rabbis, the time from k'rias Shema of the morning has arrived!"

Why were the Rabbis reminded specifically about k'rias Shema of Shacharis?

My father, Dr. Larry Ciment, explains that the rabbis were actually pondering their exile and yearning for salvation; they were saying that instead of always merely having *emunah* and blindly believing (כל אותו הלילה) in redemption, as signified by *Emes V'Emunah* of the nighttime *Shema*, the rabbis wanted a more apparent actual salvation signified by the *Emes V'Yatziv* ("stand upright") that culminates the *Shema* of *Shacharis*. (LC)

הרי אני כבן שבעים שנה ולא זכיתי שתאמר יציאת מצרים בלילות עד שדרשה בן זומא.

I am like seventy years old and wasn't able to say that [the story of] the Exodus from Egypt should be said at night until Ben Zoma expounded…

What's the relevance of Ben Zoma?

Ben Zoma said in *Avos* (4:1): "Who is wise? One who learns from all people," and Rabbi Elazar ben Azaryah was just a fledgling rabbi who didn't know his ideas would be accepted until he remembered that *derashah*. (David Barth)

ברוך המקום ברוך הוא ברוך שנתן תורה לעמו ישראל ברוך הוא.

Blessed is [G-d] the Place, Blessed He, Blessed is He that gave
the Torah to Israel.

What is the relevance of this berachah of the Torah's importance by the Four Sons?

Children's potential success or failure, and ultimate wisdom, wickedness, simplicity, or lack of awareness, is determined through the prism of their dedication to Torah values. (AC)

כנגד ארבעה בנים דברה תורה.

Corresponding to four sons the Torah talks.

Does the Torah talk?

Here is an unusual wording of *k'neged*, and furthermore, does the Torah talk (*dibrah*)?

The word *k'neged* here may be a euphemism for a mother, as in "עֵזֶר כְּנֶגְדּוֹ." Therefore, this could be read: "As for the mother (*k'neged*), there are four consequences (*banim* can mean sons or consequences) to how she delivers (*dibrah*) her Torah," i.e., the mother is responsible for teaching her offspring the ways of the world. The Torah then is not "speaking," but the *k'neged*, the mother, is speaking the Torah, of which there are four possible outcomes: the *chacham*, the *rasha*, the *tam*, and the *she'eino yodei'a lishol*. The children's outcomes are dependent on some level on their nurturing from their mother! (AC)

חכם/רשע/תם מה הוא אומר?

The wise/wicked/simple son, what does he say?

Why "Mah hu omer"?

In general, you can tell a lot about a person by how they speak. You can be defined by how you speak. In that sense, the sons are *"Mah hu omer"*—they are defined by "what" (*mah*) they say (*hu omer*)! (AC)

Why not tzaddik and rasha?

Is a *chacham* about wisdom or about faith? "אִם אֵין יִרְאָה אֵין חָכְמָה" means that being a *chacham* is predicated not on wisdom but on faith/practice. The opposite of a *rasha* then is not a *tzaddik* but a *chacham*. True wisdom is not discernable without fear of G-d. (AC)

הקהה את שניו/ואף אתה אמר לו כהלכות הפסח.

Hit his tooth/And you will say to him like the halachos of Pesach.

Responses to the chacham and rasha

When you speak to a *chacham*, you should tell him in a **"nose"** way (ואף אתה אמר לו); don't show him things outright, but make him smell it and then look/discover it on his own. (AC). When you speak to a *rasha*, knocking out his tooth (שניו) is knocking out the *shin* in *rasha* (רשע), making him a רע—friend. Showing some commonality can help turn a *rasha* into a friend! (Alisa Barth)

והיא שעמדה לאבותינו ולנו שלא אחד בלבד עמד עלינו לכלותנו אלא שבכל דור ודור עומדים עלינו לכלותנו והקדוש ברוך הוא מצילנו מידם.

And this is what stands for us and our fathers; that no one alone has destroyed us entirely; rather in each and every generation they stand on us to destroy us and G-d saves us from their hands!

Why we are standing today?

The reason we are standing alive today is because our enemies are never united; they are עומדים and not עומד, i.e., as one. G-d makes it that our enemies never unite effectively. Consider the Israeli War of Independence in 1948! (AC)

אלו הכניסנו לארץ ישראל ולא בנה לנו את בית הבחירה דיינו.

If we would enter Eretz Yisrael and would not build the
Chosen Home (Beis Hamikdash) it would have been enough.

Would it really be dayenu?

The common interpretation of *dayenu* is "it would have been enough"
or "sufficed for us." But would it really have been enough for us not to
have a Beis Hamikdash?

Dayenu may be ד' יינות—it may be saying that we still would be having
four cups of wine, even if we didn't have a Beis Hamikdash. The four
cups represent the four expressions of *geulah*, and the final culmination
of *v'lakachti* was vague enough to include all those permutations listed
in the rhyme! (AC)

Shavuos

WHY DOES SHAVUOS COINCIDE
WITH *PARASHAS BAMIDBAR?*

כָּךְ הִיא דַּרְכָּהּ שֶׁל תּוֹרָה: פַּת בְּמֶלַח תֹּאכַל,
וּמַיִם בִּמְשׂוּרָה תִּשְׁתֶּה, וְעַל הָאָרֶץ תִּישַׁן, וְחַיֵּי
צַעַר תִּחְיֶה, וּבַתּוֹרָה אַתָּה עָמֵל.

*Such is the way of Torah: Bread with salt you shall eat,
water in small measure you shall drink, and upon the
ground you shall sleep; live a life of deprivation and toil in
Torah…(Avos 6:4)*

--- QUESTIONS ---

1. Why all the negativity? As we accept the Torah on Shavuos, is this "life of asceticism" described above really the optimal way to live or pursue a Torah-observing life? It sounds so depressing! Why can't we just all just live happy, chilled, and calm?

2. In a soon-to-be related question, when it comes to providing medical care, isn't it puzzling that the Talmud says, "*Permission is granted to the doctor to heal*"? Shouldn't it say, "It is a mitzvah to try to heal your fellow neighbor"?

3. How do we understand why we sing "מַה טֹּבוּ אֹהָלֶיךָ יַעֲקֹב מִשְׁכְּנֹתֶיךָ יִשְׂרָאֵל—How goodly are your tents, O Yaakov, your dwellings,

O Yisrael," even though this was said/composed by our arch-enemy Bilaam, the evil prophet?

ANSWERS

Parashas Bamidbar begins with our traveling in the desert. The midrash (*Tanchuma, Beshalach*) explains that G-d circuitously took us to Israel, making us suffer in the desert for forty years because: "If each person had their own field or vineyard, they would not learn Torah…by feeding them the *mann* (מָן) and making them drink from the well, the Torah settles within them." The unfortunate truth is that when we have so many amenities, human nature is to neglect or forget our reliance on G-d. The *Ramban* on the Torah explains that ideally, when man becomes ill, this should be an opportunity to get close to G-d and yearn for His direct healing; man should not solicit care from a doctor but instead rely on G-d. Since we are not *zocheh* to this closeness, however, we have *permission* to seek care, but ideally we should strive for an existence in which we can just rely on G-d. The point (obviously in the extreme here) is that we need to be reminded that our amenities and luxuries tend to cloud our true reliance on Hashem.

Parashas Bamidbar always falls out next to Shavuos to remind us that a true Torah life is only achieved by a mindset of living a simple, non-voracious lifestyle. Homiletically: "בְּרֵאשִׁית," in the beginning, "שְׁמוֹת וַיִּקְרָא," names [you are] called, "בְּמִדְבַּר" but only in a *midbar* bare of all excesses, "דְּבָרִים," can you truly become something!

Now the Tanna in *Avos* finally makes sense: He isn't saying "suffer by eating a little and drinking a bit, and also learn Torah," but rather he is saying that by suffering, to some extent, you can actually recognize your reliance on G-d and thus dedicate yourself more to a Torah way of life. *Bamidbar* is the gateway to a Torah existence.

My father, Dr. Larry Ciment, explains: Later on, in *Sefer Bamidbar*, when Bilaam realized he wasn't going to be able to curse Israel at the behest of the Moavite king Balak, he resorted to blessing them. He did so because he knew that "too much of a good thing won't be good for long"! He thus was cursing them with blessings, in effect saying, "How goodly are your tents, O Yaakov, *but will your dwellings be the same?*" The challenge of the Jewish People will not be how they will act when they are comfortable with their lives, not when they are struggling in tents (similar to the midrash above)!

Balak understood the hint and, in fact, the next paragraph in the Torah details how Israel sinned:

וַיֵּשֶׁב יִשְׂרָאֵל בַּשִּׁטִּים וַיָּחֶל הָעָם לִזְנוֹת אֶל בְּנוֹת מוֹאָב.

And Israel dwelled in Shitim and they started to sin with the daughters of Moav. (Bamidbar 25:1)

By **dwelling** comfortably in Shitim, Israel easily and unfortunately sinned. Perhaps the reason this (Mah Tovu) has become a childhood song is because this is our perpetual challenge—only by making a *midbar* in the midst of our comfort can we ultimately claim victory.

—————— TAKEAWAY MESSAGES ——————

Why all the negativity in *Avos* about eating measly salted bread and sleeping on the ground? Human nature is that the amenities make us forget how much we rely on Hashem. This is the challenge of Bilaam that we sing about: "Too much of a good thing won't be good for long." We need to find the *midbar* among the comforts to ensure our Torah observance: "כָּךְ הִיא דַּרְכָּהּ שֶׁל תּוֹרָה...וְחַיֵּי צַעַר תִּחְיֶה, וּבַתּוֹרָה אַתָּה עָמֵל."

"בְּרֵאשִׁית," in the beginning, "שְׁמוֹת וַיִּקְרָא," names [you are] called, "בְּמִדְבַּר" but only in a *midbar* bare of all excesses, "דְּבָרִים," can you truly become something! The lesson of *Bamidbar* is that Torah is best absorbed when we bare ourselves of excesses.

Why does Shavuos coincide with *Parashas Bamidbar*? Only a *midbar* can retain the Torah.

ABOUT THE AUTHOR

Ari Judah Ciment, son of Larry and Helen Ciment, has been practicing pulmonary and critical care medicine in Miami Beach, Florida, since 2008. In addition to many medical field achievements, he has been an invited grand-rounds lecturer for several hospitals and universities.

Dr. Ciment served as adjunct professor on Jewish medical ethics at Touro College and has arranged several medical ethics symposiums, most notably with the renowned ethicist Rabbi Avraham Steinberg, as well as BU ethicist Michael Grodin. He is currently president of the medical staff at the Mount Sinai Medical Center. His hobbies include basketball, tennis, guitar, and writing the weekly *dvar Torah* for Beth Israel Congregation. He lives with his wife, Elissa, and their three children, Tehila, Jack, and Sam, in Miami Beach, Florida.

MOSAICA PRESS
BOOK PUBLISHERS

Elegant, Meaningful & Bold

info@MosaicaPress.com
www.MosaicaPress.com

The Mosaica Press team of
acclaimed editors and designers
is attracting some of the most
compelling thinkers and teachers
in the Jewish community today.
Our books are available around
the world.

HARAV YAACOV HABER
RABBI DORON KORNBLUTH